THE ARDEN SHAKESPEARE

GENERAL EDITORS: HAROLD F. BROOKS AND HAROLD JENKINS

MACBETH

THE ARDEN EDITION OF THE WORKS OF WILLIAM SHAKESPEARE

MACBETH

Edited by
KENNETH MUIR

METHUEN & CO LTD
11 New Fetter Lane, London, E.C.4

The general editors of the Arden Shakespeare have been W. J. Craig (1899–1906), succeeded by R. H. Case (1909–1944) and Una Ellis-Fermor (1946–1958). Present general editors: Harold F. Brooks and Harold Jenkins.

Henry Cuningham's edition of *Macbeth* first published 1912
It was reprinted five times
Seventh edition (Kenneth Muir), revised and reset, 1951
Eighth edition, 1953
Reprinted, with minor corrections, 1955
Reprinted, with minor corrections and new appendix, 1957
Reprinted, with minor corrections and new appendix, 1959
Ninth edition, 1962
Editorial Matter © 1962 Methuen & Co.
Reprinted twice
Reprinted 1968

9.4

S.B.N. 416 47320 2

PRINTED IN GREAT BRITAIN BY RICHARD CLAY (THE CHAUCER PRESS), LTD.,
BUNGAY, SUFFOLK AND BOUND BY BURN AND CO., LTD., ESHER

CONTENTS

GENERAL EDITOR'S PREFACE

WHEN it was proposed, in 1946, to re-issue the Arden Shakespeare, little more was intended than a limited revision, bringing introductions and collations into line with the work of recent years and modifying appendices whenever additions were necessary or the material had been accepted into the common body of knowledge. In the main part of each volume the form of the original page was to be undisturbed, in order that the stereotype plates of those originals might still be used. This meant that practically no alterations could be made in the text, which was based on the Cambridge edition of 1863–6 (revised, 1891–3), and that any alterations in the commentary must be so arranged as to occupy the same space as the notes which they replaced.

It had been recognized from the first that in the case of a few plays it might be necessary to modify this restriction and it soon became clear that the first two volumes, *Macbeth* and *Love's Labour's Lost*, would prove more costly to produce if the stereotypes were retained than if they were abandoned. The two editors, therefore, who had gallantly endeavoured to preserve the original lay-out of the pages, found themselves freed from this necessity when their work was done or partly done, so that much of it had to be done again. As conditions became more stable, it became possible also to consider sparing their successors what they had experienced and at last to allow all editors to start afresh without tying them to the Cambridge text or to the lay-out of the original pages.

Thus a major change of policy came about by degrees, as the conditions of the years immediately after the war began to allow of it, and what had begun as a revision became a new edition.

This meant that publishers, editors, and general editor were faced with an entirely new responsibility: that of establishing the text of each play in place of a text which had hitherto been prescribed. Since we were unwilling to suspend activities until textual critics should be agreed that a text had been established as nearly authoritative for our day as that of the 1891–3 edition was held to be for its own, we decided to continue the work begun, in full awareness of the difficulties involved in publishing an edition such as this at a moment when there is not yet full agreement on a generally acceptable text. Each individual editor would thus be responsible for the text of his play, as well as for the introductions, collations, commentary and appendices.

The policy of the original edition in respect of introductions, commentary and appendices remains what it has always been; the lines laid down by those scholars who first designed its form have proved their worth throughout the past half-century. The introductions, though the emphasis must vary with the nature of the given play, include, together with the results of the editor's own thought and investigation, a survey of as many as possible of those studies which throw light upon the nature of the play or the problems surrounding it. The general commentary, which we have kept in its original position, at the foot of the page, provides such brief notes as may be required for the elucidation of specific passages or textual problems or for general comment and comparison; these often, therefore, serve to illustrate the general account given in the introduction.

The policy in respect of text is of necessity neither so simple nor so consistent as that of the editors of the original series, who were enjoined to use as their base the Cambridge text of 1891–3, and in most cases did so willingly, believing it to be as nearly authoritative as could be. Much has happened in the last fifty years, through the great extension of palæographical, bibliographical and textual scholarship;

and our better understanding of (among other things) the nature and relations of Folio and Quarto texts has led us not always into more certainty, but sometimes rather into wholesome and chastened uncertainty. Each editor's text must now be his individual concern, since each play presents its own group of problems. Some of us may prove to have solved these in a way which posterity will repudiate. But an attempt will be made in every case to present the evidence for the editor's decisions fairly and to give at the same time representation to solutions other than that editor's own.

UNA ELLIS-FERMOR

LONDON, 1952

PREFACE

THE original Arden *Macbeth*, edited by Henry Cuningham, first appeared in 1912. The present edition owes much to its predecessor, many of the notes being used with little or no change; but there are substantial alterations. The introduction is new; the text (for which Mr. Cuningham was not responsible) has been revised, and several hundred small alterations have been made in it—most of them consisting of a return to the First Folio; nearly all the notes contain alterations, and many are entirely new; and the appendices are new. There are, in fact, so many alterations that it was not possible to print from the old stereos.

Mr. Cuningham disagreed with the General Editor of the series, and was not allowed to print his own text: he was thereby constrained to make a number of protests in the notes, which are happily now superfluous. Some of the differences between the present edition and Mr. Cuningham's are caused by a change of attitude to the authenticity of the text. In 1912 it was still possible for Mr. Cuningham to say:

> "It is admitted by all competent scholars that the text of *Macbeth* has been more or less vitiated by the interpolation or additions of some dramatist other than Shakespeare."

But it is now generally agreed that such interpolations and additions are at least fewer than Mr. Cuningham imagined.

It may be as well to mention one or two points about the present volume. First, the relevant parts of Holinshed's *Chronicle* are printed in the appendix, but, in order to save space, other parts have been curtailed. Secondly, the sections of the Introduction devoted to Date and Interpolations contain criticism necessary for the understanding of the final section, which is devoted to interpretation. Thirdly, though many of the annotations deal with questions of poetic imagery, I hope I have not lost sight of the fact that *Macbeth* is an acting play.

I am indebted to previous editors of the play, especially H. H. Furness, Jr. (1903), Sir Herbert Grierson (1914), and Dr. J. Dover Wilson (1947). I am grateful to many of my colleagues for assistance on different points, and particularly to Mr. Harold Fisch who has checked the collations and criticized the introduction. Professor P. Alexander has generously given me advice on textual matters; Professor R. Peacock supplied me with useful information; Mr. Roy Walker lent me the MS. of his valuable study, *The Time is Free*, and gave me permission to make use of it in my notes; Mr. J. M. Nosworthy sent me some unpublished notes; and, above all, Professor U. Ellis-Fermor has been all that a General Editor should be. I should add that Cleanth Brooks' essay in *The Well Wrought Urn* arrived too late for me to use it, though we agree on a number of points.

KENNETH MUIR

UNIVERSITY OF LEEDS
Christmas, 1950

NOTE TO EIGHTH EDITION

I have taken the opportunity of correcting misprints, and of making various alterations. I am indebted to Mr. J. C. Maxwell and to Professor J. Dover Wilson for numerous suggestions and corrections. I have added an appendix on Henry N. Paul's recent book.

K. M.

LIVERPOOL, 1952

NOTE TO NINTH EDITION

It is now ten years since the publication of the Seventh Edition and I have taken the opportunity of substituting passages from Buchanan and Leslie in place of those from Stewart, of revising the section of the Introduction dealing with Sources, and of co-ordinating the various additional notes.

K. M.

LIVERPOOL, 1961

INTRODUCTION

1. Text

The Tragedie of Macbeth was first published in the Folio of 1623, following *Julius Caesar*, and preceding *Hamlet*. As the play is mentioned in the Stationers' Register as one of those " as are not formerly entred to other men," it may be assumed that there was no Quarto. Acts and scenes, with certain exceptions mentioned in the notes, are indicated in the Folio, but not the *dramatis personæ*.

Macbeth was printed from a prompt-copy, or from a transcript of one,[1] as the text contains duplicated stage directions, characteristic of such a source.[2] The text was branded by the Cambridge editors as " one of the worst printed of the plays "; and they suggested that it was printed from a transcript of the author's MS., " which was in great part not copied from the original but *written to dictation*." There is little or no evidence of dictation, but there are a number of mistakes which could be explained on the assumption that the transcriber of the play for the printer was familiar with it on the stage and reproduced actors' blunders. Dr. Dover Wilson, whose theory this is,[3] instances " Gallowgrosses," " quarry," " tale Can," and " Rebellious dead." [4] The first two of these may well be actors' blunders; but I think it most unlikely that an actor would change the simple " hail Came " into the unintelligible " tale Can," or that he would change the straightforward " Rebellion's head " into the obscure " Rebellious dead." The last example suggests that here at least the transcriber *misheard* the actor. But it is quite possible for a transcriber to make blunders which

---

[1] Cf. Chambers, *William Shakespeare*, i. 471; Greg, *The Editorial Problem in Shakespeare*, p. 147; *Macbeth*, ed. Wilson, p. 87; Bald, *The Review of English Studies*, 1928, p. 429.

[2] Cf. II. iii. 81 and III. v. 33.   [3] *Op. cit.* p. 89.

[4] Cf. I. ii. 13; I, ii. 14; I. iii. 97-8; IV. i. 97. But I retain the last of these readings.

seem to be aural rather than visual.[1] The explanation
is simple. I imagine that most transcribers of verse
say the lines to themselves—aloud or to their inner ear
—and are liable to make the same kind of mistake as
someone copying from dictation. Indeed, they are really
dictating to themselves. Such mistakes are more likely
to appear where the transcriber is not required to respect
every letter and comma of the original, and where he is
familiar with the handwriting.

The play is abnormally short, one of the shortest in
the whole canon. Dr. Greg remarks—

" Whether the multiplicity of very brief scenes is mainly due to
cutting or to an unusual dramatic technique is perhaps uncertain;
but there is clear evidence of cutting at some points in short abrupt
lines accompanied by textual obscurities, and there are also some
difficulties of construction." [2]

Professor F. P. Wilson thinks that some of the cutting may
have been due to censorship.[3] R. C. Bald, referring to
the stage directions for torches in the daylight scene, I. vi.
argues that they must refer either to an indoor performance
at the Blackfriars Theatre, or to a night performance at
the Court,

" for it is only at the Court that night performances are recorded at
this period." [4]

The shortness of the play, he thinks, suggests a Court
performance. But the torches can be otherwise explained,[5]
and though I do not doubt that the play was performed
at Court, I find it difficult to believe that scenes cut for
such a performance would not be preserved, as they might
be needed when the play was next performed in the public
theatre.

But that there have been some interpolations is generally agreed; and there may have been some cuts to balance
them. The text is disfigured by mislineation, which suggests that something has been added to, or subtracted
from, the text, to the confusion of the printer or of the

---

[1] In copying Wyatt's poems from MSS. for my edition, I made one or
two mistakes of this kind.
[2] *Op. cit.* p. 147.   [3] Cited Greg, *op. cit.* 147.
[4] *R.E.S.* iv. pp. 429-31.   [5] See note to I. vi.

transcriber. Dr. Wilson says that this mislineation is most apparent in the second scene of the play and that it " grows noticeably less as the play goes forward," and that the process of abridgement was partly responsible for it.[1] It must be pointed out, however, that Dr. Wilson departs from the Folio lineation in only five places in I. ii.; and in some of these the Folio is defensible.[2] He departs from the Folio lineation much more in I. iii. and in II, iii. where more than twenty lines are affected by mislineation, though he does not suspect abridgement there. Mr. John Masefield, however, does.[3] It would be dangerous to offer any theory about the mislineation. Human error, of one kind or another, must serve as an explanation, though there may well have been cuts to make room for the Hecate interpolations.

Mr. Flatter stands alone in his belief that the Folio text of *Macbeth* shows no traces of editorial interference, and that Shakespeare's producing hand may be discerned in it.[4] But Mr. Traversi also warns us against assuming that difficulties in the text can be explained by the fact that there have been omissions:

" The verse of *Macbeth* is often, at first reading, so abrupt and disjointed that some critics have felt themselves driven to look for gaps in the text. Yet the difficult passages do not look in the least like the result of omissions, but are rather necessary to the feeling of the play." [5]

The present text is, I believe, closer to that of the First Folio than any since the seventeenth century, especially with regard to lineation. In this I have probably been influenced by Mr. Flatter, though I could not always accept his views without qualification. I agree that Shakespeare's irregularities were deliberate, but it is not always possible to distinguish between such irregularities

---

[1] *Op. cit.* p. 90.
[2] He departs from the F lineation at I. ii. 33-5, 38, 42-3, 60-1. The F may be right in all these except the last. In I. iii. Wilson departs from F in the following lines: 81-3, 111-14, 131-2, 140-3, 149-53. In II. iii. he departs from F at 54-6, 59-61, 64-5, 84-5, 103-5, 121-3, 137-41.
[3] *Thanks Before Going*, 1947, p. 161.
[4] *Shakespeare's Producing Hand*, 1948, p. 94.
[5] *Approach to Shakespeare*, p. 89.

and those for which transcriber or printer is responsible.[1]
This being so, some compromise is inevitable.

I have also restored some of the Folio's capitals, where
they seem to assist the meaning, in titles, personifications,
and technical terms.

2. DATE

The first recorded performance of *Macbeth* is in Dr.
Simon Forman's manuscript, *The Bocke of Plaies and Notes
therof per Formans for Common Pollicie*[2] (i.e. as affording
useful lessons in the common affairs of life), which describes
a performance at the Globe in the Spring of 1611:

In Mackbeth at the Glob, 16jo [*for* 1611], the 20 of Aprill [Sat.],
ther was to be obserued, firste, how Mackbeth and Bancko, 2 noble
men of Scotland, Ridinge thorowe a wod, the[r] stode before them
3 women feiries or Nimphes, And saluted Mackbeth, sayinge 3 tyms
vnto him, haille Mackbeth, king of Codon; for thou shalt be a kinge,
but shall beget No kinges, &c. then said Bancko, what all to mackbeth
And nothing to me. Yes, said the nimphes, haille to thee Bancko,
thou shalt beget kings, yet be no kinge. And so they departed &
cam to the Courte of Scotland to Dunkin king of Scots, and yt was
in the dais of Edward the Confessor. And Dunkin bad them both
kindly wellcome. And made Macbeth forth with Prince of Northumberland, and sent him hom to his own castell, and appointed mackbeth
to prouid for him, for he wold Sup with him the next dai at night,
& did soe. And mackbeth Contriued to kill Dunkin, & thorowe
the persuasion of his wife did that night Murder the kinge in his own
Castell, beinge his gueste. And ther were many prodigies seen that
night & the dai before. And when Mackbeth had murdred the kinge,
the blod on his hands could not be washed of by Any means, nor from
his wiues handes, which handled the bloddi daggers in hiding them,
By which means they became moch amazed and Affronted. the
murder being knowen, Dunkins 2 sonns fled, the on to England, the
other to Walles, to saue themselues. They beinge fled, they were
supposed guilty of the murder of their father, which was nothinge
so. Then was Mackbeth crowned kinge, and then he for feare of
Banko, his old companion, that he should beget kings but be no kinge

---

[1] Compare, for example, my treatment of Macbeth's aside (I. iii. 127 ff.)
with the printing of 149-55 in the same scene. Mr. Flatter is most valuable
in his suggestions about the metrical rules governing the entrance of characters,
and the metrical relation of asides to the remainder of the dialogue. I accept
the principles, though there seem to be exceptions. But Mr. Flatter's book
would have been even more valuable if he had applied his theories to a good
Quarto, where one would expect to find Shakespeare's producing hand in
greater evidence.   [2] Ashmolean MS. 208.

him selfe, he contriued the death of Banko, and caused him to be Murdred on the way as he Rode. The next night, being at supper with his noble men whom he had bid to a feaste to the whiche also Banco should haue com, he began to speake of Noble Banco, and to wish that he wer there. And as he thus did, standing vp to drincke a Carouse to him, the ghoste of Banco came and sate down in his cheier be-hind him. And he turninge About to sit down Again sawe the goste of banco, which fronted him so, that he fell into a great passion of fear and fury, vtterynge many wordes about his murder, by which, when they hard that Banco was Murdred they Suspected Mackbet.

"Then Mack dove fled to England to the kings sonn, And soe they Raised an Army, And cam into scotland, and at dunston Anyse ouerthrue Mackbet. In the mean tyme whille macdouee was in England, Mackbet slewe Mackdoues wife & children, and after in the battelle mackdoue slewe mackbet.

"Obserue Also howe mackbets quen did Rise in the night in her slepe, & walke and talked and confessed all, & the docter noted her wordes." [1]

Although this performance, in 1611, is the first of which we have a definite record, we can be certain that the play was in existence four years before, because of echoes in contemporary plays. In *Lingua* (pub. 1607) there are possible echoes of II. i, and what seems to be a parody of the sleep-walking scene. There are references to Banquo's ghost in *The Puritaine*, IV. iii. 89:

> and in stead of a Iester, weele ha the ghost ith
> white sheete sit at vpper end a' th' Table. . . .

[1] This account has been regarded as a Collier forgery because i. Forman relies partly on Holinshed (e.g. "3 women feiries or Nimphes"); ii. he does not mention the Cauldron scene or the prophecies of the apparitions, which might have been expected to interest a professional astrologer; iii. he gives an impossible date (April 20 did not fall on a Saturday in 1610); and iv. the Globe, being an "open" theatre, was rarely occupied before May. But the authenticity of *The Bocke of Plaies* was finally settled by Dr. J. Dover Wilson and Dr. R. W. Hunt in an article in *The Review of English Studies*, July 1947. Collier in his transcription of the account of the performance of *The Winter's Tale* misread "coll pixci" as "Coll Pipci": he would not have failed to recognize the word if he had forged the original. It is impossible to deduce very much about the characteristics of the play in 1611, as Forman probably did not write the description immediately after the performance, and his memories of the performance became mixed with his memories of Holinshed. We cannot assume, for example, that the first two scenes of the play were cut or non-existent, that Macbeth was made Prince of Northumberland, that there was an early reference in the play to Edward the Confessor, that there was a scene in which Macbeth and his wife tried in vain to wash the blood off their hands, and that there was no Cauldron scene. Cf. J. M. Nosworthy's article on "Macbeth at the Globe" (*The Library*, 1948).

and in Beaumont and Fletcher's *Knight of the Burning Pestle*, v. i. 26 ff.:

> When you art at thy Table with thy friends,
> Merry in heart, and fild with swelling wine,
> I'll come in midst of all thy pride and mirth,
> Invisible to all men but thy self,
> And whisper such a sad tale in thine ear
> Shall make thee let the Cup fall from thy hand,
> And stand as mute and pale as Death it self.

The Puritaine was published, and *The Knight of the Burning Pestle* probably acted, in 1607. Allowing for the necessary interval for the writing, performing, and publishing of the former play, it is fairly certain that *Macbeth* was being performed in 1606. On the other hand, the reference to the King's Evil (IV. iii.) and the two-fold balls and treble sceptres of Banquo's descendants (IV. i.) must have been written after the accession of James I.[1]

The play was therefore written, we may assume, between 1603 and 1606. The allusions to equivocation (II. iii. 9 ff.) and the hanging of traitors (IV. ii. 46 ff.) must have been written after the trial of Father Garnet (28 March, 1606) for complicity in the Gunpowder Plot. The words " yet could not equivocate to heaven " imply that the speech was written after Garnet's death by hanging (3 May). Equivocation had been mentioned by Shakespeare in *Hamlet* (v. i.), but in the Spring and Summer of 1606 it had become a burning topic. John Chamberlaine wrote to Winwood on 5 April:

> So that by the Cunning of his Keeper, *Garnet* being brought into a *Fool's Paradise*, had diverse Conferences with *Hall, his fellow Priest in the Tower*, which were overheard by *Spialls* set on purpose. With which being charged he stifly denied it; but being still urged, and some Light given him that they had notice of it, he *persisted still, with Protestation upon his Soul and Salvation, that there had passed no such Interlocution:* till at last being *confronted* with *Hall*, he was driven *to confess;* And being now asked in this Audience how he could salve this *lewd Perjury*, he answered, *that so long as he thought they had no Proof he was not bound to accuse himself: but when he saw they had Proof, he stood not long*

---

[1] The play as a whole might have been written earlier, these passages being interpolations; but the " two-fold balls and treble sceptres " do not read like an interpolation.

in it. And then fell into a large Discourse of defending *Equivocations*, with many weak and frivolous Distinctions.[1]

Garnet admitted that equivocation was justifiable only when used for a good object;[2] but he argued that if the law be unjust, then there is no treason.[3] He prayed " for the good Success of the great Action, concerning the Catholick Cause in the beginning of the Parliament " and then denied that this referred to the Gunpowder Plot.[4] He claimed that he could not reveal the plot because he was told of it in Confession, though as James I pointed out:

" For first, it can neuer be accounted a thing vnder Confession, which he that reueals it doth not discouer with a remorse, accounting it a sinne whereof hee repenteth him; but by the contrary, discouers it as a good motion, and is therein not dissuaded by his Confessor, nor any penance enioyned him for the same . . . at the last hee did freely confesse, that the party reuealed it vnto him as they were walking and not in the time of Confession . . . he confessed, that two diuers persons conferred with him anent this Treason; and that when the one of them which was *Catesby*, conferred with him thereupon, it was in the other parties presence and hearing; and what a Confession can this be in the hearing of a third person? "[5]

When Garnet was asked if it were well to deny on his priesthood that he had written to Greenwell, or had conference with Hall, knowing his denial to be false, he replied that in his opinion, and that of all the schoolmen, equivocation may be confirmed by oath or sacrament, without perjury, " if just necessity so require."[6] At his trial Garnet excused a man who had perjured himself on his death-bed with the words: " It may be, my Lord, he meant to equivocate."[7] Finally, I may quote Dudley Carleton, who in a letter to John Chamberlaine on May 2 mentions the postponement of Garnet's execution and his surprise when told he was to die. Carleton tells his correspondent that the Jesuit shifts, falters and equivocates,

[1] Winwood, *Memorials*, ii. 205-6.
[2] *Calendar of State Papers (Domestic)*, 1603-10, p. 306.
[3] *Op. cit.* p. 308.   [4] *State Trials*, i. 254.
[5] James I, *A Premonition* in *Political Works* (1918), pp. 156-7.
[6] *Calendar*, etc., p. 313 (28 April).   [7] *State Trials*, i. 266.

but "will be hanged without equivocation."[1] This grim jest, worthy of the Porter, is quoted by Mr. Stunz in his article on the date of *Macbeth*.[2] He goes on to argue that the Porter's references to drunkenness and lechery are also aimed at Garnet, who comforted himself with sack to drown sorrow,[3] and was falsely accused of fornication with Mrs. Vaux, a slander he repudiated in a speech he made on the scaffold. But there seems to me to be no such implication in the passages about drink and lechery. Some critics have argued that Shakespeare inserted allusions to equivocation in order to please the taste of James I or of the public; but although they doubtless did please the public, there is every reason to believe that Shakespeare with his views on Order would be horrified at the "dire combustion" of the Gunpowder Plot and would have agreed with his royal master on the subject:

> And so the earth as it were opened, should haue sent foorth of the bottome of the *Stygian* lake such sulphured smoke, furious flames, and fearefull thunder, as should haue by their diabolicall *Domesday* destroyed and defaced, in the twinkling of an eye, not onely our present liuing Princes and people, but euen our insensible Monuments. . . .[4]

Dr. Leslie Hotson has shown that Shakespeare must have been personally interested in the Gunpowder Plot:

> When we consider that most of the traitors were native to his own countryside; that he had known Catesby and Grant from his childhood; that Tresham, Catesby, Grant, and the Winters were cousins and allies of the Bushells who were to be connected by marriage with his daughter, Judith; that in London the plotters frequented the Mermaid Tavern . . .; that . . . Ben Jonson had dined with Catesby and Winter only a few days before the explosion was to have torn to bits the Earl of Southampton and the brothers of his friends Thomas Russell and William Leveson, it seems that the peculiar

---

[1] *Calendar*, etc., p. 315. Garnet was not alone in his views. Father Strange argued that the accused "can use equivocation, if he is unjustly interrogated, when it is a matter of prison, danger of death or torture" (quoted Hotson, *I, William Shakespeare*, p. 196). Cf. Strange's statement "that Catholics do hold that they may lawfully equivocate" and said that he "did hold it lawful also" (S.P. 14/17/No. 32, *Calendar*, p. 270, 12 Dec. 1605). There is a treatise on Equivocation in the Bodleian, probably by Gerard, with corrections in Garnet's hand. (Printed 1851, ed. Jardine.)

[2] *English Literary History*, 1942.

[3] *Calendar*, p. 305.

[4] James I, *Workes*, 1616, p. 224.

horror of the dark design and its end in blood and revenge must have taken more hold on his feelings than we have suspected.[1]

Nor is there reason to doubt that Shakespeare agreed with the King, and most of his subjects, on the damnableness of equivocation. Devout Catholics like Anne Vaux were equally scandalized by Garnet's conduct: she remarked that she was sorry to hear that he was privy to the Plot, as he had made many protestations to the contrary.[2] At about the time *Macbeth* was first performed, the King, saved from death by what he regarded as a miracle, praised the wisdom of the Venetian Republic for the measures she had taken against the Jesuits:

" O blessed and wise Republic . . . how well she knows the way to preserve her liberty; for the Jesuits are the worst and most seditious fellows in the world. They are slaves and spies, as you know." He then embarked on a discourse about the Society. By an able induction from all the kingdoms and provinces of the world he demonstrated that they have always been the authors and instruments of all the great disturbances which have taken place.[3]

These quotations will give some idea of the climate of opinion in which *Macbeth* was written. Lord Salisbury's *Answer to Certain Scandalous Papers*—an exposure of equivocation—was being " greedily read " as early as 5 February 1606;[4] but equivocation became a still more burning topic at the time of Garnet's trial and execution which must have preceded the writing of the Porter's speech.

There are various other scraps of evidence about the date. The price of wheat was low in the three years 1605–7; but as the farmer who hanged himself on the expectation of plenty was an old joke, we cannot assume that the Porter's allusion refers to any particular year.[5] The reference to French hose (II. iii. 14) seems to imply that it was close-fitting, but the joke was an old one, and

[1] Hotson, *I, William Shakespeare*, pp. 197-8. That Shakespeare had actually known Catesby and Grant is questionable. But the whole chapter, pp. 172-202, contains interesting sidelights on *Macbeth*.

[2] *Calendar*, p. 299. See also Garnet's letter to Anne Vaux, *op. cit.* p. 309.

[3] *Calendar of State Papers (Venetian)*, x, p. 361. June 14, 1606.

[4] *Calendar of State Papers (Domestic)*, p. 286. Cited by Chambers.

[5] Cf. *P.M.L.A.*, l. p. 712.

too much reliance cannot be placed on it.[1] Shakespeare
need not have heard of Matthew Gwynne's entertainment
at St. John's College, Oxford, on the occasion of James I's
visit on 27 August 1605, for though this was based on the
prophecies of the three Weird Sisters the poet knew his
Holinshed. Nor need he have known of the investiture
of Sir David Murray as Lord Scone, which was fancifully
compared by Hunter to the investiture of Macbeth as
Thane of Cawdor. All these facts, inconclusive as they
are, do nothing to disturb the probability that *Macbeth*
was written in 1606—a date that is supported by various
metrical tests.[2]

There are, however, two difficulties about this dating.
As Bradley pointed out,[3] there are a number of parallels
between *Macbeth* and *Sophonisba*; and these impelled
Sir Edmund Chambers to put Shakespeare's play early
in 1606 and supported Dr. Dover Wilson's argument that
the references to Garnet were added for a Court performance. As *Sophonisba* was entered in the Stationers' Register
on 17 March, one may doubt whether Marston could
have got his play written and performed in the few weeks
which were supposed to have elapsed between the first
performance of *Macbeth* earlier in the year and the entry
of *Sophonisba*. The relevant passages in Marston's play
are all an integral part of the text and the most significant
are in Act I, which he probably wrote first.[4]

---

[1] Cf. note *loc. cit.* Malone quoted Anthony Nixon's *Black Year*, 1606:
" Gentlemen this year shall be much wronged by their taylers, for their
consciences are now much larger than ever they were, for where they were
wont to steale but half a yard of brood cloth in making up a payre of breeches,
now they do largely nicke their customers in the lace too, and take more than
enough for the new fashion's sake, besides their old ones." D. C. Allen has
shown that this was copied from a pamphlet of 1591.

[2] E.g. there are many more overflows in *Macbeth* than in the other three
" great " tragedies, and in one place there are nine successive overflows;
there are many more light-endings (O. 2, H. 8, L. 5, M. 21) and in this respect
Macbeth approaches *Antony and Cleopatra*.

[3] *Shakespearean Tragedy*, p. 471.

[4]   (i) *Sophonisba*, I. ii. 5-27; *Macbeth*, III. iv. 35. On the importance
         of ceremony. Bradley omits this.

       (ii) *Sophonisba*, I. ii.; *Macbeth*, I. ii. 49-51. Quoted below.

      (iii) *Sophonisba*, I. ii. Cf. wounded Carthalon with the bloody Sergeant
         in *Macbeth*, I. ii.

But need we assume that Marston was the debtor? There is reason to believe that Shakespeare was influenced by *Antonio and Mellida*,[1] and I think it can be shown that he was influenced by *Sophonisba* also. By far the most striking parallel is the following:

> three hundred saile
> Upon whose tops the *Roman* eagles streachd
> Their large spread winges, which fan'd the evening ayre
> To us cold breath, for well we might discerne
> *Rome* swam to *Carthage*.

> From Fiffe, great King
> Where the Norweyan Banners flowt the Skie,
> And fanne our people cold.

The Marston passage is more obvious than Shakespeare's: for whereas eagles, by a quibble, can readily be imagined as fanning cold air to the enemy, it is more difficult to see the aptness of the lines in which the inanimate Norweyan banners actively fan the Scots' army. I assume with Mr. Nosworthy that the second scene of *Macbeth* is substantially authentic,[2] and that we should not, therefore, rely on a convenient interpolator to account for this and other echoes from *Sophonisba*. It is more likely that Shakespeare picked up one of Marston's best images from the second scene of *Sophonisba* than that Marston imitated several passages from one of the weakest scenes in *Macbeth* —though it may have been better in its original form,

---

(iv) *Sophonisba*, I. ii. " yet doubtfull stood the fight "; *Macbeth*, I. ii. 7, " Doubtful it stood."

(v) *Sophonisba*, I. ii. " when loe, as oft we see "; *Hamlet*, II. ii. 499, 505, " for loe . . . But as we often see."

(vi) *Sophonisba*, III. ii. " Greefe fits weake hearts, revenging virtue men "; *Macbeth*, IV. iii. 214-5. And compare the ends of these scenes.

(vii) *Sophonisba*, IV. i. " I know thy thoughts "; *Macbeth*, IV. i. " He knows thy thought." Both these are in witch scenes.

(viii) *Sophonisba*, V. iii. " Small rivers murmur, deep gulfes silent flow "; *Macbeth*, IV. iii. 209-10. But this is a favourite quotation from Seneca.

[1] F. Radebrecht, *Shakespeare's Abhängigkeit von John Marston*, 1918. Cf. Thorndike, *Relations of " Hamlet " to Contemporary Revenge Plays*, *P.M.L.A.* xvii. pp. 200-1. Radebrecht is reviewed by Charlton in *M.L.R.* xvii. I owe these references to H. Harvey Wood's edition of Marston. See my letters in *T.L.S.* October 1948.

[2] *Review of English Studies*, April 1946.

before cutting—while he remained uninfluenced by later and greater scenes.

One other parallel remains to be mentioned. In the anonymous play, *Cæsar's Revenge*, are the lines:

> Why thinke you Lords that tis ambitions spur
> That pricketh *Cæsar* to these high attempts,
> Or hope of Crownes, or thought of Diademes.
>
> —(1468-70)

The resemblance to *Macbeth*, I. vii. 25-7 (spur . . . prick . . . ambition) is not likely to be fortuitous. *Cæsar's Revenge* was entered in the Stationers' Register in June 1606; but the play is old-fashioned in style, and might well have been written in the previous reign. We must assume that Shakespeare was the borrower in this case too.

If, therefore, Shakespeare borrowed from these two plays, very little remains of the case that a *Macbeth* existed before 1606. It has been suggested by Dr. Dover Wilson that the passage about the hanging of traitors (IV. ii. 44-63) is an interpolation, as it is prose in the middle of a verse scene.[1] This is not impossible; but there is no means of telling whether it was interpolated five minutes or five years after the scene was originally completed. Dr. Wilson suggests further that the " milk of concord " and the " King's Evil " passages [2] were interpolated in 1606 for a Court performance. This is also possible; but the same caveat applies as before—that there was an interpolation does not prove any great lapse of time between the composition of the original scene and its revision. Then Dr. Wilson thinks that the second scene of the play must have been written soon after the Hecuba speeches in *Hamlet;* but the resemblance can better be explained as a deliberate attempt on Shakespeare's part to adopt a style suitable for " epic " narrative, on the model of Marlowe's account of the fall of Troy in *Dido* and Kyd's account of the battle in *The Spanish Tragedy.* Nothing can be deduced about the date of the scene in *Macbeth.* Lastly Dr. Wilson argues that the play has been cut so

---

[1] *Op. cit.* p. xxxi.
[2] IV. iii. 91-100, 140-60. Cf. Wilson, pp. xxxi-xxxiii.

expertly—apart from what he regards as clumsy cuts for which Middleton was responsible in I. ii.—that only Shakespeare could have performed the operation.[1] This is a large assumption, and is linked with the theory that there was a scene between Macbeth and his wife between I. iii. and I. iv.; that there was a later scene in which Lady Macbeth went with knife in hand to murder Duncan, and another dialogue between her and her husband; that Banquo in the original play made his position clear on the accession of Macbeth, and showed that he was not acquiescing in Macbeth's crimes; that the appearance of the Third Murderer was not mysterious in the original play; and that Macduff's desertion of his wife was adequately explained.[2] I find it impossible to accept any of these hypotheses, not only because there is no positive evidence for them, but because the play would greatly suffer from any one of these speculative additions. Two more dialogues between Macbeth and his wife before the murder of Duncan would be dramatically disastrous—" Enough—or too much," as Blake remarked; for Macbeth to play, or even intend to play, a passive role in the murder would detract from his tragic stature; Banquo's conduct requires no explanation; and any explanation of the Third Murderer or of Macduff's " desertion " would detract from the atmosphere of suspicion so necessary in this part of the play.

Nor can I find any real evidence that *Macbeth* was first performed in Edinburgh before the death of Queen Elizabeth, or, for that matter, that Shakespeare had ever visited Scotland. Saintsbury's opinion that there are two strata in *Macbeth* is based on the characteristics of the second scene of the play, which have been explained above. The possibility that Shakespeare derived his portrait of Lady Macbeth from Stewart's *Metrical Chronicle* is, I believe, remote; and even if it were less remote, we need not assume that he read that poem in the Scottish capital,

[1] *Op. cit.* p. xxxiii.

[2] Lady Blakeney was not aware that her husband was the Scarlet Pimpernel! See Wilson, *op. cit.* pp. xvi, xxxiv-xxxix and my notes on I. ii., I. iv. 35, I. v. 68, I. vii. 48; III. i. 1-10, 129; IV. ii. 1, IV. iii. 99-100, IV. iii. 140-59.

for he might have been lent a copy in England after James'
accession had brought a flood of Scotsmen to London.[1]

It is reasonable to assume, therefore, that the play
was first performed in 1606, first at the Globe, and afterwards at Court—perhaps with a few minor alterations,
and perhaps before King Christian of Denmark, who was
in England in July and August of that year on a visit
to his brother-in-law, James I. It would be hazardous to
attempt a more precise dating of the play.[2]

3. INTERPOLATIONS

It would be a fruitless task to detail all the passages
in *Macbeth* which, by one critic or another, have been
regarded as spurious. I have referred to many of them
in the notes to individual passages. The more important
ones are as follows:

(i) Act I, Scene i. Cuningham thought it was
written by Middleton.

(ii) Act I, Scene ii. The Clarendon editors and
Cuningham suspected this scene was by Middleton. As
I have suggested, Shakespeare was deliberately writing
in an " epic " style.[3]

[1] Shakespeare's hypothetical debt to Stewart is discussed below under
Sources, pp. xxxix-xliv.

[2] Mr. Stunz argues that as James touched for the evil at about the time
of Garnet's execution (cf. C.S.P. (*Venetian*) p. 344: " These last few days
the King has been attending to his devotions, which, according to the custom
of the country, occupy Holy Week. He has touched many for Scrofula,
they say with hopes of good effects, remembering the earlier cases of healing
conferred by his hand ") and as there were bad harvests abroad which sent
up the price of English wheat, the play must have been performed before
August 1606. Stunz dates it May-June. But I doubt whether it is possible
to tie it down so exactly, or whether we can estimate how long the play took
to write. James was touching as early as 6 November 1604. J. M. Robertson
argues in *Literary Detection* (1931) that the play was written in 1601-2.
H. N. Paul *S.A.B.*, October, 1947, pp. 149-54, suggests that the play was
first performed at Hampton Court on August 7, 1606. J. G. McManaway,
Shakespeare Survey, 2, p. 149, thinks that this " was most certainly the first
performance of Shakespeare's abbreviated version." Mr. Paul also argues
that IV. iii. 97-100 were interpolated, and that they were suggested to
Shakespeare by Marston's entertainment before James I on 31 July, in which
Concordia was to deliver a Latin oration on Concord, Peace and Unity—
three words used in the alleged interpolation. This is quite possible.

[3] Cf. Nosworthy, *Review of English Studies*, 1946. He has since suggested
privately that the battle descriptions might originally have formed part of a
" prologue armed ". Cf. *Troilus and Cressida*.

(iii) Act I, Scene iii, 1-37. The Clarendon editors and Cuningham thought these lines were by Middleton.

(iv) Act II, Scene iii, 1-22. Coleridge and the Clarendon editors thought these lines were interpolated by the actors, and presumably also the bawdy dialogue which follows, 26-42.

(v) Act III, Scene v. Most editors regard this scene as spurious.

(vi) Act IV, Scene i, 39-43, 125-32. Many editors regard these lines as spurious.

(vii) Act IV, Scene ii, 30-64. Cuningham thought this passage was spurious.

(viii) Act IV, Scene iii, 140-60. The Clarendon editors believed this to be an interpolation.

(ix) Act v, Scene ii. The Clarendon editors doubted the authenticity of this scene.

(x) Act v, Scene ix. The Clarendon editors thought this passage showed " evident traces of another hand."

Most of these do not require further discussion. Mr. Nosworthy has proved the authenticity of Nos ii and x. Professor Knights and others have defended Nos. i and iii. No one who regards Nos. vii-ix as spurious has offered any serious evidence.[1] There remain Nos. iv-vi. No. iv is worth discussing merely because it was an aberration of one of the greatest of critics; with regard to Nos. v and vi, I agree with previous editors that the passages are spurious, but I think it has been too easily assumed that the interpolator was Middleton.

(A) *The Porter Scene*

I have said enough, in discussing the date of the play, to indicate some of the contemporary significance of the Porter scene. Few critics would now agree with Coleridge that the soliloquy with which the scene begins was, apart from one obviously Shakespearean phrase, interpolated by the players.[2]

---

[1] Nor need we pursue that prince of disintegrators, J. M. Robertson, in his attempts to divide the authentic from the spurious in *Literary Detection*.

[2] Coleridge's *Shakespearean Criticism*, ed. Raysor, i. pp. 75-8. Coleridge had no love for low jokes; on the other hand he could not help noticing the Shakespearean ring of the phrase, " the primrose way to the everlasting bonfire." So, by giving the low jokes to another writer, and retaining for Shakespeare an indisputably Shakespearean phrase, Coleridge was able to safeguard the dramatist's moral, as well as his poetical, reputation.

The scene is theatrically necessary, because the actor who plays Macbeth has to change his costume and wash his hands, and (as Capell suggested) it was necessary " to give a rational space for the discharge of these actions." Shakespeare himself was fully conversant with theatrical necessities; but if these were the sole reason for the scene's existence it might have been added by another hand.

Some scene there had to be between the exit of Macbeth and the entrance of Macduff. But this does not explain why Shakespeare should choose or permit a drunken Porter, when a sober Porter, singing an aubade, as in one of the German versions, might seem to do as well. Comic relief is a convenient, but question-begging, term; for Shakespeare, we might suppose, could have used lyrical relief, if relief were needed. As Coleridge pointed out, Shakespeare never introduced the comic " but when it may react on the tragedy by harmonious contrast." A great dramatist does not laboriously create feelings of tension and intensity to dissipate them in laughter. Sometimes he may use humour as a laughter-conductor, so as to prevent the audience from laughing in the wrong place, and at the wrong things, thereby endangering the sublimity of the hero. In the present case, too, it is impossible to agree with those critics who think the function of the Porter is to take the present horror from the scene. On the contrary, the effect of the Porter's scene is almost the opposite of this. It is there—I do not say for the groundlings, but for the more judicious—in order to increase the horror of the situation. We are never allowed to forget, throughout the scene, the crime that has been committed and is about to be discovered. If we laugh, it is not the laughter of oblivion.

It is, perhaps, in accordance with the Scottish national character that a Porter in his cups should talk in true Calvinistic fashion of damnation. In his opening words he identifies himself with the traditional figure of the miracle plays, the porter of hell-gate,[1] who was expected to make jests, but who was something more than a jester. The purpose of linking the Porter with this traditional character was two-fold: first, because it transports us

[1] Hales, *Notes and Essays on Shakespeare*, 1884, pp. 273-90.

from Inverness to the gate of Hell, without violating the unity of place, for Shakespeare has only to tell us the name of the place we were in before. It is the gate of hell because Lady Macbeth has called on the murthering ministers, because Macbeth has called on the stars to hide their fires, and because hell is a state, and not a place, and the murderers might say with Mephostophilis—

> "where we are is hell,
> And where hell is, there must we ever be."

Shakespeare's second reason for recalling the miracle plays was that it enabled him to cut the cable that moored his tragedy to a particular spot in space and time, so that it could become universalized on the one hand, or become contemporary on the other. Macbeth's tragedy might therefore appear as a second Fall, with Lady Macbeth as a second Eve; or it could appear as terrifyingly contemporary. As Mr. Bethell puts it,

the historical element distances and objectifies what is contemporary, and the contemporary element gives current significance to an historical situation. The equivocators, for example, had conspired to kill the king, as Macbeth was doing: and Macbeth's own regicide involved him in a life of equivocation. The whole atmosphere of treason and distrust which informs *Macbeth* found a parallel in the England of the Gunpowder Plot, so that a passing reference serves to define an attitude both to the Macbeth regime and to contemporary affairs.[1]

The reference to treason in the Porter's speech looks back to the executed Thane of Cawdor, the gentleman on whom Duncan had built an absolute trust; and it looks forward to the dialogue between Lady Macduff and her son, and to the long testing of Macduff by Malcolm —which shows the distrust and suspicion which grow from equivocation and hypocrisy. Later in the play, Macbeth complains of

> th' equivocation of the fiend
> That lies like truth;

and of those juggling fiends

> That palter with us in a double sense,
> That keep the word of promise to our ear,
> And break it to our hope.

[1] *Shakespeare and the Popular Dramatic Tradition*, 1944, p. 46. P. Ure points out (N.Q., 28 May, 1949) that the chapter added to Warner's *Albion's England* (1606) dealing with the story of Macbeth is immediately followed by one on the Gunpowder Plot.

Indeed, as Dowden pointed out,[1] Macbeth on his next appearance is compelled to equivocate. Later in the same scene there is an even more striking equivocation:

> Had I but died an hour before this chance,
> I had liv'd a blessed time; for from this instant
> There's nothing serious in mortality;
> All is but toys: renown and grace is dead;
> The wine of life is drawn, and the mere lees
> Is left this vault to brag of.

The audience knows, as Macbeth himself was to know—though he here intended to deceive—that the words are a precise description of the truth about himself. Macbeth's own equivocation, by an ironical twist, becomes merely an aspect of truth. It is a brilliant counterpart to the equivocation of the fiend that lies like truth: it is the equivocation of the murderer who utters truth like lies. Equivocation therefore links up with one of the main themes of the play, and the equivocator would have earned his place in the Porter scene if Father Garnet had never lived.

Similarly, the unnaturalness of the avaricious farmer is contrasted with the images of natural growth and harvest which are scattered through the play; and he is connected with the equivocator, because Garnet went under the alias of Farmer. Even the tailor has his place in the scheme of the play, because of the clothing imagery which is so abundant in it.[2]

Nor is the style of the scene un-Shakespearean. Bradley pointed out resemblances between Pompey's soliloquy on the inhabitants of the prison in *Measure for Measure* and the Porter's soliloquy and between the dialogue of Pompey with Abhorson (IV. ii. 22 ff.) and the dialogue that follows the Porter's soliloquy.[3] We may go further and suggest that one of the Porter's speeches, often bowdlerized out of existence, provides a valuable clue to one theme of the play. He is speaking of the effects of liquor, in answer

---

[1] *New Shakespeare Society Transactions* (1874).
[2] Not only the image of the ill-fitting garments pointed out by Miss Spurgeon, *Shakespeare's Imagery*, pp. 325-7. Cf. notes on II. iii. 6, 9, 16,
[3] *Shakespearean Tragedy*, p. 397.

to Macduff's question: " What three things does drink especially provoke? "

Marry, Sir, nose-painting, sleep and urine. Lechery, Sir, it provokes, and unprovokes: it provokes the desire, but it takes away the performance. Therefore much drink may be said to be an equivocator with lechery: it makes him, and it mars him; it sets him on, and it takes him off; it persuades him, and disheartens him; makes him stand to, and not stand to: in conclusion, equivocates him in a sleep, and giving him the lie, leaves him.

Drink " provokes the desire, but it takes away the performance "; and this contrast between *desire* and *act* is repeated several times in the course of the play. Lady Macbeth, in invoking the evil spirits, begs them not to allow compunctious visitings of nature to shake her fell purpose,

> nor keep peace between
> Th' effect and it:

That is, intervene between her purpose and its fulfilment. Two scenes later she asks her husband:

> Art thou afeard
> To be the same in thine own act and valour
> As thou art in desire?

In the last scene in which the weird sisters appear (IV. i.), Macbeth gives some variations on the same theme:

> The flighty purpose never is o'ertook,
> Unless the deed go with it. From this moment,
> The very firstlings of my heart shall be
> The firstlings of my hand. And even now,
> To crown my thoughts with acts, be it thought and done . . .
> This deed I'll do, before this purpose cool.

This passage is linked with one at the end of the Banquet scene, where Macbeth tells his wife:

> Strange things I have in head, that will to hand,
> Which must be acted, ere they may be scanned.

The opposition between the hand and the other organs and senses recurs again and again. Macbeth observes the functioning of his own organs with a strange objectivity: in particular, he speaks of his hand almost as though it had an independent existence of its own.

He exhorts his eye to wink at the hand; when he sees the imaginary dagger, he decides that his eyes have been made the fools of the other senses, or else worth all the rest; later in the same speech his very footsteps seem, as it were, to be divorced from himself:

> Hear not my steps, which way they walk, for fear
> The very stones prate of my where-about;

and, after the murder of Duncan, both criminals are obsessed by the thought of their bloody hands. Macbeth speaks of them as " a sorry sight " and as " hangman's hands "—the hangman had to draw and quarter his victim; Lady Macbeth urges him to wash the " filthy witness " from his hand; and in the great speech that follows her exit, Macbeth asks:

> What hands are here? Ha! they pluck out mine eyes.
> Will all great Neptune's ocean wash this blood
> Clean from my hand? No, this my hand will rather
> The multitudinous seas incarnadine,
> Making the green one red.

In the first line of this quotation the hand–eye opposition appears in its most striking, most hallucinated, form. Lady Macbeth persists in her illusion that a little water clears them of the deed—an illusion she has to expiate in the sleep-walking scene. Just before the murder of Banquo, Macbeth invokes Night:

> Scarf up the tender eye of pitiful day,
> And, with thy bloody and invisible hand,
> Cancel, and tear to pieces, that great bond
> Which keeps me pale.

The bloody hand has now been completely detached from Macbeth and become a part of Night. Later in the play we are reminded of the same series of images when Angus declares that Macbeth feels

> His secret murthers sticking on his hands.[1]

[1] The hand–eye opposition was possibly suggested by the Biblical injunctions to pluck out the eye that offends, and to cut off the hand that offends; for these occur in chapters which are echoed elsewhere in the play. In *Matt.* vi. there are references to the single eye and to the fowls of the air, mentioned by Macduff's son; *Matt.* v is echoed several times in the scenes relating to the murder of Banquo; *Matt.* xviii contains references to the

The Porters words on lechery have yet another significance. They are written in an antithetical form:
*provokes—unprovokes; provokes—takes away; desire—peform-
ance; makes—mars; sets on—takes off; persuades—disheartens;
stand to—not stand to.* Here concentrated in half a dozen
lines we find one of the predominant characteristics of
the general style of the play—it consists of multitudinous
antitheses. The reader has only to glance at any page
of the play.[1] We may link this trick of style with the
" wrestling of destruction with creation "[2] which Mr.
Wilson Knight has found in the play, and with the opposition he has pointed out between night and day, life and
death, grace and evil. Mgr. Kolbe likewise speaks of
the play as a " picture of a special battle in a universal
war "—the war, that is, between sin and grace—and he
declares that

this idea is portrayed and emphasized in words and phrases more than
400 times. . . . Not a single scene in the play is without the colour.
And the whole effect is enhanced by the two-fold contrast we have
already observed,—Darkness and Light, as a parable, Discord and
Concord as a result.[3]

But the play contains many antitheses which are not to
be found under such headings as Angel and Devil, good
and evil. It may even be suggested that the iterative
image of ill-fitting garments is a kind of pictorial antithesis, a contrast between the man and his clothes, as in
the lines—

> Now does he feel his title
> Hang loose about him, like a giant's robe
> Upon a dwarfish thief.

Another recurrent image—not mentioned by Miss Spurgeon
—may be regarded as a contrast between the picture and
the thing depicted:

---

everlasting fire and to offending " one of these little ones " (cf. IV. ii. 68);
Mark ix contains the same references; and *Luke* xi mentions Beelzebub
three times, and also knocking. Cf. note to II. ii. 58 and R. Walker, *op. cit.*

[1] E.g. in the First Act: i. 4, 11; ii. 26, 67; iii. 38, 41, 45, 51, 53, 61,
64-5, 81, 124, 131, 138, 141; v. 20-3, 49, 57, 68; vii. 6, 15, 20-1, 44, 46, 53,
82. *Much Ado* also contains much antithesis.

[2] *The Imperial Theme*, p. 153.   [3] *Shakespeare's Way*, 1930, pp. 21-2.

> the sleeping and the dead
> Are but as pictures: 'tis the eye of childhood
> That fears a painted devil.
>
> This is the very painting of your fear.
>
> Shake off this downy sleep, death's counterfeit,
> And look on death itself!   Up, up, and see
> The great doom's image!

These images are linked with the equivocation, deceit, and treachery which have been noted by more than one critic as constituting one of the main themes of the play. These too are a contrast between appearance and reality.[1]

The style of the Porter's speech is not alien to that of the rest of the play.   It possesses the antithetical characteristics of the verse, suitably " transprosed " for semi-comic purposes.   The whole scene is linked so closely with the rest of the play, in content as well as in style, that it is impossible to regard it as a barbarous interpolation of the actors.   The antithetical style is a powerful means of suggesting the paradox and enigma of the nature of man,

> The glory, jest, and riddle of the world,

the conflict within him between sin and grace, between reason and emotion, and the shadow which falls

> Between the potency
> And the existence
> Between the essence
> And the descent.

This discussion of the authenticity of the scene has led us imperceptibly into a consideration of the play as a whole; and this in itself may serve to show that the Porter is an integral part of the play.   We might almost apply Bishop Wordsworth's remark on the scene—though he meant something rather different: " I believe it may be read with edification."

[1] Cf. Knight, *The Wheel of Fire*, 1949, pp. 140-59; Knights, *Explorations*, pp. 18 ff.; T. Spencer, *Shakespeare and the Nature of Man*, pp. 153-62.

(B) *The Hecate Scenes*

Two songs were interpolated in III. v. and IV. i. from Middleton's *The Witch*, a play which was not printed until 1778. It has, however, come down to us in a transcript by Ralph Crane, one of the scriveners of the King's Men. He states that the play was " long since acted by His Majesty's servants at the Blackfriars "; and, as the company did not act there before the autumn of 1609, it can be assumed that the play was written after that date. The transcript has been roughly dated 1620-7, so that " long since " is likely to have been before 1620, and perhaps before 1615.[1] Lawrence argues that *The Witch* was written soon after Jonson's *Masque of Queenes*, and suggests that the same performers, the same dances, and the same costumes were used.[2] This is plausible enough; but we cannot tell how long the performers and costumes would be available, if indeed they were available at all. Dr. Wilson thinks 1609-10 is a " highly probable date " for *The Witch*. But it may be that Middleton did not start writing for the King's men before 1614, and that *The Witch* was not written until 1616.[3]

It is impossible to determine when the two songs were added to *Macbeth*. Forman's account in 1611 does not help us one way or the other, because he does not mention the Cauldron scene. Perhaps the astrologer thought that no profitable moral " for common policy " could be drawn from the equivocating prophecies, which might warn spectators not to believe in the prophecies of even respectable astrologers.[4] One would like to think that Shakespeare was dead and buried, or at least living in retirement at Stratford, before his fellows spoilt his play. It is reasonable to assume that Shakespeare himself would have been called in to revise the play, if he had been available. On the whole I am inclined to think that the play

---

[1] Cf. Greg, *Elizabethan Dramatic Documents*, pp. 358-9; F. P. Wilson's article on Crane in *The Library*, vii. 194-215; Chambers, *Elizabethan Stage*, ii. 510; Dover Wilson, *op. cit.* pp. xxvii-xxviii.

[2] *Shakespeare's Workshop*, pp. 28-33.

[3] Cf. Bald, *Modern Language Review*, xxxii. p. 43.

[4] Forman successfully prophesied the day of his own death, and the sceptical have therefore suspected that he took his own life.

was contaminated after the performance witnessed by Forman, and possibly—if the same performers and costumes were used—soon afterwards.

But was Middleton himself responsible? or was he equally the victim of vandalism? Mr. J. M. Nosworthy points out that

> The Hecate of Middleton's *The Witch* is a very different creature from the *prima donna* and *prima ballerina* of *Macbeth*. She is coarse, brusque and colloquial, speaking mainly in blank verse . . . and never in octosyllabic couplets.

He goes on to argue that

> There is no reason why the Hecate so rudely thrust into *Macbeth* should not have had all the properties of her namesake in *The Witch*. Close comparison of the two plays has convinced me that, of all contemporary claims to the Hecate scenes, Middleton's is, in fact, the weakest.[1]

Mr. Nosworthy is surely right, and I believe that the Hecate passages (III. v.; IV. i. 39-43, 125-32) were all written by an anonymous writer, not without poetic ability, who was instructed to explain and introduce the two songs and the dance which had been interpolated from *The Witch*. It was then found necessary to make certain other alterations in the play. Perhaps some cuts were made in I. ii. iii. and iv.; and apparently there was some re-arrangement of scenes later in the play.

Fifty years ago it was conjectured by Crosse[2] that III. vi. should follow IV. i. and he suggested that it was shifted to its present position, on the interpolation of the Hecate scene, so as to prevent the juxtaposition of two witch scenes. Lenox and the Lord, Crosse argued, converse on matters which have not yet occurred, and of which Macbeth was ignorant until informed by Lenox at the end of IV. i. Chambers points out that Macbeth decides (III. iv. 132-3) to go on the following morning to the Weird Sisters, and IV. i. presumably takes place only a few hours after the end of the Banquet scene. Macbeth at the same time declares that he will send to-morrow to Macduff; and yet in III. vi. we hear that his messenger

---

[1] *The Review of English Studies*, April 1948, p. 138.
[2] *Notes and Queries*, 22 October 1898.

has already been repulsed by Macduff, and that the latter has fled to England. A considerable interval is therefore required between III. iv. and III. vi. It might be added that Macbeth's spy at Fife must have been singularly incompetent not to discover that Macduff had fled until after the " Lord " had told Lenox. Now Shakespeare has elsewhere deliberately departed from chronological sequence for the sake of some dramatic effect,[1] and his dramatic time is seldom realistic, but in this case the loss of dramatic surprise at Macduff's flight (IV. i. 142) is a heavy price to pay for some increase of irony (IV. i. 82). I think we must assume (1) that III. vi. originally followed IV. i. and (2) that Lenox's speeches in one scene or the other originally belonged to another character. This scene, III. vi., would then be an effective means of expanding the brief anouncement that Macduff had fled at the end of IV. i. There is, however, a difficulty. The Banquet scene and the Cauldron scene would thereby be juxtaposed, and the furniture of the former would have to be removed. This might be done by drawing a traverse on the departure of the guests in the Banquet scene; or there might be an interval; or III. vi. may consist of an amalgam of two scenes, one of which came before, and one after, the Cauldron scene.[2]

Middleton was himself influenced by *Macbeth* when he wrote *The Witch* as the following parallels will show:

(i) " For the maid servants and the girls o' th' house,
    I spic'd them lately with a drowsy posset."
    (IV. iii. 17) " Francisca is watching late at night to encourage the perpetration of a murder " (Steevens). Cf. *Macbeth*, II. ii. 6.

(ii) " the innocence of sleep " (IV. iii. 47). Cf. *Macbeth*, II, ii. 35.

(iii) " There's no such thing " (IV. iii. 78).
    " Francisca when she undeceives her brother, whose imagination has been equally abused " (Steevens). Cf. *Macbeth*, II. i. 47.

---

[1] *Troilus and Cressida*, III. iii. must come chronologically before III. ii.

[2] But see note on III. iv. 131 and *M.L.N.* xv. p. 81. R. Walker, *The Time is Free*, Chap. 5, has a detailed defence of III. vi. which brushes aside the difficulties; but J. Q. Adams in his edition, 1931, argues that the scene is spurious.

(iv) " I'll rip thee down from neck to navel " (v. i. 16).   Cf.
    Macbeth, i. ii. 22.

(v)   " Why shak'st thy head so,
    And look'st so pale and poorly? " (iii. ii. 145-6).
    Cf. *Macbeth*, i. vii. 37; ii. ii. 64, 71.

There are also a number of parallels with the Witch scenes
in *Macbeth*, which may be explained by the fact that the
two dramatists drew on similar sources for their information.
Some of these parallels are with the Hecate scenes.

Lamb, in a famous passage, described the differences
between Middleton's witches and the Weird Sisters:

> His witches are distinguished from the witches of Middleton by
> essential differences. These are creatures to whom man or woman
> plotting some dire mischief might resort for occasional consultation.
> Those originate deeds of blood, and begin bad impulses to men.   From
> the moment that their eyes first met Macbeth he is spellbound.   That
> meeting sways his destiny.   He can never break the fascination.   These
> witches can hurt the body; those have power over the soul.   Hecate,
> in Middleton, has a son, a low buffoon: the hags of Shakespeare have
> neither child of their own, nor seem descended from any parent.   They
> are foul Anomalies, of whom we know not whence they are sprung
> nor whether they have beginning or ending.   As they are without
> human passions, so they seem to be without human relations.   They
> come with thunder and lightning, and vanish to airy music.   This is
> all we know of them.   Except Hecate, they have no names; which
> heightens their mysteriousness.   Their names, and some of the pro-
> perties, which Middleton has given to his hags, excite smiles.   The
> Weird Sisters are serious things.   Their presence cannot co-exist
> with mirth.   But in a lesser degree, the Witches of Middleton are fine
> creations.   Their power, too, is, in some measure, over the mind.
> They raise jars, jealousies, strifes, *like a thick scurf o'er life*.[1]

It may be observed, however, that the weird sisters do
not plant the seeds of evil in Macbeth; that they have
no power over the innocent; that hatred and the love of
power are, alas, human passions; and that Lamb had
no reason to suppose that the Hecate scenes were spurious
—as they doubtless are.[2]

---

[1] *Specimens of English Dramatic Poets.*
[2] " The speeches of the three weird sisters . . . are prevailingly tetra-
meter with a trochaic cadence, the rhythm which Shakespeare almost always,
if not always, adopts in songs and in lyrical passages hardly to be told from
songs . . . The fact that the speeches of Hecate and the First Witch

4. SOURCES

The main source of *Macbeth*, and perhaps the only one, was Holinshed's *Chronicles;* but Kempe, in his *Nine Daies Wonder* (1600), refers to what was apparently a ballad on the subject, and ballads were frequently based on plays:

I met a proper vpright youth, onely for a little stooping in the shoulders, all hart to the heele, a penny Poet whose first making was the miserable stolne story of Macdoel or Macdobeth or Macsomewhat, for I am sure a Mac it was though I neuer had the maw to see it.

Kempe proceeds to advise its author to " leaue writing these beastly ballets, make not good wenches prophetesses for little or no profit "—which may well be a reference to the three Weird Sisters. As Kempe seems very vague about the details it is difficult to deduce anything definite from this reference: but he presumably would not speak of a stolen story if it were merely taken from Holinshed, and it is reasonable to assume that the ballad was based on a play—perhaps on a play with which Kempe was not personally acquainted. Shakespeare may have seen this ballad, and may have known the play on which it was based.[1]

(III. v. 4-43; IV. i. 39-43, 125-32) are in iambic measures creates, I think, a strong presumption against their Shakespearean authorship. . . . What is more, the metre of these speeches of Hecate—dull, mechanical, regular, touched with favour and prettiness—is in striking and almost amusing contrast with the grotesqueness, the freedom, the bold roughness of the colloquies and incantations of the weird sisters " (D. L. Chambers, *The Metre of* " *Macbeth* "; quoted Lawrence, *op. cit.* pp. 36-7).

[1] Collier professed to discover the following entry in the Stationers' Register: " 27 die Augusti 1596. Tho. Millington—Thomas Millington is likewyse fyned at ijs vjd for printinge of a ballad contrarye to order, which he also presently paid. *Md. the ballad entituled the taming of a shrew. Also one other Ballad of Macdobeth.*" Unfortunately the italicised words are almost certainly a modern fabrication. See Greg's remarks, *The Library*, VIII, 418, and *M.L.N.* 1930. Mrs. Stopes mentions, *Shakespeare's Industry*, pp. 95-6, that between 14 July 1567 and the following March there was performed " a tragedie of the King of Scottes; to ye which belonged the scenery of Scotland and a gret castle on the other side " (Harl. MS., 146, fo. 15). This might be an early play on Macbeth. A play called *Malcolm, Kyng of Scottes* is mentioned in Henslowe's diary (April 1602), perhaps about the Malcolm of Shakespeare's play, but more probably about Duncan's grandfather and predecessor on the throne.

Mrs. C. C. Stopes argued [1] that Shakespeare was acquainted with William Stewart's *Buik of the Croniclis of Scotland*, an enormous poem of over 42,000 lines which remained in manuscript until 1858. It was written 1531-5 by order of Queen Margaret, for the use of her son, James V. Mrs. Stopes' essay was written in 1897, but it has not found many supporters. She does not give any example of a real verbal parallel between Stewart and Shakespeare. Although " till the warldis end " may be compared with " the crack of doom " (IV. i. 117), it may be noted that Lancelot Andrewes, in his sermon on the coronation of James I, speaks of the King's descendants, " who shall (wee trust, and pray they may) stretch their line to the world's end."

It seems to me that the resemblances between Stewart and Shakespeare are accidental, and that any poet expanding the bare facts of the story would tend to develop Lady Macbeth's character in the same way. From Holinshed Shakespeare would learn that Donwald committed the murder of Duff *through setting on of his wife*, who *bare no lesse malice in hir heart towards the king* and showed Donwald *the meanes wherby he might soonest accomplish it*. Although Donwald *abhorred the act greatlie in heart, yet through instigation of his wife* he bribed the servants to do the deed. In the section of the *Chronicles* relating to Macbeth himself Shakespeare would have read that *his wife lay sore upon him to attempt the thing, as she was verie ambitious, burning in vnquenchable desire to beare the name of a queene*. From these hints of the ambition of the wife and the moral scruples of the murderer, it would not be difficult for any dramatist to deduce that Lady Macbeth called her husband a coward, bade him play the hypocrite, and herself pretended great indignation after the murder to cover up their guilt. Even the real or feigned swoon of Lady Macbeth need not necessarily have been suggested by the pretended swoon of Donwald. Nor would it be difficult for two poets independently to have arrived at the idea of Banquo's descendants reigning till the end of the world from Holinshed's " long order of continuall descent.' (Matthew Gwinn, indeed, made his three sibyls prophecy to Banquo's descendants *imperium sine fine*.)

It is more likely, as M. H. Liddell and H. N. Paul have argued,[1] that Shakespeare had read Buchanan's *History of Scotland* in its original Latin. His hero is, perhaps, nearer to Buchanan's portrait of Macbeth than to Holinshed's. Buchanan says he

> was a man of penetrating genius, a high spirit, unbounded ambition, and, if he had possessed moderation, was worthy of any command however great; but in punishing crimes he exercised a severity, which, exceeding the bounds of the laws, appeared oft to degenerate into cruelty.

Holinshed speaks of him merely as a " valiant gentleman." The account given by Buchanan of King Kenneth's remorse is likewise closer than Holinshed's to Macbeth's:

> His soul disturbed by a consciousness of his crime, permitted him to enjoy no solid or sincere pleasure; in retirement the thoughts of his unholy deed tormented him; and, in sleep, visions full of horror drove repose from his pillow. At last, whether in truth an audible voice from heaven addressed him, as is reported, or whether it were the suggestion of his guilty mind, as often happens with the wicked, in the silent watches of the night, he seemed thus to be admonished.

Buchanan's statement that " the command of Cumberland was always considered the next step to the crown " is nearer to Macbeth's lines (I. iv. 48-50) than the corresponding passage in Holinshed.

Mr. Paul has also argued that Shakespeare knew Leslie's *De Origine, Moribus, et Rebus Gestis Scotorum* (1578), in which the Weird Sisters are devils disguised as women, as they may be in Shakespeare's play, and in which there is a genealogical tree of Banquo's descendants with roots, leaves and fruit. This may well have caught Shakespeare's eye and left its mark on the imagery of Acts III and IV, though he had used this imagery before.[2] Leslie, moreover, makes no mention of Macbeth's accomplices, he stresses the way in which Lady Macbeth persuaded her husband by showing him how the deed could be successfully accomplished—as Donwald's wife does in Holinshed—he speaks of the " most

---

[1] Ed. *Macbeth* (1903); *The Royal Play of Macbeth* (1950).

[2] Cf. " root " (III. i. 5), " stick deep " (III. i. 48), " seeds " (III. i. 69), and " snake " (III. ii. 13; III. iv. 28), the last two being suggested by the fruit and the serpentine trunk of the tree in the picture.

holy king Duncan," and he gives a more vivid account than Holinshed of Macbeth's reign of terror.[1]

In any case, there is no doubt that Holinshed was the main source of the play, and that Shakespeare combined the account of the murder of King Duff with the later account of Macbeth. He may have got some hints about witchcraft from Holinshed's story of the noblemen who conspired with witches against King Duff; and he certainly took several details from the murder of Duff by Donwald and his wife, including the incitement by the wife, the fact that the King was a guest of the murderer and had just given him presents, the murder of the chamberlains whom Donwald and his wife had sent to bed drunk, the pretended indignation of Donwald, and the various portents accompanying the murder. But in Holinshed's account the murder is carried out by four of Donwald's servants who remove the body from the castle. Holinshed's marginalia read almost like a running commentary on the play and they may have given hints to Shakespeare on the dramatic treatment of the subject:

A giltie conscience accuseth a man. . . . Donwald's wife counselled him to murther the king. . . . The womans euill counsell is followed. . . . Donwald a verie dissembler. . . . Prophecies mooue men to vnlawfull attempts . . . women desirous of high estate. . . . Mackbeth's guiltie conscience. . . . Mackbeths dread. . . . His crueltie caused through feare. . . . Mackbeths confidence in wizzards. . . . Macbeth recoileth (cf. v. ii. 23). . . . Mackbeths trust in prophecies.

The voice that cried "Sleep no more" was probably suggested by the voice heard by King Kenneth after he had murdered his nephew—as described by Holinshed or Buchanan. One or two details were derived from the account of Edward the Confessor's reign, and by a lucky chance touching for the king's evil was topical as well as historically accurate. But the main plot was taken from Holinshed's account of Macbeth, though with many alterations.[2] Shakespeare keeps close to the chronicler in his account of Macbeth's meeting with the Weird Sisters and in the scene between Macduff and Malcolm in England.

---

[1] See Appendices B and C. Paul believes that Shakespeare also consulted Skene's *Scots Acts*; but he did not need to read this book in order to make Duncan " a good and modest prince " and Macbeth " a cruel tyrant."

[2] R. A. Law, *University of Texas Studies in English* (1952), has a useful list of thirty-five incidents in the play which are not to be found in Holinshed. Most of these, however, are inevitable results of dramatizing the story.

In these two scenes there are a number of verbal parallels, partly because in both places Holinshed uses direct speech. Elsewhere Shakespeare occasionally uses single words which may have been suggested by the *Chronicle*, but not many.

The following are the most striking differences: (i) Duncan, as depicted by Holinshed, is younger than in the play, and he is depicted as a feeble ruler. By making the victim old and holy and by passing over his weaknesses, Shakespeare deliberately blackened the guilt of Macbeth. (ii) There are three campaigns described in Holinshed which are condensed into one in the play: the defeat of Macdonwald's rebellion, the defeat of Sweno, and the defeat of Canute, who came with a new fleet to avenge his brother Sweno's overthrow. (iii) Macbeth in the *Chronicle* has a genuine grievance against Duncan, who by proclaiming his son Prince of Cumberland went against the laws of succession, and took away from Macbeth the prospect of the throne; which he had every reason to hope for, since he could claim it on behalf of his wife and her son by her first husband. Shakespeare suppresses these facts, partly because he wished for dramatic reasons to accentuate Macbeth's guilt and to minimize any excuses he might have had, and partly for accidental reasons. Macbeth was the murderer of James I's ancestor, and could not be depicted in a favourable light, and because of " the triumph of primogeniture during the twelfth and thirteenth centuries" [1] the method of succession which existed in Macbeth's day was not fully understood in Shakespeare's, even by Holinshed. (iv) Banquo and others were accomplices in the murder of Duncan, which was carried out as an open political assassination. This was altered, partly because it was more dramatic for Macbeth and his wife to bear the whole responsibility for the murder, and partly because Banquo's reputation as James I's ancestor has to be safeguarded. James had a particular dislike of political assassination, even of manifest tyrants. [2] Shakespeare

---

[1] Wilson, *op. cit.*, p. ix.

[2] Cf. James, *The Trew Law of Free Monarchies*, in *Political Works*, ed. McIlwain, pp. 60-1, 66: " And although there was neuer a more monstrous persecutor, and tyrant nor *Achab* was: yet all the rebellion, that *Elias* euer raised against him, was to flie to the wildernes: where for fault of sustentation, he was fed with the Corbies. . . . Vnder the lawe, *Ieremie* threateneth

therefore took the details of the murder from Donwald's murder of Duff. (v) Shakespeare omits the ten years' good rule by Macbeth between the murder of Duncan and the murder of Banquo. It would obviously have ruined the play by breaking it into two and by interfering with Shakespeare's conception of the workings of conscience. (vi) Shakespeare invents the Banquet scene and the appearance of the ghost of Banquo. (vii) He omits the story of Macduff's refusal to assist in the building of Dunsinane Castle. It would have been difficult to dramatize and was not strictly relevant to the main theme of the play. (viii) The Cauldron scene is based on the three prophecies mentioned by Holinshed, but Shakespeare substitutes the Weird Sisters for " a certeine witch, whom hee had in great trust." (ix) In the *Chronicle*, Macbeth surrounded Macduff's castle with a great power. It was more economical dramatically to use murderers. (x) The testing of Macduff by Malcolm is given in full in Holinshed (and it is also to be found in Boece, Bellenden, and Stewart); but Shakespeare omits—at least in the existing text—the fable of the Fox and the Flies and adds other vices to those mentioned by Holinshed. In the *Chronicle* the testing of Macduff occurs after he has heard of his wife's death. Shakespeare's alteration enabled him to motivate Malcolm's suspicions. (xi) In the *Chronicle* Macbeth flees from Dunsinane Castle and is pursued by Macduff to Lunfannaine—an incident which would have been dramatically irrelevant. (xii) Shakespeare invents the sleep-walking scene and the presumed suicide of Lady Macbeth. Holinshed says nothing about the fate of Macbeth's wife or of Donwald's.

---

the people of God with vtter destruction for rebellion to *Nabuchadnezar* . . . who although he was an idolatrous persecutor, a forraine King; a Tyrant, a vsurper of their liberties; yet in respect they had once receiued and acknowledged him for their king, he not only commandeth them to obey him, but euen to pray for his prosperitie, adioyning the reason to it; because in his prosperitie stood their peace . . . that king whom *Paul* bids the *Romanes obey* and serue *for conscience sake*, was *Nero* that bloody tyrant, an infamie to his aage, and a monster to the world, being also an idolatrous persecutor. . . . The wickednesse therefore of the King can neuer make them that are ordained to be iudged by him, to become his Iudges." One wonders what James would have said of the assassination of Athaliah, though approved by scripture, and of Racine's glorification of it.

As there is nothing to show that Shakespeare had studied Holinshed's sources, and as there may have been a source play, there is no point in discussing the variants of the Macbeth story in Fordun, Andrew of Wintoun, Boece, or Bellenden; and there would be still less point in trying to isolate the " historical " Macbeth; for few would agree with Sir Herbert Tree's remark that " we must interpret Macbeth, before and at the crisis, by his just and equitable character as a king that history gives him." [1]

It has been suggested by Sir Herbert Grierson that Shakespeare derived from Holinshed's *Chronicles*

the tone and atmosphere of the Celtic and primitive legends of violent deeds and haunting remorse. . . . Story after story told him of men driven by an irresistible impulse into deeds of treachery and bloodshed but haunted when the deed was done by the spectres of conscience and superstition.[2]

---

[1] Cited by Knights, *Explorations*, p. 15. Hales, *Essays and Notes on Shakespeare*, p. 291, mentions ironically that Macbeth, historically speaking, was a good churchman. Hooker, *Ecclesiastical Polity*, provides the evidence: " Will any man deny that the Church doth need the rod of corporal punishment to keep her children in obedience withal? Such a law as Macabeus made among the Scots, that he which continued excommunicate two years together, and reconciled not himself to the Church, should forfeit all his goods and posessions." Cf. Holinshed, *op. cit.* pp. 171-2.

In Wyntoun's *Original Chronicle*, Macbeth is begotten by the Devil on a witch:

> " Gottyn he was on ferly wise.
> His modyr to woddis made rapayr
> For the delyte of haylsum ayr.
> Swa scho past apon a day
> Til a wode hir for to play;
> Scho met of casse withe a fayr man,
> Neuir nane sa fayr, as scho thoucht than,
> Befor than had scho seyn withe sycht. . . ."

This man, who is none other than the Devil, tells her

> " that hir son suld be
> A man of gret state and bounte,
> And no man sulde be borne of wif
> Off powar to reiff hym his lif."
> (VI, xviii. 1900 ff.)

Wyntoun describes a dream of Macbeth that he is hunting with Duncan when they encounter the three weird sisters. This dream had become a reality in Boece, who also substitutes Banquo for Duncan, and adds the prophecy about his descendants. Holinshed used Bellenden's translation of Boece as well as the original. See Stopes, *op. cit.* pp. 78-109 and Wilson, *op. cit.* pp. viii-xi. [2] *Macbeth*, ed. Grierson, 1914, pp. xviii-xix.

This is true; but it should be added that there is little evidence of remorse in Holinshed's account of Macbeth, and it is only implied in his treatment of Donwald.

5. MACBETH, 1606-1948

Most of the great actors and actresses during the past three hundred years have appeared in *Macbeth*, from Burbage to Mr. John Gielgud; but between 1674 and 1744 the play was performed only in D'Avenant's adaptation.[1] Garrick restored most of Shakespeare's text [2] and Macready most of the rest.

Although the play was regularly acted, it evoked little interesting criticism until the end of the eighteenth century, presumably because there was little disagreement about it. There would be some dissentients when Johnson complained of the meanness of some of Shakespeare's language,[3] but he probably expressed the general view when he summarized the play in these words:

" This play is deservedly celebrated for the propriety of its fictions, and solemnity, grandeur and variety of its action; but it has no nice discrimination of character; the events are too great to admit the influence of particular dispositions, and the course of the action necessarily determines the conduct of the agents.

" The danger of ambition is well described; and I know not whether it may not be said, in defence of some parts which now seem improbable, that, in Shakespeare's time, it was necessary to warn credulity against vain and delusive predictions.

" The passions are directed to their true end. Lady Macbeth is merely detested; and though the courage of Macbeth preserves some esteem, yet every reader rejoices at his fall."

---

[1] E.g. I. v. opens with a dialogue between Lady Macbeth and Lady Macduff; Act II. ends with a scene in which the Macduffs encounter the witches on the blasted heath; a scene between Macbeth and his wife, expressing her remorse, is interpolated in Act IV.; the testing of Macduff by Malcolm is cut; and much of the poetry appears in a debased form.

[2] But Garrick inserted the following death speech of his own composition:
" Tis done! the scene of life will quickly close.
Ambition's vain delusive dreams are fled,
And now I wake to darkness, guilt, and horror;
I cannot bear it! let me shake if off—
It will not be; my soul is clog'd with blood—
I cannot rise! I dare not ask for mercy—
It is too late, hell drags me down; I sink,
I sink,—my soul is lost for ever!—Oh!—Oh! "

[3] Cf. note on I. v. 51.

But when these words were published in 1765 the attitude implied in them was already breaking down: the performances of Garrick and Mrs. Siddons directed people's attention to the characters they played; the rise of the novel and the spread of *sensibility* put more emphasis on character than on plot; and the growth of romanticism completed what sensibility had begun. William Richardson analysed the character of Macbeth in 1774; at about the same time Whately compared Macbeth and Richard III; Cumberland followed on the same subject in *The Observer;* and J. P. Kemble answered Whately in the same year. There were a few remarks on *Macbeth* in Morgann's *Essay on the Dramatic Character of Falstaff* (1777).[1]

Coleridge's surviving remarks on *Macbeth* are mostly concerned with the first act. Some of them are valuable, but I find it difficult to agree with Mr. Raysor when he says that Coleridge's " psychological genius is most apparent in the analysis of *Macbeth*." [2] Hazlitt in *Characters of Shakespeare's Plays* owed something to Coleridge and Lamb, and something, perhaps, to Whately; but his essay is the most satisfying written on the play up to this date. He shows that the play is distinguished from the other great tragedies by " the wildness of the imagination and

---

[1] Richardson, *A Philosophical Analysis and Illustration of some of Shakespeare's Remarkable Characters* (1774); Whately, *Remarks on Some of the Characters of Shakespeare* (1785, but written 1770); J. P. Kemble, *Macbeth Reconsidered* (1786); and *The Observer* (1786). Whately argued: " Macbeth has an acquired, though not a constitutional, courage, which is equal to all ordinary occasions; and if it fails him upon those which are extraordinary, it is, however, so well formed as to be easily resumed as soon as the shock is over. But his idea never rises above manliness of character." Kemble regarded these remarks as " villifying " and argued " That Shakespeare has not put into any mouth the slightest insinuation against the personal courage of Macbeth is in itself a decisive proof that he never meant his nature should be liable to so base a reproach." But the disagreement between these two critics was really verbal. Richardson was mainly concerned with the drawing of morals. " Thus, by considering the rise and progress of a ruling passion, and the fatal consequences of its indulgence, we have shown, how a beneficent mind may become inhuman: and how those who are naturally of an amiable temper, if they suffer themselves to be corrupted, will become more ferocious and more unhappy, than men of a constitution orginally hard and unfeeling " (*op. cit.* edn. 1784, p. 85).

[2] Cf. notes on I. i; I ii. 7-23; I. iii. 41-2; I. iv. 22-7; II. iii. Raysor's remark is quoted from his Introduction to his edition of Coleridge's *Shakespearean Criticism*, p. lviii.

the rapidity of the action." [1]   Nor should it be forgotten
that Hazlitt was the best of dramatic critics and that in
praising Mrs. Siddons he often made revealing remarks
about the play itself. Mrs. Siddons' own analysis of the
character of Lady Macbeth, though not well written,
shows that the great actress had thought deeply about
the part she played so often, and the well-known account
of her first experience of learning the part shows that
she was moved by the play with which she moved
others:

" I went on with tolerable composure, in the silence of the night
(a night I can never forget), till I came to the assassination scene,
when the horrors of the scene rose to a degree that made it impossible
for me to get farther. I snatched up my candle and hurried out of
the room in a paroxysm of terror. My dress was of silk, and the
rustling of it, as I ascended the stairs to go to bed, seemed to my panic-
struck fancy like the movement of a spectre pursuing me. . . . I
clapt my candlestick down upon the table, without the power of putting
the candle out, and threw myself on my bed, without daring to stay
even to take off my clothes." [2]

Apart from De Quincey's great essay *On the Knocking
at the Gate in Macbeth* there is little to detain us between
Hazlitt and Dowden (*Shakespeare, His Mind and Art*, 1875),
except G. Fletcher, whose *Studies of Shakespeare* (1847)
have been lately praised. The merit of Fletcher's analysis
is that he does not subordinate everything else to the character of the protagonists, and that he shows that Macduff
and his Lady

" are the chief representatives in the piece, of the interests of loyalty
and domestic affection, as opposed to those of the foulest treachery
and the most selfish and remorseless ambition."

But our respect for Fletcher diminishes when we find him
saying that Macbeth, being intensely selfish,

"is incapable of any true moral repugnance to inflicting injury upon
others; it shrinks only from encountering public odium "—

or that the poetry delivered by Macbeth

" springs exclusively from a morbidly irritable fancy ";

and finally expires when he characterizes Macbeth's

[1] Edn. 1906, p. 12.   [2] Campbell, *Life of Mrs. Siddons*, 1834, ii. p. 35.

soliloquy (v. iii. 22-8) as " mere *poetical whining* over his own most merited situation." [1]

R. G. Moulton wrote a fine essay on the all-pervasive irony of the play and a less satisfactory one on Macbeth and his wife. The former is partly spoiled by a moralizing strain, and the latter by his assumption that because Macbeth offers only practical objections to the murder of Duncan he has no moral ones—Lady Macbeth being regarded as an embodiment of the inner life. [2]

After this date the interpretations of *Macbeth* multiply like the villainies of the merciless Macdonwald. Kirke argues that the terrible dreams that shake Macbeth and his wife are caused by " a remorse in which there lurks no hope of redemption. It is the remorse of the damned." [3] J. C. Carr thinks the murder of Duncan " had long been the subject of conjugal debate "; and Symons contrasts Macbeth's attempt to stand against the temptation with Lady Macbeth's prayer for power to carry out the deed. [4] This brings us to Bradley, whose *Shakespearean Tragedy* (1904) contains the most influential of all criticisms of the play.

Later criticism by Robert Bridges, Maeterlinck, Sir Herbert Grierson, Professor W. C. Curry, Mr. John Masefield, Mr. Wilson Knight, Professor L. C. Knights, Mr. J. Middleton Murry, and Dr. Dover Wilson is mentioned in the next section of the introduction. We need only notice here first, a reaction against elaborate character analysis and an increasing emphasis on the poetry of the play; secondly, a greater understanding of *Macbeth* as an acting play; and thirdly, an examination of the play, from the standpoint of Elizabethan demonology.

---

[1] *Op. cit.* pp. 109 ff. and 166.
[2] *Shakespeare as a Dramatic Artist*, 1885.   [3] *Atlantic Monthly*, 1895.
[4] Symons, *Studies in Two Literatures*, 1897, pp. 24 ff. A word is due to the ingenious Libby who, in *Some New Notes on Macbeth*, 1893, demonstrated to his own satisfaction that Ross is the real villain of the play, who first gets the Thane of Cawdor executed on a false charge of treachery, then murders Banquo, disguised as the Third Murderer, is Macbeth's agent in the murder of Macduff's family, and then, seeing that Macbeth's power is on the wane, he deserts to Malcolm and is rewarded with an earldom.

6. THE PLAY

Macbeth, as we have seen, was first performed in the year 1606; that is to say, it comes after *Hamlet, Othello, Measure for Measure,* and *King Lear,* and before *Antony and Cleopatra* and *Coriolanus.* The play is linked to *Hamlet* in more ways than one:[1] Macbeth's shrinking from the murder of Duncan, and the infirmity of purpose with which his wife charges him, are similar to Hamlet's inability to carry out the instructions of the Ghost though Macbeth's act is " evil " and Hamlet's (at least in his conscious opinion) is " good." Macbeth also resembles Claudius in that both are murderers and usurpers. Macbeth is (consciously) willing to jump the life to come, and we cannot imagine him on his knees; Claudius tries to repent: but both are led from crime to crime in their attempt to achieve security. Macbeth may, in a sense, be regarded as a humanization of Claudius: Shakespeare wished to get inside the skin of a murderer, and to show that the Poet for the Defence, though he extenuates nothing, can make us feel that we might have fallen in the same way, so that we may even assent to Professor Alexander's application of Donne's words:[2]

" Thou knowest this man's fall, but thou knowest not his wrestling; which perchance was such that almost his very fall is justified and accepted of God."

Though Macbeth is *a miserable, and a banished, and a damned creature, yet* he is God's *creature still and contributes something to his glory even in* his *damnation.*[3] We have the same feeling about his crime as we do about Angelo's—and the echoes from *Lucrece* pointed out in the Appendix show the link between lust and murder in Shakespeare's mind—because just as Angelo learns that he must not judge Claudius, so the audience learns not to judge Angelo.

[1] Cf. Stopes, *Shakespeare's Industry*, pp. 72-77, and Draper's article in *Bull. Hist. Med.* x. R. Walker, *op. cit.* chap. 9, says that " if *Hamlet* is a study of moral man in an immoral society, *Macbeth* is a study of immoral man in a moral universe." Cf. Max Plowman's *The Right to Live.*

[2] *Shakespeare's Life and Art*, p. 173.

[3] Donne, ed. Hayward, 1929, p. 663.

Othello was " an honourable murderer "; Macbeth is a noble and gifted man who falls into treachery and crime, not deluded into believing that he has any justification for his deeds, but knowing them precisely for what they are. In *King Lear*, the evil is concentrated in the savage quartet, Goneril, Regan, Edmund, and Cornwall, who are able to bring about the ruin of better people than themselves by making use of their weaknesses—pride, credulity, and lust.[1] In *Macbeth*, the evil is transferred from the villains to the hero and heroine.

Macbeth is Shakespeare's " most profound and mature vision of evil "; [2] " the whole play may be writ down as a wrestling of destruction with creation "; [2] it is " a statement of evil "; [3] " it is a picture of a special battle in a universal war, and the battleground is in the souls of Macbeth and his wife "; [4] and it " contains the decisive orientation of Shakespearean good and evil." [5] The play, we may add, is about damnation; and a modern dramatist with a taste for fancy titles might have called it *The Primrose Way*. Yet in order to show how his hero comes to be damned, in order to present a convincing image of damnation, Shakespeare had to describe and create the good which Macbeth had sacrificed; so that although there is no play in which evil is presented so forcibly, it may also be said that there is no play which puts so persuasively the contrasting good. This is done by means of the characters, certainly, though Duncan and Malcolm, the Macduffs, the messenger who comes to warn Lady Macduff, and even Banquo are little to place in the scales against the Macbeths and the Weird Sisters. It is done more effectively by means of imagery, symbolism,

[1] Charlton, *Shakespearean Tragedy*, 1948, pp. 14, 189, argues the *Macbeth* was written before *Lear* because Shakespeare's themes became progressively more primitive from *Hamlet* to *Lear*, *Hamlet* dealing with the civilized world, *Othello* with a clash of two worlds, *Macbeth* with the period when the moral sense was emerging, and *Lear* with the primitive human family, when man was near the animal level. But surely in Duncan and Edward the Confessor and in the frequent references to Christian conceptions there is evidence that Professor Charlton is wrong about the play.

[2] Knight, *The Wheel of Fire*, 1949, p. 140; *The Imperial Theme*, p. 153.
[3] Knights, *Explorations*, p. 18.   [4] Kolbe, *Shakespeare's Way*, p. 20.
[5] Traversi, *Approach to Shakespeare*, p. 86.

and iteration. The image of the ill-fitting garments, pointed out by Caroline Spurgeon, I have already discussed;[1] the contrast between light and darkness is part of a general antithesis between good and evil, devils and angels, evil and grace, hell and heaven.[2] The image of the deed too terrible to look at requires no interpretation;[3] and the disease images in IV. iii. and in the last act clearly reflect both the evil which is a disease, and Macbeth himself who *is* the disease from which his country suffers. Mr. Wilson Knight has an essay on the " life-themes " in the play, which he classes under the headings of Warrior-honour, Imperial magnificence, Sleep and Feasting, and Ideas of creation and nature's innocence.[4] He makes the point that Lady Macbeth " wins largely by appealing to Macbeth's ' valour '." [5] All through the play Shakespeare continually juggles with the different meanings of " honour." Both the words and the wounds of the bloody sergeant are said to smack of honour; but so also do the titles bestowed by Malcolm at the end of the play. " Honour " thus means both " worth " and the titles that reward it. An anonymous " Lord " pines for " free honours," and he speaks as a Chorus. Macbeth in the last act laments that he has mouth-honour instead of honour, where the word means reverence or respect; just as in the first act he wishes to wear the golden opinions he has purchased by his bravery.

The ambiguity of *honour* is best brought out in the exchange between Macbeth and Banquo just before the murder of Duncan:

> If you shall cleave to my consent, when 'tis,
> It shall make honour for you.
> So I lose none
> In seeking to augment it, but still keep
> My bosom franchis'd, and allegiance clear,
> I shall be counsell'd.

---

[1] Cf. p. xxxi. *ante*, and the note on v. ii. 21-2.
[2] Kolbe, *op, cit.* pp. 21-2. See p. xxxiii. *ante*, and e.g I. iv. 41, 50; I. v. 51; II. i. 4; I. iv. 7, 9; III. ii. 46, 52; IV. i. 48; IV. iii. 22; V. i. 23.
[3] Cf. II. ii. 53; II. iii. 76; III. iv. 60; IV. i. 113; V. v. 20.
[4] *The Imperial Theme*, p. 125.   [5] *Op. cit.* p. 127.

Closely connected with "honour" are the feudal ideas of "duties" and "service," the repetition of which helps to create a picture of an orderly and closely-knit society, in contrast to the disorder consequent upon Macbeth's initial crime. The naturalness of that order, and the unnaturalness of its violation by Macbeth, is emphasized by the images of planting and sowing, and the images of sleep and milk contrast with the images of unnatural disorder and the reiteration of fear and blood.[1] The contrast is most apparent in the lines which express so violently Lady Macbeth's violation of her sex:

> " I have given suck, and know
> How tender 'tis to love the babe that milks me:
> I would, while it was smiling in my face,
> Have pluck'd my nipple from his boneless gums,
> And dash'd the brains out, had I so sworn. . . ."

By such means Shakespeare builds up the order of Nature and examines the nature of order; so that the violation of order in the state by the assassination of Duncan is seen to be an unnatural horror, inevitably attended by portents.[2]

Nevertheless the presentation of the good which counterbalances the evil is done most effectively through Macbeth and his wife, who are unwilling witnesses to the good they renounce. Macbeth is aware that the deed he contemplates is evil from the very beginning. He admits that its "horrid image" makes his hair stand on end, and his heart knock against his ribs. Although he never discusses with his wife the morality of the murder, although he hardly faces it himself, every word he speaks shows

[1] I am indebted here to at least four critics, Knight, Knights, Traversi, and Kolbe. See also an eloquent passage in Masefield's lecture, *Shakespeare and Spiritual Life* (*Recent Prose*, 1932, pp. 270 ff.) on the significance of the portents in *Macbeth*.

[2] Presumably the riding images, mentioned by Miss Spurgeon, suggest only that Macbeth is riding for a fall. She also records four reverberation images which, she thinks, suggest the "overwhelming and unending nature of the consequences or reverberations of the evil deed." It may be worth noting that Erasmus in the same colloquy echoed in III. i. has the following passage: " I would desire to have a certain honourable renown of my name, which may Eccho again throughout the whole world, and which may become more famous with my age, and at last may grow more renowned after my death " (trans. H.M. 1671, p. 478).

that he is struck to the soul with a realization of the horror
of the deed. The half-demented language he uses immediately after the murder expresses fear, but not of
detection; and although he fears Banquo for prudential
reasons, he fears him also because of his own sense of guilt.
Macbeth is never in doubt of the difference between good
and evil; nor is Lady Macbeth, not even in the speech
in which she deliberately chooses evil as a means of achieving the " good " of the crown; nor, indeed, is the audience.
Inexorably the action rams home the well-worn moral
that " Crime does not pay," that " all the perfumes of
Arabia will not sweeten this little hand," and that, to those
who destroy life, life itself becomes merely " a tale told by
an idiot." [1]

To some critics, however, the play has seemed to be
lacking in inevitability and coherence. Robert Bridges
complained that the Macbeth we have cause to admire could
never have committed the murder of Duncan, and that
Shakespeare deliberately throws dust in the eyes of the
audience, not clearly telling them whether Macbeth
decided to murder Duncan before the beginning of the
play, or whether the idea was imposed upon him by the
witches, or whether he was urged to it by his wife— [2]

" We may combine the two latter motives, and see hell and home
leagued against him: the difficulty lies in the unknown quantity of
the first motive, his predisposition; which, if it be allowed to be only
in the exact balance required for these two agencies to carry it, is still
contradictory to the picture of nobility impressed upon us by Shakespeare."

A Macbeth who feels the horror of the deed as deeply as
Shakespeare's hero (thinks Bridges) would not be able to
commit it. The argument is that Shakespeare sacrifices
psychological consistency to theatrical effect. Professor
Stoll makes a similar point, though without regarding this
characteristic of the play as necessarily a fault. As he
points out— [3]

[1] Murry, *Shakespeare*, pp. 331-6, has a good passage on the use of time in
Macbeth to reveal the damnation of the murderers. Cf. also Spender's
article (*Penguin New Writing*, No. 3) in which he discusses the same subject
from a different angle; and R. Walker, *The Time is Free*, *passim*.

[2] Bridges, *The Influence of the Audience on Shakespeare's Dramas*, ed. 1927, p. 14.

[3] *The Review of English Studies*, xix. p. 27.

" If Macbeth had been thwarted or (to use Holinshed's word) ' defrauded,' as having, at this juncture, a better title to the throne than Malcolm, or had thought himself better fitted to rule; or, again, if Duncan had not borne his faculties so meek and been so clear in his great office, as in the tragedy, but not the chronicle he is; why, then, Macbeth's conduct in killing him would have been more reasonable and more psychologically in keeping, to be sure, but less terrible, less truly tragic."

Shakespeare was not so much concerned with the creation of real human beings, but with theatrical, or *poetical*, effect. He was fascinated by the very difficulty of making the psychologically improbable, by sheer virtuosity, appear possible. According to Schücking,[1] Shakespeare made

" the bold experiment of a character with a strongly marked mixture of qualities of which the one seems almost to preclude the other. . . . So he creates a hero such as Macbeth, who is a moral coward and for a while a henpecked husband, who in critical moments is rebuked like a schoolboy by his wife and who, on the other hand, proves himself a lion on the battlefield.[2] Or the same character is brutal enough to murder his crowned guest, but retains notwithstanding the nobility of spirit—or superstitious fear of fate?—to feel the disgracefulness of assassinating his victim in his sleep so deeply as to become possessed of the idea of having incurred the punishment of eternal insomnia. In this case, too, the interpretation has only too often missed the meaning of the author. By unduly simplifying the complicated psychological facts it has done less than justice to the wonderful and unique results of that hazardous antithetical character-construction which was favoured by the style of the time."

It is only fair to Shakespeare to add, and Professor Stoll does not always make full allowance for this, that ideas about what is psychologically possible change from age to age, and that what Bridges thought impossible seemed perfectly possible to the readers of Timothy Bright and even, to judge from criticism of the play, right down to the end of the nineteenth century.[3] Bridges

---

[1] *The Baroque Character of the Elizabethan Tragic Hero*, 1938, pp. 21-2.

[2] It should be said, however, that many lions have been tame at home.

[3] I am constrained to add that conversely Shakespeare's contemporaries would have been baffled by the psychology of Margaret, the heroine of Bridges' own *Palicio*, who betrays her lover in the hope that with the failure of his conspiracy he will abandon politics, and devote himself to her happiness. We are not meant to regard her as half-witted. Bridges could not blame the Victorian audience for the faults of his plays, as he blamed Shakespeare's, as they were not really intended for the stage. There is a good reply to Bridges in J. I. M. Stewart's *Character and Motive in Shakespeare* (1949).

under-estimates the potentialities for evil in the virtuous, and for virtue in the wicked; and there is reason to believe that the sheep and goats of our "judgement here" are not necessarily the same as those of "the life to come." "Our life is but a mingled yarn, good and ill together." Besides all this, there is something artificial in Bridges' assumption that if Macbeth has enough predisposition to be driven to murder by wife and witches combined he is too ignoble to be the tragic hero envisaged by the dramatist. For it is never possible to determine the exact share of blame to be allotted after a crime to the three factors, heredity, environment, and personal weakness; and only the morally complacent could witness a good performance of *Macbeth* without an uneasy feeling that if they had been so tempted they might conceivably have so fallen. We cannot divide the world into potential murderers and those who are not. It consists of imperfect human beings, more or less ignorant of their own selves, and not knowing (though they have been told often enough) the way to be happy. If they commit evil it is because they hope thereby to avoid another evil, which seems to them for the moment to be worse, or obtain another good, which seems attractive if only because it is not in their possession. The direct cause of sin, as Thomas Aquinas explains, is the

"*adherence to a mutable good*, and every sinful act proceeds from an inordinate desire for some temporal good; and that one desires a temporal good inordinately is due to the fact that *he loves himself inordinately*." [1]

Macbeth has not a predisposition to murder; he has merely an inordinate ambition that makes murder itself seem to be a lesser evil than failure to achieve the Crown.

Lady Macbeth, however, accuses her husband of having proposed the murder to her before Duncan announced his intention of visiting Inverness, before time and place cohered. This made Coleridge argue that the murder had been discussed before the opening of the play, and led Bradley to suggest ingeniously that

[1] Curry, *Shakespeare's Philosophical Patterns*, pp. 111-12. The italicized words are direct quotations from Thomas Aquinas.

" If they had had ambitious conversations, in which each felt that some half-formed guilty idea was floating in the mind of the other, she might naturally take the words of the letter, as indicating much more than they said." [1]

Dr. Dover Wilson uses this passage (I. vii. 47-52) to support his theory that in the original play there was another scene between Macbeth and his wife after he met the Weird Sisters, and before he knew that Duncan was coming to Inverness, and that this scene was afterwards cut by Shakespeare himself. He rejects Coleridge's view that the murder had been discussed earlier, because he thinks that Macbeth's aside (I. iii. 130 ff.)

" depicts the terror of Macbeth's soul when the idea of murder *first* comes to him ";

and that Lady Macbeth's soliloquy at the beginning of I. v. proves that " so far he has refused to entertain any but honourable thoughts." [2] But Macbeth's aside, by a common Shakespearean convention, does not so much express the birth of murderous thoughts as refer back to the guilty start to which Banquo calls attention earlier in the scene,[3] a start which could not be explained earlier without holding up the action of the scene.[4] It could either represent the birth of guilt, or else show that Macbeth's mind has been

" rendered temptable by a previous dalliance of fancy with ambitious thoughts ".[5]

Lady Macbeth's soliloquy does not prove that her husband did not have these thoughts, or what Bradley calls " some vaguer dishonourable dream ": they prove only that she believed, and rightly, it appears, that Macbeth's conscience or conventionality was liable to prevent him from achieving the Crown by foul means, even though he may have proposed the murder when the question was merely theoretical.

[1] Bradley, *op. cit.* pp. 480-4.   Cf. Charlton, *op. cit.* p. 166.
[2] *Op. cit.* p. xxxvi.   [3] I. iii. 51.
[4] Just as the soliloquy at the end of *Hamlet*, Act II, expresses the thoughts which had been passing through the hero's mind during the recitation of the Hecuba speeches.
[5] Coleridge, *op. cit.* i. 68.

I do not find, therefore, the inconsistency of which Bridges speaks; nor do I think there is enough evidence to support Dr. Dover Wilson's theory of a former version of the play in which all was clear.[1] Even if Lady Macbeth refers to a time between I. iii. and I. iv. Shakespeare might (and, in my opinion, would) have left the scene unwritten.

In the same essay, Bridges speaks of Macbeth's *poetic imagination*. In this opinion he was following Bradley, who had argued that

"Macbeth's better nature—to put the matter for clearness' sake too broadly—instead of speaking to him in the overt language of moral ideas, commands and prohibitions, incorporates itself in images which alarm and horrify. His imagination is thus the best of him, something usually deeper and higher than his conscious thoughts; and if he had obeyed it he would have been safe." [2]

Sir Herbert Grierson goes even further, and paradoxically compares Macbeth to Bunyan, in that

"his own deepest thoughts and feelings come to him as objective experiences, as visions of the bodily eye, as voices that ring in the ear. . . . The obscure processes of his own soul translate themselves into the voices and visions, and their significance is a better clue to the working of his moral being than are his articulate statements. He may profess contempt of moral scruples and supernatural inhibitions, and declare that if he were safe in this world he would 'jump the life to come'. The voices that he hears and the visions that he sees give him the lie." [3]

We are here on very dangerous ground. It is perfectly legitimate to disagree with Moulton who had argued that Macbeth's soliloquy in I. vii. shows that he was deterred not by moral scruples but by a fear of the consequences; for the imagery of the speech shows that Macbeth is haunted by the horror of the deed, and impresses that horror on the audience.[4] But if we go further and pretend that

---

[1] See above p. xxiii. It is unreasonable to praise Shakespeare as the perfect artist on the strength of a hypothetical version of the play at the same time as one assumes that Shakespeare cut the play in such a way as to spoil the earlier perfection.

[2] *Op. cit.* p. 352.   [3] Grierson, *ed. cit.* pp. xxv-xxvi.

[4] Cf. K. Muir, *Penguin New Writing*, No. 28 (Summer 1946), p. 114, and Bradley, *op. cit.* p. 352: "His conscious or reflective mind, that is, moves chiefly among considerations of outward success and failure, while his inner being is convulsed by conscience."

this poetic imagery is a proof that Macbeth had a powerful imagination, that he was in fact a poet, we are confusing real life and drama. Every character in a poetic play may speak poetry: but this poetry does not necessarily reflect their poetic dispositions—it is merely a medium. The bloody sergeant utters bombastic language, not because he is himself bombastic, but because such language was considered appropriate to epic narration. The First Murderer quotes Samuel Daniel,[1] and gives us a lovely vignette of twilight,[2] not because he was of a literary turn of mind, but because Shakespeare was a poet, and in the second passage required some verbal scene-painting. So, too, with Macbeth, we may say his imagery expresses his unconscious mind (that poetry can do this is one of the greatest advantages it has over realistic drama) but we must not say he is therefore a poet.[3]

Maeterlinck speaks of the way in which the " essence of the dramatic poet's art consists in speaking through the mouth of his characters without appearing to do so," and he declares that the mode of life in which the protagonists of *Macbeth*

" are steeped penetrates and pervades their voices so clearly, animates and saturates their words to such a degree that we see it much better, more intimately and more immediately than if they took the trouble to describe it to us. We, like themselves, living there with them, see from within the houses and the scenery in which they live; and we do not need to have those surroundings shown to us from without any more than they do. It is the countless presence, the uninterrupted swarm of all those images that form the profound life, the secret and almost unlimited first existence of the work. Upon its surface floats the dialogue necessary to the action. It seems to be the only one that our ears seize; but, in reality, it is to the other language that our instinct listens, our unconscious sensibility, our soul, if you like; and, if the spoken words touch us more deeply than those of any other poet, it is because they are supported by a great host of hidden powers." [4]

The characters are thus subordinated to the poetry, rather than (as in much nineteenth-century criticism) the poetry to the characters. Lascelles Abercrombie in his *Idea of*

[1] III. i. 111. [2] III. iii. 5-8.
[3] Hamlet, despite the sublime poetry of the soliloquies, tells Ophelia " I am ill at these numbers," i.e. " I am no good at writing poetry."
[4] Tr. by Alex. Teixeira de Matos, *Fort. Rev.*, Ap. 1910, pp. 696-9. Cf. H. Fluchère, *Shakespeare : Dramaturge Elisabéthain*, 1948, p. 300.

Great Poetry has a brilliant discussion of why we enjoy tragedy which seems a version of " the mere evil of life." In answering this question he provides an eloquent analysis of *Macbeth*. In the last act of the play, the hero's world " turns into a blank of imbecile futility "; yet he

" seizes on the appalling moment and masters even this: he masters it by knowing it absolutely and completely, and by forcing even this quintessence of all possible evil to live before him with the zest and terrible splendour of his own unquenchable mind." [1]

Abercrombie quotes Macbeth's words when he hears of his wife's death and comments:

" Tragedy can lay hold of no evil worse than the conviction that life is an affair of absolute inconsequence. . . . And precisely by laying hold of this and relishing its fearfulness to the utmost, Macbeth's personality towers into its loftiest grandeur. . . . We see not only what he feels, but the personality that feels it; and in the very act of proclaiming that life is a tale told by an idiot signifying nothing personal life announces its virtue, and superbly signifies itself." [2]

The fallacy here is simply that Abercrombie is confusing the powers of expression possessed by Macbeth with the poetic powers of Shakespeare himself. Once again it must be emphasized that because Shakespeare makes Macbeth talk as only a great poet could talk, we are not to assume that Macbeth is a great poet: he is merely part of a great poem. His consummate expression of the meaninglessness of life signifies only that life is meaningless to him: it cannot be taken to signify that he has overcome that meaninglessness in the very act of expressing it. Nor, of course, does it mean that Shakespeare was expressing his own pessimistic ideas about the universe. What gives satisfaction to the spectator or reader is not the comprehension of experience by Macbeth, but the poet revealing experience through the mouth of his hero. Macbeth by his own actions, has robbed life of meaning. Shakespeare restores meaning to life by showing that Macbeth's nihilism results from his crimes.[3]

[1] *Op. cit.* p. 176.

[2] *Op. cit.* p. 177. But it should be added that Abercrombie is one of the best critics of our time, and one would like a comprehensive selection of his prose.

[3] On the other hand Macbeth is not just a callous criminal. Tragic heroes, as James points out in the preface to *The Princess Casamassima*, must

For Macbeth, though a tragic hero, is a criminal; and though he arouses our sympathies more than Richard III does, he has some resemblances to him, as the earliest critics of the play pointed out.[1] The difference between the two characters is mainly the result of Shakespeare's increasing understanding of human nature.   All his mature tragedies may be regarded as " melodrama humanized." Richard is a conscious villain, and a deliberate Machiavel; Macbeth embarks on his career of crime with anguish [2] and reluctance, " as if it were an appalling duty." [3]   He is humanized by his fears,[4] which prove him to be a man, and not the monster his oppressed subjects believe him to be.   " Those are my best dayes," he might have said, " when I shake with fear." [5]   Richard, though he suffers from the same terrible dreams, is depicted from the outside, and not without appreciation of his sardonic humour; [6] but as Macbeth goes the primrose way to the everlasting bonfire, we see with his eyes.   Richard is the villain as hero; Macbeth is a hero who becomes a villain.

It should be remembered that the Elizabethans, bred on Seneca, did not adhere to the Aristotelian dictum that the overthrow of a bad man is not a tragedy at all.   They were content with

" the high and excellent Tragedie . . . that maketh Kings feare to be Tyrants . . . that maketh vs know,
    Qui sceptra saevus duro imperio regit,
    Timet timentes, metus in authorem redit." [7]

These lines from Seneca's *Œdipus*, which, as Dr. Dover Wilson suggests, would be a suitable motto for *Macbeth*, are thus translated in *Tenne Tragedies*:

" Who so the cruel tyrant playes, and guiltlesse men doth smight,
    Hee dreadeth them that him doe dread, so feare doth cheifly light
    On causers chiefe.   A iust reuenge for bloudy mindes at last."

---

be " finely aware " and this " *makes* absolutely the intensity of their adventures, gives the maximum of sense to what befalls them.   We care . . . comparatively little for what happens to the stupid, the coarse and the blind; care for it, and for the effects of it, at the most as helping to precipitate what happens to the more deeply wondering, to the really sentient."
    [1] Cf. p. xlv. *ante.*   [2] I am thinking of the Existential " anguish " of choice.
    [3] Bradley, *op. cit.* p. 358.   [4] H. Craig, *The Enchanted Glass*, p. 232.
    [5] Donne, *Holy Spirit*, xix.   [6] Charlton, *op. cit.* pp. 24 ff.
    [7] Sidney, *The Defence of Poesie*, facs. E 4v.   Read: *duro saevus . . . auctorem*

There is also a passage in James I's *Basilikon Doron* which
forms an interesting commentary on the play—

" For a good King (after a happie and famous reigne) dieth in
peace, lamented by his subiects, and admired by his neighbours;
and leauing a reuerent renowne behinde him in earth, obtaineth the
Crowne of eternall felicitie in heauen. And although some of them
(which falleth out very rarelie) may be cut off by the treason of some
vnnaturall subiects, yet liueth their fame after them, and some notable
plague faileth neuer to ouertake the committers in this life, besides
their infamie to all posterities hereafter ":

—the " even-handed justice " of which Macbeth speaks—

" Where by the contrarie, a Tyrannes miserable and infamous
life, armeth in end his owne Subiects to become his burreaux: and
although that rebellion be euer vnlawfull on their part, yet is the
world so wearied of him, that his fall is little meaned by the rest of
his Subiects, and but smiled at by his neighbours. And besides the
infamous memorie he leaueth behind him here, and the endlesse
paine hee sustaineth hereafter, it oft falleth out, that the commiters
not onely escape vnpunished, but farther, the fact will remaine as
allowed by the Law in diuers aages thereafter." [1]

I have not quoted from King James in order to suggest
that *Macbeth* was written as a compliment to him.[2] Even
though the subject was chosen originally to gratify the King,
since it combines two themes on which he was an expert
—witchcraft and his own ancestry—and even though
Shakespeare mentions touching for scrofula, and pre-
nuptial chastity, two other subjects in which James was
interested,[3] he did not drag these things into the play as
irrelevant flattery. Still less ought we to assume that
Shakespeare's treatment of Banquo was circumscribed by
royal susceptibilities, or that the dialogue between Macduff
and Malcolm on the nature of Kingship was inserted to
please James.[4]

Nor, to return to the Senecan conception of tragedy
as applied to *Macbeth*, should we imagine that Shakespeare's

---

[1] *Political Works*, ed. McIlwain, p. 19.

[2] Cf. Draper's article in *Eng. Stud.* 72 and Wilson, *op. cit.* pp. xliv-xlv.

[3] McIlwain, *op. cit.* p. 34: " yee must keepe your bodie cleane and vn-
polluted, till yee giue it to your wife, whom-to onely it belongeth. . . .
Be not ashamed then, to keepe cleane your body, which is the Temple of
the holy Spirit." James ascribed his success in touching for the evil to prayer.
Cf. notes to iv. iii. 99-100, 140-59.   [4] Cf. Wilson, *op. cit.* p. xliv.

imagination was cabined, cribbed, confined by this, any more than he was bound within the Senecan form and structure. His imaginative perception of the human heart made it increasingly difficult for him to regard any character as a mere villain—even Iachimo repents—and *Macbeth* is the story of a noble and valiant man who is brought to his damnation, presented in such a way as to arouse our pity and terror.[1] For though, in the last resort, Macbeth is damned by his own sin, he is sorely tempted. " The power of divels," wrote George Giffard in 1603,

" is in the hearts of men, as to harden the heart, to blind the eyes of the mind, and from the lustes and concupiscences which are in them, to inflame them vnto wrath, malice, enuie, and cruell murthers: . . . And about these things they work continually, and with such efficacy, that without the power of the glorious passion and resurrection of our Lord Jesus Christ, which we haue by faith, they cannot be withstood." [2]

So James himself declared that the devil allures persons,

" euen by these three passions that are within our selues: Curiositie . . . thirst of reuenge, for some tortes deepely apprehended: or greedy appetite of geare." [3]

Shakespeare could not represent devils in a tragedy because they had acquired comic associations; but witches were tragic creatures who,

" for the sake of certain abnormal powers, had sold themselves to the devil." [4]

We do not know Shakespeare's personal opinion of witchcraft—whether he accepted the tenets of James's *Dæmonologie*, or whether he adhered to the sceptical position of Reginald Scot which seems to us to be so much more sane. But the belief in witchcraft could be used by him for dramatic purposes at a time when almost everybody supposed that witches were

" channels through which the malignity of evil spirits might be visited upon human beings." [5]

---

[1] Cf. Charlton, *op. cit.* p. 182.
[2] *A Dialogue concerning Witches and Witchcrafts*, ed. 1843, pp. 22-3.
[3] *Workes*, p. 98.   [4] Curry, *Shakespeare's Philosophical Patterns*, p. 61
[5] *Ibid.* p. 61.

Professor Curry has argued that the Weird Sisters are in
reality demons, or devils, in the form of witches; but

" Whether one considers them as human witches in league with the
powers of darkness, or as actual demons in the form of witches, or as
merely inanimate symbols, the power which they wield or represent
or symbolize is ultimately demonic." [1]

It should be noted, however, that the Weird Sisters
tempt Macbeth only because they know his ambitious
dreams; and that even so their prophecy of the crown
does not dictate evil means of achieving it—it is morally
neutral. Macbeth himself never thinks of blaming the
Weird Sisters for tempting him to the murder of Duncan,
though he blames the " juggling fiends " who have lulled
him into a false sense of security. He knows that the
first step along the primrose path was taken on his own
responsibility:

> " And as Hell fires, not wanting heat, want light;
> So these strange witchcrafts, which like Pleasure be,
> Not wanting faire inticements, want delight,
> Inward being nothing but deformity;
> And doe at open doores let fraile powers in
> To that straight building, Little-ease of sinne." [2]

The first crime is inspired by ambition; the remainder,
from the murder of the grooms to the slaughter of Macduff's
family, are inspired by fear, a fear that is born of guilt.
Timothy Bright distinguished between neurotic fears and
those that are caused by the pangs of conscience:

" Whatsoeuer molestation riseth directly as a proper obiect of
the mind, that in that respect is not melancholicke, but hath a farther
ground then fancie, and riseth from conscience, condemning the
guiltie soule of those ingrauen lawes of nature, which no man is voide
of, be he neuer so barbarous. This is it, that hath caused the prophane

[1] Curry, op. cit. pp. 59, 61. Curry points out that " their control over
the primary elements of nature, the rationes seminales, would seem to indicate
that the Weird Sisters were demons disguised as witches." It should be pointed
out, however, that the Weird Sisters do not claim this power, though Macbeth
assumes that they have it, and that they call up their " masters " in IV. i.
Kittredge, Complete Works of Sh. p. 1114, argues, however, that the Weird
Sisters are norns. " They were great powers of destiny, great ministers of
fate. They had determined the past; they governed the present; they
not only foresaw the future, but decreed it." Douglas, Aen. iii. translated
parcae by " weird sisters."
[2] Greville, Caelica, cii. 19-24.

poets to haue fained Hecates Eumenides, and the infernall furies; which although they be but fained persons, yet the matter which is shewed vnder their maske, is serious, true, and of wofull experience." [1]

These are the terrible dreams that nightly shake Macbeth and his wife; and the apocalyptic imagery that precedes and follows the murder of Duncan may be ascribed to the same cause, rather than to Macbeth's poetic temperament. Plutarch, in his *Morals*, declares that

" wickednesse ingendering within it selfe . . . displeasure and punishment, not after a sinfull act is committed, but euen at the very instant of committing, it beginneth to suffer the pain due to the offence . . . wheras mischieuous wickednesse frameth of her selfe, the engines of her owne torment . . . many terrible frights, fearfull perturbations and passions of the spirit, remorse of conscience, desperate repentance, and continuall troubles and vnquietnesse." [2]

Before the end of the play Macbeth, having " supped full with horrors," is no longer tortured by such " fearfull perturbations": this is the measure of his damnation. As Professor Curry says—

" in proportion as the good in him diminishes, his liberty of free choice is determined more and more by evil inclination and . . . he cannot choose the better course." [3]

Although, as we have seen, the murders after the first are all motivated by a frantic desire for security, there are differences between them. The murder of Banquo is not merely due to his knowledge of the Weird Sisters' prophecy which makes him a menace to Macbeth; nor is it due merely to the promise that Banquo's descendants would inherit the throne—powerful though both

---

[1] Bright, *A Treatise of Melancholy*, p. 193.

[2] *Morals*, tr. P. Holland, pp. 545-6. Cited by Campbell, *Shakespeare's Tragic Heroes*, and by Charlton, *op. cit.* p. 187.

[3] Curry, *op. cit.* p. 105. I dissent, therefore, from Wilson Knight's opinion, expressed in *The Wheel of Fire*, p. 155, that Macbeth " contends for his own individual soul against the universal reality . . . and emerges at last victorious and fearless." I dissent still more from this sentence on Macbeth in *Christ and Nietzsche*, p. 85: " Starting with the disrupted, anxious, accents of a nervous wreck, he is, poetically, a new man after the first murder, dramatically a more violent one after the second, and philosophically a noble, though unrepentant, creature of sublime and courageous self-knowledge and superb poetry at the close when at last an honest and therefore sin-free relation to the world is established."

motives might be.[1]   Macbeth fears Banquo's "royalty of nature," the "dauntless temper of his mind," and his wisdom.   He fears them because they are a standing reproach to his own nature, now stained with crime—

> " under him
> My genius is rebuk'd."

He vaguely hopes that by murdering Banquo he will rid himself of this reproach; yet the act merely ensures that the reproach will be eternal.   We may, perhaps, apply what M. Sartre says of murder to the killing of Banquo. He argues that the murderer perpetuates the intolerable situation for which he did the deed by the very act of murder: for he kills his victim because he hates being the other's *object*, and by the murder this relationship is rendered irremediable.   The victim has taken the key of this alienation into the tomb with him:

" The death of the other constitutes me as irremediable object, exactly as my own death would do.   So hatred is transformed into frustration even in its triumph." [2]

Some think that Banquo scarcely deserves the compliment of admiring hatred, in that he seems to have come to terms with evil.   Before the murder, he is determined to lose no honour in seeking to augment it;   and after the murder, with suspicion of Macbeth in his mind, he declares:

> " In the great hand of God I stand; and thence
> Against the undivulg'd pretence I fight
> Of treasonous malice."

Yet at the beginning of the third act we find that he has done nothing to implement his vow, and Bradley argues that

[1] Without raising the vexed question of how many children Lady Macbeth had, we may observe that there is no certainty that Macbeth had any. " Bring forth men-children only " (I. vii. 72) seems to imply that he expected children; but " barren sceptre " (III. i. 61) may mean, though not necessarily, that he was without children.   S. Freud, *Collected Papers*, IV, 1934, pp. 328 ff., suggests that " it would be a perfect example of poetic justice in the manner of the talion if the childlessness of Macbeth and the barrenness of his Lady were the punishment for their crimes against the sanctity of geniture."

[2] Sartre, *L'Etre et le Néant*, p. 483 (paraphrased).

" He alone of the lords knew of the prophecies, but he has said nothing of them. He has acquiesced in Macbeth's accession, and in the official theory that Duncan's sons had suborned the chamberlains to murder him." [1]

Although we may well agree with Dr. Dover Wilson that we should not treat Shakespeare as if he were a historian; although this interpretation of Banquo's character, that " he has yielded to evil," seems to be contradicted by Macbeth's tribute later in the same scene; and although James I might not have approved of an unflattering portrait of his reputed ancestor: yet, nevertheless, Dr. Wilson's theory of a cut at this point is too convenient to be convincing, and we may reasonably doubt whether, according to James' theories of Divine Right, Banquo ought to have behaved loyally to Macbeth until Malcolm set foot on Scottish soil. As we have seen, James condemned rebellion even against manifest tyrants. There was nothing new in this, and the Tudors would all have agreed with every word in this passage from *The Trew Law of Free Monarchies*:

" The wickednesse therefore of the King can neuer make them that are ordained to be iudged by him, to become his Iudges. . . . Next, in place of relieuing the commonwealth out of distresse (which is their onely excuse and colour) they shall heape double distresse and desolation vpon it; and so their rebellion shall procure the contrary effects that they pretend it for." [2]

Even a bad king keeps order in the commonwealth, and except where his lusts or passions are involved, he will generally favour justice. If there is no king, James thought, " nothing is vnlawfull to none." Yet he was also careful to point out that

" the duty and alleageance, which the people sweareth to their prince, is not only bound to themselues, but likewise to their lawfull heires and posterity . . . it is alike vnlawful (the crowne euer standing full) to displace him that succeedeth thereto, as to eiect the former: For at the very moment of the expiring of the king reigning, the nearest and lawful heire entreth in his place: And so to refuse him, or intrude

[1] Bradley, *op. cit.* pp. 384-5. R. Walker, *op. cit.* chap. 5, argues from the dialogue following Banquo's soliloquy that he is not "fishing for an understanding with Macbeth " but " is anxious to tell him nothing and get away as quickly as possible."
[2] *Political Works*, ed. McIlwain, p. 66.

another, is not to holde out vncomming in, but to expell and put out their righteous King." [1]

It is surely clear that Banquo ought not to have awaited Malcolm's invasion of Scotland before taking any steps against the usurper: he should have defended the son's title to the throne on the death of Duncan.[2]

The long dialogue between Macbeth and the murderers of Banquo looks back to John's temptation of Hubert and Claudius' temptation of Laertes. It shows us a Macbeth we have only glimpsed before, a smooth-tongued " politician," well able to " beguile the time." If it be said that the two murderers would have been content to do the deed without all this persuasion—that they only wanted the cash—it may be answered that Macbeth

" wanted to subdue their wills. One sees him pacing the floor and weaving words like spells round the two wretches, stopping every now and then to eye them hard and close." [3]

He wants them to do the deed out of hatred of Banquo, and not out of the need of money, so that he himself shall be relieved of some part of the guilt—so that he can cry, " Thou canst not say I did it." His speech about dogs, regarded by some as the least necessary speech in the play, meet for the cutter's pencil, serves to present one aspect of the *order*, which he himself is destroying.[4] There is one significance of this scene which up till now has not been fully appreciated—the echoes from the Sermon on the Mount by which Macbeth, all unconsciously, bears witness to the ethic he has violated.[5]

The later murder of Macduff's family, also executed by underlings, is a pointless massacre which proves to be Macbeth's own death-warrant. It is not calculated to achieve a particular end: destruction, though originating in fear, has come to be an end in itself.

According to Coleridge the other protagonist, the accomplice as well as the temptress of Macbeth, is not the

[1] *Op. cit.* p. 69.

[2] James had no legitimate reason to complain of the portrait of Banquo who, in the *Chronicles*, was Macbeth's accomplice.

[3] Granville-Barker, *op. cit.* p. xl.   [4] Knights, *op. cit.* p. 24.

[5] Cf. note on III. i. 87-8.

monster, the fiend-like queen, that most eighteenth-century critics assumed her to be:

" on the contrary, her constant effort throughout the play was to *bully* conscience. She was a woman of a visionary and day-dreaming turn of mind; her eye fixed on the shadows of her solitary ambition; and her feelings abstracted, through the deep musings of her absorbing passion, from the common-life sympathies of flesh and blood. But her conscience, so far from being seared, was continually smarting within her; and she endeavours to stifle its voice, and keep down its struggles, by inflated and soaring fancies, and appeals to spiritual agency." [1]

It is true that Lady Macbeth is not naturally depraved or conscienceless (any more than Satan was): but she deliberately chooses evil, her choice being more deliberate than her husband's. Macbeth speaks of ambition being his only spur; but he would never have overcome his reluctance to commit murder without the chastisement of his wife's tongue. She, not metaphorically or symbolically, but in deadly earnest, invokes the powers of darkness to take possession of her; and, as Professor Curry has cogently argued,

" Her prayer is apparently answered; with the coming of night her castle is . . . shrouded in just such a blackness as she desires. She knows also that these spiritual substances study eagerly the effects of mental activities upon the human body, waiting patiently for evidences of evil thought which will permit them entrance past the barriers of the human will into the body to possess it. They tend on mortal thoughts. For, says Cassian: ' It is clear that unclean spirits cannot make their way into those bodies they are going to seize upon, in any other way than by first taking possession of their minds and thoughts.' Thus, instead of guarding the workings of her mind against the assaults of wicked angels, Lady Macbeth deliberately wills that they subtly invade her body and so control it that the natural inclinations of the spirit toward goodness and compassion may be completely extirpated. . . . And without doubt these ministers of evil do actually take possession of her body even in accordance with her desire." [2]

Mrs. Siddons was right when she said that Lady Macbeth,

---

[1] *Op. cit.* ii. 270-1. Probably the reporter of the *Bristol Gazette* was not quite accurate in his account of what Coleridge said. Macbeth and his Lady together, Freud declared, *Collected Papers*, IV, 1934, p. 333, " exhaust the possibilities of reaction to the crime, like the two disunited parts of the mind of a single individuality."   [2] Curry, *op. cit.* pp. 86-7.

" having impiously delivered herself up to the excitements of hell
. . . is abandoned to the guidance of the demons she has invoked." [1]

The great actress's realization of this fact is one of the reasons
why her performance of the part was more effective than
that of any other actress, and why naturalistic interpretations are foredoomed to failure. We need not
necessarily assume that Shakespeare himself believed in
demoniacal possession, any more than we need decide
whether he followed Reginald Scot in his views on witchcraft, or King James in his views on Divine Right: but
that he intended Lady Macbeth to be literally possessed
it is difficult to doubt. Such an interpretation explains
the unnatural darkness, and the equally unnatural portents
on the night of the murder,[2] as it explains what Professor
Curry calls the " demoniacal somnambulism " of the sleep-
walking scene.[3]

Some critics have sentimentalized the character of Lady
Macbeth and have argued that her cry,

> " The Thane of Fife
> had a wife . . ."

shows that " as a woman she can still feel for a murdered
woman." On the other hand, Bradley agreed with
Campbell when he insisted " that in Lady Macbeth's
misery there is no trace of contrition." [4]   But this, surely,
is to take the sleep-walking scene too literally. Although
Lady Macbeth's obsession with the blood-stains on her
hand, and particularly with the *smell* of the blood, might
be interpreted as evidence that she fears detection, it also
symbolizes, as plainly as if she had cried it from the house-
tops, her consciousness of guilt and the outrage she has
committed on her own soul. It must be admitted, however,
that a second personality which speaks through the patient's
mouth, confessing sins and sometimes relating memories,
was thought to be a characteristic of demoniacal somnambulism.[5] It may be said that the night without stars,

---

[1] Quoted in *New Variorum*, pp. 472-3.
[2] Cf. Masefield, *Recent Prose*, pp. 270-2.
[3] *Op. cit.* p. 90.   [4] Bradley, *op. cit.* p. 378.
[5] Curry, *op. cit.* p. 90.

the prodigies accompanying the murder, and the sleep-walking of Lady Macbeth can all be explained without bringing in the supernatural at all—and this fact may well reflect an ambiguity in Shakespeare's mind. The audience could take them either way, though the supernatural way was to Shakespeare's original audience the more natural. On the other hand it must be admitted that the miraculous scene in the third act where we see that the crime has not brought the criminals closer together, but has set an impassable barrier between them—this picture " of the haunted desert of their souls " which shows that Lady Macbeth now realizes (what her husband knew at the time of the murder) what it is they have done—does not require, and may even be thought to exclude, that Lady Macbeth should still be actively possessed: and the Banquet scene itself, in which she recovers for a while and for the last time some semblance of her will, is not easy to reconcile with the demoniac theory; for in that case Satan would seem to be divided against himself, on the one hand driving Macbeth to exhibit his guilt, and on the other enabling Lady Macbeth to shield him.[1] So in the sleep-walking scene, whether her involuntary confessions (so poignant that, as Bradley remarked,[2] for the moment

" all the language of poetry . . . seems to be touched with unreality, and these brief toneless sentences seem the only voice of truth ")

are the outpourings of her repressed conscience, or the treacherous words of the demon within her, we need not deny her (what Shakespeare must have given her) pity—

[1] The ghost of Banquo has been regarded as an hallucination, like the air-drawn dagger, but clearly it was something more than a projection of guilt. The ghost of Hamlet's father was invisible to Gertrude, though few would question its objective existence. Banquo's ghost appeared to Macbeth only because he alone was guilty; and the manifestation would have been the same whether the ghost was indeed Banquo's and had come to demand vengeance or whether, as Professor Curry thinks (*op. cit.* pp. 73, 75), it is an infernal illusion created by devils to bring Macbeth to his material ruin. Devils " are able to assume bodies of air, condensing it by virtue of their angelic natures insofar as is necessary for the forming of assumed bodies. . . . Demons are enabled to induce in the imaginations of men, either waking or asleep, whatever visions and hallucinations they please."

[2] *Op. cit.* p. 400.

as well as the terror she has never failed to arouse.   There is pity even in Dante's *Inferno*.

The fact that we no longer believe in demons, and that Shakespeare's audience mostly did, does not diminish the dramatic effect for us; for with the fading of belief in the objective existence of devils, they and their operations can yet symbolize the workings of evil in the hearts of men. It is not only the superstitious, but the guilty, to whom sleep is " a verie hell and a place of damned persons," for it presents unto them

" terrible visions and monstrous fancies; it raiseth diuels, fiends and furies, which torment the poore and miserable soule; it driueth her out of her quiet repose by her owne fearfull dreames, wherewith she whippeth, scourgeth and punisheth herselfe (as it were) by some other, whose cruell and vnseasonable commandementes she doth obey." [1]

The changes in custom and belief do not seriously detract from the universality of the tragedy.

Nor need we suppose that cuts and alterations have greatly damaged the unity and power of the play.[2]   Some critics, indeed, have complained that most of the characters in the play are " flat " and lacking in individuality, and that certain scenes are undramatic and even dull.   The levelling of the characters is, however, a legitimate dramatic device, which has the effect of focusing attention on the main characters.   Rosse, Angus, the Old Man, the other Lord, Lenox, the two Doctors, and the Waiting Gentlewoman have scarcely any recognizable traits, and the characteristics of Rosse and Lenox seem to be self-contradictory: but together these characters form a chorus which comments on the action of the play.

The other complaint, that certain scenes are undramatic, I have, perhaps, already answered, at least by implication. It is not altogether accidental that some of the scenes which earlier critics regarded as of doubtful authenticity, or as

---

[1] Plutarch, *Morals*, tr. Holland, p. 260.   Cited by Campbell, *Shakespeare's Tragic Heroes*, p. 212.   A. A. Smirnov, *Shakespeare*, 1937, p. 72, even argues that " the conversations of Macbeth with the witches and phantoms, like the famous dialogue of Ivan Karamazov with the devil, are but the inner dialectical struggle of Macbeth with himself.   This struggle is projected on the supernatural plane, just as the socio-historical events arising from Macbeth's concrete actions are projected on the spiritual plane."

[2] See pp. xxiii.-xxiv. *ante.*

irrelevant compliments to King James, or as concessions to the taste of the groundlings, or even as pieces of relaxed writing, have now come to be regarded as essential to the understanding of the play. The Porter scene,[1] the passage about dogs,[2] the speech on the King's Evil,[3] the first two scenes of the play,[4] and the dialogue between Macduff and Malcolm [5] in Act IV, Scene iii have been discussed elsewhere: but it may be worth while to add a note on the last of these passages which has been condemned as long-drawn-out and absurd. Harley Granville-Barker, who thinks there is a lack of spontaneity in the writing of the scene, points out its importance in the scheme of the play. It is the starting-point of the play's counter-action, the audience need a breathing-space, and

" That Malcolm might be what his self-accusation would make him, that Macduff might be Macbeth's spy, that each then should turn from the other in loathing, and that Macduff should not be too easily convinced of the truth—all this is necessary as a solid foundation for the moral dominance of the rest of the play by these two. And the whole matter must be given space and weight to the measure of its importance." [6]

The scene can also be defended as a " mirror for magistrates "—a discussion on the contrast between true royalty and tyranny that is very germane to the matter.[7] It can demonstrate effectively how Macbeth's misrule has made even the good suspect the good of treachery. Perhaps, too, as Professor Knights has suggested,[8] the scene acts as a choric commentary:

" We see the relevance of Malcolm's self-accusation. He has ceased to be a person. His lines repeat and magnify the evils that have already been attributed to Macbeth, acting as a mirror wherein the ills of Scotland are reflected. And the statement of evil is strengthened by contrast with the opposite virtues."

Professor Charlton complains [9] of critics who treat Shakespeare's characters " as plastic symbols in an arabesque of esoteric imagery " or as " rhythmic ripples intoned in a chromatic ritual "; and though we may doubt

---

[1] Cf. notes on the scene and pp. xxv, ff.　　　　[2] Cf. p. lxvi.
[3] Cf. note on IV, iii. 140-59.　　[4] Cf. notes on I. i., I. ii., and I. ii. 7-23.
[5] Cf. p. xliv. and note on IV. iii.　　[6] *Op. cit.* p. xlviii.
[7] Wilson, *op. cit.* p. xliv.　　[8] *Op. cit.* p. 28.　　[9] *Op. cit.* p. 1.

whether these phrases aptly describe the practice of post-Bradleian critics, we may agree that the poetic dramas of Shakespeare are plays to be performed, and not merely poems to read. On the other hand the distinction between art and life must be preserved, as it is not always preserved in the psychological critics of the past century and a half. Shakespeare wrote plays which happen to be poems, as well as poems which happen to be plays—and it is not always easy to preserve a nice balance between the two parts of this statement. Then, again, in the process of analysing one of the tragedies, we are only too apt to fossilize the living substance of the original, and to impose a modern, or an Elizabethan, meaning on its stranger and less formulable significance. For what the groundlings or even the "judicious" thought in Shakespeare's day may be as far from a complete, a Shakespearean, under-standing of *Macbeth* as the speculations of an Andrew Bradley. The plays are so vast and so complex that we can make statements about them which seem contradictory, and yet both express some aspect of the truth. We may, indeed, call *Macbeth* the greatest of morality plays, at the same time as we are aware that Shakespeare transcends the sublime story of a human soul on the road to damnation and that he shows us also indomitable energy burning *in the forests of the night,* cherubim *horsed upon the sightless couriers of the air, Pity, like a naked new-born babe, striding the blast,* the very *frame of things disjoint,* and human life, a brief candle quenched in the dust of death, in all its splendours and miseries, and even in its crimes, not

> " a tale
> Told by an idiot, full of sound and fury,
> Signifying nothing."

We may not agree with Campbell when he spoke of *Macbeth* " as the greatest treasure of our dramatic literature " or with Mr. Masefield, who called it " the most glorious" of Shakespeare's plays; but glory it certainly has, of a peculiar richness and intensity, which the poet seldom equalled and " the achieve of, the mastery of the thing " which he surpassed, perhaps, only in *King Lear.*

MACBETH

DRAMATIS PERSONÆ

DUNCAN, *King of Scotland.*

DONALBAIN,
MALCOLM, } *His Sons.*

MACBETH,
BANQUO, } *Generals of the King's Army.*

MACDUFF,
LENOX,
ROSSE,
MENTETH, } *Noblemen of Scotland.*
ANGUS,
CATHNESS,

FLEANCE, *Son to Banquo.*

SIWARD, *Earl of Northumberland, General of the English Forces.*

YOUNG SIWARD, *his Son.*

SEYTON, *an Officer attending on Macbeth.*

BOY, *Son to Macduff.*

AN ENGLISH DOCTOR.

A SCOTTISH DOCTOR.

A SOLDIER.

A PORTER.

AN OLD MAN.

LADY MACBETH.

LADY MACDUFF.

GENTLEWOMAN *attending on Lady Macbeth.*

[HECATE].

THREE WITCHES.

Lords, Gentlemen, Officers, Soldiers, Murderers, Attendants,
and Messengers.

The Ghost of Banquo, and other Apparitions.

SCENE: *In the end of the Fourth Act, in England; through*
the rest of the play, in Scotland.

THE TRAGEDY OF MACBETH

ACT I

SCENE I.—*An open place.*

Thunder and lightning.   Enter three WITCHES.

1 *Witch.* When shall we three meet again?
   In thunder, lightning, or in rain?
2 *Witch.* When the hurlyburly's done,
   When the battle's lost and won.

(I. i.)
   1. again?] again *Hanmer.*   2. or] and *Hanmer, Capell.*

Scene 1] Cuningham thought that this scene was spurious, because no dramatic object was gained by its introduction. Granville-Barker (*Preface*, xxvi) concurred: " Apart from such an opening being un-Shakespearean, the lines themselves are as little like Shakespeare as Hecate is, and have indeed all the tang of the Hecate lines. . . . The scene . . . is a poor scene and a pointless scene." But, as Coleridge remarked (*Shakespearean Criticism*, ed. Raysor, i. 68) " the true reason for the first appearance of the Weird Sisters, [is to strike] the keynote . . . of the whole play. . . ." Coleridge likewise suggests that the opening of the play should be contrasted with that of *Hamlet:* " In the latter the gradual ascent from the simplest forms of conversation to the language of impassioned intellect, yet still the intellect remaining the *seat* of passion; in the *Macbeth* the invocation is made at once to the imagination, and the emotions connected therewith " (*op.*

cit. i. 67). So Knights, *Explorations,* p. 18, declares that each theme of the play " is stated in the first act. The first scene, every word of which will bear the closest scrutiny, strikes one dominant chord."

   1. Hanmer's emendation, though generally accepted, is superfluous.

   3. *hurlyburly*] uproar, tumult, confusion, esp. the tumult of edition or insurrection. See Halle, *Chronicle* (1548), *Hen. VIII*, 231 *a:* " In this tyme of insurrection, and in the rage of horley borley." The word occurs in Golding's *Ovid*, IX. 510 and in Marlowe, *Dido*, IV. i. 10, and there is a close parallel in Seneca, *Agam.* (tr. Studley), I, Chor. " One hurly burly done." Cf. note v. iii. 45 *post.* Knights (*op. cit.* p. 18) suggests that the word " implies more than the tumult of insurrection. Both it and ' When the Battaile's lost, and wonne ' suggest the kind of metaphysical pitch-and-toss which is about to be played with good and evil."

3 *Witch.* That will be ere the set of sun.   5

1 *Witch.* Where the place?

2 *Witch.*   Upon the heath.

3 *Witch.* There to meet with Macbeth.

1 *Witch.* I come, Graymalkin!

2 *Witch.* Paddock calls.

3 *Witch.* Anon!   10

All. Fair is foul, and foul is fair:

    Hover through the fog and filthy air.   [*Exeunt.*

SCENE II.—*A camp.*

Alarum within. Enter KING DUNCAN, MALCOLM, DONAL-
BAIN, LENOX, *with Attendants, meeting a bleeding Captain.*

Dun. What bloody man is that? He can report,

    As seemeth by his plight, of the revolt

    The newest state.

9-11. Paddock . . . fair] *Singer (1856), Hunter, Globe, Kittredge, Wilson;
one line spoken by All* Padock calls anon: faire is foule, and foule is faire *Ff; two
lines ending* anon! fair *Pope;* Paddock calls.—Anon! *Rowe and Capell, subst.*

Sene II

Duncan] *Capell;* King] *F 1.* Captain] *Ff;* Sergent *Old Camb. Edd.*

8. *Graymalkin*] or Grimalkin, a grey cat; with the toad, a common witches' familiar. Cf. " brinded cat " (IV. i. 1 *post*). " Malkin " is a diminutive of Mary. Upton observes that " to understand this passage we should suppose one familiar calling with the voice of a cat, and another with the croaking of a toad." Cf. James, *Dæmonologie* (*Workes*, 1616), p. 103: " either in likenes of a Dog, a Cat, an Ape, or such-like other beast; or else to answere by a voice onely." Cf. Scot, *Discouerie of Witchcraft*, ed. 1930, p. 6: "Some say they can keepe divels and spirits in the likenesse of todes and cats."

9-11. *Paddock . . . fair*] Printed as one line in the Folios. Most editors retain the speech-prefix, *All*, and divide into two lines. Hunter's re-arrangement, which I have adopted, allows the witches to speak in turn.

It is obviously improbable that Shakespeare intended all the witches to address the paddock, the familiar of one.

9. *Paddock*] a toad. The word is still found in provincial English. But Cotgrave seems to regard the word as equivalent to *grenouille*, a frog, and not to *crapaud*, a toad. Topsell, *History of Serpents*, 1608, p. 187, refers to the " Padock or crooked back Frog "—" It is not altogether mute, for in time of perrill . . . they have a crying voyce, which I have often times prooved by experience " (quoted by Furness, Jr.).

11. *Fair . . . fair*] Farmer pointed out the proverbial character of this phrase, and quoted Spenser's *Faerie Queene*, IV. viii. 32: " Then faire grew foule, and foule grew faire in sight." R. Walker, *The Time is Free*, chap. 1, points out that the picture of Sclaunder in stanza 26

Mal.   This is the Sergeant,
Who, like a good and hardy soldier, fought
'Gainst my captivity.—Hail, brave friend!   5
Say to the King the knowledge of the broil,
As thou didst leave it.

5. Hail, brave friend] Haile: haile brave friend *F 2, 3, 4.* 6. the knowledge]
thy knowledge *Walker.*

may have contributed to Shakespeare's picture of the witches. Furness, Jr., quotes Nashe, *Terrors of the Night* (1594, ed. McKerrow, I. p. 361): "euery thing must bee interpreted backward as Witches say their Pater-noster, good being the character of bad, and bad of good." The line is the first statement of one of the main themes of the play, of " the reversal of values " (Knights).

Scene II

The authenticity of this scene has been questioned by Cuningham, following Clark and Wright; but it has been successfully defended by modern critics, inc. Knights, Nosworthy, *Review of English Studies,* April 1946, and Flatter, *Shakespeare's Producing Hand* (1948). It may, however, have been badly cut. See Introduction, p. xxii.

Theobald and Capell, followed by most modern editors, deduced from I. iii. 39 and from Holinshed that Sc. II. was laid at Forres. But Macbeth —assuming he is Bellona's bridegroom—was fighting in Fife (l. 50) which, as Wilson points out, is 100 miles from Forres, and could not be in two places at once. The two battles have been run together in place as well as in time. Cf. note on I. iii. 91. The Captain begins to tell the story of the second phase of the battle (ll. 30-43), i.e. with the Norweyan lord; and Rosse completes the tale (ll. 53-9). But not even an audience of Scotsmen would notice the geographical difficulties.

R. Walker, *op. cit.* chap. 2, argues for the authenticity of this scene by showing that in Sc. III. " Shakespeare means us to give most of our attention to Macbeth's reception of the news, not to the news and its bearers. He achieves this by a measure of repetition."

1. *bloody*] Kolbe points out, *Shakespeare's Way,* p. 3, that " blood " is mentioned over 100 times in the course of the play. Dowden makes a similar observation.

3. *Sergeant*] Steevens suggests that Shakespeare borrowed the term from Holinshed, who mentions that Duncan sent a Sergeant at Arms to bring up the chief rebels to answer the charges preferred against them, but they slew him. Cf. Appendix.

3, 5, 7. The various attempts which have been made to regularize the metre are superfluous. The gap in 5 may indicate a pause for a gesture, and there might be a pause in 7 while the wounded captain collects himself to speak. Flatter (*op. cit.*) defends many of the irregularities in the metre in a similar way.

5. *my captivity*] This may have been suggested by Holinshed's mention of a Captain Malcolme, who was beheaded by Makdowald in an earlier phase of the revolt. But Case thinks that Malcolm merely means that the Captain had resisted an attempt to take him prisoner.

6. *broil*] Cf. *I. Hen. IV.* I. i. 3 and *Oth.* I. iii. 87.

7-23. According to Cuningham this is " a corrupt piece of bombast."

Cap.   Doubtful it stood;
As two spent swimmers, that do cling together
And choke their art.   The merciless Macdonwald
(Worthy to be a rebel, for to that   10
The multiplying villainies of nature
Do˙ swarm upon him) from the western isles
Of Kernes and Gallowglasses is supplied;
And Fortune, on his damned quarrel smiling,
Show'd like a rebel's whore: but all's too weak;   15
For brave Macbeth (well he deserves that name),
Disdaining Fortune, with his brandish'd steel,
Which smok'd with bloody execution,
Like Valour's minion, carv'd out his passage,

9. Macdonwald] Macdonnell *F 2, 3, 4.*   10. for to that] for, to that, *Capell.*
11. villainies] villaines *F 2, 3.*   13. Gallowglasses] *F 2;* Gallowgrosses *F 1.*
14. quarrel] *Hanmer;* quarry *Ff.*   19. carv'd] *Ff;* carved *Rowe.*

It may be corrupt; but, as Nosworthy has argued (*op. cit.*) its style
may be compared with the "epic"
style of the Pyrrhus speeches in
Hamlet and the corresponding passage in Marlowe's *Dido.* Coleridge,
Shakespearean Criticism (p. 67), makes
the same comparison: "the epic is
substituted for the tragic, in order
to make the latter be felt as
the *real-life* diction." Cf. Bradley,
Shakespearean Tragedy, pp. 389-90.
    9. *Macdonwald*] Holinshed's form
is Makdowald. Knights, *Explorations,*
p. 20, suggests that Shakespeare
"consciously provided a parallel
with the Macbeth of the later acts."
    10. *to that*] i.e. to that end.
    11-12. *The . . . him*] i.e. like lice.
    13. *Kernes and Gallowglasses*] See
Holinshed, Appendix, p. 174. The
"kern" was a light-armed foot-
soldier; one of the poorer class
among the "wild Irish," from whom
such soldiers were drawn. Stani-
hurst in his Introduction to Holinshed's *Irish Historie* (p. 45*a*) says
that "Kerne signifieth . . . a shower
of hell, because they are taken for
no better than for rakehels, or the
diuels black gard, by reason of the
stinking sturre they keepe, where-

soeuer they be." The "gallowglass" was a horseman armed with
a sharp axe, defined by *O.E.D.* as
"one of a particular class of soldiers
or retainers formerly retained by
Irish chiefs." According to Stani-
hurst (*op. cit.*) the gallowglass uses
"a kind of pollax for his weapon.
These men are commonlie weieward
rather by profession than by nature,
firm of countenance, tall of stature,
big of lim, burlie of body, well and
stronglie timbered, cheeflie feeding
on beefe, porke and butter." Both
words occur in *2 Henry VI.* IV. ix.
26-7: "A puissant and a mighty
power of gallowglasses and stout
kerns."
    14. *quarrel*] This, the emendation
of Hanmer, inasmuch as it occurs
in the corresponding passage in
Holinshed, may be regarded as
certain. The Clar. Edd. point out
that Fairfax in *Godfrey of Bulloigne*
uses "quarry" (xi. 28) as well
as "quarrel" (vii. 103) for the
square-headed bolt of a cross-bow.
The Folio printers, therefore, may
readily have printed *quarrel* as *quarry.*
    15. *rebel's whore*] Nosworthy com-
pares *Ham.* II. ii. 515: "strumpet,
fortune."

Till he fac'd the slave;　　　　　　　　　　20
which ne'er shook hands, nor bade farewell to him,
Till he unseam'd him from the nave to th' chops,
And fix'd his head upon our battlements.

Dun. O valiant cousin! worthy gentleman!

Cap. As whence the sun 'gins his reflection,　　25
Shipwracking storms and direful thunders break,
So from that spring, whence comfort seem'd to come,
Discomfort swells. Mark, King of Scotland, mark:
No sooner justice had, with valour arm'd,
Compell'd these skipping Kernes to trust their heels, 30
But the Norweyan Lord, surveying vantage,
With furbish'd arms, and new supplies of men,
Began a fresh assault.

21. Which] *Ff;* Who *Pope;* And *Capell.* ne'er] never *F 4;* bade] bid *F 4.*
22. nave] nape *Hanmer, Warburton.* th' chops] *Ff;* the chaps *Reed (1803).*
26. thunders break] *Pope;* Thunders: *F 1;* thunders breaking *F 2-4.* 28.
Discomfort swells] Discomforts well'd *Johnson (conj. Thirlby);* Discomfort wells
Capell. 29. had,] *F 1-3;* had *F 4, Globe.* 32. furbish'd] (furbisht) *Rowe;*
furbusht *Ff.*

20. Half a line, and probably more, seems to be missing here, perhaps deliberately cut. The *Which* of the following line may refer either to Macbeth, or to Macdonwald, or to Fortune (whose slave he is). If it refers to Macbeth, the polite expression contrasts with the impolite action.

21. *shook hands*] i.e. bade farewell. Cf. Lyly, *Euphues* (ed. Arber, p. 75): " you would inueigle me to shake hands with chastitie."

22. *unseam'd*] Note the tailoring metaphor, of which there are many in the course of the play.

22. *nave*] i.e. navel, but not so used elsewhere. The words were perhaps confused in Elizabethan English. Cf. Massinger, *Parliament of Love,* II. iii. " His body be the navel to the wheel ". Steevens quoted Marlowe, *Dido,* II. i. 256:

" Then from the navell to the throat at once
He ript old *Priam.*"

22. *chops*] i.e. jaws.

24. *cousin*] Macbeth and Duncan were both grandsons of King Malcolm.

25-8. *As . . . swells*] Nosworthy compares *Ham.* II. ii. 506-11. R. Walker, *op. cit.* chap. 2, suggests that " the storms and thunders at once recall the witches, and inform us from what source the danger threatens; and we remember that the Witches go to meet Macbeth. ' Shipwracking ' storms is the very subject of the Witches' next consultation. Macbeth is the source whence comfort seemed to come. From just that quarter danger threatens. . . . Let the King of Scotland mark the omen! . . . The Sergeant . . . is of course unconscious of the undertone of meaning."

25. *reflection*] i.e. shining.

27. *spring*] i.e. source, but possibly suggested by day-spring with its comforting associations.

31. *surveying vantage*] i.e. seeing his opportunity (Wilson). Cf. *Rich. III.* v. iii. 15: " Let us survey the vantage of the ground."

Dun.   Dismay'd not this
   Our captains, Macbeth and Banquo?
Cap.   Yes;
   As sparrows eagles, or the hare the lion.   35
   If I say sooth, I must report they were
   As cannons overcharg'd with double cracks;
   So they
   Doubly redoubled strokes upon the foe:
   Except they meant to bathe in reeking wounds,   40
   Or memorize another Golgotha,
   I cannot tell—
   But I am faint, my gashes cry for help.
Dun. So well thy words become thee, as thy wounds:
   They smack of honour both.—Go, get him surgeons. 45
                          [*Exit Captain, attended.*

33-4. Dismay'd . . . Banquo?] *verse Pope; prose Ff.*   34-5. Yes; . . .
lion] *Pope; two lines, ending* Eagles; Lyon: *Ff.*   37. over-charg'd with]
overcharg'd; with *Theobald.*   38. So they] *Steevens; begins* 39 *Ff; ends*
37 *Globe (1878), Kittredge;* They *so conj. Keightley.*   39. upon] on *F 2, 3, 4.*
40. reeking] recking *F 2, 3.*   42-3. I cannot . . . help] *Rowe; lines end* faint,
help *Ff.*   45. *Enter Rosse and Angus*] *Ff; Enter Ross, Steevens; Enter Ross and
Angus, after* strange (48) *Dyce; after* here? (46) *Old Camb., Wilson.*

33-4. Duncan's speech is printed as prose in the Folio, and though the Clar. Edd., following Douce, assumed that "captains" should be pronounced "capitains" to make the line regular (cf. *3 Hen. VI.* iv. vii. 30: "A wise stout captain, and soon persuaded"), the word is nearly always dissyllabic in Shakespeare, and it might be better to print the speech as prose. In which case the Captain's "Yes" would be printed with 35.

38. *So they*] Abbot suggests that this short line should be detached from the beginning of 39 (as it is in the Folio) and added to 37—reading *o'ercharg'd* for the sake of the scansion. But I suspect that a line or more is missing between 36 and 37, 37 beginning a new sentence.

39. *Doubly redoubled*] cf. *Rich. II.* i. iii. 80.

42-3. *I . . . help.*] Flatter, *op. cit.* p. 101, defends the F arrangement of these lines on the grounds that the broken line ("I . . . faint") allows the captain to exhibit faintness, and that the short line at the end marks the place where attendants go to his assistance. Wilson thinks the whole speech is the ruin of a longer one. Perhaps a wounded soldier may be forgiven some slight incoherence.

45. S.D. *Enter . . . . Angus*] Steevens says that "as Ross alone is addressed, or is mentioned in this scene, and as Duncan expresses himself in the singular number as in line 49, Angus may be considered a superfluous character. Had his present appearance been designed, the King would naturally have taken some notice of him." But cf. i. iii. 100 which makes it certain that his presence in this scene was intended.

Enter ROSSE AND ANGUS.

Who comes here?
Mal.   The worthy Thane of Rosse.
Len. What a haste looks through his eyes! So should he
      look
That seems to speak things strange.
Rosse.   God save the King!
Dun. Whence cam'st thou, worthy Thane?
Rosse.   From Fife, great King,
Where the Norweyan banners flout the sky,   50
And fan our people cold.   Norway himself,
With terrible numbers,
Assisted by that most disloyal traitor,
The Thane of Cawdor, began a dismal conflict;
Till that Bellona's bridegroom, lapp'd in proof,   55

47.] *Hanmer; lines end* eyes? strange. King. *Ff.*   47. a haste] hast
F 2, 3, 4. 48. seems] teems *conj. Johnson;* comes *Collier (ed. 2).*   51-2.]
Finger, Globe, Chambers, Grierson, Kittredge, etc.; lines end cold. numbers,
Sf, Arden (ed. 1), Wilson, etc. 54. began] 'gan *Pope.*

47-9. *What . . . king*] Hanmer's
arrangement of these lines is probably
correct.
   47. *a haste*] The line would be
better without the article.
   47. *look*] Perhaps copied in error
from " looks," which in F is in the
previous line. Cf. *A.C.* v. i. 50:
" The business of this man looks
out of him."
   48. *seems*] i.e. " whose appearance
corresponds with the strangeness of
his message." Cf. i. v. 29 *post*, and
1 Hen. IV. iii. ii. 162: " thy looks
are full of speed."
   50. *flout*] Elwin, quoted in the
New Variorum, suggests that Rosse
" describes the previous advantages
of the rebels in the present tense,
in order to set the royal victory in
the strongest light of achievement."
Keightley rearranges the lines and
inserts " did " before " flout." The
meaning must be that the Norweyan
banners made the Scots cold with
fear, and not, as Malone supposed,

that the captured banners serve to
cool the conquerors. Cf. Marston,
Sophonisba, i. ii.:
   " Upon whose tops the *Roman*
      eagles stretch'd
   Their large spread winges, which
      fanned the evening ayre
   To us cold breath."
See Introduction, p. xxiii. Cf. also
K. John, v. i. 72.
   53. *traitor*] Holinshed says the
Thane of Cawdor was condemned at
Forres for treason; but makes no mention of his having assisted the invaders.
   55. *Bellona's bridegroom*] i.e. Macbeth. Chapman, *Iliad*, v. 590,
cited by Wilson (from P. Simpson)
speaks of " great Mars himselfe,
matcht with his femall mate,/The
drad Bellona." Douce remarks
that " Shakespeare has not called
Macbeth . . . the *God of War*, and
there seems to be no great impro-
priety in *poetically* supposing that
a warlike hero might be *newly
married* to the Goddess of War."

Confronted him with self-comparisons,
Point against point, rebellious arm 'gainst arm,
Curbing his lavish spirit: and, to conclude,
The victory fell on us;—
Dun.   Great happiness!
Rosse. That now   60
Sweno, the Norways' King, craves composition;
Nor would we deign him burial of his men
Till he disbursed at Saint Colme's Inch
Ten thousand dollars to our general use.
Dun. No more that Thane of Cawdor shall deceive   65

---

57. point, rebellious arm] *Ff;* point rebellious, arm *Theobald, Globe, Chambers.*
60-1.] *Johnson, Steevens (1778); lines end* King, composition: *Ff; one line*
(*omitting* That) *Pope.* 63. Inch] ynch, *F 1;* hill *F 2, 3, 4.*

Shakespeare knew that " the fire-eyed *maid* of smoky war " (*1 Hen. IV.* IV. i. 114) was not a bride.

Granville-Barker suggests that Bellona's bridegroom may not be Macbeth. But though Shakespeare was condensing three campaigns into one, there would have been no point in making some other general responsible for the victory over Sweno, in defiance of his source. Nosworthy compares *Ham.* II. ii. 512.

55. *lapp'd in proof*] i.e. clad in armour of proof—approved or tested. Cf. *Rich. III.* II. i. 115.

56. *Confronted . . . self-comparisons*] i.e. faced him with equal courage and skill; " gave him a Roland for his Oliver," as Craig says. But R. Walker, *op. cit.* chap. 2, points out that Macbeth is to match the Thane of Cawdor in treachery as well as in valour.

57. Theobald's punctuation, wisely rejected by Cuningham, the New Clarendon, Kittredge and Wilson, " obliterated a characteristic feature of Shakespeare's style " (Simpson, quoted Wilson). Nosworthy compares *Ham.* II. ii. 492.

58. *lavish*] i.e. insolent. Cf. *2 Hen. IV.* IV. iv. 63:

" When rage and hot blood are his
          counsellors,
When means and lavish manners
          meet together."

58. *to conclude*] To Wilson " this sudden conclusion suggests abridgement "; but if one were not looking for evidence of abridgement, one would not suspect it here.

60. *That now*] For the construction cf. II. ii. 7, 23, *post.*

61. *Sweno*] Steevens thought, from the irregularity of the metre, that *Sweno* was only a marginal reference, thrust into the text, and that the line originally read " That now the Norways' king craves composition."

63. *Saint Colme's Inch*] Steevens says that " Colmes " is here a dissyllable. *Colmes'-ynch*, now called Inchcomb, is a small island lying in the " Frith of Edinburgh " (i.e. the Firth of Forth). Saint Colmes'-kill Isle (Pope's emendation) is Iona, in the Hebrides, a totally different place. Cf. Appendix, p. 177.

64. *dollars*] First coined *cir.* 1518, some five hundred years later.

Our bosom interest.—Go pronounce his present death,
And with his former title greet Macbeth.
Rosse. I'll see it done.
Dun. What he hath lost, noble Macbeth hath won.
[*Exeunt.*

SCENE III.—*A heath.*

Thunder.   Enter the three Witches.

1 *Witch.* Where hast thou been, Sister?
2 *Witch.* Killing swine.
3 *Witch.*   Sister, where thou?
1 *Witch.* A sailor's wife had chestnuts in her lap,
   And mounch'd, and mounch'd, and mounch'd: " Give
   me," quoth I:—   5
   " Aroynt thee, witch! " the rump-fed ronyon cries.

66. interest.—Go] trust.   *conj. Capell.*   67. greet] great *F 2, 3, 4.*

Scene III

5.] Pope; *two lines ending* mouncht: I. *Ff.*   6. Aroynt] Anoynt *F 3.*

68. *former title*] R. Walker, *op. cit.*
chap. 2, points out that the last title
applied to the Thane of Cawdor was
" that most disloyal traitor."

Scene III

2. *Killing swine*] Steevens quotes
from *A Detection of Damnable Driftes,*
etc., 1579: " She came on a tyme
to the house of one Robert Lath-
burie . . . who, dislyking her dealying
sent her home emptie; but presently
after her departure, his hogges fell
sicke and died, to the number of
twentie."

6. *Aroynt thee*] Cf. *Lear,* III. iv. 129:
" And aroint thee, witch, aroint
thee "; the only other passage
where the word seems to occur.
The origin of the word is unknown,
though it has been the subject of
numerous conjectures. Ray, in his
North Country Words, 1691, thus explains: " Ryntye, by your leave,
stand handsomly "; as " ' Rynt

you, witch,' quoth Bessie Locket to
her mother; Proverb: Cheshire."
Halliwell, *Dict. of Archaic and Provincial Words,* says that, according
to Wilbraham, " rynt thee " is an
expression used by milkmaids to a
cow when she has been milked, to
bid her get out of the way. Cuningham suggests the word may have
some relation to the north-country
and Scottish word *runt,* a term applied
in contempt to an old woman. In
any case, the word seems to mean
' begone.'
   " A term of exorcism " (Grierson).
   6. *rump-fed*] This is variously explained. (i) "fed on offals" (Steevens).
Cf. Jonson, *Staple of News,* II. iii. 78:
   " And then remember, meat for my
      two dogs;
   Fat flaps of mutton, kidneyes,
      rumps of veale,
   Good plentious scraps."
(ii) " fat-bottomed; fed or fat-
tened in the rump " (Nares).

Her husband's to Aleppo gone, master o' th' *Tiger:*
But in a sieve I'll thither sail,
And like a rat without a tail;
I'll do, I'll do, and I'll do.   10
2 *Witch.* I'll give thee a wind.

(iii) " Nut-fed " (Dyce. Cf. Killan's Dictionary: " *Rompe.* Nux myristica vilior, cassa, inanis." The sailor's wife was eating chestnuts.

(iv) " fed on the best joints, pampered " (Clar.). Though Cuningham points out that this explanation does not go well with "ronyon," the first does not suggest the wife of a master of the *Tiger.* I incline to (iv).

6. *ronyon*] a mangy, scabby creature, and hence a term of abuse. Cf. *Merry Wives,* IV. ii. 195: " You witch, you hag, you baggage, you polecat, you ronyon! "

7. th' *Tiger*] a favourite name for ships in Shakespeare's day. Cf. *T.N.* v. i. 65.

8. Several quotations are given by Steevens in the 1821 Variorum as to the powers of witches in this respect. The New Variorum quotes from Pitcairn, *Criminal Trials,* I. ii. 217, about Agnis Tompson (Sampson), who confessed that, accompanied by 200 other witches, " all they together went to Sea, each one in a riddle or cive, and went into the same very substantially, with flaggons of wine, making merry and drinking by the way in the same riddles or cives, to the Kirke of North Barrick in Lowthian." Cf. *Newes from Scotland,* 1924, p. 13.

9. *tail*] Steevens mentions it as a belief of the times, that though a witch could assume the form of any animal she pleased, the tail would still be wanting, and that the reason given by some old writers for such a deficiency was, that though the hands and feet by an easy change might be converted into the four paws of a beast, there was still no

part about a woman which corresponded with the length of tail common to almost all our four-footed creatures.

10. *I'll do*] Kittredge, *Witchcraft in Old and New England,* p. 13, explains: " she will take the shape of a rat in order to slip on board the *Tiger* unnoticed. This, and not to use her teeth, is the object of the transformation. Then she will bewitch the craft and lay a spell upon the captain. There is no question of scuttling the ship." This is doubtless correct, though some editors have supposed that the witch in the shape of a rat would gnaw through the hull and make the ship spring a leak (Clarendon) or through the rudder and make the ship drift helplessly (Grierson, prob. from Paton, *Few Notes on Macbeth*).

11. *a wind*] Witches were supposed to sell winds. See Nashe, *Terrors of the Night,* 1594 (ed. McKerrow, i. 359): " Farre cheaper maye you buy a winde amongst them than you can buy wind or faire words in the Court. Three knots in a thred, or an odde (? olde) grandams blessing in the corner of a napkin, will carrie you all the world ouer." Also his *Will Summers Last Will and Testament,* 1600 (ed. McKerrow, iii. ll. 1219-22):

" For, as in *Ireland* and in *Denmarke* both

Witches for gold will sell a man
  a winde,

Which, in the corner of a napkin
  wrapt,

Shall blow him safe unto what
  coast he will."

Hunter quotes G. Fletcher, *The Russe Commonwealth,* 1591 (inc. in

1 *Witch.* Th' art kind.

3 *Witch.* And I another.

1 *Witch.* I myself have all the other;

　　And the very ports they blow,　　　　　　　15

　　All the quarters that they know

　　I' th' shipman's card.

　　I'll drain him dry as hay:

　　Sleep shall neither night nor day

　　Hang upon his penthouse lid;　　　　　　　20

　　He shall live a man forbid.

　　Weary sev'n-nights nine times nine,

---

15. very] various *conj. Johnson*　ports] points *Pope.*　　18. I'll] (Ile) *Ff;*
I will *Pope, etc.*　　　22. sev'n-nights] *Theobald;* Seu'nights *Ff;* se'nnights
Globe, etc.

Hakluyt's *Voyages,* Everyman ed. ii. 326-7) on the Laplanders: "Though for enchanting of ships that saile along their coast . . . and their giving of winds good to their friends, and contrary to other, whom they meane to hurt by tying of certaine knots upon a rope (somewhat like to the tale of Æolus his windbag) is a very fable, devised (as may seeme) by themselves, to terrifie sailers for comming neere their coast." See also Drayton, *The Moon Calfe,* 865 ff. (ed. Hebel, iii. 188):

"She could sell windes to any one
　　that would,
　Buy them for money, forcing
　　them to hold
　What time she listed, tye them
　　in a thrid,
　Which ever as the Sea-farer undid
　They rose or scantled, as his
　　Sayles would drive,
　To the same Port whereas he
　　would arive."

14. *other*] i.e. others. Cf. *Philip.* ii. 3.

15. *very . . . blow*] " the exact ports the winds blow upon " (Cuningham); but the meaning is rather that contrary winds keep the ship out of every port, and we must assume either that " from " is understood (Abbott),

or else that " ports " is the subject (Wilson).

17. *Shipman's card*] The circular piece of stiff paper on which the 32 points of the compass are marked, and hence the compass itself. But as Hunter (*New Illustrations of Shakespeare,* ii. 167) points out, the word also meant *chart;* and Dyce likewise quotes Sylvester, *Du Bartas, The Triumph of Faith,* 1641, where " my Card and Compasse " translates " Mon Quadrant et ma Carte marine." Cf. *Ham.* v. i. 149: " we must speak by the card."

18. *I'll*] Most editors unnecessarily accept Pope's sophistication.

19-20. *Sleep . . . lid*] Compare Macbeth's later insomnia.

20. *penthouse lid*] The eyelid slopes like the roof of a penthouse. Malone quotes Dekker, *Gul's Horne Booke* (ed. McKerrow, p. 33): " The two eyes are the glasse windowes at which light disperses itselfe into every roome, having goodly penthouses of haire to overshadow them "; and Drayton, *David and Goliath,* 373:

" His brows like two steep pent-
　　houses hung down
　Over his eyelids."

21. *forbid*] " as under a curse, an interdiction " (Theobald).

Shall he dwindle, peak, and pine:
Though his bark cannot be lost,
Yet it shall be tempest-tost.   25
Look what I have.

2 *Witch.* Show me, show me.

1 *Witch.* Here I have a pilot's thumb,
Wrack'd, as homeward he did come.   [*Drum within.*

3 *Witch.* A drum! a drum!   30
Macbeth doth come.

All. The Weïrd Sisters, hand in hand,
Posters of the sea and land,
Thus do go about, about:
Thrice to thine, and thrice to mine,   35
And thrice again, to make up nine.
Peace!—the charm's wound up.

29. wrack'd] (wrackt) *Ff;* wreckt *Theobald (ed. 2), Globe, Chambers.*
32. Weïrd] *Theobald, Wilson;* weyward *Ff;* weyard *Keightley;* weird *modern Edd. generally.*

23. *dwindle*] The passage may have been suggested by the account in Holinshed of the bewitchment of King Duff (Appendix, p. 170). Scot, *Discoverie of Witchcraft,* xii. 16, has "*A charme teaching how to hurt whom you list with images of wax, etc.*" Waxen figures were stuck with needles or melted before a slow fire; and as the figure wasted, so wasted the person intended to be harmed. Cf. Webster, *Duchess of Malfi,* iv. i. 73:
"It wastes me more,
Than were't my picture, fash-
ion'd out of wax,
Stucke with a magical needle, and
then buried," etc.

23. *peak*] i.e. become emaciated. Cf. *Ham* ii. ii. 594.

24. Knight, *The Wheel of Fire* (1949), p. 157, applies this couplet to Macbeth; but surely *his* bark is lost.

30. *drum*] It is curious that though Banquo and Macbeth are alone, their arrival is announced by a drum.

32. *Weïrd*] I have adopted Theobald's spelling. The Folio spelling of *wayward* is repeated at i. v. 8 and ii. i. 20. It is also to be found in

Heywood, *The Late Witches of Lancashire* (1633): "one of the Scottish wayward sisters." He may have been influenced by the Folio spelling. Elsewhere in the Folio, however, the word is spelt *weyard,* which probably indicates how it was pronounced. The word comes from O.E. *wyrd,* M.E. *werd* (i.e. fate). Cf. Holinshed, Appendix, p. 178, "the weird sisters, that is (as ye would say) the godesses of destinie."

33. *Posters*] i.e. persons who travel post, swiftly.

35-6. *Thrice . . . nine*] Odd numbers, and especially multiples of three and nine, were affected by witches. Cf. iv. i. 2 *post.* The Clar. Edd. cite Ovid, *Metam.* xiv. 58 and vii. 189-91. Golding translates the latter:
"The starres alonly faire and
bright did in the welken shine.
To which she lifting up her
handes did thrise hir selfe encline:
And thrise with water of the
brooke hir haire besprincled shee:
And gasping thrise she opte her
mouth."

37. *wound up*] i.e. "set in readiness for action" (*O.E.D.*).

Enter MACBETH *and* BANQUO.

Macb. So foul and fair a day I have not seen.
Ban. How far is't call'd to Forres?—What are these,
So wither'd and so wild in their attire,   40
That look not like th' inhabitants o' th' earth,
And yet are on't?   Live you?   or are you aught
That man may question?   You seem to understand me,
By each at once her choppy finger laying
Upon her skinny lips: you should be women,   45
And yet your beards forbid me to interpret
That you are so.
Macb.   Speak, if you can:—what are you?
1 *Witch.* All hail, Macbeth! hail to thee, Thane of Glamis!
2 *Witch.* All hail, Macbeth! hail to thee, Thane of Cawdor!
3 *Witch.* All hail, Macbeth!   that shalt be King here-
after.   50

39. Forres] (Foris) *Pope;* Soris *Ff.*   44. Choppy] (choppie) *Ff;* chappy
Collier.

38. *So . . . seen*] Cf. I. i. 11. Dowden
(p. 249) comments on this parallel
that Shakespeare intimated by it
" that, although Macbeth has not
yet set eyes upon these hags, the
connection is already established
between his soul and them. Their
spells have already wrought upon his
blood." Elwin, *Shakespeare Restored,*
1853, thinks it means " *Foul* with
regard to the *weather,* and *fair* with
reference to his *victory.*" But Wilson
quotes James I, *Dæmonologie,* 1924,
p. 39, to the effect that the Devil can
" thicken and obscure so the aire,
that is next about them [witches]
by contracting it strait together, that
the beames of any other mans eyes
cannot pearce thorow the same, to
see them." [*Workes,* 1616, p. 114.]

39. *How . . . call'd*] Stopes, *Shakespeare's Industry,* p. 98, says this is a
" peculiarly Scottish idiom." Mr.
David D. Murison, however, editor
of *The Scottish National Dictionary,*
informs me privately that though
" an old speaker in N.E. Scotland
might use those very words " it

might also have been used in England.
Brougham, quoted in Webster's
New International Dictionary for a
similar use of the word " call,"
" *might* have picked it up in Edinburgh." Murison concludes that it is
" most highly improbable that Shakespeare meant it for a Scotticism."

43. *question?*] " Are ye any beings
with which man is permitted to hold
converse, or of whom it is lawful to
ask questions? " Wilson refers to
Ham. I. i. 45 and I. iv. 43, and
points out that " Spirits might not
speak unless first addressed."

44. *choppy*] i.e. chapped. Cotgrave,
Dict. 1611, has " Fendu: *gaping,
chappie.*" Wilson, following Bradley,
suggests that the gesture means that
the witches refuse to speak to Banquo;
they reply directly to Macbeth.

46. *beards*] Cf. *Merry Wives,* IV. ii.
202: " By yea and no, I think the
'oman is a witch indeed.   I like not
when a 'oman has a great peard.""

48. *Glamis*] To Shakespeare the
word was dissyllabic. Cf. I. v. 15,
54; II. ii. 41, etc.

Ban. Good Sir, why do you start, and seem to fear
   Things that do sound so fair?—I' th' name of truth,
   Are ye fantastical, or that indeed
   Which outwardly ye show?   My noble partner
   You greet with present grace, and great prediction   55
   Of noble having, and of royal hope,
   That he seems rapt withal: to me you speak not.
   If you can look into the seeds of time,
   And say which grain will grow, and which will not,
   Speak then to me, who neither beg, nor fear,   60
   Your favours nor your hate.
1 *Witch.* Hail!
2 *Witch.* Hail!
3 *Witch.* Hail!
1 *Witch.* Lesser than Macbeth, and greater.   65
2 *Witch.* Not so happy, yet much happier.
3 *Witch.* Thou shalt get kings, though thou be none:
   So all hail, Macbeth and Banquo!
1 *Witch.* Banquo and Macbeth, all hail!
Macb. Stay, you imperfect speakers, tell me more.   70
   By Sinel's death I know I am Thane of Glamis;

57. rapt] *Pope;* wrapt *Ff.*   59. not] rot *conj. Porson MS.*   68-9.] *Given
to all three witches, Lettsom apud Dyce ed. 1866, Hudson, and conj. Cuningham.*

51. *start*] a sign of guilty thoughts (Coleridge).

43. *fantastical*] imaginary. The word is used by Holinshed in the context ("some vaine fantasticall illusion") and Craig quotes Scot, *Discoverie of Witchcraft,* "these prestigious things which are wrought by witches are fantasticall."

55-6. *present . . . hope*] "There is here a skilful reference to the thrice repeated 'Hail' of the witches" (Hunter).

56. *having*] estate, possession, fortune. Cf. *T.N.* III. iv. 379.

57. *rapt*] i.e. *extra se raptus* (Steevens). Cf. 143 *post.* The Folio was inconsistent in the spelling of this word (Clarendon).

58. *seeds of time*] "Demons," says Curry, *Shakespeare's Philosophical*

Patterns, p. 48, "know the future development of events conjecturally though not absolutely. . . . If time is the measure of movement of corporeal things and if corporeal things move and develop according to the impulses latent in that treasury of forces called *rationes seminales,* then these seeds of matter may literally be called the seeds of time and demons have the power of predicting which grain will grow and which will not."

68, 69. I am inclined to agree with Cuningham that both these lines should be assigned to *all* the weird sisters.

71. *Sinel's*] Shakespeare got the name from Holinshed (cf. Appendix, p. 178). The word "Finele" was mis-transcribed "Synele" by Boece.

But how of Cawdor? the Thane of Cawdor lives,
A prosperous gentleman; and to be King
Stands not within the prospect of belief,
No more than to be Cawdor.   Say from whence   75
You owe this strange intelligence? or why
Upon this blasted heath you stop our way
With such prophetic greeting?—Speak, I charge you.

[*Witches vanish.*

Ban. The earth hath bubbles, as the water has,
And these are of them.—Whither are they vanish'd? 80
Macb. Into the air; and what seem'd corporal,
Melted as breath into the wind.   Would they had stay'd!
Ban. Were such things here, as we do speak about,
Or have we eaten on the insane root,
That takes the reason prisoner?   85

78. With . . . you] *so Pope; two lines Ff.*   81-2. Into . . . stay'd]
three lines in Ff ending corporall, Winde. stay'd;   *two lines ending* melted stay'd;
Capell *and most modern Edd.*   84. on] of *F 4.*

and so the name reached Holinshed
(Wilson).

73. *prosperous*] Cawdor's aid to the
invader was secret and not discovered until after Macbeth had
left the battlefield.   This would seem
to be the only way of explaining
this epithet and Macbeth's surprise.
But the point is not made clear, and
there may have been a bad cut.   An
audience would not notice that
anything was wrong.

74. *prospect*] range of vision.   Cf.
T.N. III. iv. 90: " the full prospect
of my hopes."

75-6. *whence* . . . *intelligence*]
rhyme, presumably accidental.   Cf.
II. iii. 130-2 *post.*

76. *owe*] own.

78. The Folio line-division leaves
room for a necessary pause after
" greeting! "

79. *bubbles*] Wilson interprets this
to mean " illusions " and refers to
O.E.D., which, however, quotes this
line as an illustration of the ordinary
meaning of the word.   Banquo
simply means that the witches have
vanished like a bubble.

81-2. *Into . . . stay'd*] The lines are
easier to speak if " melted " is placed
at the beginning of the line as in F.
The second of these lines is printed
as two by F to indicate the significant
pause after *wind.*

81. *corporal*] i.e. corporeal, a form
which Shakespeare never uses.   Cf.
Ham. III. iv. 118: " incorporal air."

82. *as . . . wind*] Coleridge,
Shakespearean Criticism, i. 69, notes
the appropriateness of the simile to
a cold climate; and Wilson adds
that it is also apt to a Scotch mist.

84. *on*] For this common usage,
compare v. i. 61 *post* and *M.N.D.*
II. i. 266.

84. *the insane root*] i.e. which pro-
duces insanity.   This may be hem-
lock, henbane, or deadly nightshade.
Steevens quotes Greene, *Never Too
Late* (ed. Grosart, p. 195): " you
haue eaten of the rootes of Hemlock,
that makes men's eyes conceipt vn-
seene obiects."   Cf. IV. i. 25 *post.*
Malone quotes Plutarch, *Life of
Antonius* (Temple ed. p. 63).   The
Roman soldiers in the Parthian
War were driven by hunger " to

Macb. Your children shall be kings.
Ban.   You shall be King.
Macb. And Thane of Cawdor too; went it not so?
Ban. To th' selfsame tune, and words. Who's here?

Enter ROSSE *and* ANGUS.

Rosse. The King hath happily receiv'd, Macbeth,
    The news of thy success; and when he reads   90
    Thy personal venture in the rebels' fight,
    His wonders and his praises do contend,
    Which should be thine, or his: silenc'd with that,
    In viewing o'er the rest o' th' selfsame day,
    He finds thee in the stout Norweyan ranks,   95
    Nothing afeard of what thyself didst make,
    Strange images of death. As thick as hail,
    Came post with post; and every one did bear

91. rebels'] *Theobald;* Rebels *Ff;* rebel's *Johnson.*   96. afeard] afraid *F 4.*
97-8. hail Came.] *Rowe;* tale Can *Ff;* tale, Came *Malone (conj. Johnson).*

tast of rootes that were never eaten before; among the which there was one that killed them, and made them out of their wits. For he that had once eaten of it, his memorye went from him, and he knew no manner of thing." Douce quotes Batman, *Uppon Bartholome de propriet. rerum.* xviii. 87: " Henbane . . . is called *Insana,* mad, for the use thereof is perillous, for if it be eate or dronke, it breedeth madness . . . is called commonly *Mirilidium,* for it taketh away wit and reason." The Clar. Edd. suggest that Shakespeare was thinking of the Mekilwort berries, mentioned by Holinshed (Appendix, p. 176). Boece speaks of them as deadly nightshade, which " troubleth the minde, bringeth madnes if a fewe of the berries be inwardly taken " (Gerard, *Herball*).

88. *To . . . words*] Banquo quibbles on " went " (Wilson). J. M. Nosworthy points out that in all accounts of the episode Macbeth and Banquo joked about the " prophesies."

91, 95. Referring to the two

phases of the fight, against Macdonwald, and against Norway.

92-3. *His wonders . . . his*] There is a conflict in Duncan's mind between his astonishment at the achievement and his admiration for Macbeth.

93. *Which . . . his*] R. Walker, *op. cit.,* comments that " in Macbeth's rebel heart that is the very question."

93. *that*] " the mental conflict just described " (Clarendon).

97. *images of death*] Cf. Virgil, *Aen.* II. 369: " plurima mortis imago " (Sprague). See Empson, *Seven Types of Ambiguity,* 1930, pp. 58-9.

97. *thick as hail*] Rowe's emendation is generally accepted. Though Johnson retained the Folio reading, and explained, " posts arrived as fast as they could be counted," Dyce showed that whereas " thick as tale " is unknown, " thick as hail " is common. He instances, e.g. Harington, *Orlando Furioso,* xvi. 51 (1591). It is twice used by Holinshed, not far from *Macbeth* sources.

Thy praises in his kingdom's great defence,
And pour'd them down before him.
Ang.   We are sent,   100
To give thee from our royal master thanks;
Only to herald thee into his sight,
Not pay thee.
Rosse. And, for an earnest of a greater honour,
He bade me, from him, call thee Thane of Cawdor: 105
In which addition, hail, most worthy Thane,
For it is thine.
Ban.   What! can the Devil speak true?
Macb. The Thane of Cawdor lives: why do you dress me
In borrow'd robes?
Ang.   Who was the Thane, lives yet;
But under heavy judgment bears that life   110
Which he deserves to lose.   Whether he was combin'd
With those of Norway, or did line the rebel

102-3. Only . . . pay thee] *one line, Singer.*   108-9. The Thane . . .
yet;] *so Capell; three lines Ff ending* liues: Robes? yet.   109 borrow'd] his
borrowed *F 2, 3, 4.*   111-14. Which . . . know not;] *so Malone; five lines
in Ff ending* loose, Norway, helpe, labour'd not:; *four lines ending* was Rebell
both not; *Pope.*   112. did] *else* did *F 2, 3, 4.*

100. *pour'd*] continues image of
" hail " (Wilson).
104. *for . . . honour*] R. Walker,
op. cit., suggests that as Rosse has
been given no message from Duncan
which would justify this phrase, he
" has become an oracle, repeating
the greatest promise of the Witches."
At least Macbeth may take it as such.
104. *earnest*] " mony giuen for the
conclusion, or striking vp, of a
bargaine " (Cotgrave).
106. *addition*] " a Title given to a
Man over and above his Christian
and Sirname, shewing his Estate,
Degree, Mystery, Trade, Place of
dwelling, etc." (Blount, Law Dict.
(1670)).
108-9. *dress . . . robes*] This image
recurs throughout the play. Cf.
Spurgeon, *Shakespeare's Imagery,* pp.
325-7.
111-14. Wilson remarks that the
mislineation in the Folio suggests
adaptation.   But there is a good deal
of mislineation in F where adapta-

tion is not suspected. Granville-
Barker (*Preface,* p. xxvii) remarks
that it is strange that Angus should
say these words of Cawdor.   " Shakespeare was not apt to leave things
in such a muddle at the beginning
of a play."   But perhaps the muddle
helps to create the atmosphere of
" deceitful appearance, and consequent doubt, uncertainty, and
confusion " (Knights, *op. cit.* p. 18).
R. Walker, *op. cit.* chap. 2, explains: " The poet is shifting the
emphasis from the former thane of
Cawdor's particular faults which
are past to a statement in general
terms which ostensibly describes
those faults but actually foreshadows
also the faults, the ' treasons capital '
that will ' overthrow ' the new
thane of Cawdor.   He achieves his
purpose by casting this slight haze
of doubt over the particular faults and
speaking in the most positive and
arresting terms of the general sins
that are common to both cases."

With hidden help and vantage, or that with both
He labour'd in his country's wrack, I know not;
But treasons capital, confess'd and prov'd,   115
Have overthrown him.

Macb. [*Aside*]   Glamis, and Thane of Cawdor:
The greatest is behind. [*To Rosse and Angus*] Thanks
for your pains.—
[*To Banquo*] Do you not hope your children shall be
kings,
When those that gave the Thane of Cawdor to me
Promis'd no less to them?

Ban.   That, trusted home,   120
Might yet enkindle you unto the crown,
Besides the Thane of Cawdor. But 'tis strange:
And oftentimes, to win us to our harm,
The instruments of Darkness tell us truths;
Win us with honest trifles, to betray's   125
In deepest consequence.—
Cousins, a word, I pray you.

Macb.   [*Aside*] Two truths are told,
As happy prologues to the swelling act
Of the imperial theme.—I thank you, gentlemen.—
[*Aside*] This supernatural soliciting   130
Cannot be ill; cannot be good:—

114. wrack] wreck *Theobald.*   116. S.D.] *Rowe.*   117. S.D.] *White.*
120. trusted] thrusted *conj. Malone.*   125. betray's] betray us *Rowe.*   126-7.]
One line in Capell.   127. S.D.] *Rowe.*   131-2. good:—If ill,] *so Ff;*
lines divided after ill, Rowe, etc.

112. *line*] strengthen, reinforce.
Cf. *Hen. V.* II. iv. 7: "To line and
new repair our towns of war."
120. *home*] thoroughly, fully, largely
(Cotgrave). Cf. *Cym.* III. v. 92.
121. *enkindle you*] "excites you to
hope for" (Bradley). Banquo does
not think of foul play.
122-6. *But . . . consequence*] The
application to Macbeth is obvious.
123. *to win . . . harm*] Cf. James,
Dæmonologie in *Workes*, 1616, p. 98:
"for that old and craftie serpent
being a Spirit, he easily spies our
affections, and so conformes himself
thereto to deceiue vs to our wracke."

128. *the swelling act*] Cf. *Hen. V.*
Prol. 3-4:

" A kingdom for a stage, princes to
act,
And monarchs to behold the
swelling scene."

130-1. The " sickening sea-saw
rhythm completes the impression of
' a phantasma, or a hideous dream ' "
(Knights, *op. cit.* p. 20). Flatter also
supports the F lineation. Knight,
The Wheel of Fire, 1949, p. 153,
comments: " This is the moment
of the birth of evil in Macbeth—
he may indeed have had ambitious

If ill, why hath it given me earnest of success,
Commencing in a truth?　I am Thane of Cawdor:
If good, why do I yield to that suggestion
Whose horrid image doth unfix my hair,　　　　135
And make my seated heart knock at my ribs,
Against the use of nature?　Present fears
Are less than horrible imaginings.
My thought, whose murther yet is but fantastical,
Shakes so my single state of man,　　　　　　140
That function is smother'd in surmise,
And nothing is, but what is not.
Ban. Look, how our partner's rapt.

135. hair] *Rowe;* Heire *Ff.*   139. murther] murder *Steevens* (*1778*).
140-2. Shakes . . . not] *so Ff; lines end* function is rapt.   *Pope and most modern Edd.*

thoughts before, may even have intended the murder, but now for the first time he feels its oncoming reality."

135. *horrid image*] i.e. of himself murdering Duncan.

137. *Against . . . nature*] contrary to my natural habit (Kittredge).

137. *fears*] objects of fear. Cf. *M.N.D.* v. i. 21: "Or in the night, imagining some fear."

139. *fantastical*] imaginary. Cf. i. iii. 53 *ante.*

140-2. I have restored the F arrangement of these lines, as nearly every actor speaks them thus and, I think, correctly.

140. *single . . . man*] Steevens observes that "*double* and *single* anciently signified *strong* and *weak.*" Cf. *Oth.* i. ii. 14: "As double as the Duke's," and *2 Hen. IV.* i. ii. 207: "Is not . . . your wit single?" and cf. i. vi. 16 *post.* But Grierson—I think rightly—says that *single* here means "indivisible" and the phrase as a whole "my composite nature —body, spirits, etc., made one by the soul." Thought Wilson regards a reference to the microcosm pointless in this context, I believe that such a reference is made. Cf. *J.C.* ii. i. 63-9, where the same phrase,

"state of man" occurs, and where the reference to the microcosm is explicit.

141. *function*] The intellectual activity which is revealed in outward conduct: but the word is applied to action in general, whether physical or mental. "All powers of action are oppressed and crushed by one overwhelming image in the mind, and nothing is present to me but that which is really future. Of things now about me I have no perception, being intent wholly on that which has no existence" (Johnson).

142. *nothing . . . not*] Knight, *The Wheel of Fire,* 1949, p. 153, says this is "the text of the play. Reality and unreality change places." Coleridge, *op. cit.* i. 69-70, says: "So truly is the guilt in its germ anterior to the supposed cause and immediate temptation . . . a confirmation of the remark on the early birth-date of guilt."

143. *rapt*] Cf. line 57 *ante.* According to Flatter's rules, Banquo should not be made to complete Macbeth's line; but it is difficult to regard either Macbeth's asides or Banquo's speeches as linked together metrically.

Macb. [*Aside.*] If Chance will have me King, why, Chance
    may crown me,
  Without my stir.

Ban.   New honours come upon him,   145
    Like our strange garments, cleave not to their mould,
    But with the aid of use.

Macb.   [*Aside.*] Come what come may,
    Time and the hour runs through the roughest day.

Ban. Worthy Macbeth, we stay upon your leisure.

Macb. Give me your favour: my dull brain was
    wrought   150
    With things forgotten.   Kind gentlemen, your pains
    Are register'd where every day I turn
    The leaf to read them.—Let us toward the King.—
    [*To Banquo*] Think upon what hath chanc'd; and
    at more time,
    The Interim having weigh'd it, let us speak   155
    Our free hearts each to other.

Ban.   Very gladly.

Macb. Till then, enough.—Come, friends.   [*Exeunt.*

---

144. If . . . crown me,] *so Rowe; two lines in Ff.*   149-54. Give
. . . time], *so Pope; seven lines in F ending* fauour forgotten registred, leafe,
them vpon time,; *six lines ending* favour: forgotten. register'd them King
time *Knight.*   154. S.D.] *Rowe.*   155. The] I' th' *conj. Steevens;* In
the *Keightley.*   157. Till . . . friends] *so Pope; two lines in Ff.*

    145. *come*] Probably the participle,
not the finite verb.

    146. *Like . . . mould*] Another
image taken from clothes.

    148. *Time . . . hour*] Grant White,
Words and their Uses, 1871, p. 237,
says: "Time and the hour in this
passage is merely an equivalent of
time and tide—the time and tide
that wait for no man." Shakespeare
may use "runs" intransitively;
but Cuningham thinks it is used
transitively, meaning, "runs the
roughest day through." Dyce, *Few
Notes,* etc., 1853, p. 119, remarks
that "this expression is not infre-
quent in Italian"—e.g. "*il tempo e
così l'ora*" (Pulci).

    150. *favour*] pardon.

    150. *wrought*] agitated. Cf. *Oth.*
v. ii. 345.

    151. *things forgotten*] i.e. which he
is trying to recall. He is lying.

    152-3. *register'd . . . them*] i.e. in
his brain.

    155. *The Interim*] Steevens says,
"Thus intervening portion of time
is personified; it is represented as
a cool impartial judge; as the
pauser Reason." Malone, however,
believes it is used adverbially. The
word is here printed in the Folio with
a capital letter and in italics, as in
J.C. ii. i. 64, but not elsewhere in
the Folio.

SCENE IV.—*Forres.   A room in the palace.*

Flourish.   Enter DUNCAN, MALCOLM, DONALBAIN, LENOX,
and Attendants.

Dun. Is execution done on Cawdor?   Or not
Those in commission yet return'd?
Mal.   My Liege,
They are not yet come back; but I have spoke
With one that saw him die: who did report,
That very frankly he confess'd his treasons,   5
Implor'd your Highness' pardon, and set forth
A deep repentance.   Nothing in his life
Became him like the leaving it: he died
As one that had been studied in his death,
To throw away the dearest thing he ow'd,   10
As 'twere a careless trifle.
Dun.   There's no art
To find the mind's construction in the face:
He was a gentleman on whom I built
An absolute trust—

Scene IV

S.D. *Forres . . . palace*] Capell; *not in Ff.*   1. Is . . . not] *so Capell;*
Is . . . Cawdor? *one line in Ff.*   Or] *F 1;* Are *F 2, 3, 4.*   2-8. My . . .
died] *so Pope; seven lines in F ending* back. die: hee Pardon, Repentance: him,
dy'de,   9-10. studied . . . To] studied, . . . death, To *Keightley;* studied
. . . death To *Dyce (ed. 2).*

Scene IV

This scene, says Knights, *Explorations,* p. 21, " suggests the natural order which is shortly to be violated. It stresses natural relationships . . . honourable bonds and the political order . . . and the human ' love ' is linked to the more purely natural by images of husbandry." Cf. Knight, *The Imperial Theme,* p. 126, and Traversi, *Approach to Shakespeare,* p. 88.

1. *Or*] Cuningham suggests that the reading of the First Folio may be correct, the verb being understood.

2. *in commission*] charged with the duty.

9. *studied*] A theatrical term, meaning " learnt by heart."

10-11. *To . . . trifle*] R. Walker compares III. i. 67-8, *post.*

11-12. *There's . . . face*] " We cannot construe or discover the disposition of the mind by the lineaments of the face " (Johnson). Baldwin compares Juvenal, *Satires,* ii. 8 ff. " *Frontis nulla fides.*" The irony of the speech is pointed by the immediate entrance of Macbeth, as critics have observed.

Enter MACBETH, BANQUO, ROSSE, *and* ANGUS.

          O worthiest cousin!
The sin of my ingratitude even now   15
Was heavy on me.   Thou art so far before,
That swiftest wing of recompense is slow
To overtake thee: would thou hadst less deserv'd,
That the proportion both of thanks and payment
Might have been mine! only I have left to say,   20
More is thy due than more than all can pay.
Macb. The service and the loyalty I owe,
In doing it, pays itself.   Your Highness' part
Is to receive our duties: and our duties
Are to your throne and state, children and servants; 25
Which do but what they should, by doing everything
Safe toward your love and honour.
Dun.   Welcome hither:
I have begun to plant thee, and will labour
To make thee full of growing.—Noble Banquo,
That hast no less deserv'd, nor must be known   30
No less to have done so, let me infold thee,
And hold thee to my heart.
Ban.   There if I grow,
The harvest is your own.
Dun.   My plenteous joys,
Wanton in fulness, seek to hide themselves

17. That] The *Jennens.* wing] *F 1;* wine *F 2, 3, 4;* wind *Rowe.*
23-7. In . . . honour] *so Pope; six lines in Ff ending* selfe. Duties: State,
should, Loue Honor.   27. Safe] Shap'd *Hanmer;* Fief'd *Warburton;* Fiefs
conj. idem; Serves *conj. Heath;* saf'd *conj. Malone;* Slaves *conj. Kinnear;*
Sole *conj. Orson.* your] you *conj. Blackstone.* love] Life *Warburton.*   30.
That] Thou *Pope.* nor] and *Rowe.*

19-20. *That . . . mine*] i.e. that I might have been able to give you thanks and reward in proportion to your merits. *O.E.D.* quotes this passage and defines " proportion " as " the action of making proportionate."

22-7. Coleridge, *Shakespearean Criticism,* i. 70, declares that " Macbeth has nothing but the commonplaces of loyalty, in which he hides himself. . . . *Reasoning* instead of joy . . . the same language of *effort* . . . at the moment that a new difficulty suggests a new crime."

27. *Safe . . . honour*] " with a sure regard to your love and honour " (Clarendon) or " to confer security on you whom we love and honour."

28. *plant*] Cf. *A.W.* II. iii. 163: " It is in us to plant thine honour where we please to have it grow."

In drops of sorrow.—Sons, kinsmen, Thanes,   35
And you whose places are the nearest, know,
We will establish our estate upon
Our eldest, Malcolm; whom we name hereafter
The Prince of Cumberland: which honour must
Not unaccompanied invest him only,   40
But signs of nobleness, like stars, shall shine
On all deservers.—From hence to Inverness,
And bind us further to you.
Macb. The rest is labour, which is not us'd for you:
I'll be myself the harbinger, and make joyful   45
The hearing of my wife with your approach;
So, humbly take my leave.
Dun.   My worthy Cawdor!

---

35. Sons] Sons and *conj. Cuningham.*

33-5. *My . . . sorrow*] Cf. *R.J.* III.
ii. 102-14; *M.A.* I. i. 26-9; and
W.T. v. ii. 49-50. Malone quotes
Lucan, *Phars.* ix. 1038:
" —lacrymas non sponte cadentes
    Effudit, gemitusque expressit
        pectore laeto
    Non aliter manifesta potens
        abscondere mentis
    Gaudia, quam lacrymis."
34. *Wanton*] unrestrained, perverse.
35. *Sons, kinsmen*] Cuningham
wanted to mend the metre by inserting " and " between these two
words. But there must be a pause
while Duncan masters his emotion.
Adams thinks that two scenes have
been run together or at least that
portions of the text are lost because
(i) we lose a day while Macbeth
makes enquiries about the weird
sisters, (ii) the weak Duncan suddenly exhibits strength by arranging
for his son to succeed him, and
(iii) announces in an unexpected
and brief clause—almost unintelligible—that he proposes to visit
Macbeth at Inverness. Bradley and
Wilson also suspect a cut. But see
Thaler, *Shakespeare and Democracy*,
pp. 88-105, for a refutation of Adams.
(i) Shakespeare was not realistic in

his treatment of time; (ii) Duncan
was not weak, and even if he were,
a sudden announcement is not in-
compatible with weakness; (iii) the
clause is intelligible enough—though
I too suspect there may have been
a cut here.
37. *establish our estate*] settle the
succession.
39. *The . . . Cumberland*] " The
crown of Scotland was originally not
hereditary. When a successor was
declared in the life-time of a king, as
was often the case, the title of *Prince
of Cumberland* was immediately bestowed on him as the mark of his
designation. Cumberland was at
that time held by Scotland of the
crown of England as a fief "
(Steevens).
45. *harbinger*] an officer of the
household whose duty it was to
provide lodgings for the king, hence
" forerunner."
47-53. Granville-Barker, *Preface*,
p. xxvii, remarks that " the dis-
closure of Macbeth's mind, not in a
soliloquy, but in two rather ineptly
contrived asides, is surely, in such a
play and with such a character, un-
Shakespearean." Fleay suspected this
passage was written by Middleton.

Macb. [*Aside.*] The Prince of Cumberland!—That is a step
    On which I must fall down, or else o'erleap,
    For in my way it lies.   Stars, hide your fires!   50
    Let not light see my black and deep desires;
    The eye wink at the hand; yet let that be,
    Which the eye fears, when it is done, to see.   [*Exit.*
Dun. True, worthy Banquo: he is full so valiant,
    And in his commendations I am fed;   55
    It is a banquet to me.   Let 's after him,
    Whose care is gone before to bid us welcome:
    It is a peerless kinsman.   [*Flourish.   Exeunt.*

SCENE V.—*Inverness.   A room in* MACBETH'S *castle.*

Enter LADY MACBETH, *reading a letter.*

Lady M. " They met me in the day of success; and I
    have learn'd by the perfect'st report, they have

48. S.D.] *Rowe.*   51. not] *Ff;* no *Hanmer.*   light] Night *Warburton.*
56. Let's] *Ff;* Let us *Pope, etc.*

Scene v

S.D. Inverness . . . castle.] *Capell*

But the imagery is Shakespearean.
Compare 49 with I. vii. 27; 50 with
I. v. 50 and II. i. 5; and 52 with
several passages in which eye and
hand are opposed. See Introduction,
p. xxix and cf. Spurgeon, *Shakespeare's
Imagery*, pp. 329.

50. *Stars*] " Macbeth apparently
appeals to the stars because he is
contemplating night as the time for
the perpetration of the deed. There
is nothing to indicate that this scene
took place at night " (Clarendon).
Cf. Lady Macbeth's speech I. v. 50-4.
R. Walker, *op. cit.* compares 41 *ante*
and comments: " it is the signs of
nobleness in his own nature that
he would obscure."

52. *wink at*] seem not to see, con-
nive. Cf. Introduction, p. xxxi.

52. *be*] i.e. be done.

56. *banquet*] Cuningham suggests
that this is what we now call dessert
—a slight refection, consisting of
cakes, sweetmeats and fruit, and
generally served in a room to which

the guests removed after dinner;
but as the ordinary sense of the word
is common in Shakespeare and as
several critics have stressed the importance of banquets in the play,
as a visible sign of the concord
violated by Macbeth's crimes—see,
e.g., Knight, *The Imperial Theme*—it
is unlikely that Shakespeare here
intended the restricted sense of the
word.

58. *kinsman*] Macbeth was Duncan's first-cousin.

Scene v

1. *success*] Although the common
sense of this word in Shakespeare's
day was " issue," " sequel " or
" consequence " of a thing, it is used
here and at I. iii. 90 *ante* in the modern
sense. Cf. note to I. vii. 4 *post.*

2. *the perfect'st report*] " the best
intelligence " (Johnson); " my own
experience " (Clarendon); Rosse's
report of the King's intention to
invest Macbeth with the thaneship

more in them than mortal knowledge.　When
I burn'd in desire to question them further, they
made themselves air, into which they vanish'd.　5
Whiles I stood rapt in the wonder of it, came
missives from the King, who all-hail'd me, ' Thane
of Cawdor'; by which title, before, these Weïrd
Sisters saluted me, and referr'd me to the coming on
of time, with 'Hail, King that shalt be!'　This have　10
I thought good to deliver thee (my dearest partner
of greatness) that thou might'st not lose the dues
of rejoicing, by being ignorant of what greatness is
promis'd thee.　Lay it to thy heart, and farewell."
Glamis thou art, and Cawdor; and shalt be　　　15
What thou art promis'd.—Yet do I fear thy nature:
It is too full o' th' milk of human kindness,
To catch the nearest way.　Thou wouldst be great;
Art not without ambition, but without

---

8. Weïrd] *Cf. 1. iii. 32.*　　10. be!] be hereafter *conj. Upton.*　　13. the]
thy *conj. Capell.*　　15. be] be—*Kittredge.*　　17. human] *Rowe;* humane *Ff.*
human kindness] humankindness *conj. Moulton.*

---

of Cawdor (Leighton). Johnson's
explanation, implying that Macbeth
had made enquiries about the weird
sisters, is clearly right.

7. *missives*] messengers. Cf. *A.C.*
II. ii. 74: " Did gibe my missive
out of audience."

7. *all-hailed*] Florio, *Worlde of
Wordes,* 1598, gives as meanings of
salutare, " to greet, to salute, to
recommend, to all-haile."

14. *farewell*] R. Walker, *op. cit.*
chap. 3, comments that Macbeth
does not mention Banquo. " He
has suppressed the one piece of news
that would show the flaw in the
plot against Duncan, and deliberately made his wife believe that the
prophecy . . . is a secret of which
he was the sole possessor." But we
only hear the second half of the
letter.

15-29. *Glamis. . . . withal*] Stewart,
Modern Language Review, 1945, p.

173, points out that " the speech
will be satisfactory if we only admit
that the portrayal of Lady Macbeth,
and of her relations with her husband,
are factors in it; and that a certain
distortion of Macbeth's character is
entailed in this.　On Macbeth himself the speech does indeed throw new
and useful light, such as is desirable
in an exposition, for we chiefly
gather from it that he is not likely
to be immediately wholehearted in
villainy and that some spiritual
struggle is to be expected of him.
But the speech is also charged with
certain feelings of Lady Macbeth's
which lead her to exaggerate what
she pervertedly regards as her
husband's insufficiencies, and this
renders more striking and terrible
our first impression of her." Lady
Macbeth suddenly realizes " forces
in his nature that may militate against
her designs. These she does not

The illness should attend it: what thou wouldst highly,
That wouldst thou holily; wouldst not play false,   21
And yet wouldst wrongly win; thou'dst have, great
    Glamis,
That which cries, "Thus thou must do," if thou have it;
And that which rather thou dost fear to do,
Than wishest should be undone. Hie thee hither,   25
That I may pour my spirits in thine ear,

22-3. And . . . it] *so Pope; three lines in Ff ending* winne. cryes, it;
23. "Thus . . . do "] *so Hunter; final inverted commas placed after* undone,
Pope; placed after have it, *Hanmer, Capell.*   25. Hie] *F 4;* High *F 1,*
2, 3.

review 'objectively' but magnifies
in passion and scorn. And this
should be clear to us. For we already
know that Macbeth has murder in
his thoughts."

15. *shalt be*] Lady Macbeth, in repeating the words of the Third Sister,
instinctively checks herself at the word
King, and substitutes a reticent phrase
(Kittredge).

17. *th' milk . . . kindness*] Cuningham points out that it is essential
to remember the radical significa-
tion of the words *kind, kindness*, as
meaning *natural* and *nature*. Moulton,
Shakespeare as a Dramatic Artist, p. 149,
therefore suggests that we should
read *humankind* as meaning *human
nature;* "and that the sense of the
whole passage would be more
obvious if the whole phrase were
printed as one word, not 'human
kindness' but 'humankind-ness'"
—that shrinking from the unnatural
which is a marked feature of the
practical man. "The other part of
the clause, *milk* of humankindness,
no doubt suggests absence of hardness: but it equally connotes natural
inherited traditional feelings imbibed
at the mother's breast." But cf.
K. Lear, I. iv. 364: "This milky
gentleness and course of yours," and
line 48 *post* (" take my milk for gall ")
which certainly suggest that *milk*
implies an absence of hardness; and
humane was the only spelling down
to the end of the eighteenth century,

when *human* was substituted in
certain senses, leaving *humane* as a
distinct word, with distinctive meanings. There is therefore no reason
for altering the text. Lady Macbeth
implies that her husband is squeamish
and sentimental. She may also imply
that he is bound by traditional
feelings. See headnote to Sc. IV.
ante and the reference to " the milk
of concord " (IV. iii. 98). Cf. Appendix A., p. 188.

20. *illness*] evilness, wickedness.
The word was not used for " sickness " in Shakespeare's day.

22-5. *thou'dst . . . undone*] The
chief difficulty here is the extent of
the quotation. Pope put the whole
passage in inverted commas, and he
has been followed by most editors
(i.e. " Thus . . . undone "). Hanmer,
Capell, Verity, Wilson and others
end the quotation at the end of line
23. Hunter (*Illustrations*, ii. 172)
only marks " Thus thou must do "
as such. I think he is right, because
that which cries, the crown, and
if " it " were part of the quotation,
one would expect " me " instead.
As Verity explains, " thou'ldst have "
has two objects, the crown (23) and
the murder by which the crown
may be obtained (24-5). Cuningham wished to follow Keightley and
emend the second " thou " in 23 to
" thou'ldst. " But Shakespeare
wisely avoided the more logical
form because he already had a pleth-

And chastise with the valour of my tongue
All that impedes thee from the golden round,
Which fate and metaphysical aid doth seem
To have thee crown'd withal.

Enter a Messenger.

What is your tidings? 30

Mess. The King comes here to-night.
Lady M.   Thou'rt mad to say it.
Is not thy master with him? who, were't so,
Would have inform'd for preparation.

Mess. So please you, it is true: our Thane is coming;
One of my fellows had the speed of him,   35
Who, almost dead for breath, had scarcely more
Than would make up his message.
Lady M.   Give him tending:
He brings great news. [*Exit Messenger.*] The raven
        himself is hoarse,
That croaks the fatal entrance of Duncan

---

28. impedes thee] thee hinders *F 2, 3.*   38. He . . . hoarse] *one line,*
Rowe; two lines, Ff.

ora of *wouldsts* and there could be
no doubt of the meaning.

27. *chastise*] The accent is on the
first syllable. Cf. *Rich. II.* II. iii. 104.

28. *golden round*] cf. IV. i. 88.

29. *metaphysical*] supernatural.

29. *seem*] cf. I. ii. 48 *ante.*

30. *tidings*] singular or plural, like
" news." Cf. *A.Y.L.I.* v. iv. 159:
" these tidings "; *A.C.* IV. xiv. 112:
" this tidings." Flatter suggests that
Lady Macbeth's question should
form a line with the messenger's
speech which follows, so as to allow
for a dramatic pause after *say it.*

31. *The King . . . to-night*] R.
Walker, *op. cit.* chap. 3, makes the
ingenious suggestion that as Lady
Macbeth has been thinking of her
husband as King, she thinks for a
moment that the messenger refers
to him and not to Duncan.

31-3. *Thou'rt . . . preparation*] Lady
Macbeth, in replying to the messenger, discloses what has been
passing in her own mind, and then,

observing the man's surprise, she
adds a not very convincing explanation.

33. *inform'd*] absolute or intransi-
tive.

35. *had the speed of*] Cf. *M.A.* I. i.
142: " I would my horse had the
speed of your tongue." But the
phrase in *Macbeth* means " out-
distanced," in *M.A.* " went as
fast as."

37. *tending*] Shakespeare does not
elsewhere use this word as a substantive.

38-9. *The raven . . . croaks*] Some
think that the reference is to the
breathless messenger, but lack of
breath does not cause hoarseness.
As Hunter says, the phrase means
" even the raven . . . has more
than its usual harshness "; or
perhaps, as Manly suggests, the
implication is that " the approach
of an ordinary guest might be announced by a magpie, but for such
a visit as Duncan's the hoarse

Under my battlements.   Come, you Spirits   40
That tend on mortal thoughts, unsex me here,
And fill me, from the crown to the toe, top-full
Of direst cruelty!   make thick my blood,
Stop up th' access and passage to remorse;

croaking of a raven would alone be appropriate." Collier cites Drayton, *Barons' Wars*, v. 42:

"The ominous raven with a dismal cheer,
Through his hoarse beak of following horror tells."

The lines, however, were altered by Drayton (ed. Hebel, ii. 95):

"The ominous Raven, often he doth heare,
Whose croking, him of following Horror tells."

Cf. also *Oth.* IV. i. 21: "As doth the raven o'er the infected house, Boding to all"; and Nashe, *Terrors of the Night* (ed. McKerrow, i. 346) on the raven also: "A continuall messenger hee is of dole and misfortune."

39. *entrance*] This word is a trisyllable. The retention of *e* is frequently required *metri gratia*, when a mute is followed by a liquid. Cf. III. vi. 8 and *T.N.* I. i. 32, "remembrance."

40. *Come, you Spirits*] Wilson comments: "All critics have noticed the effect of the metrical pause before "Come" and the tremendous lines that follow." But to judge from the fact that editors have followed Davenant in reading "Come, all you spirits," the statement is an exaggeration. Darmesteter supports this emendation by comparing Hughes, *Misfortunes of Arthur*, I. ii: (an echo of the opening lines of Seneca's *Medea*):

"Come, spiteful fiends, come heaps of furies fell,
Not one by one, but all at once!"

Steevens suggested a repetition of "Come"; and Cuningham argued

for "Come, you ill spirits." Nevertheless these emendations spoil the effectiveness of the passage and deprive the actress of the chance of taking the long breath she obviously needs. Malone quotes Nashe, *Pierce Penilesse*, ed. McKerrow, i. 230, where he thinks "Shakespeare might have found a particular description of these spirits and of their office": "The Second kind of Diuels, which he most imployeth, are those Northerne *Marcii*, called the spirits of reuenge, & the authors of massacres, & seedesmen of mischiefe; for they haue commission to incense men to rapines, sacriledge, theft, murther, wrath, furie, and all manner of crueltles, & they commaund certaine of the Southern spirits (as slaues) to wayt vpon them, as also *Arioch*, that is tearmed the spirite of reuenge."

Burton, *Anatomy of Melancholy*, I. ii. 1, 2 mentions nine kinds of bad spirits. See Introduction, p. lxix, for a comment on this invocation.

41. *mortal thoughts*] "murderous, deadly, or destructive designs" (Johnson). Cf. III. iv. 80 and IV. iii. 3.

42. *crown . . . toe*] Baret's *Alvearie* has: "From the top to the toe, *a capite ad calcem usque*."

42. *top-full*] Cf. *K.J.* III. iv. 180.

43. *make . . . blood*] Wilson compares *W.T.* I. ii. 171 and *K.J.* III. iii. 42-7. She means "so that pity cannot flow along her veins" and reach her heart (Bradley).

44. *remorse*] compassion, tenderness. Cf. *M.V.* IV. i. 20. "Used anciently to signify repentance not only for a deed done but for a thought conceived" (Clarendon).

That no compunctious visitings of Nature　　45
Shake my fell purpose, nor keep peace between
Th' effect and it!　Come to my woman's breasts,
And take my milk for gall, you murth'ring ministers,
Wherever in your sightless substances
You wait on Nature's mischief!　Come, thick Night, 50
And pall thee in the dunnest smoke of Hell,
That my keen knife see not the wound it makes,
Nor Heaven peep through the blanket of the dark,
To cry, " Hold, hold! "

46. peace] pace *Travers (conj. Johnson);* space *conj. Bailey.*　　　47. it]
F *3, 4,* hit F *1, 2.*　　　53. blanket] blank height *conj. Coleridge.*

45. *compunctious*] Not used elsewhere by Shakespeare.

46-7. *nor . . . it*] " use the restraining power of a peacemaker . . . between my purpose and the achievement of it." (New Clar.) Steevens
quotes Brooke, Romeus and Juliet
(1562), 1781 ff:
　　　" the lady no way could
Kepe trewse betweene her greefes
　　and her."

48. *take . . . gall*] " Take away
my milk, and put gall into the
place " (Johnson); " Nourish yourselves with my milk which . . . has
turned to gall " (Delius); take =
infect (Keightley). Johnson's explanation is the best. Cuningham
compares *1 Hen. VI,* v. iv. 27:
　　　" I would the milk
Thy mother gave thee when thou
　　suck'dst her breast,
Had been a little ratsbane for
　　thy sake! "

48. *ministers*] attendant spirits
(Wilson).

49. *sightless*] invisible. Cf. I. vii.
23.

50. *Nature's mischief*] According to
Johnson this means " mischief done
to nature, violation of nature's order
committed by wickedness "; Elwin
thinks it means " both injury en-
gendered in human nature and done
to it "; and Cuningham thinks it
may mean " mischief wrought by

any natural phenomenon, such as
storm, tempest, earthquake, etc.? "
Curry's explanation of the whole
clause, *Shakespeare's Philosophical Patterns,* p. 86, is " objective, substantial
forms, invisible bad angels, to whose
activities may be attributed all the
unnatural occurrences of nature."

50-5. *Come . . . hold*]. Cf. Munday,
*The Downfall of Robert, Earl of
Huntington,* 1601 :
　　　" Muffle the eye of day,
Ye gloomie clouds (the darker than
　　my deedes,
That darker be than pitchie sable
　　night)
Muster together on these high
　　topt trees,
That not a sparke of light thorough
　　their sprayes
May hinder what I meane to
　　execute."
See *M.L.N.* 1931, and cf. III. ii. 46-7
post.

51. *dunnest*] an epithet criticised by
Johnson (*Rambler,* no. 168) as
" mean "; but the criticism was apparently recanted in his *Dictionary.*

52. *my*] Wilson and Adams assume
that Lady Macbeth originally intended to do the deed herself.　Cf.
68, 73 *post* and note on II. i. 30.　See
Introduction, p. xxv.

53. *blanket*] Johnson also objected
to the meanness of this word, and
so did Coleridge (*Shakesp. Criticism,*

Enter MACBETH.

Great Glamis! worthy Cawdor!
Greater than both, by the all-hail hereafter!   55
Thy letters have transported me beyond
This ignorant present, and I feel now
The future in the instant.

Macb.   My dearest love,
Duncan comes here to-night.

Lady M.   And when goes hence?

Macb. To-morrow, as he purposes.

Lady M.   O! never   60
Shall sun that morrow see!
Your face, my Thane, is as a book, where men

62. a] *not in F 2.*

i. 73); but many parallels have
been quoted including: "The sullen night in mistie rugge is wrapp'd"
(Drayton, *Mortimeriados*, l. 694, ed.
Hebel, i. 329); "Spread thy close
curtain, love-performing night" *R.J.*
III. ii. 5); *1 Hen. VI.* II. ii. 2; and
Lucrece, 788. Whiter, in his
Specimen of a Commentary, 1794, pp.
153-84, quotes so many passages
which link *pall*, *hell*, *knife* and *dark*
with the stage that it is impossible
not to believe that they were associated in Shakespeare's mind. "The
peculiar and appropriate dress of
Tragedy is a *pall* and a *knife*. When
Tragedies were represented, the
stage was hung with black . . . on
the same occasions, the *Heavens*, or
the Roof of the Stage, underwent
likewise some gloomy transformation." But although the passage as
a whole was suggested by the stage,
the metaphor of the blanket is quite
simple, and can only refer to the
blanket spread by the dark over the
earth. It implies a "sleeping world"
(Clarendon).

55. *all-hail hereafter*] Lady Macbeth
"speaks as if she had heard the words
as spoken by the witch, and not
merely read them as reported in
her husband's letter" (Clarendon).

Yet the audience would not notice
the discrepancy, and it may be noted
that the letter does use the phrase
"all-hailed" (7) and that Lady
Macbeth reads only the second half
of the letter. Wilson interprets
"hereafter" to mean "that followed": and the New Clarendon
assumes that "All-hail" is an adjective. But surely hereafter = in
the future. Mrs. Siddons accepted
this reading; so, I imagine, do most
actresses.

57. *This . . . present*] i.e. this
present which is ignorant of the
future (ignorant = unknowing). Cf.
W.T. I. ii. 397.

57-8. *I . . . instant*] "I feel by
anticipation those future honours, of
which, according to the process of
nature, the *present time* would be
ignorant" (Johnson). Several critics
have supposed that a word is missing
between "feel" and "now." Cuningham suggested "even" and quoted
v. ii. 10 *post.* This is possible, but
not necessary; and it would slow
up the line, where impetuosity is
required.

62. *face*] Mrs. Siddons here looked
at Macbeth's face for the first time
in this scene.

62. *strange*] Cf. I. ii. 48 *ante.*

May read strange matters.　To beguile the time,
Look like the time; bear welcome in your eye,
Your hand, your tongue: look like th' innocent flower,
But be the serpent under't.　He that's coming　　65
Must be provided for; and you shall put
This night's great business into my dispatch;
Which shall to all our nights and days to come
Give solely sovereign sway and masterdom.　　　70

Macb.　We will speak further.

Lady M.　　　　　　　　　　Only look up clear;
To alter favour ever is to fear.
Leave all the rest to me.　　　　　　　*[Exeunt.*

---

63. matters. To . . . time,] *Theobald;* matters, to . . . time. *F 1;*
matters to . . . time. *F 3, 4.*　　72. to fear] and fear *Theobald (ed. 2).*

63. *beguile the time*] i.e. deceive the
world, delude all observers. " The
time " often means " the present
age, i.e. men and things generally."
Cf. i. vii. 81 *post.* Steevens cites
Daniel, *Civil Wars,* viii. 709:

" He drawes a trauerse 'twixt his
　　greeuances:
Lookes like the time: his eye
　　made not report
Of what he felt within."

In *T.N.* iii. iii. 41, Shakespeare uses
the phrase to mean " wile away the
time."
65-6. *look . . . under't*] Cf. Chaucer,
Squire's Tale, 512; *2 Hen. VI.* iii. i.
228; *R.J.* iii. ii. 73 and *Rich. II.*
iii. ii. 19. The idea is ultimately
derived from Virgil, *Ecl.* iii. 93:
" latet anguis in herba." This
quotation appears in Whitney, *Choice
of Emblemes,* 1586, p. 24, with a
picture of a serpent and a straw-
berry plant and the following explanation:

" Of flattringe speeche, with sugred
　　wordes beware,
Suspect the harte, whose face
　　doth fawn and smile,
With trusting theise, the worlde
　　is clog'de with care,
And fewe there bee can scape
　　these vipers vile:

With pleasinge speche they
　　promise, and protest,
When hatefull heartes lie hidd
　　within their brest."

Wilson thinks the image shows that
Lady Macbeth intended her husband
to play a passive role (p. lvii). But
the serpent does more than hide
behind the flower—he also stings.
67. *provided for*] Cf. *1 Hen. VI.*
v. ii. 15.
68. *my dispatch*] This does not
necessarily mean that Lady Macbeth
intended to do the actual deed, but
merely that she intends to manage
the whole affair. Cf. Introduction,
p. xxiii. Wilson points out that there
is a pun on the word " dispatch."
70. *solely*] " for us alone " (New
Clar.); " absolutely " (Wilson).
71. *speak further*] The old formula
for refusing the royal assent to a bill
in Parliament was " le roi s'avisera "
(Clar.).
72. *To alter . . . fear*] " When a
person shows a disturbed countenance, it is always inferred he has
something on his mind—and that may
rouse suspicion " (Kittredge).
72. *favour*]　look,　countenance.
" Lady Macbeth detects more than
irresolution in her husband's last
speech."
73. *Leave . . . me*] Cf. notes to 65,
68 *ante.*

SCENE VI.—*The same.   Before the castle.*

Hautboys and torches. Enter DUNCAN, MALCOLM, DONAL-
BAIN, BANQUO, LENOX, MACDUFF, ROSSE, ANGUS,
and Attendants.

Dun. This castle hath a pleasant seat; the air
Nimbly and sweetly recommends itself
Unto our gentle senses.

Ban.   This guest of summer,
The temple-haunting martlet, does approve,

Scene VI

S.D. The . . . castle.] *Theobald, subst.*   1-2. the air . . .
itself] *so Rowe; first line ends* seat, *Ff.*   3. senses] sense *Capell (conj.*
Johnson).   4. martlet] *Rowe;* Barlet *Ff;* Marlet *Collier (MS.).*

Scene VI

Knights, *op. cit.* p. 22, remarks
that " the key words of the scene
are . . . all images of loves and pro-
creation, supernaturally sanctioned,
for the associations of ' temple-
haunting ' colour the whole of the
speeches of Banquo and Duncan."
Cf. Knight, *The Imperial Theme*, p.
142 and Leavis, *Education and the
University*, appendix.

Hautboys and torches] Used for the
player of the instrument and the
bearer of the torch, as well as for the
instrument and the torch. Cf. II. i.
init. Wilson omits the torches, on
the ground that they are inappropriate to one of the few sun-lit
scenes in the play. But at sundown,
torches would be needed inside the
castle, even though it was still light
outside.

1. *seat*] Reid compares Bacon,
Essays, Of Building: " Hee that
builds a faire *House*, upon an *ill
Seat*, Committeth himself to Prison.
Neither doe I reckon it an *ill Seat*
only where the Aire is unwholesome,
but likewise where the Aire is unequal; as you shall see many fine
Seats set upon a Knap of Ground
environed with higher Hills round
about it."

3. *gentle senses*] probably a proleptic
construction, in which the epithet of
the object is the result of the previous
action (cf. III. iv. 75 *post*); but
Duncan may mean that his senses
have become gentle through age.

4. *martlet*] This is now the swift,
but seems to have been the house-
martin in Shakespeare's day. According to *O.E.D.* the bird was
" formerly often confused with the
swallow and the house-martin ";
but even Gilbert White thought that
the martlet was another name for
house-martin, though he would not
confuse the swift with the martin.
B. K. Harris points out (*T.L.S.*
16/3/51) that there were martlets on
Edward the Confessor's shield.
Cf. " temple-haunting." Spurgeon,
Shakespeare's Imagery, pp. 187-90,
compares *M.V.* II. ix. 28:

    " like the martlet
    Builds in the weather on the
        outward wall."

She points out that in both contexts
a guest arrives who is to be fooled
or deceived, the hidden connection
in Shakespeare's mind being that
" martin " was a slang term for
" dupe," the word being so used by
Greene and Fletcher. This supports
the view that martlet = martin.

By his loved mansionry, that the heaven's breath   5
Smells wooingly here: no jutty, frieze,
Buttress, nor coign of vantage, but this bird
Hath made his pendent bed, and procreant cradle:
Where they most breed and haunt, I have observ'd
The air is delicate.

Enter LADY MACBETH.

Dun.   See, see! our honour'd hostess.—   10
The love that follows us sometime is our trouble,
Which still we thank as love.   Herein I teach you,
How you shall bid God 'ild us for your pains,
And thank us for your trouble.

5. mansionry] *Theobald;* Mansonry *Ff;* masonry *Pope.*   6-10.] *Steevens* (*1793*) *arranges in five lines, ending* buttress, made they air delicate. 6. wooingly here:] wooingly: here is no *Travers* (*conj. Johnson*) wooingly: there is no *conj. Cuningham* jutty, frieze] *Steevens* (*1793*); Iutty frieze *Ff;* jutting frieze *Pope.*   8. his] this *F 4.*   8-9. cradle: . . . haunt,] *Rowe;* Cradle, . . . haunt: *Ff.*   9. most] *Rowe;* must *Ff;* much *Collier* (*ed. 2*). 10. See, see!] See! *Hanmer.*   11. sometime] sometimes *Theobald.*   13. God 'ild] *Globe;* God yield *Steevens;* God ild *Dyce;* God-ild *Capell;* God-eyld *Ff;* Godild *Hanmer;* God-yield *Johnson;* God shield *conj. Johnson.*

4. *approve*] prove. Cf. *M.V.* III. ii. 80: "Will bless it and approve it with a text."

5. *By . . . mansionry*] "by making it his favourite abode" (New Clar.). Staunton's conj. "love-mansionry" was supported by Cuningham and is not unattractive.

6. *Smell's . . . frieze*] Some think that one or two words have dropped out of this line; but there are five stresses as it stands.

6. *jutty*] "iuttie, or part of a building that iuttieth beyond, or leaneth ouer, the rest" (Cotgrave, *Dictionary*, 1611); "An outnooke or corner standing out of a house; a iettie" (Florio, *Worlde of Wordes*, 1598); "*Sporto*, a porch, a portall, a baie window, or outbutting, or iettie of a house that ietties out further than anie other part of the house, a iettie or butte. Also the eaues or penteis of a house" (*ibid.*). Cf. *Hen. V.* III. i. 13: "jutty."

7. *coign of vantage*] "a position (properly a projecting corner) affording facility for observation or action" (*O.E.D.*).   Old French *coing* or *coin* is the corner-stone at the exterior angle of a building; and perhaps, as Johnson explained, the phrase means merely "convenient corner." Hunter mentions that in *Porta Linguarum Trilinguis* an advantage is described as "a something added to a building, as a jutting."

10. *delicate*] soft. Cf. *W. T.*III . i. 1.

11-14. *The love . . . trouble*] A difficult speech, but not corrupt. It means: "Love sometimes occasions me trouble, but I thank it as love notwithstanding; this should teach you to pray God to reward me for the trouble you yourself are taking."

13. *God'ild us*] i.e. God reward us. Hunter refers to a passage in Palsgrave's *Lesclarcissement*, 1530, p. 441*b*:

Lady M.   All our service,
In every point twice done, and then done double,   15
Were poor and single business, to contend
Against those honours deep and broad, wherewith
Your Majesty loads our house: for those of old,
And the late dignities heap'd up to them,
We rest your hermits.
Dun.   Where's the Thane of Cawdor?   20
We cours'd him at the heels, and had a purpose
To be his purveyor: but he rides well;
And his great love, sharp as his spur, hath holp him
To his home before us.   Fair and noble hostess,
We are your guest to-night.
Lady M.   Your servants ever   25
Have theirs, themselves, and what is theirs, in compt,
To make their audit at your Highness' pleasure,
Still to return your own.
Dun.   Give me your hand;
Conduct me to mine host: we love him highly,
And shall continue our graces towards him.   30
By your leave, hostess.   [*Exeunt.*

17-20. Against . . . hermits] *so Pope; Ff end lines* broad, House: Dignities, Ermites.   23. as] at *F 2.*   26. theirs, in compt,] *Hanmer;* theirs in compt, *Ff;* theirs, in compt: *Capell.*   29. host:] Host *F 1, 2.*   30. continue] continue, *Ff;* continue in *conj. Cuningham.*

" We use ' God yelde you ' by manner of thanking a person." Cf. *A.Y.L.I.* v. iv. 56 and *A.C.* IV. ii. 33.

16. *single*] simple, weak. Cf. I. iii. 140 *ante.*

20. *We . . . hermits*] " We as *hermits* or *beadsmen* shall always pray for you " (Steevens). Cf. *T.A.* III. ii. 41 add *T.G.* I. i. 17.

22. *purveyor*) providor (Cotgrave). His office was to travel before the King in his progresses to different parts of the realm, and to see that everything was duly provided, and generally, to make provision for the

royal household. The office was restrained by 12 Chas. II. c. 24.

26. *in compt*] subject to account (Steevens).

30. This line scans awkwardly and it is probable, as Cuningham urges, that it should read " continue in." Cf. *Temp.* II. i. 184; *M.M.* II. i. 276, 196; and *Mac.* v. i. 28.

31. *By your leave*] " As the custom was, he kisses Lady Macbeth's cheek. What better climax and ending could the scene have? " (Granville-Barker).

SCENE VII.—*The same.   A room in the castle.*

Hautboys and torches.   Enter, and pass over the stage, a Sewer,
and divers Servants with dishes and service.   Then enter
MACBETH.

Macb. If it were done, when 'tis done, then 'twere well
It were done quickly: if th' assassination
Could trammel up the consequence, and catch
With his surcease success; that but this blow
Might be the be-all and the end-all—here,   5

Scene VII

1-2. well It . . . quickly: if] well, It . . . quickly: If *Ff;* well. It . . .
quickly, if *Travers.*   4. surcease success] success, surcease *conj. Johnson.*
5. end-all—here,] end all   Heere, *Ff;* end-all here, *Hanmer;* end all—Here,]
Rowe (ed. 1); end-all—Here.   *Warburton;* end-all . . . here, *Wilson.*

Scene VII

Enter . . . a Sewer] From the French
essayeur, and meant originally one
who tasted of each dish to prove
that there was no poison in it.   Afterwards it was applied to the chief
servant, who directed the placing of
the dishes on the table.

1-28. Macbeth's soliloquy has been
taken as the supreme expression of
his "visual imagination" (Wilson)
and as a proof that he was worried
only by practical considerations
(Moulton). See Introduction, p. xlvii,
and Empson, *Seven Types of Ambiguity,* 1930, pp. 64-5.

1-2. *If it . . . if*] The notion of
placing a full stop at the end of the
first line and taking "It were done
quickly" as part of the next sentence is ingenuity misplaced, though
Kemble, Macready and Irving
adopted it.

1-7. *If it . . . come*] This passage
must be considered as a unit. "If
the assassination were ended once
for all as soon as accomplished, then
it were well to do it quickly: if it
could prevent any consequences and
obtain success by his death, in such
a way that this blow might kill
Duncan and not lead to any re-

prisals, here, only here, in this world,
we would risk what might happen in
the next world." Or, as Bethell
puts it more briefly: "If there
were no ill-consequences in this life
I should be quite satisfied, for I
should ignore the question of a
future state."

2. *It . . . quickly*] R. Walker compares *John,* xiii. 27: "And after
the soppe, Satan entered into him.
Then said Iesus vnto him, That thou
doest, doe quickly." Both Duncan
and Jesus have "almost supped,"
when the betrayer leaves the chamber.
The allusion to the Last Supper may
have suggested to Shakespeare the
chalice, 11 *post.*

3. *trammel up*] i.e. entangle as in a
net. A trammell (Fr. *tramail*) was
a net for partridges (Cotgrave) or
for catching fish. But *trammel* also
meant to fasten the legs of horses
together, so that they could not
stray, or to teach them to amble;
and Cuningham thought that Shakespeare may have been thinking of an
iron device for suspending pots over
a fire, the meaning being "hang up"
the consequences.

3. *catch*] metaphor suggested by
"trammel."

But here, upon this bank and shoal of time,
We'd jump the life to come.—But in these cases,
We still have judgment here; that we but teach
Bloody instructions, which, being taught, return
To plague th' inventor: this even-handed Justice   10

6. shoal] *Theobald;* Schoole *F 1, 2.*   10-1. th'inventor . . . Commends]
not in F 2, 3, 4, Rowe.   10. this] thus *conj. Mason.*

4. *his surcease*] Cuningham, following Clarendon, thought that " his "
must refer to " consequence " rather
than to " Duncan." *Surcease* (O. Fr.
sursis, from *surseoir*) a legal term,
meaning the stop or stay of pro-
ceedings, is not elsewhere in Shakespeare used as a substantive. But
in *Lucrece,* l. 1766 (" If they surcease
to be that should survive ") it is
used in a phrase meaning " die," and
I believe the word here is a euphemism
for death—one of several in the play
—and that " his " refers to Duncan.

4. *success*] Cuningham suggests that
the word is not used here in the more
modern sense of " prosperous issue,"
but rather meaning simply the issue,
sequel or consequence of an action,
whether good or bad. This would
make " trammel up the consequence "
and " catch . . . success " almost
identical in meaning, as indeed
Staunton takes them to be. It seems
to me better to take *success* in its
usual modern sense. Cuningham
further suggests that the word may
have the sense of " succession " as
in *W.T.* I. ii. 394:
" Our parents' noble names,
   In whose success we are gentle."
Perhaps, like *surcease,* an Empsonian
ambiguity.

5. *end-all—here*] Rowe's punctuation. The Folio full-stop after
" end-all " cannot be retained in a
modern text; but most editors have
debased Shakespeare's intentions. As
Simpson points out, *Shakespeare's
Punctuation,* pp. 82-3, " The meaning
as well as the movement of the verse
suggest the close connection of the
words ' Heere, But heere.' The

pause is the most powerful of which
blank verse is capable. At that final
monosyllable the rhythm gathers
like a wave, plunges over to the
line beyond, and falls in all its weight
and force on the repeated word.
The check given to the line fits in
admirably with the brooding, hesitat-
ing mood of the speaker."

6. *bank and shoal*] Theobald's brilliant emendation for " Schoole " is
now generally accepted, especially
as " schoole " is a possible seventeenth
century spelling of " shoal." Theobald explained, " This *Shallow,* this
narrow Ford, of humane Life, opposed
to the *great Abyss* of Eternity." Heath,
however, *Revisal of Shakespeare's Text*
(1765), argued for bank (= bench)
and school. So also did Elwin, *Shakespeare Restored* (1853): " If here only,
upon this bench of instruction, in
this school of eternity, I could do
this without bringing these, my pupil
days, under suffering, I would hazard
its effect on the endless life to come."
Bethell, *The Winter's Tale* (1947),
pp. 126-7, is one of the few modern
critics to defend " school." He
adopts the suggestion of the Rev. G.
Shaw that " bank " is the judical
bench, probably from O.F. *banc.*
The word was certainly current in
this sense in Shakespeare's time.
Bethell says: " Time is thus seen
as the period of judgment, testing,
or ' crisis,' and as a school; corresponding to these meanings we
have later in the speech, ' judgment here ' and ' teach Bloody instructions.' " If we reject this interpretation, it should not be because
it is less *poetic* in the stock sense—

Commends th' ingredience of our poison'd chalice
To our own lips.   He's here in double trust:
First, as I am his kinsman and his subject,
Strong both against the deed; then, as his host,
Who should against his murtherer shut the door,   15

11. ingredience] *Ff, Kittredge, Wilson;* ingredients *Pope.*

cf. Keats' parable of the world as a school (*Letters,* 1935, p. 336)—but because Shakespeare often couples words together like " bank and shoal " (though Bethell denies this) and the preposition " upon " fits " bank " but not " school." It seems to me probable that Shakespeare intended " shoal "; but that, by an unconscious pun, " bank " suggested " judgment " and " schoole " suggested " teach . . . instructions . . . taught " a few lines below.

7. *jump*] i.e. risk. Cf. *Cym,* v. iv. 188: " Jump the after-enquiry at your own peril." But it might perhaps mean " skip over " or " evade " (the thought of the life to come).

7. *life to come*] i.e. the future life, though Keightley thought it meant the remaining years of Macbeth's own life on earth and compared *T.C.* III. ii. 180:

" True swains in love shall in the world to come
    Approve their truths by Troilus."

But this means the world generations hence, not during the lifetime of Troilus. Some think that in *W.T.* IV. iii. 31 (" For the life to come I sleep out the thought of it "), Autolycus was speaking of his future life on earth. But surely Shakespeare was echoing the prayer-book phrase (" the life of the world to come ") both here and in *Macbeth.*

8. *have judgment*] i.e. receive sentence. See Hall, *Chronicles,* 244: " He confessed the inditement and had judgment to be hanged."

8. *here*] referring back to " here " (5, 6).

8. *that*] i.e. " so that," or " in that."

10. *plague th' inventor*] Wilson compares Seneca, *Hercules Furens,* 735-6:
   " Quod quisque fecit, patitur:
        auctorem scelus
     Repetit suoque premitur exemplo
        nocens."
Heywood translates:
   " What eche man one hath done,
        he feeles: and guilt to th'
        author theare
     Returnes, and th'hurtfull with
        their owne example punisht
        bee."
Grierson suggests that the adjacent description of the good king (739-41) may have been echoed in Macbeth's description of Duncan (16 ff.). Heywood translates:
   " what man of might with fauour
        leades his lande,
     And of his own lyfe lorde reserues
        his hurtlesse handes to good,
     And gently doth his empyre guide
        without the thyrst of blood,
     And spares his soule. . . ."
Malone quotes (from a different text), Bellenden's translation of Boece (1941, II. p. 154): " Schort tyme eftir Makbeth returnit to his innative cruelte, and became furious, as the nature of all tyrannis is quhilkis conquessis realmes be wrangwis menis, traisting all pepill to doo siclike cruelteis to him as he did afoir to vtheris." This passage introduces the murder of Banquo. The corresponding passage in Holinshed contains the phrase " least he should be serued of the same cup." Cf. 11 *post.* See Appendix, p. 180.

10. *even-handed*] impartial.

11. *Commends*] offers.

11. *ingredience*] For the spelling cf. IV. i. 34. Originally a misspelling of the plural, it was subsequently

Not bear the knife myself.   Besides, this Duncan
Hath borne his faculties so meek, hath been
So clear in his great office, that his virtues
Will plead like angels, trumpet-tongu'd, against
The deep damnation of his taking-off;   20
And Pity, like a naked new-born babe,
Striding the blast, or heaven's Cherubins, hors'd
Upon the sightless couriers of the air,
Shall blow the horrid deed in every eye,

16. bear] bare *conj. Daniel.*   17. his] this *F 2, 3.* faculties]
Faculty *F 3.*   22. cherubins] Cherubin *F, Grierson, Kittredge;*
cherubim *D'avenant.*   23. couriers] *Pope;* (Curriors *Ff);* coursers
Theobald (Warburton).

confused with the singular, *ingredient.*
   17. *faculties*] powers, prerogatives
of the crown.   Still used in this
sense in ecclesiastical law.
   18. *clear*] free from guilt or stain.
   19. *Will . . . trumpet-tongu'd*]
" suggests the Last Judgment "
(Wilson). Garrick used to make a
long pause after " Angels " to indicate that the epithet agreed with
" virtues." But this is unlikely;
" trumpet-tongu'd " means either
" using their trumpets for speech "
or, more likely, " with voices as
clear, penetrating, and musical, as
trumpets."
   20. *taking-off*] cf. III. i. 104 *post,*
and *Lear* v. i. 65.
   21. *Pity*] R. Walker, *op. cit.* chap.
3, notes that " the babe whose brains
the she-devil would dash out is pity,
striding the blast of the storm of evil."
   22. *Striding*] i.e. bestriding.
   22. *blast*] Wilson comments: " i.e.
(*a*) of the trumpet, (*b*) the tempest
of horror and indignation aroused by
the deed."   But I do not understand
how Pity—and still less how a naked
new-born babe—can stride the blast,
i.e. the sound, of a trumpet. But
" blast," by a hidden pun, was
doubtless suggested by " *trumpet-*
tongu'd "—and perhaps Wilson
meant this.
   22. *Cherubins*] Cf. " He rode vpon
the Cherubyns and did flye; he

came flyenge with the winges of the
wynde " (Ps. xviii. 10—Coverdale).
The Psalter of Shakespeare's day
had " Cherubims . . . flying vpon
the wings "; the Metrical Psalter
read " On Cherubes and on Cherubins "; but Shakespeare always
uses the form *cherubins.* Cf. Spenser,
Hymne on Heavenly Beautie, 92-4.
Although " from the beginning of
the seventeenth century *cherubim*
began to be preferred by scholars
to *cherubims* " (*O.E.D.*), Shakespeare
is unlikely to have known that
cherubim was a plural; and a knowledge of Hebrew could not have
been called into being by a desire
to avoid an excess of sibilants.
Cherubins involves less change in the
text than *cherubims,* besides being
Shakespeare's invariable form of
the plural. But see *N.Q.* (25/12/
1886) where it is pointed out that
Batman in 1582 speaks of the
" order of Cherubin " and says that
" Cherubin are the highest com-
panies of Angelles."
   23. *sightless couriers*] invisible run-
ners, i.e. the winds. Cf. I. v. 49 *ante.*
Steevens cites Warner, *Albion's England,* 1602, II. xi: " The scouring
winds that sightless in the sounding
air do fly." Elwin interprets " blind
and invisible "; and the horses in
Blake's painting " Pity " are blind.

That tears shall drown the wind.—I have no spur   25
To prick the sides of my intent, but only
Vaulting ambition, which o'erleaps itself
And falls on th' other—

Enter LADY MACBETH.

How now! what news?
Lady M. He has almost supp'd. Why have you left the
chamber?
Macb. Hath he ask'd for me?
Lady M.   Know you not, he has?   30
Macb. We will proceed no further in this business:
He hath honour'd me of late; and I have bought
Golden opinions from all sorts of people,
Which would be worn now in their newest gloss,
Not cast aside so soon.
Lady M.   Was the hope drunk,   35
Wherein you dress'd yourself? Hath it slept since?

27. itself] its sell *conj. Landor.*   28. th' other—] *Rowe;* th' other. *Ff;* th'
other side *Hanmer, Kittredge (subst.);* the other. *Globe.*   30. not, he has?]
not? he has. *conj. Capell.*   33. sorts] sort *Theobald.*

24-5. *blow . . . wind*] "Alluding to
the remission of the wind in a
shower" (Johnson) and "also to an
object blown into the eye, causing it
to fill with tears" (Elwin). Cf.
Lucrece, 1788-90; *T.C.* IV. iv. 55.

25-8. *I have . . . other—*] "I have
no spur to stimulate my guilty intention except ambition—ambition
which is like a too eager rider, who
in vaulting into the saddle o'erleaps
himself and falls on the other side
of the horse." Hunter explains:
"lights on the opposite side of what
was intended; that is, dishonour
and wretchedness, instead of glory
and felicity." Wilson mentions that
vaulting into one's saddle was a
much admired feat. But Grierson,
following Steevens, suggests that
"Shakespeare may be thinking of a
too furious rider who, leaping too
high at an obstacle, clears it indeed
but falls on the other side." Cf.
I. iv. 48-50 *ante.* Cuningham wanted

to insert "side" after "other" to
regularize the metre; but the
entrance of Lady Macbeth interrupts
the soliloquy and fills in the gap. I
cannot agree with Wilson that
"Macb. is exhausted by his passion"
and that *therefore* Shakespeare "makes
him end with an unfinished sentence;
a weary gesture supplying the gap."
The images from horsemanship, *spur*
and *vaulting*, were suggested by
hors'd and *couriers* above.

34. *would*] i.e. should. Cf. IV.
iii. 23 *post.*

34. *worn*] another clothing image.
Cf. *dress'd* (36).

35, 36. *Was . . . since*] cf. *John,*
IV. ii. 116-17:
"O where hath our intelligence
    been drunk?
Where hath it slept?"

36. *dress'd*] Another clothing image
which has been altered by some
editors to *'dressed* (= addressed) and
bless'd, so as to avoid a mixed

And wakes it now, to look so green and pale
At what it did so freely?   From this time
Such I account thy love.   Art thou afeard
To be the same in thine own act and valour,   40
As thou art in desire?   Would'st thou have that
Which thou esteem'st the ornament of life,
And live a coward in thine own esteem,
Letting " I dare not " wait upon " I would,"
Like the poor cat i' th' adage?
Macb.   Pr'ythee, peace.   45
I dare do all that may become a man;
Who dares do more, is none.
Lady M.   What beast was't then,
That made you break this enterprise to me?
When you durst do it, then you were a man;

39. afeard] afraid *F 4.*   41, 43. have . . . And] leave . . . And *or*
have . . . Or *conj. Johnson.*   45. adage?] *Capell;* Addage. *Ff.*   47. do]
Rowe; no *Ff,* Hunter, *who gives the whole of 47 to Lady M.*

metaphor. But *dress'd* is clearly suggested by *worn* and may be intended by Lady Macbeth as a sarcastic reference to it (Abbott).

37. *green and pale*] i.e. with a hangover.

38. *did*] Bulloch's conj. " dared " is attractive at first sight; but " did " refers to the orgy of which Hope repents.

39. *afeared*] Cf. I. iii. 96 *ante.*

40-1. *act . . . desire*] cf. II. iii. 29-37 and Introduction, p. xxix.

42. *ornament of life*] i.e. the crown.

45. *cat i' th' adage*] Heywood, *Three Hundred Epigrammes* (Spenser Society, p. 28) " The cate would eate fyshe, and would not wet her feete." Cf. " Le chat aime le poisson, mais il n'aime pas à mouiller la patte."

47. *do more*] Rowe's emendation is supported by *M.M.* II. iv. 134:

" Be that you are,
   That is, a woman; if you be
   more, you're none."

47. *none*] i.e. " superhuman or devilish " (Wilson) or " subhuman."

47. *beast*] The whole force of the passage lies in the direct dramatic contrast to *man* in the previous line. Cf. *R.J.* III. iii. 109-13; " Art thou a man? . . . fury of a beast."

48. *That . . . me?*] Chambers and others use this to show that the murder was discussed before the action of the play or in a lost scene (Koester, Wilson). Thaler, *Shakespeare and Democracy,* pp. 88-105, remarks: " Macbeth's *letter,* written when neither place nor time yet ' adhered,' is sufficient to explain Lady Macbeth's nervous and not necessarily accurate allusion to earlier passages between them on this subject. . . . If a scene must be sought in which Macbeth definitely yielded to his wife's urgings, this scene— *unwritten,* i.e. compressed to a mere suggestion, for reasons of artistic economy in an opening action consciously keyed to a swiftly tense crescendo—would logically come *between scenes,* after I. v. which closes with Macbeth's promise, ' We will speak further.' " Cf. Bradley, *Shakespearean Tragedy,* pp. 480-4, and Introduction, p. lv.

And, to be more than what you were, you would   50
Be so much more the man.   Nor time, nor place,
Did then adhere, and yet you would make both:
They have made themselves, and that their fitness now
Does unmake you.   I have given suck, and know
How tender 'tis to love the babe that milks me: 55
I would, while it was smiling in my face,
Have pluck'd my nipple from his boneless gums,
And dash'd the brains out, had I so sworn
As you have done to this.

Macb.   If we should fail?

Lady M.   We fail?   60
But screw your courage to the sticking-place,
And we'll not fail.   When Duncan is asleep

51. the] than *Hanmer.*

58-9.] So *Ff;* as you/Have *Steevens (1793).*
Theobald (ed. 2) fail! *Singer (ed. 2).*
these words as part of line 59.
1); We fail. *Capell.*

55. me:] *Capell;* me— *Rowe;* me, *Ff.*

59. fail?] *Ff;* fail,—
60. We fail?] *Most editors give*
We fail! *Rowe, Delius, Craig, Arden (ed.*

52. *adhere*] i.e. "not the *coherence*
of *time* with *place,* but the *adherence*
of these two with the murder"
(Capell).

54. *I . . . suck*] Cf. IV. iii. 217.
This raises the unprofitable question
of how many children had Lady
Macbeth? Wilson wisely quotes
Eckermann, *Conversations,* 18 April
1827: "Whether this be true or
not does not appear; but the lady
says it, and she must say it, in order
to give emphasis to her speech."
There is no reason to think that
Shakespeare was referring to Lady
Macbeth's child by her first husband,
who is not mentioned by Holinshed.
Cf. I. v. 48 *ante.*

57. *pluck'd . . . gums*] Coleridge
says that this passage "though
usually thought to prove a merciless
and unwomanly nature, proves the
direct opposite: she brings it as the
most solemn enforcement to Macbeth
of the solemnity of his promise to
undertake the plot against Duncan.
Had *she* so sworn, she would have
done that which was most horrible
to her feelings, rather than break

the oath; and as the most horrible
act which it was possible for imagination to conceive, as that which was
most revolting to her own feelings,
she alludes to the destruction of
her infant, while in the act of suck-
ing at her breast. Had she regarded
this with savage indifference, there
would have been no force in the
appeal; but her very allusion to it,
and her purpose in this allusion,
shows that she considered no tie so
tender as that which connected her
with her babe" (*op. cit.* ii. 271).

58-9. *sworn . . . this*] Flatter, *op.
cit.,* p. 127, pleads for a restoration
of the Folio lineation. This makes a
less awkward enjambement, allows
for a greater emphasis on the words
dash'd, brains out, and *sworn,* and leaves
room for a pause after Lady Mac-
beth's scornful question in the
following line.

58. *the brains*] "The" frequently
takes the place of the possessive pro-
noun "his."

60. *We fail?*] Mrs. Siddons tried
"We fail?", then "*We* fail!" and
finally "We fail." Critics have

(Whereto the rather shall his day's hard journey
Soundly invite him), his two chamberlains
Will I with wine and wassail so convince,   65
That memory, the warder of the brain,
Shall be a fume, and the receipt of reason
A limbeck only: when in swinish sleep
Their drenched natures lie, as in a death,
What cannot you and I perform upon   70
Th' unguarded Duncan? what not put upon
His spongy officers, who shall bear the guilt
Of our great quell?
Macb.   Bring forth men-children only!
For thy undaunted mettle should compose
Nothing but males.   Will it not be receiv'd,   75
When we have mark'd with blood those sleepy two
Of his own chamber, and us'd their very daggers,
That they have done't?

69. lie] *F 2;* lyes *F 1.*   72-3. officers, . . . quell?] Officers? . . . quell.
Ff. 77. and] *not in conj. Capell.*

argued in favour of all three. I have
kept the Folio punctuation, though
" the note of interrogation in the
Folio is frequently equivalent to the
note of exclamation " (Cuningham).

61. *But . . . sticking-place*] But =
only. Murry, *Shakespeare*, pp. 328-9,
describes the significance of this
image, derived perhaps from the
screwing up of the strings on a viol.
Cf. *T.N.* v. i. 125. But Paton and
Liddell think the metaphor was
suggested by a soldier screwing up
the cord of his cross-bow to the
" sticking-place." cf. l. 80 below.

64. *chamberlains*] gentlemen-of-the-
bedchamber.

65. *convince*] overpower, *convincere.*
Cf. IV. iii. 142.

66-8. *memory . . . only*] The old
anatomists divided the brain into
three ventricles, in the hindmost of
which, viz. the cerebellum, they
placed the memory, Cf. *L.L.L.* IV.
ii. 70. Memory, the warder of the
cerebellum, warns the reason against
attack; and where converted by
intoxication into a fume of smoke,

it fills the brain, the receptable of
reason, which thus becomes like an
" alembic " or cap of a still. Cf.
Temp. v. i. 67:

   " the ignorant fumes that mantle
   Their clearer reason."

68. *limbeck*] The corrupt form of
" alembic," a word adopted into
most European languages from the
Arabic of the Moorish alchemists of
Spain. Cf. Appendix E.

69. *drenched*] drowned. Wilson
suggests a pun on " drench " = a dose
of medicine administered to an
animal. Cf. " swinish " (67).

72. *spongy*] drunken. Cf. *M.V.*
I. ii. 108.

73. *quell*] i.e. murder. Used as a
substantive only in this passage by
Shakespeare. It is from the same
root as " kill," i.e. O.E. *cwellan.*
Florio, *Worlde of Wordes*, 1598, has
" Mazzare: *to kill, to slay, to quell.*"
Cf. *2 Hen. IV.* II. i. 58: " a man-
queller."

74. *mettle*] i.e. material, spirit.
The same word as " metal " from
which it had not been distinguished.

Lady M.   Who dares receive it other,
      As we shall make our griefs and clamour roar
      Upon his death?
Macb.   I am settled, and bend up   80
      Each corporal agent to this terrible feat.
      Away, and mock the time with fairest show:
      False face must hide what the false heart doth know.

                                        [*Exeunt.*

75-8. *Will . . . done't*] As Curry has pointed out, *Shakespeare's Philosophical Patterns*, p. 119, Macbeth becomes entirely converted to the murder as soon as his wife puts forward a practical scheme. It is irrelevant, as Wilson says, p. lix, that the plan is absurd. It satisfies him, which is all that matters to her. *receiv'd* = accepted as true. Cf. *M.M.* I. iii. 15-16:

      "For so I've strew'd it in the
        common ear,
      And so it is receiv'd."

78. *other*] otherwise. Cf. *Oth*, IV. ii. 13.

79. *As*] inasmuch as.   Wilson compares this scheme with Lady Macbeth's fainting after the murder.

80. *bend up*] Kittredge suggests that the metaphor from a crossbow is linked with I. vii. 61, *ante*.

81. *Each . . . agent*] Cf. I. iii. 81 and *Hen. V.* III. i. 16:

      "Hold hard the breath and bend
        up every spirit
      To his full height."

82-3. *Away . . . know*] Echoing her advice of I. v. 64-5. Hunter absurdly suggested that the final couplet should be spoken by Lady Macbeth. She would not speak in this regretful tone at this point.

82. *mock the time*] i.e. delude all observers.

ACT II

SCENE I.—*The same. Court within the castle.*

Enter BANQUO, *and* FLEANCE, *with a torch before him.*

Ban. How goes the night, boy?
Fle. The moon is down; I have not heard the clock.
Ban. And she goes down at twelve.
Fle.   I take 't, 'tis later, Sir.
Ban. Hold, take my sword.—There's husbandry in heaven;
   Their candles are all out.—Take thee that too.   5
   A heavy summons lies like lead upon me,
   And yet I would not sleep: merciful Powers!
   Restrain in me the cursed thoughts that nature
   Gives way to in repose!—Give me my sword.

ACT II

Scene 1

S.D. *Court within the castle*] Capell. *lines Ff; one line, Rowe.*   4. Hold . . . heaven;] *two lines Ff; one line, Rowe.*   7-9. And . . . repose!] *So Rowe; Ff three lines ending* sleepe: thoughts repose.

Scene 1

S.D. *a torch*] Dyce remarks that " in the stage-direction of old plays, ' a Torch ' sometimes means a *torch-bearer.*" Cf. I. vi. *init.* But here Fleance probably acts as torch-bearer.

4. *husbandry*] thrift, economy. Florio, *Worlde of Wordes*, 1598, has " Parsimonia, *parcimonie, sparing, husbandrie.*" Cf. I. iv. 50, I. v. 50, *ante.*

5. *Their*] referring presumably to the inhabitants of heaven.

5. *candles . . . out*] Cf. *R.J.* III. v. 9: " Night's candles are burnt out."

5. *that*] i.e. shield, targe, cloak, dagger, or " belt with dagger " (Wilson).

6. *summons*] i.e. to sleep.

7-9. *merciful . . . repose*] " Banquo . . . cannot help dreaming of the three Weird Sisters. . . . In his extremity he importunes precisely that order of angels which God, in his providence, has deputed to be concerned especially with the restraint and coercion of demons, namely, Powers " (Curry, *Shakespeare's Philosophical Patterns*, p. 81). Kolbe suggests that Shakespeare echoes the Hymn of Compline, i.e. presumably,

   " Procul recedant somnia
      Et noctium phantasmata."

46

Enter MACBETH, *and a Servant with a torch.*

Who's there?　　　　　　　　　　　　　　　　10
Macb. A friend.
Ban. What, Sir! not yet at rest?　The King's a-bed:
　He hath been in unusual pleasure, and
　Sent forth great largess to your offices.
　This diamond he greets your wife withal,　　15
　By the name of most kind hostess, and shut up
　In measureless content.
Macb.　　　　　　　　Being unprepar'd,
　Our will became the servant to defect,
　Which else should free have wrought.
Ban.　　　　　　　　　　All's well.
　I dreamt last night of the three Weïrd Sisters:　20
　To you they have show'd some truth.
Macb.　　　　　　　　I think not of them:
　Yet, when we can entreat an hour to serve,
　We would spend it in some words upon that business,
　If you would grant the time.
Ban.　　　　　　　　At your kind'st leisure.

13. and] *So Jennens; begins line 14 Ff.*　　14. offices] *Ff;* officers *Rowe.*
16. and shut up] *Begins next line* And shut up *F 1;* And shut it up *F 2, 3;* and
's shut up *Hanmer;* and shut him up *conj. Kinnear.*　　19. All's well] Sir,
all is well *conj. Steevens.*　20. Weïrd] *Theobald;* weyward *F.*　24. kind'st]
F 1; kind *F 3, 4.*

14. *offices*] i.e. servants' quarters, though Malone and others have supported Rowe's emendation, *officers.* Chambers suggests " a case of the use of the abstract for the concrete."

15. *diamond*] Holinshed mentions that Donwald was presented with an honourable gift by King Duff on the night of the murder. See Appendix, p. 171.

16. *shut up*] This means either " wrapped in " (Chambers) or " concluded " (Steevens). Duncan has ended his day in measureless content. Cf. Spenser, *Faerie Queene,* IV. ix. 15: " And for to shut vp all in friendly loue "; *A.W.* I. i. 197: " Whose baser stars do shut us up in wishes "; and *T.C.* I. iii.—58: " In whom the tempers and the minds of all Should be shut up."

17-19. *Being . . . wrought*] i.e. As we were unprepared, our desire to give liberal hospitality to the king could not be fulfilled.

20-1. *I . . . truth*] Cuningham though these words were a " veiled incitement to Macbeth "; but they are perfectly compatible with innocence.

22. *we*] " Now that the crown is within his grasp, he seems to adopt the royal ' we ' by anticipation " (Clarendon). But, as Chambers argues, Macbeth is too good an actor to use the kingly " we." It probably means " you and I " and " would " (23) = should.

Macb. If you shall cleave to my consent, when 'tis,   25
   It shall make honour for you.
Ban.   So I lose none
   In seeking to augment it, but still keep
   My bosom franchis'd, and allegiance clear,
   I shall be counsell'd.
Macb.   Good repose, the while!
Ban. Thanks, Sir: the like to you.   30
          [Exeunt Banquo and Fleance.
Macb. Go, bid thy mistress, when my drink is ready,
   She strike upon the bell. Get thee to bed.—
          [Exit Servant.
   Is this a dagger, which I see before me,

25-6. when 'tis . . . you.] *so Rowe; one line Ff.*

25. *cleave . . . 'tis*] i.e. become or remain an adherent of my party when it exists, *or*, follow my advice when the time comes. Macbeth is purposely ambiguous. His words can mean that he wants Banquo to support his claim to the crown in the event of Duncan's natural death, or they can be regarded as a bribe. Case suggests "when 'tis" means "when we have our talk". The phrase *to be of consent* meant *to be accessory.* Cf. *A.Y.L.I.* II. ii. 3: "Some villains . . . Are of consent and sufferance in this." *Consent* also meant a party united by common agreement, or adherence to an opinion. *O.E.D.* quotes Florio's *Montaigne:* "Even those which are not of our consent, doe flatly inhibite . . . the use of the sacred name." The word was often spelt *concent* down to the sixteenth century, and was thus liable to confusion with musical *concent*, when this latter word was introduced. In some passages, it is difficult to say which of the two was meant. For *consent*, meaning counsel or advice, Wilson refers to *W.T.* v. iii. 136.

26-8. *honour . . . clear*] Bradley, *Shakespearean Tragedy*, pp. 383-4, thinks that "Banquo fears a treason-able proposal." Wilson thinks that Banquo supposes Macbeth to refer only to Duncan's death in the course of nature. Liddell believes that Banquo means by *honour*, its feudal sense of *lordship;* i.e. that his honours must be of "free tenure" as far as Macbeth is concerned. He carries the notion further in *allegiance clear,* i.e. such fealty as no man may owe to more than one lord. It seems to me that Bradley is right, and that we must interpret *franchis'd* as *free from guilt,* and *clear* as *innocent.* Banquo is telling Macbeth that he will only join his party if there is to be no foul play. As Grierson points out, there is a play on the two senses of "honour" which can either mean the distinction accorded to worth or the honourableness that merits such distinction. Some honours are bought only with the loss of honour.

30. See note on II. ii. 12-13, *post.*
31. *drink*] i.e. the posset. Cf. note on II. ii. 6 *post.*
33. *Is . . . dagger?* "the dagger should not be in the air, but on a table; he thinks it real at first" (Chambers). "Macbeth is to wait for the bell; and to wait is to sit" (Wilson). But if the scene is laid

The handle toward my hand? Come, let me clutch
   thee:—
I have thee not, and yet I see thee still.   35
Art thou not, fatal vision, sensible
To feeling, as to sight? or art thou but
A dagger of the mind, a false creation,
Proceeding from the heat-oppressed brain?
I see thee yet, in form as palpable   40
As this which now I draw.
Thou marshall'st me the way that I was going;
And such an instrument I was to use.—
Mine eyes are made the fools o' th' other senses,
Or else worth all the rest: I see thee still;   45
And on thy blade, and dudgeon, gouts of blood,
Which was not so before.—There's no such thing.

34. thee:—] thee: *Ff*; thee—*Rowe.*   41. As . . . draw.] *Walker*
and Keightley end line at me *(42) with subsequent re-arrangement.*

in the courtyard, would there be a
table? And would it not be impossible for a man like Macbeth to
sit at such a moment? The speech
is not realistic; but in answer to
Chambers it may be said that if
Macbeth really thought the dagger
a real one he would not begin with
a question, and such a question.
Seymour, *Remarks*, etc., 1805, I. 196,
argues that the actor should not
express terror, but confidence and
animation. But there is surely an
undertone of horror in the speech
(59). Curry, *Shakespeare's Philosophical Patterns*, p. 84, suggests that the
dagger " is an hallucination caused
immediately, indeed, by disturbed
bodily humours and spirits but
ultimately by demonic powers, who
have so controlled and manipulated
these bodily forces as to produce
the effect they desire."
  36. *sensible*] i.e. capable of being
perceived by the senses, perceptible.
Florio, *Worlde of Wordes:* " Per-
cettible, *perceivable, sensible.*" Johnson quotes Hooker, *Ecclesiastical
Polity*, I. vii. I: " By reason man

attaineth unto the knowledge of
things that are and are not *sensible*,"
  39. *heat-oppressed*] fevered (Wilson).
  41. The short line is filled out by
the action of drawing the dagger
(Chambers).
  42. *marshall'st me*] The dagger
seems to move towards the room
where Duncan sleeps.
  44. *Mine . . . senses*] This conflict
between the senses is mentioned
several times in the course of the
play. See Introduction, p. xxix.
  46. *dudgeon*] haft, handle. Originally the word meant a kind of wood
used for the handles of knives and
daggers, and thus came to mean the
hilt of a dagger made from this wood.
Gerard, *Herball*, speaking of the
root of the box-tree, says: " Turners
and cutlers, if I mistake not the
matter, do calle this woode *dudgeon*,
whence they make dudgeon hafted
daggers." And Cotgrave, *Dict.*, 1611,
has " Dague à roëlles: *A Scottish
dagger; or Dudgeon haft dagger*"; i.e.
one turned with little spiral rings
to give a better grip.
  46. *gouts*] drops, Fr. *goutte.*

It is the bloody business which informs
Thus to mine eyes.—Now o'er the one half-world
Nature seems dead, and wicked dreams abuse   50
The curtain'd sleep: Witchcraft celebrates
Pale Hecate's off'rings; and wither'd Murther,
Alarum'd by his sentinel, the wolf,
Whose howl's his watch, thus with his stealthy pace,
With Tarquin's ravishing strides, towards his design 55

51. sleep:] sleeper *conj. Steevens* Witchcraft] Now witchcraft *D'avenant,
Rowe, Kittredge.*   55. strides] *Pope;* sides *Ff.*

48. *informs*] takes shape (O.E.D.);
gives false impression (Kittredge).

49, 50. *o'er . . . dead*] " over our
hemisphere all action and motion
seem to have ceased " (Johnson).
Malone compares a passage from
the opening scene of the second part
of Marston, *Antonio and Mellida,*
1602, I. i. 3-8:
  " 'Tis yet dead night, yet al the
      earth is cloucht
  In the dull leaden hand of snoring
      sleepe:
  No breath disturbs the quiet of
      the ayre.
  No spirit moves upon the breast
      of earth,
  Save howling dogs, night-
      crowes, and screeching owls,
  Save meager ghosts, *Piero,* and
      black thoughts."

50. *wicked dreams*] cf. 7-9 *ante.*

50. *abuse*] deceive.

51. *sleep: Witchcraft*] Various attempts have been made to regular-
ise the line, by inserting " now "
between these two words (Davenant),
or by changing " sleep " to " sleeper."
But the pause was probably deliberate.

52. *Hecate's*] Cf. note on III. ii. 41
post. Hecate was the goddess of
classical and medieval witchcraft.
Jonson, *Masque of Queenes* (1609)
says " She was belleeu'd to gouerne
in witchcraft; and is remembered in
all theyr inuocations." Baldwin,
Shakespeare's Small Latine, ii. 437,

quotes Golding's explanatory inter-
polation in *Metam.* vii. 74-5:
  " Of whom the witches holde
      As of their goddesse."
The word is a dissyllable here. Cf.
Lear, I. i. 112:
  " The mysteries of Hecate and the
      night."

52. *offerings*] rituals (Wilson) or
" mysteries."

54. *Whose . . . watch*] Craig
interprets: " His (the murderer's)
way of knowing the passage of the
night." Cf. *Luc.* 370: " Which
gives the watch-word to his hand
full soon." But " his " probably
refers to " wolf," who howls at
regular intervals, as the sentinel calls
out, and " watch " = watchword.
Wilson gives " timepiece " as an
alternative meaning.

55. *Tarquin's*] Warburton com-
pares *Luc.* 162-8:
  " Now stole upon the time the
      dead of night,
  When heavy sleep had clos'd up
      mortal eyes,
  No comfortable star did lend his
      light,
  No noise but owls' and wolves'
      death-boding cries:
  Now serves the season that they
      may surprise
  The silly lambs, pure thoughts
      are dead and still,
  While Lust and Murder wakes
      to stain and kill."

Moves like a ghost.—Thou sure and firm-set earth,
Hear not my steps, which way they walk, for fear
Thy very stones prate of my where-about,
And take the present horror from the time,

56. sure] *Capell* (*conj. Pope*); sowre *F;* sound *Pope.*   57. which way
they] *Rowe;* which they may *Ff.*

Cf. II. i. 5, 52, 53 and II. ii. 3. See
Appendix C on the relation between
Macbeth and *Lucrece.*

55. *ravishing*] transferred epithet.

55. *strides*] Pope's emendation is
certain, though Johnson and Knight
object to "stride" as implying
violence or impetuosity. Yet the
word is coupled with "tedious" in
Rich. II. i. iii. 268 and with "soft"
in *Faerie Queene,* IV. viii. 37. Tarquin
stalks to the chamber of Lucrece
(*Luc.* 365). Case refers to "the
long tip-toe stealing steps one takes
in order to avoid sound by planting
the feet as seldom as possible."
Liddel reads *slides* and quotes
Cooper's *Thesaurus;* "Lapsus ser-
pentum, *the sliding, gliding, or creeping
of a serpent*" and Cotgrave's *Dict.*
"Griller: *to glide, slip, slide, steal.*"
In spite of *Luc.* 305 and 362 (*creeping*
and *serpent*) few will agree with this
emendation.

56. *sure*] Pope's conj. is now universally accepted. Wilson compares
Ps. xciii. 2: "He hath made the
round world so sure: that it cannot
be moved."

57. *which . . . walk*] R. Walker,
op. cit. points out that in the dedica-
tory epistle to the Authorized Version,
the translators tell James I that on
the death of Elizabeth, many ill-
wishers expected "some thick and
palpable cloud of darkness would
so have overshadowed this Land,
that men should have been in doubt
which way they were to walk." The
resemblance is probably accidental,
though it is not impossible that the
writer had seen a performance of
Macbeth, or that the phrase had been
used in a sermon or pamphlet

written on the accession of King
James.

58. *Thy . . . prate*] "A reminiscence
of *Luke* xix. 40" (Chambers): "I
tell you if these should hold their
peace, the stones would cry"
(Geneva). But I suggest the following passage, though less familiar, is
closer: "For the stone shall cry
out of the wal, & the beame out
of the timber shal aunswere it"
(*Hab.* ii. 11). The neighbouring
stanzas fit the *Macbeth* context:
"Thou hast consulted shame to
thine owne house, by destroying
many people, and hast sinned against
thine owne soule. . . . Woe vnto
him that buildeth a towne with
blood, and erecteth a citie by in-
iquitie. . . . But the *Lord is in his
holy Temple;* let all the earth *keepe
silence* before him" (vv. 10, 12, 20).
Cf. with v. 20 "The Lord's anointed
temple" (II. iii. 69 *post*).

58. *where-about*] i.e. whereabouts.
Shakespeare uses "where" as a
substantive in *Lear,* I. i. 264: "a
better where."

59. *take . . . time*] "Whether to
take horror from the time means not
rather to *catch it* as communicated,
than *to deprive the time of horror,*
deserves to be considered" (Johnson).
"Macbeth asks that the earth . . .
shall not hear his steps, for if it does
so the very stones will speak and
betray him—thereby breaking the
silence and so lessening the horror.
'Take' combines two construc-
tions. On the one hand, 'for fear
they take the present horror from
the time' expresses attraction, identi-
fication with the appropriate setting
of his crime. But 'take' is also an

Which now suits with it.—Whiles I threat, he lives: 60
Words to the heat of deeds too cold breath gives.

[A bell rings.

I go, and it is done: the bell invites me.
Hear it not, Duncan; for it is a knell
That summons thee to Heaven, or to Hell.   *[Exit.*

SCENE II.—*The same.*

Enter LADY MACBETH.

Lady M. That which hath made them drunk hath made me
bold:
What hath quench'd them hath given me fire.—Hark!
—Peace!

Scene II

S.D. *The same.*] *Capell.*
end lines fire, shriek'd, night. open:
shriek'd night open: snores possets.

imperative, expressing anguish and
repulsion. 'Which now sutes with
it' implies acceptance, either gloat-
ing or reluctant according to the
two meanings of the previous line"
(Knights, *Explorations*, p. 23). I do
not think Johnson's first alternative
is plausible. As Wilson says, Macbeth "speaks as if watching himself
in a dream"; and in this queer
state of objectivity he wants the
details of the scene to be in keeping
with the deed.
61. *Words . . . gives*] Although this
line has been regarded as an interpolation and a "feeble tag" (Clarendon) it can be paralleled in many
scenes in the canon. The opposition
between words and deeds was a
main theme in *Hamlet*, and it recurs
in a different form in *Macbeth* (see
Introduction, p. xxix). The singular verb with a plural subject is
common in Shakespeare. "There is
here a double reason for it . . . the
exigency of the rhyme, and . . . the
occurrence, between the nominative
and verb, of two singular nouns, to
which, as it were, the verb is at-
tracted" (Clarendon).

2-6. What . . . possets,] *so Rowe; Ff*
charge Possets,; *Knight ends lines* fire.

63-4. *Hear . . . Hell*] cf. III. i. 140
post and *Rich. III.* I. i. 118-20:

"I do love thee so,
That I will shortly send thy soul
to heaven,
If Heaven will take the present
at our hands."

F. M. Smith, *P.M.L.A.*, 1945, compares *Rich. III.* v. iii. 313-14.

Scene II

The scene follows on with hardly
a break; and there is no break
between scenes ii. and iii. Liddell
says that at Kenilworth, with which
Shakespeare may have been familiar,
there was "a large courtyard with
a flight of steps in one corner leading
up to the sleeping-rooms. . . . In
these quadrangular houses the hall
occupied one side of the building,
and out of this, at one end, a flight
of steps led to a lobby which opened
on the guest-chamber. . . . In the
theatre this lobby would, of course,
be the usual gallery or balcony at
the back of the stage. Duncan and
his two grooms of the chamber would
naturally be lodged in the guest-
chamber; back of this would be

It was the owl that shriek'd, the fatal bellman,
Which gives the stern'st good-night. He is about it.
The doors are open; and the surfeited grooms   5
Do mock their charge with snores: I have drugg'd
    their possets,
That Death and Nature do contend about them,
Whether they live, or die.
Macb.   [*Within.*]   Who's there?—what, ho!
Lady M. Alack! I am afraid they have awak'd,
And 'tis not done:—th' attempt and not the deed   10
Confounds us.—Hark!—I laid their daggers ready;
He could not miss 'em.—Had he not resembled
My father as he slept, I had done't.—My husband!

8. S.D.] *Johnson and Steevens* (1773).   10. attempt . . . deed] *Camb.*
(conj. Hunter); attempt, and . . . deed, *Ff;* attempt, and . . . deed *Rowe,*
Pope, Hanmer; attempt and . . . deed, *Warburton, Johnson, Var. '73, Singer*
(ed. 2).

the 'second chamber,' occupied by
Donalbain and another. Such an
arrangement would be familiar to
the Elizabethan audience, and explains clearly the action of the
scene."

3. *the fatal bellman*] cf. Webster,
Duchess of Malfi, IV. ii. 173:
" I am the common Bellman,
   That usually is sent to con-
     demn'd persons
   The night before they suffer ";
and Spenser, *Faerie Queene,* v. vi. 27,
where the cock is called " the natiue
Belman of the night." Liddell
quotes from *Phraseologia Generalis,*
1681, a reference to the " bellman
which goeth before a corps, *praeco
feralis.*" Thus " the stern'st good-
night is the last good-night of death."

5. *grooms*] serving-men; menial
servants of any kind.

6. *possets*] Malone quotes Randle
Holmes, *Academy of Armourie,* 1688,
bk. iii. p. 84: " posset is hot milk
poured on ale or sack, having sugar,
grated bisket, eggs, with other ingredients boiled in it, which goes all
to a curd." Cf. note on II. ii. 31
ante, and Middleton, *The Witch,*
IV. iii. 17:

" For the maide-servants, and the
   girles o' the house,
  I spic'd them lately with a
   drowsie posset."

8. *Who's there?*] Macbeth loses
control over himself, and breaks out
into an exclamation, fancying he
hears a noise (see l. 14). The S.D.
was added by Steevens in place
of the Folio " Enter." Chambers
makes Macbeth enter above, for a
moment; and Booth thinks the line
was spoken by one of the drunken
grooms. Wilson is doubtless right
when he says that the Folio S.D.
merely means that the player is to
speak, and that it is far more effective
for Macbeth to be unseen here than
seen.

10. *attempt . . . deed*] Critics have
quarrelled about the punctuation of
this line—unnecessarily, as the Folio
commas emphasize the words *attempt* and *deed,* and the meaning is
brought out in modern punctuation
by the omission of the commas.
Lady Macbeth discovers later that
the attempt *with* the deed also confounds them.

12-13. *Had . . . done't*] Wilson
links these lines with his theory that

Enter MACBETH.

Macb. I have done the deed.—Didst thou not hear a noise?
Lady M. I heard the owl scream, and the crickets cry.   15
    Did not you speak?
Macb.   When?
Lady M.   Now.
Macb.   As I descended?
Lady M. Ay.
Macb. Hark!
    Who lies i' th' second chamber?
Lady M.   Donalbain.
Macb. This is a sorry sight.   20
Lady M. A foolish thought to say a sorry sight.
Macb. There's one did laugh in's sleep, and one cried,
    " Murther! "
        That they did wake each other: I stood and heard
            them;
        But they did say their prayers, and address'd them
        Again to sleep.
Lady M.   There are two lodg'd together.   25

14. I . . . noise?] *one line, Rowe, two lines Ff.*   16. Did . . . descended?] *Macb.* Did . . . speak? *Lady M.* When? Now? *Macb.* As . . . descended. *conj. Hunter; Macb.* Did . . . speak? *Lady M.* When? *Macb.* Now, as I descended. *Conj. Fleay (Shakespeariana, Dec. 1884, ap. Camb.).* 17. Ay] *Rowe;* I *Ff;* I! *Chambers.*   18-19. Hark! . . . chamber?] *so Steevens (1793); one line Ff.*   22-5. There's . . . sleep.] *so Rowe; Ff end lines* sleepe, other: Prayers, sleepe.

there was an earlier version of the play. See Introduction, p. xxv. Adams believes that at II. i. 30 two scenes, separated in time, have been run together and, possibly, that an intervening scene has been omitted. This omitted scene, he thinks, represented Lady Macbeth in her attempt to kill Duncan without assistance. But neither the alleged break in the metre, nor the fact that several hours are supposed to pass in 200 lines, can be regarded as strong arguments for this fantastic theory. Faustus' last soliloquy takes only five minutes to deliver, though an hour is supposed to pass.

13. *husband*] Only here does she call him that.

15. *cricket*] According to Grimm the cricket foretold death.

16-20. Murry comments, *Shakespeare*, p. 329, that we can almost hear " the snapping of the strings " —referring back to I. vii. 61.

20. *sorry*] miserable, sad, pitiable.

22. *and . . . Murther!*] cf. II. i. 7 *ante.*

24. *address'd them*] prepared themselves. Cf. *M.V.* II. ix. 19: " and so have I address'd me."

25. *two*] Malcolm and Donalbain, not the two grooms. " The picture of the sons, half waking while their

Macb. One cried, "God bless us!" and, "Amen," the other,
   As they had seen me with these hangman's hands.
   List'ning their fear, I could not say, "Amen,"
   When they did say," God bless us."
Lady M.   Consider it not so deeply.
Macb. But wherefore could not I pronounce "Amen"?   30
   I had most need of blessing, and "Amen"
   Stuck in my throat.
Lady M.   These deeds must not be thought
   After these ways: so, it will make us mad.
Macb. Methought, I heard a voice cry, " Sleep no more!
   Macbeth does murther Sleep,"—the innocent Sleep; 35

27. hands.] hands: *Ff; hands, Rowe.*   31-2. I . . . throat.] *one line Ff.*
32. thought] thought on *Hanmer.*   34-5.] *Johnson; Ff not in inverted commas;*
quotation extends to feast (39) Hanmer.

father is murdered, adds to the horror of the situation " (Chambers). But it is curious, if the princes are in the same room, that Lady Macbeth mentions only the younger.

27. *As*] i.e. as if. Cf. *Lear*, III. iv. 15: " Is it not as this mouth should tear this hand? "

27. *hangman*] The hangman had to draw and quarter his victim, and the word is sometimes used loosely for " executioner." Cf. *M.V.* IV. i. 125: " hangman's axe."

28. *List'ning*] Cf. *J.C.* IV. i. 41: " Listen great things."

32. *thought*] In support of Hanmer's emendation, Cuningham cites III. ii. 11 *post* and *T.N.* v. i. 324.

34-9. *Methought . . . feast*] Perhaps suggested by a passage in Holinshed's account of King Kenneth. See Appendix, p. 172. It cannot be determined from the Folio where the voice is supposed to end, but Johnson's arrangement has been followed by nearly all subsequent editors. " the innocent . . . feast " " is a comment made by Macbeth upon the words he imagined he heard " (Clarendon).

34. *sleep no more*] Cf. III. ii. 16-26, III. iv. 141 and v. i. *passim.* Cf. also note on I. iii. 19. Kolbe analyses

the sleep references in *Shakespeare's Way*, pp. 5-10, and Murry in his *Shakespeare*, pp. 332 ff. Cf. Knight, *The Wheel of Fire*, 1949, pp. 126-7. The whole passage is reminiscent of Ovid, *Metam.*, xi. 624:

  " Pax animi, quem cura fugit, qui corpora duris
    Fessa ministeriis mulces reparasque labori ";

which is thus translated by Golding (ed. Rouse, xi. 723-6):

  " O sleepe (quoth shee), the rest of things: O gentlest of the Goddes,
  Sweete sleepe, the peace of mynd, with whom crookt care is aye at oddes:
  Which cherrishest mennes weery limbes appalld with toyling sore,
  And makest them as fresh to woork, and lustye as before."

Malone suggested there was an echo of Sidney's sonnet (No. 39):

  " Come, Sleepe, O Sleepe, the certaine knot of peace,
  The baiting place of wit, the balme of woe."

(Cf. *balm, feast, knits.* The 1591 ed. of *Astrophel and Stella* misprinted *baiting* as *bathing.* Cf. *bath.*) There is

Sleep, that knits up the ravell'd sleave of care,
The death of each day's life, sore labour's bath,
Balm of hurt minds, great Nature's second course,
Chief nourisher in life's feast;—
Lady M.   What do you mean?
Macb. Still it cried, "Sleep no more!" to all the house: 40
"Glamis hath murther'd Sleep, and therefore Cawdor
Shall sleep no more, Macbeth shall sleep no more!"
Lady M. Who was it that thus cried? Why, worthy Thane,
You do unbend your noble strength, to think
So brainsickly of things. Go, get some water,   45
And wash this filthy witness from your hand.—

---

36. sleave] *Steevens (conj. Seward)*; Sleeue F. 39. feast;—] feast.—*Theobald*;
Feast. *Ff.*   41-2.] *Hanmer; inverted commas not in Ff.*

---

another close parallel in Seneca,
Her. Fur. (1065-7):
         " tuque, O domitor
Somne malorum, requies animi,
Pars humanae melior vitae."
Jasper Heywood translates thus:—
    " And thou O tamer best
O sleepe of toyles, the quietnesse
       of mynde,
Of all the lyfe of man the better
       parte."
It seems probable that " balm of
hurt minds " was suggested by the
situation in *Hercules Furens*, where
the Chorus invokes Sleep to cure
the madness of the hero.
    36. *sleave*] " a slender filament of
silk obtained by separating a thicker
thread " (*O.E.D.*). But it seems
also to mean " coarse silk." See
Florio, *Worlde of Wordes* " Sfilazza:
*any kinde of raveled stuffe, or sleaue
silk. . . .* Capitone, *a kinde of course
silke called sleaue silke.*"
    38, 39. *second . . . nourisher*) Pud-
ding appears anciently to have been
the first course at dinner, the joint
or roast being the " second "—*the
pièce de résistance.* Steevens quotes
Chaucer, *Squire's Tale*, 347: " The
norice of digestioun, the slepe."
Wilson makes the admirable point

that " course " (meaning *race* or
career) suggested to Shakespeare the
other meaning of the word.
    39. *Chief . . . feast*] This may also
have been suggested by an alternative meaning of *ravell'd* (36).
Ravel, or ravelled, bread was whole
meal bread, and could be regarded
as " chief nourisher." See Harrison,
England (1877), i. 154: " The
raueled is a kind of cheat bread
also."
    41-2. *Glamis . . . more*] Johnson
thought the voice said only, " Glamis
hath murther'd sleep," the rest
being Macbeth's comment; but it
is difficult to distinguish between
the voice of conscience speaking
directly through Macbeth, and the
same voice speaking (as he imagines)
from outside him. Bradley comments that the voice " denounced
on him, as if his three names gave
him three personalities to suffer in,
the doom of sleeplessness."
    44. *unbend*] Cf. i. vii. 80 (Wilson).
    45. *brainsickly*] Shakespeare uses
the adj. " brainsick " six times but
not the adv. elsewhere.
    46. *wash*] Cf. v. i. 59 *post.*
    46. *witness*] evidence. Cf. *M.V.*
i. iii. 100.

Why did you bring these daggers from the place?
They must lie there: go, carry them, and smear
The sleepy grooms with blood.

Macb.   I'll go no more:
I am afraid to think what I have done;   50
Look on't again I dare not.

Lady M.   Infirm of purpose!
Give me the daggers.   The sleeping, and the dead,
Are but as pictures; 'tis the eye of childhood
That fears a painted devil.   If he do bleed,
I'll gild the faces of the grooms withal,   55
For it must seem their guilt.   [*Exit.—Knocking within.*

Macb.   Whence is that knocking?—
How is't with me, when every noise appals me?
What hands are here?   Ha! they pluck out mine eyes.
Will all great Neptune's ocean wash this blood

---

47. *Why . . . place?*] It is difficult
to perform the scene so as to make
plausible Lady Macbeth's delay in
noticing the daggers. Presumably
at lines 20, 27, the daggers were in
one hand, perhaps concealed behind
Macbeth's back.

51. *infirm of purpose*] Cf. Introduction, p. l.

54. *painted devil*] Cf. Webster,
White Devil, III. ii. 151: "Terrify
babes, my Lord, with painted devils."

55-6. *gild . . . guilt*] Knowles
points out that these words are a
"taunt at Macbeth, reminding him
of his own arrangement, and the
imbecility that prevents him from
carrying it into execution." The
grim pun is rather a sign of the im-
mense effort of will needed by Lady
Macbeth to visit the scene of the
crime. Those who find it distasteful
should read more genteel authors.
Cf. "golden blood" (II iii. 112
post); *John*, II. i. 316: "armours
. . . gilt with Frenchmen's blood";
and *2 Hen. IV.* IV. v. 129: "England
shall double gild his treble guilt."

58. *hands . . . eyes*] See Introduction, p. xxx.

R. Walker, *op. cit.* chapter 4, quotes
Matt. xviii. 9: "And if thine eye
cause thee to offend, plucke it out,
and cast it from thee: it is better
for thee to enter into life with one
eie, then hauing two eyes to be
cast into hell fire." He links this verse
with *Luke*, xi. 34-6, and the knocking
at the gate with *Luke* xi. 9-10. It
may be added Beelzebub is mentioned three times in the same chapter, and by Shakespeare a few lines
later (II. iii. 4); and that the hell
fire of *Mat.* xviii. reappears also in
the Porter scene.

59-62. *Will . . . red*] Upton,
Critical Observations, 1746, compares
Sophocles, *Oedip. Tyrannos*, 1227;
Steevens compares Catullus, *In Gel-
lium;* but Shakespeare is more likely
to have read Seneca, *Phaedra*, 715-8
(cited by Cunliffe):

" Quis eluet me Tanais? aut quae
          barbaris

Maeotis undis Pontico incumbens
    mari?

Non ipse toto magnus Oceano
    pater

Tantum expiarit sceleris."

Clean from my hand?   No, this my hand will rather   60
The multitudinous seas incarnadine,
Making the green one red.

61. incarnadine,] *Rowe;* incarnardine, *Ff.*   62. green one red.] *F 4;*
Greene one, Red *F 1, 2, 3;* green, One red— *Johnson;* green—one red.
Steevens, 1778 (conj. Murphy).

Studley translates:

" What bathing lukewarme Tanais
   may I defilde obtaine,
Whose clensing watry Channell
   pure may washe mee Cleane
   againe?
Or what Meotis muddy meare,
   with rough Barbarian wave
That boardes on Pontus roring
   Sea? Not Neptune graund-
   sire grave
With all his Ocean foulding
   floud can purge and wash
   away
This dunghill foule of stane."

Cf. the following passage from Seneca,
Hercules Furens, 1323-9 (1330-6):

" Quis Tanais aut quis Nilus aut
   quis Persica
Violentus unda Tigris aut Rhenus
   ferox
Tagusve Hibera turbidus gaza
   fluens,
Abluere dextram poterit? Arc-
   toum licet
Maeotis in me gelida trans-
   fundat mare,
Et tota Tethys per meas currat
manus,
Haerebit altum facinus."

C. B. Young (cited by Wilson)
points out that Shakespeare's echo
is nearer to the original than Heywood's version of the italicized line
(" And al the water thereof shoulde
now pas by my two handes ").
Shakespeare might, perhaps, have
amalgamated the two passages in
translation. But, as Young also
points out, " Haerebit " etc. is close
to v. ii. 17 *post;* and the latter is

much closer than the Heywood
version (" Yet wil the mischiefe
deep remayne "). It is therefore
highly probable that Shakespeare
knew the original. Chambers compares what is probably an independent imitation of Seneca in
Marston, *The Insatiate Countess,* v. i.:

" Although . . . the waves of all the
   northerne sea,
Should flow for ever, through
   these guiltie hands,
Yet the sanguinolent staine
   would extant be."

61. *multitudinous seas*] Not referring
to the multitude of creatures in the
seas, not the many-waved ocean
but the countless masses of waters
on the surface of the globe (Malone).
Cf. Munday and Chettle, *Death of
Robert, Earl of Huntingdon,* 1601, II. ii.
(Dodsley, ed. Hazlitt, viii. 268) " The
multitudes of seas dyed red with
blood."

61. *incarnadine*] The word was
used in Shakespeare's days as adj.
and sb. but he seems to have been
the first to use it as vb. Properly it
would mean " make flesh-coloured,"
but Shakespeare obviously means
" turn blood-red." He may have
been thinking of a crimson blush.

62. *Making . . . red*] i.e. changing
the green sea into total red. Cf.
Munday and Chettle, *Downfall of
Robert, Earl of Huntington,* 1601, IV. i.
(Dodsley, ed. Hazlitt, viii. 173),
" And made the greene sea red with
Pagan blood," Chambers compares
what is possibly a Shakespearean
passage in *Two Noble Kinsmen,* v. i.
49-50:

Re-enter LADY MACBETH.

Lady M. My hands are of your colour; but I shame
    To wear a heart so white. [*Knock.*] I hear a
    knocking
    At the south entry:—retire we to our chamber.   65
    A little water clears us of this deed:
    How easy is it then! Your constancy
    Hath left you unattended.—[*Knock.*] Hark! more
    knocking.
    Get on your night-gown, lest occasion call us,
    And show us to be watchers.—Be not lost   70
    So poorly in your thoughts.
Macb. To know my deed, 'twere best not know myself.

                                      [*Knock.*

Wake Duncan with thy knocking: I would thou
    couldst!   [*Exeunt.*

64-8. To . . . knocking.] *so Pope; seven lines Ff ending* white. entry: Chamber: deed. Constancie unattended. knocking. 67. then!] then? *Ff.* 72-3. To . . . couldst!] *so Pope; four line Ff ending* deed, selfe knocking: could'st. 72. To know] T'unknow *Hanmer.* 73. Wake . . . thy] Wake, Duncan, with this *D'avenant, Theobald.*

"Thou mighty one, that with thy
    power has turn'd
    Great Neptune into purple."
Simpson, *Shakespeare's Punctuation*, shows that in the Folio, a comma often follows a stressed word.

67-8. *Your . . . unattended*] "Your firmness has deserted you" (Chambers).

69. *night-gown*] dressing-gown or *robe de chambre.* "In Macbeth's time and for centuries later, it was the custom for both sexes to sleep without other covering than that belonging to the bed" (Grant White). If Macbeth and his wife were found in ordinary clothing, it would bring suspicion on them.

72. *To know . . . myself*] "If I must look my deed in the face, it were better for me to lose consciousness altogether" (Clarendon). "Better be lost in thought than look my deed in the face" (Wilson). The latter brings out the connection between this line and Lady Macbeth's remark, to which it is an answer; but I think it means rather: "It were better for me to remain permanently 'lost' in thought, i.e. self-alienated, than to be fully conscious of the nature of my deed." Ellis-Fermor suggests the following (privately): "If I am to live on terms with this deed, I must break with my real—my former—self."

SCENE III.—*The same.*

Enter a Porter.

[*Knocking within.*

Porter. Here's a knocking, indeed! If a man were
Porter of Hell Gate, he should have old turning the
key. [*Knocking.*] Knock, knock, knock. Who's
there, i' th' name of Belzebub?—Here's a farmer,
that hang'd himself on th' expectation of plenty: 5
come in, time-server; have napkins enow about

Scene III

S.D. The same.] *Capell.*   6. time-server] *conj. Wilson;* time *Ff etc.*
enow] *F 1;* enough *F 2, 3.*

Scene III

Capell in his *Notes*, p. 13, remarks:
"Without this scene Macbeth's
dress cannot be shifted nor his
hands washed. To give a rational
space for the discharge of these
actions was this scene thought of."
This may be true, but it can be defended on other grounds. See Introduction, pp. xxiv ff. Pope relegated
the first 42 lines of this scene to
the margin. Coleridge, *Shakespearean
Criticism*, i. 75-8, declares " This low
soliloquy of the Porter, and his few
speeches afterwards, I believe to have
been written for the mob by some
other hand, perhaps with Shakespeare's consent; and that finding it
take, he with the remaining ink of a
pen otherwise employed, just interpolated the words ' I'll . . . bonfire '
(18-20). Of the rest not one syllable
has the ever-present being of Shakespeare." But see De Quincey's essay,
" On the knocking at the gate in
Macbeth, "*Works*, ed. Masson, x. 389:
" Hence it is, that when the deed is
done, when the work of darkness is
perfect, then the world of darkness
passes away like a pageantry in the
clouds: the knocking at the gate is
heard, and it makes known audibly
that the reaction has commenced; the
human has made its reflux upon the
fiendish; the pulses of life are beginning

to beat again; and the re-establish-
ment of the goings-on of the world
in which we live first makes us
profoundly sensible of the awful
parenthesis that had suspended
them." Hales, *Notes and Essays on
Shakespeare*, pp. 273-90, argues that
the Porter is inseparably associated
with the knocking, which is an
integral part of the play; that some
relief is necessary at this point in the
play; that the whole speech is a
powerful piece of irony, because the
man *is* Porter of hell-gate as in the
Mystery plays, and that the style
and language are Shakespearean.

2. *old*] Frequently used as a
colloquial augmentative, meaning
plentiful, great, abundant or, as
Steevens says, "*frequent*, more than
enough."

5. *th' expectation of plenty*] which
would, of course, bring low prices.
Malone compares Hall, *Satires*, iv. 6
(ed. 1597):

" Ech Muck-worme wil be riche
          with lawlesse gaine,
Altho he smother vp mowes of
          seuen yeares graine,
And hang'd himself when corne
          grows cheap again."

The passage has been used to fix the
date of the play by Malone and
others. See Introduction, p. xix.

you; here you'll sweat for't. [*Knocking.*] Knock,
knock. Who's there, i' th' other devil's name?—
Faith, here's an equivocator, that could swear in
both the scales against either scale; who com-   10
mitted treason enough for God's sake, yet could
not equivocate to heaven: O! come in, equivocator. [*Knocking.*] Knock, knock, knock.
Who's there?—Faith, here's an English tailor
come hither for stealing out of a French hose: 15

6. *time-server*] Wilson's brilliant
conj. for "time" of the Folio.
(*Edin. Bib. Soc. Trans.*, 1946, ii. pt. 4,
pp. 413-16.) The twice-repeated
"come-in" (12, 15) make it probable that the Porter also says "come
in" to the farmer, with some word
relating to his miscalculating the
time (Darmesteter); and "time-
server" is "an epithet appropriate
to all farmers, who must serve time
in its changes of season and caprices
of weather, and to this farmer in its
special sense of one who adapts his
conduct to the time with an eye to
the main chance; while, inasmuch
as 'server' also means waiter at
table, it links together the otherwise
unrelated words 'napkins' and
'farmer'." Cuningham suggests that
if the Folio reading is correct, the
meaning is probably "Come in
good time, so that you may enjoy
plenty of the everlasting bonfire and
have a good old sweat for't."

6. *napkins*] handkerchiefs.

8. *other*] The Porter cannot remember the name of another devil.

9. *equivocator*] i.e. a Jesuit (Warburton). See Introduction for the
connection between this passage and
the trial of Garnet, who went under
the name of "Farmer," so that, as
Kellett, *Suggestions*, p. 64, points out,
there is a punning link between
farmer and equivocator. Cf. *New
Variorum*, 1903, p. 355. Dowden,
New Shakes. Soc. Trans., 1874, p. 275,
thinks we "should ask whether
Shakespeare did not make the porter

use this word . . . with unconscious
reference to Macbeth, who even
then had begun to find that he could
not 'equivocate to heaven'."

15. *stealing . . . hose*] The joke
against tailors was a very old one.
Scot, *Discoverie of Witchcraft*, vii. 12,
says of Samuel's apparition: "Be-
like he had a new mantell, made
him in heaven: and yet they saie
Tailors are skantie there, for that
their consciences are so large here."
Stubbes, *Anatomie of Abuses*, 1585,
fol. 23*b*: "The Frenche hose are of
two diuers makings, for the common
Frenche hose (as they list to call
them) containeth length, breadth,
and sidenesse sufficient, and is made
very rounde. The other contayneth
neyther length, breadth, nor sidenesse (being not past a quarter of a
yarde side), whereof some be paned,
cut, and drawen out with costly
ornamentes, with Canions annexed,
reaching downe beneath their knees."
This passage is cited by Clarendon
editors who say that in *M.V.* i. ii. 80,
"Shakespeare clearly speaks of the
larger kind, the 'round hose' which
the Englishman borrows from France,
and it is enough to suppose that the
tailor merely followed the practice
of his trade without exhibiting any
special dexterity in stealing." But
Warburton thought that the Porter
referred to the latter kind of hose,
for "a tailor must be a master of
his trade who could steal anything
from thence." I agree with Wilson
that the context implies that the

come in, tailor; here you may roast your goose.
[*Knocking.*]   Knock, knock.   Never   at   quiet!
What are you?—But this place is too cold for Hell.
I'll devil-porter it no further: I had thought to
have let in some of all professions, that go the prim-   20
rose way to th' everlasting bonfire.   [*Knocking.*]
Anon, anon: I pray you, remember the Porter.
                                        [*Opens the gate.*

Enter MACDUFF *and* LENOX.

Macd. Was it so late, friend, ere you went to bed,
    That you do lie so late?
Port. Faith, Sir, we were carousing till the second cock;   25
and drink, Sir, is a great provoker of three things.

25-6] *as prose, Johnson; verse in Ff.*

tailor " had tried the trick once too often " and had been caught when the fashion changed and French hose became tight-fitting. The implication with farmer, equivocator and tailor is not merely that they go to hell for their sins, but that they are caught out by overreaching themselves.

16. *goose*] smoothing iron. But the word also means a swelling caused by venereal disease, and it may therefore have been suggested by ' sweat " (7) *via* " French " (15), and it in turn suggests " lechery " (29). As Wilson observes, the *O.E.D.* gives no instance of " cook one's goose " (= do for oneself) earlier than 1851; but in the phrase " roast your goose " there may be a reference to killing the goose that laid the golden eggs, just as the tailor ruined himself in the attempt to get rich quickly. E. A. Armstrong, *Shakespeare's Imagination*, pp. 57-65, 187-8, has some interesting remarks on the image " cluster " in Shakespeare relating to the goose, and he proves the authenticity of the Porter scene by showing its relations with other scenes in Shakespeare. Cf. in particular Launce's soliloquy

(*T.G.* IV. iv.) where we have " steals her capon's leg . . . hanged for't . . . a pissing while . . . geese . . . heave up my leg." There are close parallels with all these phrases and words in the present scene.

18. *too . . . Hell*] Shakespeare may not have been aware that in Dante's *Inferno*, xxxii-xxxiv, those who were traitors to their kin, to their country, to their friends and guests, and to their lords and benefactors are tortured together in the Ninth, or *frozen* Circle of Hell. Macbeth might be regarded as a traitor to his kinsman, Duncan, to his country, Scotland, to his friend, Banquo, to his guest, lord, and benefactor, Duncan. R. Walker, *op. cit.* noted this independently.

20. *primrose way*] Cf. *A.W.* IV. v. 56: " the flowery way that leads to the broad gate and the great fire "; and *Ham.* I. iii. 50; " the primrose path of dalliance."

22. *I . . . porter*] Addressed to the audience (Wilson). Perhaps it was, though I doubt whether Shakespeare intended this.

25. *the second cock*] i.e. 3 a.m. Cf. *R.J.* IV. iv. 3:

Macd. What three things does drink especially provoke?

Port. Marry, Sir, nose-painting, sleep, and urine.
Lechery, Sir, it provokes, and unprovokes: it provokes the desire, but it takes away the performance.   30
Therefore, much drink may be said to be an equivocator with lechery: it makes him, and it mars
him; it sets him on, and it takes him off; it persuades him, and disheartens him; makes him
stand to, and not stand to: in conclusion, equi-   35
vocates him in a sleep, and, giving him the lie,
leaves him.

Macd. I believe, drink gave thee the lie last night.

Port. That it did, Sir, i' the very throat on me: but I
requited him for his lie; and (I think) being too   40
strong for him, though he took up my legs sometime, yet I made a shift to cast him.

Macd. Is thy master stirring?

Enter MACBETH.

Our knocking has awak'd him; here he comes.

Len. Good morrow, noble Sir!

Macb.   Good morrow, both!   45

Macd. Is the King stirring, worthy Thane?

Macb.   Not yet.

Macd. He did command me to call timely on him:
I have almost slipp'd the hour.

Macb.   I'll bring you to him.

---

39. on] *Ff;* o' *Theobald.*

" the second cock hath crow'd,
The curfew bell hath rung, 'tis
three o'clock."

28-37. *Marry . . . him*] See Introduction, p. xxix. Rabelais also
thought that " Carnal concupiscence
is cooled and quelled . . . by the
means of wine " (III. xxxi.).

36. *in a sleep*] a quibble: " tricks
him *into* a sleep " and " tricks
him in a sleep," i.e. by a dream
(Elwin).

36-7. *giving . . . lie*] laying him
out, as in wrestling.

41. *took . . . legs*] a quibble on the
effect of drink, and a wrestling
action. Perhaps also an echo of
" heave up my leg " (i.e. like a
dog = urinate).

42. *made a shift*] managed.

42. *cast*] quibble on cast (= throw
in wrestling) and cast = vomit
(Wilson). But " cast " can also
mean " emit," not necessarily through
the *mouth.* And cf. v. iii. 50 *post.*

Macd. I know, this is a joyful trouble to you;
   But yet 'tis one.   50
Macb. The labour we delight in physics pain.
   This is the door.
Macd.   I'll make so bold to call,
   For 'tis my limited service.   [*Exit.*
Len. Goes the King hence to-day?
Macb.   He does:—he did appoint so.
Len. The night has been unruly: where we lay,   55
   Our chimneys were blown down; and, as they say,
   Lamentings heard i' th' air; strange screams of death,
   And, prophesying with accents terrible
   Of dire combustion, and confus'd events,
   New hatch'd to th' woeful time, the obscure bird   60

52-3. I'll . . . service] *one line Ff.*   53-4.] *Steevens ends lines at* king
so *and begins 54* From hence.   55-7. The . . . death,] *so Rowe; four lines
Ff ending* vnruly: downe, Ayre Death, 59. combustion] combustions *F 2, 3, 4.*
59-60. events, New . . . time, the] *Knight, Hudson;* Events, New . . . time.
The *Ff;* events. New . . . time, the *conj. Johnson.*   60-2. New . . . night]
so Hanmer; lines end time. Night. feuorous, Night. *Ff; lines end* time. Night,
shake. Night. *Rowe.*

51. *The . . . pain*] Cf. *Cym.,* III. ii.
34 and *Temp.,* III. i. 1-2.
   53. *limited*] appointed. Cf. *M.M.*
IV. ii. 176.
   54. *he . . . so*] " guilty self-correc-
tion " (Grierson).
   55. *The . . . unruly*] Curry,
Shakespeare's Philosophical Patterns, p.
80, says that " the storm which
rages over Macbeth's castle . . . is
no ordinary tempest caused by the
regular movements of the heavenly
bodies, but rather a manifestation
of demonic power over the elements
of nature. Indeed, natural forces
seem to be partly in abeyance . . .
the firm-set earth is so sensitized by
the all-pervading demonic energy
that it is feverous and shakes.
Macbeth senses this magnetization
(cf. II. i. 58). . . . As the drunken
Porter feels, Macbeth's castle is
literally the mouth of hell through
which evil spirits emerge in this
darkness to cause upheavals in
nature." Cf. Masefield, *Recent Prose,*
pp. 270-1. James I. *Workes,* p. 117,

says that witches " can raise stormes
and tempests in the aire, either
vpon Sea or Land, though not
vniuersally, but in such a particular
place and prescribed bounds, as
God will permit them so to trouble."
   58-60. *And . . . bird*] I have
adopted the Knight-Hudson punctuation which connects " prophesying "
with " bird." Wilson Knight suggests (privately) that the owl in *J.C.*
(I. iii. 28) " hooting and shrieking
in the market-place " and prophecy-
ing doom may be compared with
" the obscure bird "; that " new-
hatch'd " suits the bird (as it must
otherwise have suggested it—cf.
Kellett, *Suggestions,* p. 65); that
Shakespeare does not elsewhere use
" prophesying " as a gerund; and
that the build-up for four lines to a
climax, with a quiet and reserved
conclusion after " night " is typically
Shakespearean. I agree and add
only that with the usual punctuation there are two short sentences
at the end of the speech, which

Clamour'd the livelong night: some say, the earth
    Was feverous, and did shake.
Macb.   'Twas a rough night.
Len. My young remembrance cannot parallel
    A fellow to it.

Re-enter MACDUFF.

Macd.   O horror! horror! horror!
    Tongue nor heart cannot conceive, nor name thee!   65
Macb., Len. What's the matter?
Macd. Confusion now hath made his masterpiece!
    Most sacrilegious Murther hath broke ope

64-5.] *so Ff; lines end* heart, matter? *Capell, etc.*

---

prevents the actor from doing much with it; and that all editors emend Folio punctuation and lineation of this speech in one way or another. Cf. Ovid, *Metam*, xv. 791: " Tristia mille locis stygius dedit omina bubo." Pliny (tr. Holland, 1634, x. xii. 276) says " The Scritch-Owle alwaies betokeneth some heauie newes and is most execrable and accursed, and namely, in the presages of publick affaires: he keepeth euer in desarts: and loueth not only such vnpeopled places, but also that are horrible and hard of accesse. In summe, he is the very monster of the night, neither crying nor singing out cleare, but vttering a certaine heauy groane of dolefull mourning. And therefore if he be seen to fly either within cities, or otherwise abroad in any place, it is not good, but prognosticates some fearfull misfortune."

59. *combustion*] tumult, confusion, especially of a political kind. Cf. *Hen. VIII.* v. iv. 51. Hotson suspects a reference to the Gunpowder Plot.

60. *hatch'd . . . time*] Malone thought *new hatch'd* should be referred to *events*, though the events were yet to come, and he compared *2 Hen. IV.* III. i. 86, " Such things become the hatch and brood of

time." He therefore argued that *hatch'd* = hatching, and that " to " meant " to suit," or perhaps " born to." Cf. *Ham.* III. i. 173-5.

62. *feverous*] referring perhaps to the fever of the ague, which was very common in Shakespeare's day, but implying, of course, an earthquake.

65-6. *O . . . matter?*] This lineation is in accordance with the Folio. But according to Flatter, *op. cit.* p. 23, a character, entering, begins a new line, unless he is supposed to over-hear the previous conversation. Here Macduff rushes in with his tidings, and he can be heard before he actually appears. His opening words should not, therefore, be regarded as the completion of Lenox's line. Perhaps Macduff's opening words should be heard before Lenox has completed his sentence, while " What's the matter? " is an extra-metrical interjection. The usual lineation, following Capell, has the effect of making the horror too orderly and metrical; but, of course, in this scene, the lineation of which even the most conservative editors are forced to emend, it would be easy to fall into the error of finding subtleties in textual corruptions.

The Lord's anointed Temple, and stole thence
The life o' th' building!

Macb.   What is 't you say? the life?   70
Len.   Mean you his Majesty?

Macd. Approach the chamber, and destroy your sight
With a new Gorgon.—Do not bid me speak:
See, and then speak yourselves.—

　　　　　　　　　　[Exeunt Macbeth and Lenox.

　　　　　　　　　　　　　Awake! awake!—

Ring the alarum-bell.—Murther, and treason!   75
Banquo, and Donalbain! Malcolm, awake!
Shake off this downy sleep, death's counterfeit,
And look on death itself!—up, up, and see
The great doom's image!—Malcolm! Banquo!
As from your graves rise up, and walk like sprites,   80
To countenance this horror!

　　　　　　　　　　　　　　[Bell rings.

---

74. S.D.] *so Dyce; after* awake! *Ff.*　　　81. horror!] *Theobald;* horror.
Ring the Bell. *Ff.*

---

69. *The Lord's anointed temple*] Cf.
1 *Sam.* xxiv. 10: " The Lord's
anointed " and 2 *Cor.* vi. 16:
" Ye are the Temple of the living
God." Though the metaphor is
mixed, it can be regarded as short-
hand for " the temple of the Lord's
anointed "; and by putting it in
this form, Shakespeare is able to
recall both texts and to glance at
the heinous sin of regicide—David
in the context protests that he could
not put forth his hand against King
Saul. Draper, *Eng. Stud.* 72, regards
the passage as a reference to James
I.'s favourite theory of Divine Right.
Cf. II. i. 58 *ante.*

70-1 *What . . . majesty?*] Macbeth
and Lenox speak together.

77. *sleep . . . counterfeit*] Cf. *Luc.* 402,
where sleep is called " the map of
death," and *M.N.D.* iii. ii. 364:
" death-counterfeiting sleep." Baldwin, *Shakespeare's Small Latine*, I. 591,
thinks that Shakespeare may have

read at school in *Sententiae Pueriles*
the phrase " Somnus mortis imago."
Cf. Anders, *Shakespeare's Books*, p.
48.

79. *doom's image*] Compare *Lear*,
v. iii. 264: " Is this the promised
end? " " Or *image* of that *horror?* "
The Idea of doomsday is continued
in 80-1, and the word " horror " is
used there too.

81. *countenance*] " suit " or " behold," or both.

81. S.D. *Bell rings*] Theobald suggested that the words which complete the line in the Folio were a
stage direction, accidentally repeated as " Bell rings." Stage
directions often appear as impera-
tives (e.g. *Knock*, II. iii. 7 *ante*).
Lady Macbeth's opening words
complete the line if Theobald's
suggestion is adopted. Cuningham,
however, agrees with Keightley that
Macduff, in his impatience, reiter-
ates the order.

Enter LADY MACBETH.

Lady M.   What's the business,
    That such a hideous trumpet calls to parley
    The sleepers of the house? speak, speak!
Macd.   O gentle lady,
    'Tis not for you to hear what I can speak:
    The repetition, in a woman's ear,   85
    Would murther as it fell.

Enter BANQUO.

                                  O Banquo! Banquo!
    Our royal master's murther'd!
Lady M.   Woe, alas!
    What! in our house?
Ban.   Too cruel, anywhere.
    Dear Duff, I pr'ythee, contradict thyself,
    And say, it is not so.   90

Re-enter MACBETH *and* LENOX.

Macb. Had I but died an hour before this chance,
    I had liv'd a blessed time; for, from this instant,
    There's nothing serious in mortality;
    All is but toys: renown, and grace, is dead;
    The wine of life is drawn, and the mere lees   95
    Is left this vault to brag of.

86-8. O . . . anywhere.] *Theobald; one line,* O Banquo . . . murther'd.
followed by three lines ending alas: House? where *Ff.*   89. contradict]
F 1; contract *F 2, 3, 4.*   90. S.D.] *Capell;* Enter Macbeth, Lenox, and
Rosse *Ff.*

88. *in our house?*] Warburton
thought that Lady Macbeth blun-
dered with these words, and that
Banquo accordingly reproved her;
but Kittredge thinks it "a natural
expression from an innocent hostess."

91-6. *Had . . . brag of*] Bradley
points out, *Shakespearean Tragedy,* p.
359, that "this is meant to deceive,
but it utters at the same time his
profoundest feelings." I would add
that Macbeth was unconscious of
the truth of his words, though Murry,
Shakespeare, p. 332, thinks otherwise:

"The irony is appalling: for
Macbeth must needs be conscious
of the import of the words that
come from him. He intends the
monstrous hypocrisy of a conven-
tional lament for Duncan; but
as the words leave his lips they
change their nature, and become a
doom upon himself. He is become
the instrument of 'the equivocation of the fiend That lies like
truth'."

93. *mortality*] "human destiny"
(Grierson).

Enter MALCOLM *and* DONALBAIN.

Don. What is amiss?

Macb.   You are, and do not know't:
The spring, the head, the fountain of your blood
Is stopp'd; the very source of it is stopp'd.

Macd. Your royal father's murther'd.

Mal.   O! by whom?   100

Len. Those of his chamber, as it seem'd, had done 't:
Their hands and faces were all badg'd with blood;
So were their daggers, which, unwip'd, we·found
Upon their pillows: they star'd, and were distracted;
No man's life was to be trusted with them.   105

Macb. O! yet I do repent me of my fury,
That I did kill them.

Macd.   Wherefore did you so?

Macb. Who can be wise, amaz'd, temperate and furious,
Loyal and neutral, in a moment?   No man:
Th' expedition of my violent love   110
Outrun the pauser, reason.—Here lay Duncan,
His silver skin lac'd with his golden blood;
And his gash'd stabs look'd like a breach in nature

104-5. Upon . . . them.] *so Ff; three lines ending* pillows: life them. *Steevens (1793).*

96. *vault*] " A metaphorical comparison of this world vaulted by the sky and robbed of its spirit and grace, with a vault or cellar from which the wine has been taken and the dregs only left " (Elwin).   In Case's view, Macbeth is thinking of the earth as a burial vault, and so proceeds to the idea of a wine vault.

102. *badg'd*] cf. *2 Hen. VI.* III. ii. 200: " murder's crimson badge."

104-5. *Upon . . . them*] Many editors have departed from the Folio arrangement of these lines, but with insufficient justification.   Cuningham's conj. " That no man's . . ." is attractive, but not essential.   The break in the metre after *pillows* and the rhythm of 105 well express the breathless haste and horror of the speaker.

111. *pauser*] i.e. delayer.

112. *lac'd*] interlaced, in reticulate fashion.   Cf. *R.J.* III. v. 8:
    " What envious streaks
    Do lace the severing clouds in
    yonder East."
And *Cymb.* II. ii. 22:
    " white and azure laced
    With blue of heaven's own tint."
" It is not improbable that Shakespeare put these forced and unnatural metaphors into the mouth of Macbeth, as a mark of artifice and dissimulation, to show the difference between the studied language of hypocrisy and the natural outcries of sudden passion.   The whole speech, so considered, is a remarkable instance of judgment, as it consists entirely of antithesis and metaphor " (Johnson).

For ruin's wasteful entrance: there, the murtherers,
Steep'd in the colours of their trade, their daggers　115
Unmannerly breech'd with gore.　Who could refrain,
That had a heart to love, and in that heart
Courage, to make's love known?

Lady M.　　　　　　　　　　　　Help me hence, ho!

Macd. Look to the Lady.

Mal. [*Aside to Don.*] Why do we hold or tongues, that
　　most may claim　　　　　　　　　　　　　　　120
　This argument for ours?

Don. [*Aside to Mal.*] What should be spoken
　Here, where our fate, hid in an auger-hole,
　May rush, and seize us?　Let's away:
　Our tears are not yet brew'd.

120, 121, 124. S.D.] *Staunton; not in Ff.*　　120-4. Why . . . sorrow]
lines end tongues, ours? here, hole, away, brew'd. Sorrow *Ff; various alternative arrangements.*　　122. in] within *F 3, 4.*　auger-hole,] awger-hole, *F 3;*
augure hole, *F 1.*

114. *wasteful*] destructive. The
attackers enter through the breech to
lay waste the town (Kittredge).

116. *breech'd*] Doubtless suggested
by " breach " (113) and meaning
" covered as with breeches, covered
with gore up to the hilts "; and this
of course would be " unmannerly "
as contrasted with " mannerly "
breeches, i.e. the sheaths. Harris,
Modern Language Notes, xxi. 12,
quotes from Guazzo, *The Ciuile
Conversation,* tr. G. Pettie, 1586:
" you meane by your wordes to
include mee in the number of the
melancholike, which have *their wit
so breeched,* that they cannot discerne
sweete from sowre."　The italicized
words translated " le cerveau ob-
fusqué." Harris thinks that " *breech* "
was more or less current (perhaps
current only as an affectation) in
the sense of " cover over " (of the
mind, " becloud "), the original
sense being, no doubt, " cover as
with breeches." But, though affected, the image fits in with the
clothing imagery of the play.

119-25. *Look . . . motion*] These
asides are spoken while Lady Macbeth is being revived from her
fainting-fit—which may be real or
pretended. I believe the arrangement of these lines is new, though
all editors make some change in
the Folio arrangement. It is better
to have the metrical pause between
" Look to the lady " and the asides,
than between Malcolm's and Donalbain's speeches. Similarly, by pre-
serving the Folio arrangement (123-4)
a metrical gap is avoided between
the speeches of Donalbain and
Malcolm, and the *our,* by coming
at the beginning of the line, has its
proper emphasis.　Donalbain is contrasting the attitude of himself and
his brother with the suspiciously glib
emotion displayed by the Macbeths.

121. *argument*] subject or theme.
Cf. *Timon,* III. iii. 20: " So it may
prove an argument of laughter."

122. *where . . . auger-hole*] Cuningham proposes to begin the line
with " whereout " and assumes that
Donalbain means that their fate may
be " lurking in any minute spot,"
ready to rush and seize them.　Cf.

Mal. [*Aside to Don.*]   Nor our strong sorrow
  Upon the foot of motion.   125
Ban.   Look to the Lady:—
                              [*Lady Macbeth is carried out.*
And when we have our naked frailties hid,
That suffer in exposure, let us meet,
And question this most bloody piece of work,
To know it further. Fears and scruples shake us:
In the great hand of God I stand; and thence   130
Against the undivulg'd pretence I fight
Of treasonous malice.
Macd.   And so do I.
All.   So all.
Macb. Let's briefly put on manly readiness,
  And meet i' th' hall together.
All.   Well contented.
                    [*Exeunt all but Malcolm and Donalbain.*

---

125. S.D.] *Rowe; not in Ff.*   127. exposure,] exposure; *Ff.*

Cor. iv. vi. 87: "Confined Into an auger's bore." Bradley quotes Scot, *The Discoverie of Witchcraft*, i, 4.: "they (witches) can go in and out at awger holes." I suppose this passage may have suggested the image to Shakespeare; but, as Chambers points out, he may have been thinking primarily of "a hole made with a sharp point, as of an auger—or a dagger."

125. *Upon . . . motion*] "yet begun to express itself."

125. *Look . . . Lady*] Flatter, *op. cit.* p. 12, believes that a character never completes the line of another's aside; so that we should perhaps assume that these words begin a fresh line, the metrical gap being filled by stage business. It is more likely, I think, that a cut has here obscured Shakespeare's intentions.

126, 133. The circumlocutions may be explained by the clothing imagery

of the play; Shakespeare calls so many other things *clothes*, that he must call *clothes* something else; "naked frailties" = unclothed, and therefore weak, bodies.

129. *scruples*] doubts.

130-1. *hand . . . stand; and thence . . . pretence*] Note the rhymes. Perhaps two couplets have been rewritten as blank verse.

131. *pretence*] design. Cf. ii. iv. 24 *post* and *Lear*, i. iv. 75: "a very pretence and purpose of unkindness." Banquo presumably fears that Macbeth will kill Malcolm.

133. *manly readiness*] Cuningham said this meant merely "men's clothes." But it surely implies "warlike equipment or temper" (New Clar.). "Ready" frequently means *dressed*, and "unready" *undressed.* Cf. *Cym.* ii. iii. 87. Case prefers the straightforward abstract meaning.

Mal. What will you do? Let's not consort with them:　135
　　To show an unfelt sorrow is an office
　　Which the false man does easy.　I'll to England.
Don. To Ireland, I: our separated fortune
　　Shall keep us both the safer; where we are,
　　There's daggers in men's smiles: the near in blood,　140
　　The nearer bloody.
Mal.　　　　　　This murtherous shaft that's shot
　　Hath not yet lighted, and our safest way
　　Is to avoid the aim: therefore, to horse;
　　And let us not be dainty of leave-taking,
　　But shift away.　There's warrant in that theft　145
　　Which steals itself, when there's no mercy left.

　　　　　　　　　　　　　　　　　　　　　[*Exeunt.*

SCENE IV.—*Without the castle.*

Enter ROSSE *and an Old Man.*

Old M. Threescore and ten I can remember well;
　　Within the volume of which time I have seen
　　Hours dreadful, and things strange, but this sore night
　　Hath trifled former knowings.

135-41. What . . . bloody] *so Rowe; nine lines ending* doe? them: Office easie. England. I: safer: Smiles; bloody. *Ff.*　143. horse;] house, *F 2, 3, 4.*

Scene IV

S.D. *Without the castle.*] Hanmer.

137. *easy*] i.e. easily.
140. *the near*] i.e. the nearer. Cf. *Rich. II.* v. i. 88: "Better far off than near, be ne'er the near." Donalbain means Macbeth, Duncan's kinsman. Cf. *Rich. III.* II. i. 92: "Nearer in bloody thoughts, but not in blood." The phrase means, "The closer our relationship, the more likely he is to murder us."
144. *dainty*] particular.
145. *shift away*] slip off.
145. *warrant*] justification.
145-6. *theft . . . steals*] Cf. *A.W.* II. i. 33: "*Bert.* I'll steal away." "*First Lord.* There's honour in the theft."

Scene IV

　This scene, as Liddell remarks, serves as a chorus; but by means of the portents it underlines the unnaturalness of Duncan's murder, it reports the sucess of Macbeth's schemes, and it gives us a taste of Macduff's integrity.
　S.D. *Without the castle*] Theobald's localizing of the scene has been followed by all editors, presumably on the ground that Macduff arrives with the latest news from the castle.
　3. *sore*] dreadful, grievous. Cf. Scottish *sair*.
　4. *trifled . . . knowings*] i.e. made former experience seem trifling.

Rosse.   Ha, good Father,
Thou seest the heavens, as troubled with man's act,   5
Threatens his bloody stage: by th' clock 'tis day,
And yet dark night strangles the travelling lamp.
Is 't night's predominance, or the day's shame,
That darkness does the face of earth entomb,
When living light should kiss it?
Old M.   'Tis unnatural,   10
Even like the deed that's done.   On Tuesday last,
A falcon, towering in her pride of place,
Was by a mousing owl hawk'd at, and kill'd.
Rosse. And Duncan's horses (a thing most strange and
        certain)
Beauteous and swift, the minions of their race,   15
Turn'd wild in nature, broke their stalls, flung out,
Contending 'gainst obedience, as they would make
War with mankind.
Old M.   'Tis said, they eat each other.

4. Ha] Ah *Rowe.*   6. Threatens] Threaten *Rowe.*   his] this *Theobald.*
7. travelling] *F 3, 4;* trauailing *F 1, 2.*   10. should] shall *F 2.*   14. And
. . . certain)] *one line, Pope; two lines Ff.*   17-18. would make War] *so*
Steevens (1793); line 17 ends would *Ff.*   18. eat] ate *Singer.*

4. *Ha*] All editors have followed
Rowe's emendation to " Ah "; but
there seems to be no point in the
change.
    6. *Threatens*] A common use of
singular verb with plural subject.
    6. *stage*] Whiter, *Specimen of a
Commentary*, etc., pp. 160-1, shows
that this word was suggested by the
theatrical meaning of " heavens," i.e.
roof of the stage.
    7. *travelling*] The word was spelt
indifferently " travel " and " tra-
vail," and both meanings may be
intended.
    7. *lamp*] i.e. the sun.
    8. *Is 't . . . shame*] " Is night
triumphant in the deed of darkness
. . . or is day ashamed to look upon
it? " (Clarendon).
    8. *predominance*] astrological influ-
ence. Cf. *T.C.* II. iii. 138: " his
humorous predominance " and *Lear,*
I. ii. 134: " spherical predominance."

12. *towering . . . place*] Terms
of falconry. " Towering " means
mounting higher and higher in
wide circles, and " place " is the
highest " pitch " or flight attained
by the hawk before stooping. Cf.
K.J. v. ii. 149. Turberville, *Book of
Falconrie*, ed. 1611, p. 53, writes of
" the number of those Hawkes that
are hie flying and towre Hawks."
    14. *horses*] Walker conj. " horse,"
the old collective plural. Cf. IV. i.
140: " the galloping of horse."
    15. *minions*] darlings, favourites,
i.e. best of their breed. According
to Chambers the owl and the
horses symbolize the traitor who
struck the king. But it may be an
exhibition of demonic power over
the elements of nature (cf. note on
II. iii. 55) or a reflection of the
violation of the natural order which
the murder involves.
    17. *as*] as if. Cf. II. ii. 27 *ante.*

Rosse. They did so; to th' amazement of mine eyes,
    That look'd upon 't.   20

                Enter MACDUFF.

                        Here comes the good Macduff.
    How goes the world, Sir, now?
Macd.   Why, see you not?
Rosse. Is 't known, who did this more than bloody deed?
Macd. Those that Macbeth hath slain.
Rosse.   Alas, the day!
    What good could they pretend?
Macd.   They were suborn'd.
    Malcolm, and Donalbain, the King's two sons,   25
    Are stol'n away and fled; which puts upon them
    Suspicion of the deed.
Rosse.   'Gainst nature still:
    Thriftless Ambition, that will ravin up
    Thine own life's means!—Then 'tis most like
    The sovereignty will fall upon Macbeth.   30
Macd. He is already nam'd, and gone to Scone
    To be invested.
Rosse.   Where is Duncan's body?
Macd. Carried to Colme-kill,

19-20. They . . . Macduff] *so Pope; three lines, ending* so: upon 't.
Macduffe. *Ff.*   28. will] *Ff,* wilt *Warburton.* ravin up] *Theobald;* rauen
up *F 1;* raven upon *F 2, 3, 4.*   29. Thine] Its *Hanmer.* life's] *Pope;*
liues *Ff.*   33. Colmekill,] Colmeshill, *Rowe;* Colmeskill, *Johnson.*

24. *pretend*] intend. Cf. " pretence " (II. iii. 134 *ante*).

24. *suborn'd*] instigated to commit
any evil action.

27-9. *'Gainst . . . means*] R.
Walker, *op. cit.,* chap. 4, comments:
" Ostensibly the words relate to
Malcolm and Donalbain. . . . But
how much better the words describe
Macbeth! "

28. *will*] No emendation is required
as this use was common in Elizabethan
English.

28. *ravin up*] swallow greedily. Cf.
IV. i. 24 *post; M.M.* I. ii. 133:
" Like rats that ravin down their

proper bane "; and Jonson, *Every
Man in His Humour,* III. iv. 42: " I
am sure on't; for they rauen vp
more butter, then all the dayes of
the weeke beside."

31. *nam'd*] chosen.

31. *Scone*] The ancient royal city,
probably the capital of the old
Pictish kingdom, about two miles
north of Perth. The Stone of Destiny,
on which the Scottish kings were
crowned, was thought to have been
Jacob's pillow: it was purloined
by Edward I in 1296 and taken to
Westminster Abbey.

33. *Colme-kill*] See note on I. ii. 63
ante and Appendix, p. 177.

The sacred storehouse of his predecessors,
And guardian of their bones.

Rosse   Will you to Scone?   35

Macd. No cousin; I 'll to Fife.

Rosse.   Well, I will thither.

Macd. Well, may you see things well done there:—adieu!—
Lest our old robes sit easier than our new!

Rosse. Farewell, Father.

Old M. God's benison go with you; and with those   40
That would make good of bad, and friends of foes!

                               [*Exeunt.*

---

37. Well, may] *Theobald;* Well may *Ff.*   40. you;] you Sir, *F 2, 3, 4.*

36. *I will thither*] The verb of motion is sometimes omitted. Cf. *Rich. II.* i. ii. 73: "desolate will I hence and die."

37. *well . . . well*] ironical repetition of Rosse's "well."

40-1. *and with . . . foes*] Fleay and Wilson suspect an interpolation, but the couplet contains the antitheses so common through the play. "The Old Man rightly judges Rosse as a mere time-server" (Chambers). The blessing, however, is more likely to be sincere. "The Old Man blesses those who would transform bad into good and foes into friends" (Flatter).

ACT III

SCENE I.—*Forres. A room in the palace.*

Enter BANQUO.

Ban. Thou hast it now, King, Cawdor, Glamis, all,
As the Weïrd Women promis'd; and, I fear,
Thou play'dst most foully for't; yet it was said,
It should not stand in thy posterity;
But that myself should be the root and father   5
Of many kings. If there come truth from them
(As upon thee, Macbeth, their speeches shine),
Why, by the verities on thee made good,
May they not be my oracles as well,
And set me up in hope? But, hush; no more.   10

ACT III

Scene 1

S.D.] *Forres . . . palace.*] *Capell.*

ACT III. *Scene* I

1-10. *Thou . . . more*] In Holinshed, Banquo is Macbeth's accomplice in the murder of Duncan; but as he was James I's ancestor he had to be treated with some respect. For purely dramatic reasons it was obviously desirable to contrast Macbeth and Banquo, and to give Macbeth and his wife no accomplices. Bradley, *Shakespearean Tragedy*, pp. 384-5, thinks that this speech proves that Banquo has become an accessory to the murder because, out of ambition, he has kept silent about the witches and thus refrained from exposing Macbeth. Wilson argues that Shakespeare could not have depicted James I's ancestor as a cowardly time-server, and refers to Macbeth's oblique compliments later in the scene (49-52 "royalty of nature," "dauntless temper," "wisdom"). He suggests further, and rather weakly, that in the un-cut *Macbeth*, Banquo may have been working with Macduff on behalf of Malcolm. If so, the cut (which on Wilson's theory was made by Shakespeare himself) was a very queer one. Cf. Introduction, p. xxiii.

3. *play'dst*] cf. I. v. 21.

4. *stand*] Cf. *M.N.D.* v. i. 417.

10. *Sennet*] "A word chiefly occurring in the stage-directions of old plays, and seeming to indicate a particular set of notes on the trumpet or cornet, different from a flourish" (Nares).

Sennet sounded. Enter MACBETH *as King*; LADY MACBETH,
      as Queen; LENOX, ROSSE, *Lords and Attendants.*

Macb. Here's our chief guest.
Lady M.   If he had been forgotten,
      It had been as a gap in our great feast,
      And all-thing unbecoming.
Macb. To-night we hold a solemn supper, Sir,
      And I'll request your presence.
Ban.   Let your Highness   15
      Command upon me, to the which my duties
      Are with a most indissoluble tie
      For ever knit.
Macb. Ride you this afternoon?
Ban.   Ay, my good Lord.
Macb. We should have else desir'd your good advice   20
      (Which still hath been both grave and prosperous)
      In this day's council; but we'll take to-morrow.
      Is't far you ride?
Ban. As far, my Lord, as will fill up the time
      'Twixt this and supper: go not my horse the better,   25
      I must become a borrower of the night,
      For a dark hour, or twain.
Macb.   Fail not our feast.
Ban. My Lord, I will not.
Macb. We hear, our bloody cousins are bestow'd
      In England, and in Ireland; not confessing   30
      Their cruel parricide, filling their hearers

S.D. Lady . . . Lenox] *Rowe;* Lady Lenox F.   13. all-thing] *F 1;*
all-things *F 2;* all things *F 3, 4.*   15. Let your Highness] Lay your
Highness's *D'avenant, Rowe;* Set your highness' *conj. Mason.*   16. upon]
be upon *Keightley.*   20-3.] *Pope ends lines* desir'd grave, but ride?
22. take] talk *Malone;* take't *Warburton (MS.) and Keightley (ap. Camb.).*

13. *all-thing*] wholly; or every thing.
14. *solemn*] formal or ceremonious.
Cf. *M.N.D.* IV. i. 191: "We'll hold
a feast in great solemnity."
15-16. *Let . . . which*] "Command
upon " is an unusual phrase for " lay
your command upon," but such tele-
scoping is not unique in Shakespeare. Cuningham thought that
the antecedent of " which " was

" Command," Clar. Edd. thought it
was "the idea contained in the
preceding clause," and Case that it
was " your highness."
21. *still . . . prosperous*] always
. . . profitable.
25. *go . . . horse*] i.e. if my horse
go not. Cf. *Rich. II.* II. i. 300:
"Hold out my horse, and I will
first be there."

With strange invention.   But of that to-morrow,
When, therewithal, we shall have cause of State,
Craving us jointly.   Hie you to horse: adieu,
Till you return at night.   Goes Fleance with you?   35
Ban. Ay, my good Lord: our time does call upon 's.
Macb. I wish your horses swift, and sure of foot;
And so I do commend you to their backs.
Farewell.—   [*Exit Banquo.*
Let every man be master of his time   40
Till seven at night;
To make society the sweeter welcome,
We will keep ourself till supper-time alone:
While then, God be with you.
                    [*Exeunt all except Macbeth and a Servant.*
                    Sirrah, a word with you.
Attend those men our pleasure?   45
Serv.   They are, my Lord,
Without the palace gate.
Macb.   Bring them before us.
                                        [*Exit Servant.*
To be thus is nothing, but to be safely thus:
Our fears in Banquo
Stick deep, and in his royalty of nature

34-5.] *so Pope; three lines ending* Horse: Night. you? *F.*   38. I do] do
I *F 3, 4.*   41-7.] *lines end* societie welcome: alone: you. men pleasure?
Gate. us. safely thus: *F.*   41-2. night; to . . . welcome,] *Theobald;* Night,
to . . . welcome: *Ff.* 48-50. Our . . . dares;] *lines end* deepe, that dares, *Ff.*

33. *cause*] subject, matter of debate. Cf. IV. iii. 196 *post,* where
the "general cause" means the
public interest.

41-8. The Folio arrangement of
these lines cannot be right, and all
editors have made some changes.
But no editor since Rowe has kept
47 intact and the rhythm of 41-6,
as usually printed, is dreadfully
flabby. The Folio printers made the
mistake of adding " to make societie "
to the short line 41, but they realized
that 43 was a complete line. The
shortness of line 48 enables a dramatic
pause to be made after the key line,
47.

44. *While*] until. Cf. *Rich. II.*
IV. i. 269: "Read o'er the paper
while the glass doth come." This
usage is still common in the North
of England.

43. *God . . you*] i.e. God b' wi'
you (= good-bye), and so scanned.

47. *To be thus . . . thus*] i.e. to be
a king in name is nothing, but to
reign in safety is the thing. Cf. III.
ii. 6, 13-26, 32.

49. *stick deep*] like thorns (Wilson).

49-53. *royalty . . . safety*] Stewart,
Modern Language Review, 1945, p. 172,
claims rightly that " the ungrudging
recognition and boundless admiration " expressed in this speech is

Reigns that which would be fear'd: 'tis much he
   dares;   50
And, to that dauntless temper of his mind,
He hath a wisdom that doth guide his valour
To act in safety.   There is none but he
Whose being I do fear: and under him
My Genius is rebuk'd; as, it is said,   55
Mark Antony's was by Cæsar.   He chid the Sisters,
When first they put the name of King upon me,
And bade them speak to him; then, prophet-like,
They hail'd him father to a line of kings:
Upon my head they plac'd a fruitless crown,   60
And put a barren sceptre in my gripe,
Thence to be wrench'd with an unlineal hand,
No son of mine succeeding.   If 't be so,
For Banquo's issue have I fil'd my mind;
For them the gracious Duncan have I murther'd;   65
Put rancours in the vessel of my peace,
Only for them; and mine eternal jewel
Given to the common Enemy of man,
To make them kings, the seed of Banquo kings!
Rather than so, come, fate, into the list,   70
And champion me to th' utterance!—Who's there?—

69. seed] *Pope;* Seedes *Ff.*   71.] *so Pope; two lines ending* th' utterance.
there? *Ff.*

not, as some critics believe, psychologically unconvincing.   " It is surely
natural enough for Macbeth to
assert that the enemy he fears and
proposes to have assassinated is a
formidable enemy, of regal temper,
at once daring and prudent.   Any-
one who doubts this should try
writing a speech for Macbeth in
which Banquo is represented as
timid, foolish, and generally neglig-
ible."   See Introduction, p. lxvii.

55-6. *My Genius . . . Cæsar*] Cf.
A.C. II. iii. 19 and North's *Plutarch*
(Temple ed. IX, pp. 43-4): " For
thy demon, said he (that is to say,
the good angell and spirit that
keepeth thee), is afraid of his: and
being couragious and high when he
is alone, becometh fearfull and

timorous when he cometh neare
vnto the other."

62. *with*] i.e. by.   Cf. e.g. *W.T.*
v. ii. 68.   See Appendix E.

64. *fil'd*] defiled.   The word is
used by Spenser, *Faerie Queene*, III.
i. 62 and Wilkins, *Miseries of Inforc'd
Marriage* (Hazlitt's *Dodsley*, ix. p.
511).

66. *Put . . . peace*] Wilson compares *Ps.* xi. 6 and *Isa.* li. 17.   Grierson suggests the image is drawn from
the sacramental cup.

67. *eternal jewel*] immortal soul.
Cf. *Oth*, III. iii. 361: " eternal
soul."

71. *champion me*] Cuningham
thought this " must mean that Fate
is called in to be Macbeth's champion to defend his royal title ";

Re-enter Servant, with two Murderers.

Now, go to the door, and stay there till we call.
　　　　　　　　　　　　　　　　[*Exit Servant.*

Was it not yesterday we spoke together?

1 *Mur.* It was, so please your Highness.

Macb.　　　　　　　　　　　　Well then, now
Have you consider'd of my speeches?—know　　75
That it was he, in the times past, which held you
So under fortune, which you thought had been
Our innocent self?　This I made good to you
In our last conference; pass'd in probation with you,
How you were borne in hand; how cross'd; the in-
　　struments;　　　　　　　　　　　　　　　　　80
Who wrought with them; and all things else, that
　　might,
To half a soul, and to a notion craz'd,
Say, " Thus did Banquo."

1 *Mur.*　　　　　　　　　You made it known to us.

Macb. I did so; and went further, which is now

74-81.] *so Rowe; lines end* then, speeches: past, fortune, selfe. conference,
you: crost: them: might *Ff*.　　75. Have you] You have *F 3.*　speeches?—
know] *Muir; speeches:* Know *Ff; speeches?* Know. *Rowe.*　78. self?] selfe.
Ff, etc.　　　84-9.] *so Rowe; lines end* so: now meeting, predominant, goe?
man, hand beggerd' euer? *Ff*.

but Macbeth is rather challenging
Fate to the combat (*O.E.D.*).

71. *to th' utterance*] Holinshed, iii.
560a, has: " the lord Mountainie
. . . would not yeeld, but made
semblance, as though he meant to
defend the place, *to the utterance.*"
Cotgrave defines " Combatre à oul-
trance " as . . . " to *fight it out, or
to the uttermost.*"

71. S.D. *two Murderers*] Granville-
Barker says that " the text's implication is surely that they were
officers, cast perhaps for some mis-
demeanour and out of luck."

75-8. *Have . . . self*] The F punctuation is possible; but editors usually
insert a question-mark at 75, and
as Macbeth informs the murderers
that he has already told them about
Banquo's villainy at a previous con-

ference, I believe the meaning is:
" Have you considered my speeches
and [do you] know that it was he,
etc."

77. *under fortune*] beneath your
deserts.

79. *pass'd in probation*] went over
the proof.

80. *borne in hand*] i.e. deceived.
Cf. *Ham.* ii. ii. 67:
　" That so his sickness, age and
　　impotence
　Was falsely borne in hand."
Cf. also *Cym.* v. v. 43, and Wyatt,
Poems, ed. Muir, p. 15:
　" For he that beleveth bering in
　　hand
　Plowithe in water and soweth
　　in the sand."

82. *notion*] mind.

Our point of second meeting.   Do you find   85
Your patience so predominant in your nature,
That you can let this go?   Are you so gospell'd,
To pray for this good man, and for his issue,
Whose heavy hand hath bow'd you to the grave,
And beggar'd yours for ever?
1 *Mur.*   We are men, my Liege.   90
Macb.   Ay, in the catalogue ye go for men;
As hounds, and greyhounds, mongrels, spaniels, curs,
Shoughs, water-rugs, and demi-wolves, are clept
All by the name of dogs: the valu'd file
Distinguishes the swift, the slow, the subtle,   95
The housekeeper, the hunter, every one
According to the gift which bounteous Nature

93. clept] *Capell;* clipt *Ff;* cleped *Theobald;* clep'd *Hanmer.*

87-8. *gospell'd . . . man*] Cf. *Matt.*
v. 44: (Geneva) "Loue your
enemies: blesse them that curse
you: doe good to them that hate
you, and pray for them which hurt
you, and persecute you." In the
scenes relating to the murder of
Banquo there seem to be several
echoes from verses in the same
chapter. Cf. 107 "perfect" and
v. 48: 127 "shine" and v. 16;
III. iii. 16 "rain . . . come down"
and v. 45; III. iii. 11-12 "go . . .
mile" and v. 41; and perhaps
III. i. 108 "vile blows and buffets"
and v. 39; and III. i. 141, "If . . .
to-night" and v. 10—implying that
Banquo is persecuted for righteous-
ness' sake.

90. *men*] Gervinus notes that Macbeth uses the very means which had
wrought most effectually upon himself: he appeals to the manliness
of the murderers.

91-100. *Ay . . . men*] "an image
of order" (Knights).

93. *Shoughs*] "what we now call
shocks" (Johnson); a shag-haired
dog. Steevens quotes Nash, *Lenten
Stuffe,* ed. McKerrow, iii. 182:
'they are for *Vltima Theule,* the

north-seas, or *Island* [Iceland], and
thence yerke ouer . . . a trundle-
taile tike or *shaugh* or two."

93. *water-rugs*] rough-haired water
dog.

93. *demi-wolves*] "dogs bred between wolves and dogs, like the Latin
lycisci " (Johnson).

93. *clept*] called. The word was
becoming obsolete in Shakespeare's
day. Cf. *L.L.L.* v. i. 23 and *Ham.*
I. iv. 19.

94. *the valu'd file*] "The file or
list where the value and peculiar
qualities of everything are set down,
in contradistinction to what he
immediately mentions, 'the bill
that writes them all alike'"
(Steevens). Cf. 101 *post* and note
on v. ii. 8. See also *M.M.* III. ii.
144: "The greater file of the subject held the Duke to be wise." It
should be noted that *valu'd* is an
adj. from the noun *value,* not the
participle of the vb.

96. *housekeeper*] In Topsell, *History
of Four-Footed Beasts,* 1608, pp. 160,
the *housekeeper* is enumerated among
the different kinds of dogs (Clarendon).

97. *According . . . gift*] Noble

Hath in him clos'd; whereby he does receive
Particular addition, from the bill
That writes them all alike; and so of men.   100
Now, if you have a station in the file,
Not i' th' worst rank of manhood, say 't;
And I will put that business in your bosoms,
Whose execution takes your enemy off,
Grapples you to the heart and love of us,   105
Who wear our health but sickly in his life,
Which in his death were perfect.

2 *Mur.*   I am one, my Liege,
Whom the vile blows and buffets of the world
Hath so incens'd, that I am reckless what
I do, to spite the world.

1 *Mur.*   And I another,   110
So weary with disasters, tugg'd with fortune,

---

102. Not] And not *Rowe.*   say't] *Ff;* say it *Rowe.*   103. that] the *F 3, 4.*
105. heart] heart; *F.*   109-10. what I do] *line ends with* doe *Ff.*   109.
Hath] *Ff.* Have *most editors.*   111. weary] weary'd *Capell.*

compares *Eph.* iv. 7 and *Matt.*
xxv. 15.

97. *bounteous Nature*] *naturae be-*
nignitas. The phrase is used by
Erasmus in his *Colloquia* (ed. 1664,
p. 662). Rea pointed out (*Modern
Language Notes,* xxxv) that in the
same colloquy there is a comparison
between dogs and men, similar to
Macbeth's. Shakespeare may have
read the passage at school. For
convenience I give H.M.'s translation, 1671, pp. 482-3: " *Sy.* All
Dogs are contained under one
species, but into how innumerable
shapes is this special kind divided,
so that thou wouldest say that they
are distinguished in the *genus,* and
not in the *species.* Now how different
are the manners and dispositions of
Dogs even altogether of the same
special kind? *Ph.* There is a very
great variety. *Sy.* Suppose that which
is spoken of dogs, to be spoken of all
the several kinds of living creatures,
but the difference appeareth in no
kind more than in Horses. *Ph.* Thou

sayest true, but to what purpose dost
thou speak these things? *Sy.* What-
soever variety there is in the general
kinds, or in the shapes of living
creatures, or in every several creature,
imagine all this to be in man: Thou
shalt find there diverse Wolves,
Dogs of an unspeakable variety."
This passage may have been recalled to Shakespeare's mind by the
reference to *genius* (55) for Erasmus
also mentions *Genius* (*op. cit.* p. 661).

98. *clos'd*] set, like a jewel (Wilson),
or just " enclosed."

99. *addition*] cf. I. iii. 106 *ante.*

101. *file*] a pun on the two meanings of " file "—as in 94, and in the
military sense.

105. *Grapples*] Cf. *Ham.* I. iii. 63:
"Grapple them to thy soul with
hoops of steel."

111. *tugg'd*] scuffled. Cf. *W.T.*
IV. iv. 508:
            " let myself and fortune
      Tug for the time to come."
The metaphor is apparently from
a rough-and-tumble at wrestling.

That I would set my life on any chance,
To mend it, or be rid on 't.

Macb.   Both of you
Know, Banquo was your enemy.

2 *Mur.*   True, my Lord.

Macb. So is he mine; and in such bloody distance,   115
That every minute of his being thrusts
Against my near'st of life: and though I could
With bare-fac'd power sweep him from my sight,
And bid my will avouch it, yet I must not,
For certain friends that are both his and mine,   120
Whose loves I may not drop, but wail his fall
Who I myself struck down: and thence it is
That I to your assistance do make love,
Masking the business from the common eye,
For sundry weighty reasons.

2 *Mur.*   We shall, my Lord,   125
Perform what you command us.

1 *Mur.*   Though our lives—

Macb. Your spirits shine through you.   Within this hour,
      at most,
I will advise you where to plant yourselves,

113-14. Both . . . enemy] *so Rowe; one line Ff.*   127. Your . . . most]
so Pope; two lines Ff.

Drayton, *Mortimeriados,* 2725, uses
the same expression: " Fortune and
I have tugg'd together so." Cf.
Daniel's *Epistle to Southampton,* 1-2:

" He who hath neuer warr'd with
      miserie,
   Nor euer tugg'd with Fortune
      and distresse."

115. *distance*] in fencing, definite
interval of space to be kept between
the combatants (Onions); hence
enmity. Cf. Bacon, *Essays,* xv. *Of
Seditions and Troubles*: " the Dividing
and Breaking of all Factions, and
setting them at distance, or at least
distrust amongst themselves."

117. *near'st of life*] i.e. vital parts.

For the construction, cf. v. ii. 11
post and *M.M.* III. i. 17: " best of
rest."

119. *avouch*] warrant, justify. Cf.
v. v. 47 *post.*

120. *For*] On account of, because
of. Cf. Abbott, *Shaks. Gram.* § 150,
and *V.A.* 114.

121. *but*] Abbott, *Gram.* § 385,
considers that the finite verb is to
be supplied here *without* the negative,
i.e. " but (I must) wail his fall," etc.;
and compares 48 *ante.* Cuningham,
however, suggested " but " was a
corruption of " would."

122. *Who*] i.e. whom—frequent in
Shakespeare.

Acquaint you with the perfect spy o' th' time,
The moment on't; for't must be done to-night,   130
And something from the palace; always thought,
That I require a clearness: and with him
(To leave no rubs nor botches in the work),
Fleance his son, that keeps him company,
Whose absence is no less material to me   135
Than is his father's, must embrace the fate
Of that dark hour.   Resolve yourselves apart;
I'll come to you anon.

2 *Mur.*   We are resolv'd, my Lord.

Macb. I'll call upon you straight: abide within.—

                          [*Exeunt Murderers.*

It is concluded: Banquo, thy soul's flight,   140
If it find Heaven, must find it out to-night.   [*Exit.*

129. the . . . time,] *Ff;* the perfect spot, the time *conj. Tyrwhitt;* you with a *conj. Johnson;* you with the perfectry o' the time *conj. Beckett;* you, with a perfect spy, o' the time *Collier MS.*   133. (To . . . work),] To . . . Worke: *Ff.*   139. S.D.] *Theobald;* Exeunt (*after 141*) *Ff.*

129. *the perfect . . . time*] The meaning of this is much disputed. (i) the third murderer (Johnson, who emends *the* to *a*). (ii) *espyal* = exact intimation of precise time (Heath). (iii) the exact time most favourable to your purposes (Steevens, who proposes a full-stop at the end of 128). There are numerous variations of these explanations and many conjectural emendations. If Johnson's explanation is correct, it is curious that Macbeth did not introduce the two murderers to the third. In Sc. iii. they seem surprised to see him. Wilson thinks there has been a cut. Perhaps for " spy " we should read " spial " (= observation, watch— *O.E.D.*). Flatter suggests that *perfect* is the theatrical term, and that it relates to time.

131. *thought*] i.e. it being thought. Liddell quotes a similar idiom from Florio's *Montaigne,* I. xxv.: " Alwayes conditioned the master bethinke himselfe where to his charge tendeth."

131. *something*] Used adverbially, like " somewhat." Cf. *2 Hen. IV.* I. ii. 212: " a white head and something a round belly."

132. *clearness*] " So that he . . . might cleare himself " (Holinshed). Cf. Appendix, p. 180. The word also implies " completeness ". Cf. l. 133.

133. *rubs*] Editors assume that the metaphor is from the bowling-green, a " rub " being an impediment. Cf. *Ham.* III. i. 65 and *John,* III. iv. 128. But I doubt whether Shakespeare was thinking of bowls here. The word means " a roughness; an unevenness or inequality " (*O.E.D.*) in a piece of work, as well as on a green. This interpretation is supported by " botches," which means " parts spoiled by clumsy work."

SCENE II.—*The same.   Another room.*

Enter LADY MACBETH *and a Servant.*

Lady M. Is Banquo gone from court?
Serv. Ay, Madam, but returns again to-night.
Lady M. Say to the King, I would attend his leisure
    For a few words.
Serv.   Madam, I will.   [*Exit.*
Lady M.   Nought 's had, all 's spent,
    Where our desire is got without content: 5
    'Tis safer to be that which we destroy,
    Than by destruction dwell in doubtful joy.

Enter MACBETH.

How now, my Lord? why do you keep alone,
Of sorriest fancies your companions making,
Using those thoughts, which should indeed have died   10
With them they think on?   Things without all remedy
Should be without regard: what's done is done.
Macb. We have scorch'd the snake, not kill'd it:
    She'll close, and be herself; whilst our poor malice

Scene II

S.D. *The same.   Another room.*] *Capell.*   11. all] *not in Hanmer*
13. scorch'd] *Ff, Grierson, Wilson;* scotch'd *Theobald, etc.*

Scene II

1. *Is . . . court?*] " May not Lady Macbeth's suspicions have been aroused by the particularity with which she had heard her husband ask concerning Banquo's movements in III. i.? " (Furness.)

6-7. *'Tis . . . joy*] cf. III. i. 47 *ante* and 19-22 *post.*

7. *doubtful*] full of doubt, suspicious, apprehensive. W. D. Sargeaunt, *Macbeth: The Play as Shakespeare Wrote It*, 1916, thinks the line means " Than to dwell near destruction in joy doubtful (fearful) of destruction "; but the title of the book is somewhat misleading.

8-45. " One of the few strokes of pathos that are let soften the grimness of the tragedy is Lady Macbeth's wan effort to get near enough to the

tortured man to comfort him. But the royal robes, stiff on their bodies —stiff as with caked blood—seem to keep them apart " (Granville-Barker, *op. cit.* p. xli).

9. *sorriest*] cf. II. ii. 20 *ante.*

10. *Using*] Keeping company with, entertaining as companions. Cf. *Per.* I. ii. 3-7.

11. *without all remedy*] i.e. beyond all remedy. Cf. *M.N.D.* IV. i. 158: " without the peril of the Athenian law " and *W.T.* III. ii. 223:

" What's gone and what's past help
    Should be past grief."

12. *what's done is done*] Cf. I. vii. 1; v. i. 64-5.

13. *scorch'd*] slash'd, as with a knife (*O.E.D.*). Theobald's emendation is unnecessary.

Remains in danger of her former tooth.   15
But let the frame of things disjoint, both the worlds
   suffer,
Ere we will eat our meal in fear, and sleep
In the affliction of these terrible dreams,
That shake us nightly.   Better be with the dead,
Whom we, to gain our peace, have sent to peace,   20
Than on the torture of the mind to lie
In restless ecstasy.   Duncan is in his grave;
After life's fitful fever he sleeps well;
Treason has done his worst: nor steel, nor poison,
Malice domestic, foreign levy, nothing   25

---

16. But . . . suffer] *one line, Theobald; two lines, ending* dis-joynt, suffer, *F.* disjoint] become disjoint *conj. Bailey.* suffer] suffer dissolution *conj. Bailey.* But let the frame of things disjoint itself, *followed by Bailey's second conj.—conj. Cuningham.* 20. peace] *F 1;* place *F 2, 3, 4.* 22.] *one line Rowe; two lines, divided after* extasie. *Ff.*

---

15. *her former tooth*] i.e. her tooth as formerly, before she was " scorch'd."

16. *But . . . suffer*] This line, unwieldy as it is, consists of two lines, both imperfect in the Folio. Shakespeare made frequent use of short lines, but he did not have two together in the middle of a speech. Bailey's conj. given above seems to be unlike the style of the play, and Cuningham's " disjoint itself " is flat. I suspect we should keep the Folio lines, but emend the first to " But let the very frame of things disjoint." Cunningham compares *Ham.* I. ii. 20: " Our state to be disjoint and out of frame." In support of Bailey's conj. " dissolution," Cuningham quotes *T.C.* v. ii. 156: " The bonds of heaven are slipp'd, dissolved, and loosed," and *Temp.* IV. i. 154: " The great globe itself . . . shall dissolve." Wilson compares *1 Hen. IV.* III. i. 16. The metaphor is from carpentry or house-building. Macbeth would rather have the universe fall to pieces than suffer from bad dreams. Nashe, *Lenten Stuffe* (ed. McKerrow,

iii. p. 214) uses " disioynt " in an active sense.

16. *frame of things*] i.e. the universe, both the worlds, celestial and terrestrial.

18. *dreams*] Wilson says that the context (24-6 *post*) shows that he dreams he is being murdered, apparently by Banquo. This may be; but perhaps he dreams, more terribly, of murdering Duncan or Banquo—as Lady Macbeth would to do. His feeling of guilt would make him fear Banquo.

20. *gain . . . peace*] i.e. to gain the peace of satisfied ambition have sent to the peace of the grave. F 2 ruins a nice point. The critics who defend " place " on the ground that Macbeth did not gain " peace " confuse fact and intention.

21. *on . . . lie*] the metaphor is from the rack.

22. *ecstasy*] " Every species of alienation of mind, whether temporary or permanent, proceeding from joy, sorrow, wonder, or any other exciting cause " (Nares, *Glossary*).   Cf. *C.E.* IV. iv. 50.

23. *fitful*] Shakespearean coinage.

Can touch him further!

Lady M.   Come on:
Gentle my Lord, sleek o'er your rugged looks;
Be bright and jovial among your guests to-night.

Macb. So shall I, Love; and so, I pray, be you.
Let your remembrance apply to Banquo: 30
Present him eminence, both with eye and tongue:
Unsafe the while, that we
Must lave our honours in these flattering streams,
And make our faces vizards to our hearts,
Disguising what they are.

Lady M.   You must leave this.   35
Macb. O! full of scorpions is my mind, dear wife!
Thou know'st that Banquo, and his Fleance, lives.
Lady M. But in them Nature's copy's not eterne.

---

28. among] *F 1;* 'mong *F 2, 3, 4.* 30. apply] still apply *F 2, 3, 4.*
32-3. Unsafe . . . streams] *lines end* laue streames, *Ff.*

---

30. *remembrance*] a quadrisyllable.
Cf. Abbott, *Sh. Grammar*, 477.

30. *apply*] be given.

31. *Present him eminence*] i.e. assign
to him the highest rank.

32. *Unsafe . . . we*] The Folio line-
division is wrong here, and something may be missing; but the
general meaning is, "For the time
being we are unsafe, so that we
must keep our honours clean by
flattering Banquo and disguising our
hatred." Wilson comments that
Macbeth fears exposure as well as
assassination from Banquo. Grierson
points out that "flattering" has the
force of a defining genitive.

36. *full . . . mind*] It has been
suggested (*M.L.N.* lx.) that there is
a reference to the superstition that
basil propagated scorpions. Topsell,
Historie of Serpents, p. 225, says that
"*Hollerius . . .* writeth that in Italy
in his dayes, there was a man that
had a Scorpion bredde in his braine,
by continuall smelling to this herbe
Basill, and *Gesner* by relation of an
Apothecary in Fraunce, writeth likewise a storie of a young mayde, who

by smelling to Basill, fell into an
exceeding head-ach, whereof she
dyed without cure, and after her
death beeing opened, there were
found little Scorpions in her braine."
Cf. Browne, *Vulgar Errors*, II. vii. 9
(ed. Keynes, ii. 176) and the note
on v. iii. 55.

38. *nature's . . . eterne*] Usually
explained as "their holding by
'copy' from nature is not for ever."
Copy, or copyhold, is the tenure of
lands "at the will of the lord according to the custom of the manor," by
copy of the manorial court-roll.
Coke on Littleton (ed. 1670) c. ix.
§ 73: "Tenant by copy of court
roll is as if a man be seised of a
manor within which manor there is
a custom which hath been used to
have lands and tenements, to hold
to them and their heirs in fee simple,
or fee tail, or for term of life, at the
will of the lord according to the
custom of the same manor." Just as,
in the case of the tenure of the estate
being only for the life of the tenant,
the estate would revert to the lord
on the former's death, so the tenure

Macb. There's comfort yet; they are assailable:
Then be thou jocund. Ere the bat hath flown   40
His cloister'd flight; ere to black Hecate's summons
The shard-born beetle, with his drowsy hums,

42. shard-born] *F 3;* shard-borne *F 1, 2.*

of their lives by Banquo and Fleance under Nature as "lady of the manor" would cease with their deaths. But Clarkson and Warren in an exhaustive discussion of the passage (*M.L.N.* lv. pp. 483-93) argue that copyholds were not subject to arbitrary termination; that Shakespeare does not specifically refer to copy of court-roll; and that elsewhere he never uses the terms copyhold or copy of court roll at all; and that by *copy* he invariably means (i) a thing to be copied, or (ii) the result of imitation, or some variation thereof. Shakespeare, perhaps, used the legal term inaccurately; and there is another legal metaphor, 50 *post;* but I agree in the main with Clarkson and Warren, and only add that the *legal* sense of *copy* may be an undertone of the passage. Kittredge compares Massinger, *Fatal Dowry,* iv. i. "Nature's copy that she works form by," and *Oth.* v. ii. 11.

39. *There's*] i.e. in that there is.

39. *comfort*] Cf. i. ii. 27 *ante.*

40. *jocund*] a revealing adjective.

41. *cloister'd*] It may be used either literally or metaphorically.

41. *black Hecate*] As Shakespeare was aware (cf. *A.Y.L.I.* iii. ii. 2) Hecate is properly another name for Diana and Luna, so that "black" might seem to be an inappropriate epithet. Cf. "pale" (ii. i. 52). But already in *M.N.D.* (v. i. 391) Shakespeare had described Hecate almost as a personification of Night, and "black" also suggests *evil* as well as *dark.*

42. *shard-born*] i.e. dung-bred (*O.E.D.*) though most editors still interpret as "borne on scaly wings."

Either meaning would suit *A.C.* iii. ii. 20, though the latter is more appropriate to *Cym.* iii. iii. 20 and, perhaps, to the present context. It may be another quibble. Baldwin, *Shakespeare's Small Latine,* i. 635, supports *O.E.D.* Cuningham quotes a passage from Mouffet, *The Theater of Insects,* on the tree-beetle: "Some there are which fly about with a little *humming;* some with a terrible & with a formidable noise . . . but their breeding in *dung,* their feeding, life, and delight in the same, this is common to them all . . . especially in the moneths of *July* and *August,* after Sun-set, for then it flyeth giddily in men's faces with a great *humming.* . . . We call them *Dorrs* in English. . . . The sheaths of their wings are of a light red colour . . . in . . . 1574 . . . there fell such a multitude of them into the River *Severn,* that they slopt and clog'd the wheels of the Water-mils."

42. *beetle*] Armstrong, *Shakespeare's Imagination,* pp. 18-24, shows that the word belongs to an image cluster including *crow* (50), *bat* (40), *night* (43), and *deed* (44). Cf. *Lear,* iv. vi. 13-38.

42. *hums*] Armstrong, *op. cit.* pp. 44-5, shows that after *cir.* 1600 this word appears in close proximity to death. Cf. iii. vi. 42 and iv. iii. 203 *post.* Also *Hen. V.* i. ii. 202-4, where "yawning" is used:

"The sad-eyed justice, with his
              surly hum,
Delivering o'er to executors pale
The lazy yawning drone."

Armstrong might have added that "executors pale" may be compared with "that great bond which keeps me pale" (49-50 *post*).

Hath rung Night's yawning peal, there shall be done
A deed of dreadful note.
Lady M.   What's to be done?
Macb. Be innocent of the knowledge, dearest chuck,   45
Till thou applaud the deed.   Come, seeling Night,
Scarf up the tender eye of pitiful Day,
And, with thy bloody and invisible hand,
Cancel, and tear to pieces, that great bond
Which keeps me pale!—Light thickens; and the
crow   50

43-4.] *so Rowe; lines end* Peale, note. *Ff.*   46. seeling] *Ff;* sealing
Rowe.   50-1.] *so Rowe; lines end* thickens, Wood: *Ff.*   50. pale]
Ff; paled *Hudson (conj. Staunton).*

43-4. Few editors have kept the Folio arrangement of these lines.

45. *dearest chuck*] a familiar term of endearment, in grim contrast to the intended murder of Banquo.

46. *seeling*] In the language of falconry to "seel" was to sew up the eyelids of a hawk by running a fine thread through them, in order to make her tractable. Cotgrave has: "Siller les yeux. *To seele, or sow vp, the eyelids; (and thence also) to hoodwinke, blinde, keepe in darknesse, depriue of sight.*" Cf. *Oth.* III. iii. 210 and *A.C.* III. xiii. 112. R. Walker, *op. cit.* chap. 5, remarks: "Macbeth is simultaneously seeling up the eye of nature and filling his whole body with darkness." The phrase "is the precise evil counterpart of the superficially similar injunction, if thine eye offend thee, pluck it out."

49. *Cancel . . . bond*] The legal metaphor was probably suggested by a concealed pun on *seeling*/sealing (46) and also by *copy* (38). Steevens compares *Rich. III.* IV. iv. 77:

"Cancel his bond of life, dear God, I pray," and *Cym.* v. iv. 27:
        "Take this life,
And cancel these cold bonds."

Macbeth means "Cancel the bond by which Banquo and Fleance hold their lives from Nature" (New Clar.). Some think he refers to the promise

of the Weird Sisters to Banquo, but this, in view of the above quotations and 38, is unlikely.   Keightley thought "bond" should be printed "band" to rhyme with "hand." Cf. "The bands of life" (*Rich. II.* II. ii. 71).   I am inclined to agree.

50. *pale*] Staunton's impression was that this should be *paled*, on the ground that the context required a word implying *restraint, abridgement of freedom*, etc., rather than *dread;* and there is something to be said for this view. Cf. III. iv. 23 *post.* Wilson points out that "paled" would develop another aspect of "bond" and "only involves a simple *e : d* misprint." Shakespeare used the word in *Cym.* III i. 19. But, on the other hand, the word "pale" may have been suggested by the parchment. Cf. IV. i. 84-5 ("bond of fate . . . pale-hearted fear") and note of 42 *ante.* Curry, *Shakespeare's Philosophical Patterns,* p. 127, says that Macbeth "recognizes that the acts of conscience which torture him are really expressions of that outraged natural law, which inevitably reduces him as individual to the essentially human. This is the inescapable bond that keeps him pale."

50. *thickens*] Malone compares Spenser, *Shep. Cal.,* March, 115: "the welkin thicks apace."

Makes wings to th' rooky wood;
Good things of Day begin to droop and drowse,
Whiles Night's black agents to their preys do rouse.
Thou marvell'st at my words: but hold thee still;
Things bad begun make strong themselves by ill.   55
So, pr'ythee, go with me.   [*Exeunt.*

SCENE III.—*The same. A park, with a road leading to
the palace.*

Enter three Murderers.

1 *Mur.* But who did bid thee join with us?
3 *Mur.*   Macbeth.
2 *Mur.* He needs not our mistrust; since he delivers
Our offices, and what we have to do,
To the direction just.

Scene III—S.D.] *The same . . . palace.*] Rowe. subst.

50. *crow*] i.e. the rook: the carrion crow is not gregarious.

51. *Makes . . . wood*] Cuningham thought that "some words, the last rhyming with *crow*, have been carelessly omitted . . . either 'all on a row' or 'in due arow'." Few would agree.

51. *rooky*] i.e. black and filled with rooks. There have, however, been many attempts to save Shakespeare from writing this excellent line, which is regarded as tautological —"murky" (Roderick), "roky" = misty (various), "rouky" = perching, i.e. where the crow settles for the night (Cuningham), "reeky" = steamy (Wilson), "rooky" = foggy, misty (Scots and northern dial.), "rouky" = chattering (from "rouk", talk privately), "rucky" (from "ruck") = multitudinous. With the last two suggestions, cf. Meredith, *Modern Love*, "multitudinous chatterings."

52. *Good . . . drowse*] "the motto of the entire tragedy" (Dowden).

53. *Night's . . . rouse*] Steevens quotes Sidney, *Astrophel and Stella*, xcvi. 10: "In night, of Sprites the

ghastly powers do stir"; and Ascham, *Toxophilus* (ed. Arber, p. 52): "For on the nighte tyme & in corners, Sprites and theues, rattes and mise, toodes and oules . . . and noysome beastes, vse mooste styrringe, when in the dayelyght, and in open places whiche he ordenyed of God for honeste thynges, they darre not ones come, which thinge Euripides noted verye well, sayenge, *Il thinges the night, good thinges the daye doth haunt & vse.*" The quotation is from *Iphig. in Taur.* 1027.

55. *Things . . . ill*] Wilson compares Seneca, *Agam.* 115: "per scelera semper sceleribus tutum est iter" ("The safest path to mischiefe is by mischiefe open still"—Studley).

56. *So . . . me*] Either "consent to my design" or "a mere exit note" (Chambers). But cf. 45 *ante*, which implies that Macbeth is not asking his wife's advice. See on this speech Empson, *op. cit.* pp. 23-5.

Scene III

Enter three Murderers] Johnson here remarks: "The *perfect spy*

1 *Mur.*   Then stand with us.
The west yet glimmers with some streaks of day;   5
Now spurs the lated traveller apace,
To gain the timely inn; and near approaches
The subject of our watch.

3 *Mur.*   Hark! I hear horses.

Ban. [*Within.*] Give us a light there, ho!

2 *Mur.*   Then 'tis he: the rest
That are within the note of expectation,   10
Already are i' th' court.

1 *Mur.*   His horses go about.

3 *Mur.* Almost a mile; but he does usually,
So all men do, from hence to the palace gate
Make it their walk.

Enter BANQUO, *and* FLEANCE, *with a torch.*

2 *Mur.*   A light, a light!

3 *Mur.*   'Tis he.

1 *Mur.* Stand to 't.   15

6. lated] latest *F 2, 3, 4.*   7. and] *F 2;* end *F 1.*   9-10. Give . . .
expectation] *lines end* hee: expectation, *Ff.*   9. 'tis] *Ff;* it is *Pope, Arden*
(*ed. 1*).

mentioned by Macbeth in the fore-
going scene has, before they enter
upon the stage, given them the
directions which were promised at
the time of their agreement; yet one
of the murderers suborned, suspects
him of intending to betray them;
the other observes that, by his
exact knowledge of *what they were to
do* he appears to be employed by
Macbeth, and needs not to be mis-
trusted." It has been argued that
the Third Murderer was Macbeth
himself (*Notes and Queries,* 1869).
Irving thought he was the attendant
or servant mentioned in III. i.
(*Nineteenth Century,* 1877). Libby
thought he was Rosse (*New Notes
on Macbeth*). Another critic thought
he was Destiny. These theories are
all fantastic. Macbeth's agitation in
III. iv. when he hears that Fleance
has escaped is proof that he cannot

have been present at the murder of
Banquo. Shakespeare, as Wilson
suggests, introduces the Third Murderer to show that Macbeth, " tyrantlike, feels he must spy even upon his
chosen instruments."

2. *He . . . mistrust*] i.e. we need
not distrust him.

4. *to . . . just*] Exactly according
to Macbeth's instructions.

4-8. " The lovely lines . . . are
not gutter-bred " (Granville-Barker,
Preface, p. li). But " it is . . .
dangerous to speak of certain characters as being more 'poetic' than
others: in poetic drama every one
necessarily speaks poetry." (Bethell,
*Shakespeare and the Popular Dramatic
Tradition,* p. 65.)

6. *lated*] belated.

7. *timely*] in good time.

10. *note of expectation*] list of expected guests.

Ban. It will be rain to-night.

1 *Mur.*   Let it come down.

[*The First Murderer strikes out the light, while the others
                                    assault Banquo.*

Ban. O, treachery! Fly, good Fleance, fly, fly, fly!
     Thou may'st revenge—O slave! [*Dies. Fleance escapes.*
3 *Mur.* Who did strike out the light?
1 *Mur.*   Was't not the way?
3 *Mur.* There's but one down: the son is fled.
2 *Mur.*   We have lost   20
     Best half of our affair.
1 *Mur.* Well, let's away,
     And say how much is done.   [*Exeunt.*

           SCENE IV.—*A room of state in the palace.*

     A banquet prepared.   Enter MACBETH, LADY MACBETH,
           ROSSE, LENOX, *Lords, and Attendants.*

Macb. You know your own degrees, sit down: at first
     And last, the hearty welcome.
Lords.   Thanks to your Majesty.
Macb. Ourself will mingle with society,
     And play the humble host.
     Our hostess keeps her state; but, in best time,   5
     We will require her welcome.

16. S.D.] *Wilson, subst.*   17. O . . . fly!] *one line, Hanmer;*
two lines, divided after Trecherie *Ff.*   17 good] godd *F 2.*   18. S.D.]
Pope; not in Ff.   21-2. Well . . . done] *one line Ff.*

                    Scene IV

     S.D. *A room . . . palace.*] *Capell, subst.*   1-2. You . . .
welcome] *so Capell (conj. Johnson); lines end* downe: welcome. *Ff; lines end*
last majesty *Delius, Arden (ed. 1).*   1. at] to *conj. Johnson* down: at first]
down at first *conj. Johnson.*   5. best] *F 1;* the best *F 2, 3, 4.*

18. *Fleance escapes*] The turning
point of the play.

                    Scene IV

1-2. *at . . . last*] i.e. from beginning
to end. Cf. *1 Hen. VI.* v. v. 102 and
Cym I. iv. 102.
     5. *state*] originally the canopy,

then the chair of state with a canopy.
Cotgrave has "Dais or Daiz. A
*cloth of Estate, Canopie, or Heauen, that
stands ouer the heads of Princes thrones;
also, the whole State, or seat of Estate.*"
     6. *require*] request, not with the
modern meaning of demanding as
of right.

Lady M. Pronounce it for me, Sir, to all our friends;
For my heart speaks, they are welcome.

Enter first Murderer, to the door.

Macb. See, they encounter thee with their hearts' thanks.
Both sides are even: here I'll sit i' th' midst.   10
Be large in mirth; anon, we'll drink a measure
The table round.   [*Goes to door.*
There's blood upon thy face.
Mur.   'Tis Banquo's then.
Macb. 'Tis better thee without, than he within.
Is he dispatch'd?
Mur.   My Lord, his throat is cut; 15
That I did for him.
Macb.   Thou art the best o' th' cut-throats;
Yet he's good that did the like for Fleance:
If thou didst it, thou art the nonpareil.

12-13. The table . . . then] *lines end* face. then. *Ff etc.*   14. he] him
Hanmer.   15-19.] *lines end* dispatch'd? him. Cut-throats, Fleans: Non-
pareill. Sir scap'd *Ff; lines end* dispatch'd? him. good, it, Sir, scap'd. *Rowe.*

10. *Both . . . even*] i.e. there are
equal numbers on both sides of the
table. But it has been suggested
that the phrase might mean, "Lady
Macbeth's welcome has now been
answered by the guests' thanks, so
that both parties are now on a
level, *quits*."
    11. *large*] liberal, free. Cf. *A.C.*
III. vi. 93: "most large In his
abominations."
    13. *There's . . . face*] Absurd from
a naturalistic point of view, but
proper to a murderer in a poetic
play. In previous editions these
words are printed as part of the
previous line; but it is better to
have the metrical gap before these
words than after. A pause is necessary while Macbeth goes to the
door, and one is undesirable either
before or after the speech of the
murderer.
    14. *'Tis . . . within*] "I am more
pleased that the blood of Banquo
should be on thy face than in his

body" (Johnson). Hunter thinks
the words are an aside, meaning,
"It is better that the murderer
should be without the banquet than
that Banquo should be inside as a
guest"; but there is no effective
antithesis unless we construe: "the
blood is better outside thee than
inside him."
    15-19. *Is . . . 'scap'd*] This arrange-
ment of the lines eliminates the
superfluous break after *dispatch'd*,
preserves the Folio lineation in
Macbeth's speech (16-18) which
Rowe and later editors have abandoned, emphasizes *I* (16), *he* (17),
and *thou* (18), and provides an
effective pause of embarrassment
before the murderer can bring out
his confession of failure (19). This
is suggested in the Folio by printing
the line as two. But Flatter, *op. cit.*
p. 104, ends the lines with *nonpareil,
Sir, again.*
    18. *nonpareil*] paragon. Cf. *T.N.*
I. v. 273.

Mur. Most royal Sir . . . Fleance is scap'd.

Macb. Then comes my fit again: I had else been
     perfect;   20
  Whole as the marble, founded as the rock,
  As broad and general as the casing air:
  But now, I am cabin'd, cribb'd, confin'd, bound in
  To saucy doubts and fears.—But Banquo's safe?

Mur. Ay, my good Lord, safe in a ditch he bides,   25
  With twenty trenched gashes on his head;
  The least a death to nature.

Macb.   Thanks for that.—
  There the grown serpent lies; the worm, that's fled,
  Hath nature that in time will venom breed,
  No teeth for th' present.—Get thee gone; to-morrow   30
  We'll hear ourselves again.   [*Exit Murderer.*

Lady M.   My royal Lord,
  You do not give the cheer: the feast is sold,
  That is not often vouch'd, while 'tis a-making,
  'Tis given with welcome: to feed were best at home;
  From thence, the sauce to meat is ceremony;   35
  Meeting were bare without it.

20. Then . . . perfect; *so Pope; lines divided after* againe: *Ff.*   31. We'll
Well *F 3.*   31. hear ourselves] *F;* hear't, ourselves, *Theobald;* hear
ourselves *Steevens;* hear, ourselves, *Dyce.*   32. sold] cold *Pope.*   33. vouch'd]
vouched *Rowe.*   a-making,] *Hudson;* a making: *F 1;* making *F 2, 3, 4.*

20. *perfect*] Cf. III. i. 107.

21. *founded*] immoveable. Cf. *Matt.*
vii. 25.

22. *broad and general*] free and
unrestrained.

22. *casing*] surrounding.

23. *cribb'd*] shut in a hovel.

24. *saucy*] insolent, importunate.

24, 25. *safe*] Cf. III. v. 32-3.

26. *trenched*] cut.

27. *a death to nature*] enough to
kill a man (New Clarendon).

28. *worm*] serpent. Cf. *A.C.* v. ii.
243.

31. *hear . . . again*] i.e. hear each
other again, when I shall receive
a more detailed account of the affair,
and you will get your promised
reward. R. Walker, *op. cit.* chap. 5,
says, "this plural royalty will hear

himself when he hears the murderers
again; murderers and 'ourselves'
are one."

32-4. *the feast . . . welcome*] That
feast can only be considered as
sold, not given, during which the
entertainers omit such courtesies as
may assure their guests that it is
given with welcome (Dyce).

33. *vouch'd*] "warranted," "re-
commended by words of welcome."
Cf. III. i. 119.

35. *From thence*] i.e. away from
home.

35. *ceremony*] a trisyllable, as frequently in Shakespeare. Marston,
Sophonisba, I. ii. 5-27, has a discussion
on the value of ceremony, which
may either have suggested this
passage or been suggested by it.

Macb.   Sweet remembrancer!—
Now, good digestion wait on appetite,
And health on both!
Len.   May it please your Highness sit?
Macb. Here had we now our country's honour roof'd,
Were the grac'd person of our Banquo present;   40

The Ghost of BANQUO *enters, and sits in* MACBETH'S *place.*

Who may I rather challenge for unkindness,
Than pity for mischance!
Rosse.   His absence, Sir,
Lays blame upon his promise.   Please 't your Highness
To grace us with your royal company?
Macb. The table's full.
Len.   Here is a place reserv'd, Sir.   45
Macb. Where?
Len. Here, my good Lord.   What is't that moves your
    Highness?

40. S.D.] *Cf. note below; after* without it *(36) Ff.*   42. mischance!] *Pope;*
Mischance. *Ff.*   43. Please't] *Ff;* Please it *Steevens.*   47. Here . . .
Highness?] *so Capell; two lines, the first ending* Lord. *Ff.*

36. *remembrancer!*] Perhaps, as
Cuningham suggests, a playful reference to the Remembrancers, officers
of the Exchequer, of whom there
were three, i.e. The King's Remembrancer, the Lord Treasurer's Remembrancer, and the Remembrancer of First Fruits. But I can see
little resemblance between these
functionaries and Lady Macbeth
who reminds Macbeth of his duties
as host, and " remembrancer " probably means simply " one engaged
or appointed to remind another."
    39. *our . . . honour*] Not, as Wilson
suggests, " all the rank and distinction of Scotland," but Banquo.
    40. *grac'd*] gracious, gracing, or
full of grace. Cf. *Lear,* 1. iv. 267:
" a graced palace."
    40. S.D. *The Ghost . . . place*] The
Folio marks the entrance of the
Ghost after Lady Macbeth's last
speech. This may be either a pre-
mature direction to give plenty of
warning to the actor, or it may
merely indicate that on the Elizabethan stage the ghost would have
some distance to walk. According
to Forman's account the Ghost
entered as Macbeth began to speak
of Banquo. I have marked the
entrance accordingly. Wilson ad-
heres to the Folio entrance, other
editors have marked it at 43 and 45,
but the favourite place is after 39.
The Ghost appears when summoned.
    47. *Here . . . highness?*] Wilson
argues that F prints this line as two,
to mark the pause as Macbeth
recognizes the figure. Flatter, *op.
cit.* pp. 106-8, argues for the F
lineation, and remarks that by
printing " Where? " in a line by
itself, the pause comes here, thereby
obliterating the essential pause after
" Here, my good Lord "—which, in
a modern edition, should be printed
as part of line 46. There is another
pause after " highness? "

Macb. Which of you have done this?

Lords.   What, my good Lord?

Macb. Thou canst not say, I did it: never shake
    Thy gory locks at me.   50

Rosse. Gentlemen, rise; his Highness it not well.

Lady M. Sit, worthy friends.   My Lord is often thus,
    And hath been from his youth: pray you, keep seat;
    The fit is momentary; upon a thought
    He will again be well.   If much you note him,   55
    You shall offend him, and extend his passion;
    Feed, and regard him not.—Are you a man?

Macb. Ay, and a bold one, that dare look on that
    Which might appal the Devil.

Lady M.   O proper stuff!
    This is the very painting of your fear: 60
    This is the air-drawn dagger, which, you said,
    Led you to Duncan.   O! these flaws and starts
    (Impostors to true fear), would well become
    A woman's story at a winter's fire,
    Authoris'd by her grandam.   Shame itself!   65
    Why do you make such faces?   When all's done,
    You look but on a stool.

Macb.   Pr'ythee, see there!
    Behold! look! lo! how say you?

---

63. Impostors to true] *F;* Impostors of true *Hanmer;* Impostures true to
conj. Johnson; Impostures of true *Capell.*   67-8. Pr'ythee . . . you?] *so Ff;*
one line, Capell.

48. *done this*] i.e. killed Banquo.

49. *Thou . . . it*] " He has had some
strange childish notion that the
second murder would not afflict his
conscience if he did not wet his own
hands in Banquo's blood " (Grierson).

54. *upon a thought*] in a moment.
Cf. *Temp.* IV. i. 164.

56. *extend his passion*] i.e. prolong
his suffering or emotion.

59. *stuff!*] Curry, *Shakespeare's Philosophical Patterns*, p. 85, thinks
" Banquo's ghost is an infernal illusion created out of air by demonic
forces and presented to Macbeth's
sight at the banquet in order that the
murderer may be confused and utterly

confounded." But this is questionable.   See Introduction, p. lxxi.

61. *air-drawn*] drawn on the air,
or drawn through the air, or both
(Wilson).

62. *flaws*] sudden squalls or gusts
of wind, hence bursts of passion.
Cf. *Ham.* v. i. 239 and *2 Hen. VI,*
III. i. 354.

63. *to*] i.e. compared with.

65. *Authoris'd*] sanctioned, war-
ranted, given on the authority of.
The accent is on the second syllable.
Cf. *Sonnet,* xxxv. 6.

67-8. *You . . . you?*] There seems
to be no point in altering the Folio
division of these lines.

Why, what care I ?   If thou canst nod, speak too.—
If charnel-houses and our graves must send   70
Those that we bury, back, our monuments
Shall be the maws of kites.   [*Ghost disappears.*
Lady M.   What! quite unmann'd in folly?

71-2. *monuments . . . kites*] Wilson
quotes Scot, *The Discouerie of Witchcraft*, v. vi.: " Some write that
after the death of Nabuchadnezzar
his sonne Eilusmorodath gave his
bodie to the ravens to be devoured,
least afterwards his father should
arise from death." The meaning
would thus be: " To prevent
bodies from returning from the
grave, we shall have to give them
to the ravens to be devoured " (cf.
Nashe, ed. McKerrow iii. 281).

There seems to be no substance in
Harry Rowe's explanation that the
food of carnivorous birds was vulgarly
supposed to pass their stomachs undigested, the clause therefore meaning: " Our monuments will be like
the maws of kites in that they send
back those that we bury *undigested*."
But Harting, *Ornithology of Shakespeare*,
p. 46, mentions the kite's habit of disgorging the undigested portions of
food; and Miss Dorothy Sasse calls
my attention to Whitney, *Choice of
Emblemes*, 1586, p. 170, where the
emblem represents two kites, one of
which is disgorging " what appears
to be a knotted snake." Underneath
are the following verses:—
" The greedie kyte, so full his
            gorge had cloy'de,
    He could not brooke his late
            deuoured praie:
    Wherefore with griefe, vnto his
            damme he cry'de,
    My bowelles lo, alas, doe waste
            awaie.
        With that quoth shee, why
            doste thou make thy mone,
        This losse thou haste is noth-
            inge of thy owne.
    By which is mente, that they
        who liue by spoile,

By rapine, thefte, or griping
        goodes by mighte,
If that with losse they suffer
        anie foile,
They loose but that, where
        in they had no right!
    Hereof, at firste the prouerbe
        oulde did growe:
    *That goodes ill got, awaie as ill
        will goe.*"

Shakespeare may have unconsciously
remembered these verses about ill-
gotten gains, though I believe
Wilson's explanation is correct. For
the idea of a grave as a maw, compare *R.J.* v. iii. 45 ff.:
" Thou detestable maw . . .
    Gorg'd with the dearest morsel
        of the earth,
    Thus I enforce thy rotten jaws
        to open;
    And, in despite, I'll cram thee
        with more food."

Armstrong, *Shakespeare's Imagination*,
pp. 11-17, shows that " kite " belonged to a cluster of ideas in the
poet's mind, and that *bed*, *death*,
spirits, *birds*, and *food* were likely to
be mentioned in the same context.
Cf. *Ham.* II. ii. 595-620 and *W.T.*
IV. iii. 5-57. In the present context
we have *sleep* (141), *monuments* (71),
ghost (72), *birds* (124), *feed* (57),
and *maw* (72). Steevens compares
Spenser, *Faerie Queene*, II. viii. 16:

" But be entombed in the rauen
        or the Kight ";
and Malone cites Kyd, *Cornelia*,
v. i. 33-6:

" Where are our Legions ? . . .
        the vultures and the Crowes,
    Lyons and Beares, are theyr
        best Sepulchers."

Macb. If I stand here, I saw him.
Lady M.   Fie! for shame!
Macb. Blood hath been shed ere now, i' th' olden time,
    Ere humane statute purg'd the gentle weal;   75
    Ay, and since too, murthers have been perform'd
    Too terrible for the ear: the time has been,
    That, when the brains were out, the man would die,
    And there an end; but now, they rise again,
    With twenty mortal murthers on their crowns,   80
    And push us from our stools. This is more strange
    Than such a murther is.
Lady M.   My worthy Lord,
    Your noble friends do lack you.
Macb.   I do forget.—
    Do not muse at me, my most worthy friends,
    I have a strange infirmity, which is nothing   85
    To those that know me. Come, love and health to all;
    Then, I'll sit down.—Give me some wine: fill full:—
    I drink to th' general joy o' th' whole table,
    And to our dear friend Banquo, whom we miss;
    Would he were here!

Re-enter Ghost.

           To all, and him, we thirst,   90
  And all to all.
Lords.   Our duties, and the pledge.
Macb. Avaunt! and quit my sight! let the earth hide thee!

---

75. humane] *Ff;* human *Theobald (ed. 2), etc.*   76. have] hath *Johnson,*
77. time has] *Grant White;* times has *F 1;* time have *F 2, 3, 4.*

75. *humane*] Not distinguished in Shakespeare's day from *human*, and as the word may here imply both meanings, it is better to retain F spelling. Cf. *Cor.* III. i. 327:

  " It is the humane way; the other course
    Will prove too bloody."

See Empson, *op. cit.* p. 258.
75. *gentle weal*] " The *peaceable community,* the state made quiet and safe by human statutes " (Johnson). A proleptic use of the adjective, with the meaning " purged the commonwealth and thus made it gentle."

80. *mortal murthers*] i.e. deadly wounds, each of itself sufficient to effect murder. Cf. 26-7 *ante.*

90. S.D.] Grierson marks the Ghost's re-entry here. " He comes again when summoned." In the Folio the entrance is marked after 88, but cf. note on 40 *ante.*

91. *all to all*] i.e all good wishes to all. Cf. *Tim.* I. ii. 234: " All to you." Wilson suggests that the phrase means, " Let everybody drink to everybody."

Thy bones are marrowless, thy blood is cold;
Thou hast no speculation in those eyes,
Which thou dost glare with.
Lady M.   Think of this, good Peers,   95
But as a thing of custom: 'tis no other;
Only it spoils the pleasure of the time.
Macb. What man dare, I dare:
Approach thou like the rugged Russian bear,
The arm'd rhinoceros, or th' Hyrcan tiger;   100
Take any shape but that, and my firm nerves
Shall never tremble: or, be alive again,
And dare me to the desert with thy sword;
If trembling I inhabit then, protest me
The baby of a girl.   Hence, horrible shadow!   105

104. I inhabit then,] *F 1.;* I inhabit then *F 2, 3, 4;* I inhibit, then *Pope,*
Theobald, Hanmer, Warburton, Halliwell; I evade it, then *conj. Johnson;*
I inhibit then, *Capell;* I inhibit thee, *Malone (conj. Steevens), Dyce;* I exhibit,
then *A Hunter (conj. Robinson);* I inhabit here *conj. Camb.;* I inherit then,
conj. Kinnear; I, in habit then *conj. Jennens* protest] protect *F 4.*   105.
horrible] terrible *Theobald (ed. 2), Warburton, Johnson.*

94. *speculation*] i.e. the intelligence
arising in the brain but seen in the
eye, of which the eye is only the
medium, "intelligent or compre-
hending vision" (*O.E.D.*). Cf *T.C.*
III. iii. 107-11:
"but eye to eye opposed
Salutes each other with each
other's form;
For speculation turns not to itself,
Till it hath travell'd and is
mirror'd there
Where it may see itself."
See also *Oth.* I. iii. 271: "speculative
. . . instruments"; and Bullokar,
Expositor, 1616: "Speculation: the
inward knowledge or beholding of a
thing."
98. *What . . . dare*] This line
would seem to be merely a continuation of Macbeth's last speech, Lady
Macbeth's speech coming by way of
parenthesis. Flatter, *op. cit.* p. 110,
suggests that the Macbeths speak
simultaneously. This is improbable.

99-100. *bear . . . tiger*] Cf. *Hen. V.*
III. vii. 154: "Russian bear";
3 Hen. VI. I. iv. 155: "tigers of
Hyrcania." The Hircanian tiger and
the rhinoceros are mentioned on
adjacent pages of Holland's *Pliny.*
103. *dare*] Cf. *Rich. II.* IV. i. 74:
"I dare meet Surrey in a wilder-
ness"; i.e. for a fight to the death,
with none to interrupt. See also
Cor. IV. ii. 23 and *Cymb.* I. i. 167.
103. *desert*] Cf. *M.V.* II. vii. 41:
"Hyrcanian deserts."
104. *If . . . then*] Three possible
meanings: (i) If I inhabit, or house,
trembling (Wilson); (ii) if I trembling stay at home (Henley); (iii) if I
wear (in-habit) trembling (Maxwell).
105. *baby of a girl*] Not "baby of
an immature mother" (Clarendon),
but "girl's doll" cf. Bald. *S.A.B.,*
1949, pp. 220-2), or "baby girl"
(Harrison *ap.* Hudson). Cf. such a
phrase as "fool of a commentator."

Unreal mock'ry, hence!—   [*Ghost disappears.*

              Why, so;—being gone,

I am a man again.—Pray you, sit still.

Lady M. You have displac'd the mirth, broke the good
    meeting

With most admir'd disorder.

Macb.   Can such things be,

And overcome us like a summer's cloud,   110

Without our special wonder? You make me strange

Even to the disposition that I owe,

When now I think you can behold such sights,

And keep the natural ruby of your cheeks,

When mine is blanch'd with fear.   115

Rosse.   What sights, my Lord?

Lady M. I pray you, speak not; he grows worse and worse;

Question enrages him. At once, good night:—

Stand not upon the order of your going,

  But go at once.

Len.   Good night, and better health

Attend his Majesty!

Lady M. .   A kind good night to all!   120

                 [*Exeunt Lords and Attendants.*

Macb. It will have blood, they say: blood will have blood:

---

106. being gone,] be gone *F 3, 4.*   108-9. broke . . . disorder] *so Rowe;*
one line, *Ff.*   115. is] are *Malone.* sights,] *F 1;* signes *F 2, 3, 4.*
121. It . . . blood] *one line, Rowe; two lines, the first ending* say *Ff.* blood
they say: *Ff;* blood: they say, *Rowe;* blood, they say *Pope;* blood.—They
say, *Johnson.*

---

109. *admir'd*] wonderful, amaz-
ing.

109. *disorder*] " lack of self-control "
(Wilson); but there is an implied
reference to the overthrowing of
order—one of the main themes of
the play.

110. *overcome*] i.e. pass over.

111-12. *strange . . . owe*] i.e. self-
alienated or, perhaps, amazed at my
own nature. "He had thought
himself brave; now, when he sees
her unmoved at sights which appal
him, he is staggered in his estimate
of himself" (Grierson).

112. *owe*] own, as often.

115. *mine*] the natural ruby of my
cheeks.

121. *It*] i.e. the murder of Banquo.

121. *blood, they say: blood*] As
Simpson, *Shakespeare's Punctuation,* p.
78, points out, a colon often introduced a noun clause, so that the
Folio punctuation is best represented
by that of the text (Wilson). But
A. P. Rossiter argues convincingly
for the retention of F punctuation,
to preserve " the rhythm of terror."
Noble refers to *Gen.* ix. 6 and Wilson
to *Mirror for Magistrates,* ed. Campbell, p. 99: " Bloud wyll haue
bloud, eyther [at] fyrst or last."

Stones have been known to move, and trees to speak;
Augures, and understood relations, have
By magot-pies, and choughs, and rooks, brought forth
The secret'st man of blood.—What is the night?   125

123. Augures] *Ff;* Augurs *Theobald;* Auguries *Rann (conj. Steevens)* and understood] that understood *Rowe;* that understand *Warburton.*

122. *Stones*] Two possible explanations: (i) covering the corpse of the murdered man (Clar., Wilson); (ii) Paton, *Notes and Queries,* 1869, argues that this would only reveal the victim and not the murderer. (But the discovery of the corpse is the first step towards the detection of the murderer.) He suggests that the allusion may be to the rocking stones, or " stones of judgment," by which the Druids tested the guilt or innocence of accused persons. There is one near Glamis Castle, though there is no reason to believe that Shakespeare had heard of it.

122. *trees to speak*] Possibly a reminiscence of Scot, *Discouerie of Witchcraft* (1930), VIII. vi. p. 94: " This practice began in the Okes of Dodona, in the which was a wood, the trees thereof (they saie) could speake." Furness also quotes from the same work, XI. xviii. 119: " Divine auguries were such, as men were made beleeve were done miraculouslie, as when dogs spake; as at the expulsion of Tarquinius out of his kingdome; or when trees spake; as before the death of *Caesar.*" Furness adds a reference to *Georgics,* I. 476, where Virgil, speaking of the portents before that event, says:

" Vox quoque per lucos vulgo
     exaudita silentis Ingens "

Most editors, however, follow Steevens in assuming that there is a reference to *Aen.* iii. 22-68, the story of the ghost of Polydorus speaking from a tree.

123. *Augures*] i.e. auguries. In Florio's *Worlde of Wordes,* 1598, *augure* is given as an equivalent of *soothsaying, prediction.* In the 1611 edition, the word is also given as

an equivalent of *soothsayer.* Shakespeare uses the word *augury* twice, and *augurer* five times; but he also uses *augur (Son.* 107, and *Phoenix and the Turtle,* where it may mean either *soothsayer* or *omen).* Wilson thinks that *Augures* here may be a misprint for *Auguries,* but the metre is better without emendation.

123. *understood relations*] Not " reports properly comprehended " (Kittredge) or " overheard conversations " (*N.Q.* 2 Dec., 1933). Johnson explained: " the connection of effects with causes; to understand relations as an augur, is to know how those things relate to each other, which have no visible combination or dependence." This is more pointed than Schmidt's " incidents which were perceived to have reference to the question." Heath explains: " Those hidden ties by which every part of nature is linked and connected with every other part of it, in virtue whereof the whole of created nature, past, present, and to come, is truly and properly one." Cf. Appendix E.

124. *magot-pies*] i.e. magpies. (The Fr. *margot,* a familiar form of *Marguerite,* is also used to denote a magpie.)

124. *choughs*] The chough is a bird of the crow family, and the word formerly included all the smaller " chattering " species, and esp. the jackdaw. See *M.N.D.* III. ii. 21 (note in Arden ed.) and *Temp.* II. i. 265: " a chough of as deep chat."

125. *The . . . blood*] Wilson refers to a passage in James I.'s *Dæmonologie (Workes,* 1616, p. 136): " for as in a secret murther, if the dead carkasse bee at any time thereafter handled

Lady M. Almost at odds with morning, which is which.
Macb. How say'st thou, that Macduff denies his person,
    At our great bidding?
Lady M.   Did you send to him, Sir?
Macb. I heard it by the way; but I will send.
    There's not a one of them, but in his house   130
    I keep a servant fee'd.   I will to-morrow
    (And betimes I will) to the Weïrd Sisters:
    More shall they speak; for now I am bent to know,
    By the worst means, the worst.   For mine own good,
    All causes shall give way: I am in blood   135
    Stepp'd in so far, that, should I wade no more,
    Returning were as tedious as go o'er.
    Strange things I have in head, that will to hand,
    Which must be acted, ere they may be scann'd.

132. Weïrd] *Theobald;* weyard *F 1;* wizard *F 2, 3, 4;* wayward *Pope;* weird *Capell.*   134. worst. For . . . good] *Johnson;* worst, for . . . good, *Ff;* worst, for . . . good; *Rowe.*   136. Stepp'd] (Stept) *F 1;* Spent *F 2, 3, 4.*

by the murtherer, it will gush out of bloud, as if the bloud were crying to the heauen for reuenge of the murtherer, God hauing appoynted that secret supernaturall signe, for tryall of that secrete vnnaturall crime." Furness refers to Florio's *Montaigne,* II. v. (Temple ed., iii. 60).

126. *at odds with*] disputing with. Wilson comments: " A symbolical timing of the central moment of the play; borne out by the immediate reference to Macduff, who is to usher in the dawn."

127. *How say'st thou*] i.e. what do you say to this? Banquo being dead, Macbeth is driven towards the next murder.

130. *one*] Theobald conj. " thane " and White " man," but unnecessarily.

131. *fee'd*] Cf. Holinshed: " in euerie noble man's house one slie fellow or other in fee with him."

131-2. *I will . . . Sisters*] The Folio has the phrase " And betimes I will " in brackets; but Shakespeare perhaps intended the first

" I will " (131) to apply to his sending to Macduff, and it should be punctuated:

    " I will to-morrow:
And betimes I will to the weird
    sisters."

Wheelock, *Modern Language Notes,* xv, makes the same suggestion but since *betimes* means *very early* we do not remove the difficulty of the time sequence in this and the following scenes. But see Introduction, p. xxxvi.

135. *All . . . way*] i.e. everything else must take second place.

135. *I . . . blood*] Cf. *M.N.D.* III. ii. 47: " Being o'er shoes in blood, plunge in knee deep, And kill me too." And, closer, *Rich. III.* IV. ii. 63-4:

         " I am in
So far in blood that sin will pluck
    on sin."

138-9. *Strange . . . scann'd*] Cf. v. i. 145-8 *post.*

Lady M. You lack the season of all natures, sleep.   140
Macb. Come, we'll go to sleep.   My strange and self-abuse
    Is the initiate fear, that wants hard use:
    We are yet but young in deed.   [*Exeunt.*

SCENE V.—*The heath.*

Thunder.   Enter the three Witches, meeting HECATE.

1 *Witch.* Why, how now, Hecate? you look angerly.
Hec. Have I not reason, beldams as you are,
    Saucy, and overbold?   How did you dare
    To trade and traffic with Macbeth,   5
    In riddles, and affairs of death;
    And I, the mistress of your charms,
    The close contriver of all harms,
    Was never call'd to bear my part,
    Or show the glory of our art?
    And, which is worse, all you have done   10
    Hath been but for a wayward son,

144. in deed] *Theobald;* indeed *Ff.*

Scene v

1. Hecate? . . . angerly.] Hecat, . . . angerly? *Ff.*   2. are,] are?
Ff.   3. overbold?] over-bold, *Ff.*

140. *season*] Whiter, *Specimen of a Commentary,* etc., p. 147, showed that Shakespeare was thinking of the preservative power of sleep. Cf. *Luc.* 796, *M.A.* IV. i. 144, *T.C.* I. ii. 278, and *T.N.* I. i. 30.   Macbeth, it will be remembered, has murdered sleep.

141. *self-abuse*] deception, self-delusion.   Cf. II. i. 50.

142. *the initiate fear*] i.e. the fear of a novice (Grierson).

142. *hard use*] practice that hardens one (Kittredge).

143. *We . . . deed*] A " line which looks to nethermost hell " (Granville-Barker).

Scene v

This scene is probably not Shakespeare's.   See Introduction, p. xxxiii.
Hecate] The common pronunci-

ation of this name was dissyllabic, as in II. i. 52 and III. ii. 41 *ante;* and *M.N.D.* v. i. 391.   Shakespeare was possibly not responsible for the trisyllable in *1 Hen. VI.* III. ii. 64: " I speak not to that railing Hecate."

8-9. Nosworthy, *R.E.S.* Apr. 1948, argues that these lines were inserted to explain the interpolation and he explains " to bear my part " as " to take part in a previous performance."

11. *wayward son*] " We do not need Hecate to tell us that he is but a wayward son, who . . . loves for his own end. . . . Whatever he does is inevitably in pursuance of some apparent good, even though that apparent good is only temporal or nothing more than escape from a present evil " (Curry, *Shakespeare's Philosophical Patterns,* p. 131).

Spiteful, and wrathful; who, as others do,
Loves for his own ends, not for you.
But make amends now: get you gone,
And at the pit of Acheron　　　　　　　　　　15
Meet me i' th' morning: thither he
Will come to know his destiny.
Your vessels, and your spells, provide,
Your charms, and everything beside.
I am for th' air; this night I'll spend　　　　20
Unto a dismal and a fatal end:
Great business must be wrought ere noon.
Upon the corner of the moon
There hangs a vap'rous drop profound;
I'll catch it ere it come to ground:　　　　　25
And that, distill'd by magic sleights,
Shall raise such artificial sprites,
As, by the strength of their illusion,
Shall draw him on to his confusion.
He shall spurn fate, scorn death, and bear　　30
His hopes 'bove wisdom, grace, and fear;
And you all know, security
Is mortals' chiefest enemy.
　　　　　　[*Song within:* "Come away, come away," etc.

26. sleights,] *Collier;* slights, *Ff.*　27. raise] *F 1;* rise *F 2.*　33. S.D.]
Musicke, and a Song F.　*See 35.*

21. *dismal*] disastrous.

24. *vap'rous drop profound*] "This vaporous drop seems to have been meant for the same as the *virus lunare* of the ancients, being a foam which the moon was supposed to shed on particular herbs, or other objects, when strongly solicited by enchantment" (Steevens). Cf. Lucan, *Pharsalia,* VI. 669. profound = with deep or hidden qualities (Johnson), rather than " deep, and therefore ready to fall" (Clarendon).

32. *security*] i.e. over-confidence.

33. The song is to be found in Middleton, *The Witch,* III. iii. though this does not necessarily mean that he wrote the whole of this scene:—

" Come away, come away,
　Hecate, Hecate, come away!

Hec. I come, I come, I come, I come,
　With all the speed I may,
　With all the speed I may.
　Where's Stadlin?
Voice. Here.
Hec. Where's Puckle?
Voice. Here;
　And Hoppo too, and Hellwain too;
　We lack but you, we lack but you;
　Come away, make up the count.
Hec. I will but 'noint, and then I
　mount.
　　(*A Spirit like a cat descends.*
Voice. There's one comes down to
　fetch his dues,
　A kiss, a coll, a sip of blood;
　And why thou stay'st so long,
　　I muse, I muse,
　Since the air's so sweet and good.

Hark! I am call'd: my little spirit, see,   34
Sits in a foggy cloud, and stays for me.   [*Exit.*
1 *Witch.* Come, let's make haste: she'll soon be back again.
          [*Exeunt.*]

SCENE VI.—*Somewhere in Scotland.*

Enter LENOX *and another Lord.*

Len. My former speeches have but hit your thoughts,
Which can interpret farther: only, I say,
Things have been strangely borne.   The gracious
          Duncan
Was pitied of Macbeth:—marry, he was dead:—
And the right-valiant Banquo walk'd too late;   5

35. S.D. *Sing within . . . etc. F.   (See 33).*   36.] *two lines divided
after* be *Ff.*

Scene VI

1. My . . . thoughts,] *so Rowe; two lines, the first ending* Speeches, *Ff.*
5. right-valiant] *so Theobald;* right valiant *Ff.*

Hec. O, art thou come?
   What news, what news?
Spirit. All goes still to our delight:
   Either come, or else
   Refuse, refuse.
Hec. Now I'm furnish'd for the flight.
Fire. Hark, hark, the cat sings a
   brave treble in her own language!
Hec. (*going up*) Now I go, now I fly,
   Malkin my sweet spirit and I.
   O what a dainty pleasure 'tis
   To ride in the air
   When the moon shines fair,
   And sing and dance, and toy and
   kiss!
   Over woods, high rocks, and
   mountains,
   Over seas, our mistress' fountains,
   Over steep towers and turrets,
   We fly by night, 'mongst troops of
   spirits:
   No ring of bells to our ears sounds,
   No howls of wolves, no yelps of
   hounds;
   No, not the noise of water's
   breach,
   Or cannon's throat our height can
   reach.
(*Voices above*) No ring of bells, etc."

35. Hecate is taken up in the
cloud, i.e. a stage car, drawn up on
pulleys, and concealed by billowing
draperies (Wilson, who refers to
Adams, *The Globe Playhouse*, pp.
335-66).

Scene VI

The location of this scene seems
to be quite immaterial, but the conversation is unlikely to have taken
place in a room of the palace, which
was Capell's suggestion.   The scene
may have come originally after
IV. i.   See Introduction, p. xxxiv.

S.D. *another Lord*] Johnson suggested that the abbreviation *An.* (for
Angus) in the manuscript was
erroneously expanded by a transcriber into " another Lord." But
cf. the anonymity of the Old Man
in II. iv. *ante.*

3. *borne*] carried on. Cf. 17 *post,*
and *M.A.* II. iii. 229: " The conference was sadly borne," i.e. seriously conducted.

5. *walk'd too late*] Cf. Kyd, *Spanish
Tragedie,* III. iii. 39: (See *M.L.R.,* i.
54).

Whom, you may say (if 't please you) Fleance kill'd,
For Fleance fled.   Men must not walk too late.
Who cannot want the thought, how monstrous
It was for Malcolm, and for Donalbain,
To kill their gracious father? damned fact!   10
How it did grieve Macbeth! did he not straight,
In pious rage, the two delinquents tear,
That were the slaves of drink, and thralls of sleep?
Was not that nobly done?   Ay, and wisely too;
For 'twould have anger'd any heart alive   15
To hear the men deny 't.   So that, I say,
He has borne all things well: and I do think,
That, had he Duncan's sons under his key
(As, and 't please Heaven, he shall not), they should find

---

8. Who . . . the] You cannot want the *Hanmer;* We cannot want the
Keightley; Who can but want the *Collier (ed. 3);* Who can now want the
Hudson (1879. Conj. Cartwright).   11. Macbeth!] *Capell;* Macbeth? *Ff.*
14. not that] *F 1, 2;* that not *F 3, 4.*   18. his key] the key *F 2, 3, 4.*
19. and 't] *Ff;* an't *Theobald (ed. 2).* should] *F 1;* shall *F 2, 3, 4.*

"Why hast thou thus vnkindely
   kild the man?
Why? because he walkt abroad
   so late."
Ellis-Fermor suggests, privately, that
there is an undertone of meaning—
"lived too long."
  8. *want the thought*] i.e. help
thinking. Shakespeare must have
meant "can" and not "cannot";
but "this construction arises from a
confusion of thought common enough
when a negative is expressed or
implied" (Clarendon). But perhaps an ambiguity was intended, as
Empson suggests, *Seven Types of
Ambiguity,* 1930, p. 265: "Who *can*
avoid thinking, is the meaning; but
the *not* breaks through the irony into
'Who must not feel that they have
not done anything monstrous at all?'
'Who must not avoid thinking altogether about so touchy a state
matter?' This is not heard as the
meaning, however, the normal construction is too strong, and the negative acts as a sly touch of disorder."

  8. *monstrous*] probably a trisyllable,
though the dissyllable is much more
common in Shakespeare. Cf. I. v.
39 and III. ii. 30 *ante.*
  10. *fact*] act, deed. Invariably
used in Shakespeare in the sense of
"evil deed," "crime."
  12. *pious*] loyal.
  14. *Was . . . done*] Lenox apparently accepted Macbeth's story at
the time (cf. II. iii. 103); but he
may have changed his mind on
reflection, or perhaps he has been
substituted here for another character (cf. Introduction, p. xxxv), or
he may be regarded as a chorus,
rather than as a person of distinct
character. He is still serving Macbeth
in IV. i.
  17. *He . . . well*] cf. III. vi. 3 and
III. i. 80. He has managed things
successfully and cunningly.
  19. *and 't*] if it. See Abbott,
Shakespearean Grammar, § 101. Theobald's emendation to the more usual
form *an't* was unnecessary.
  19. *should*] would be sure to.

What 'twere to kill a father; so should Fleance.   20
But, peace!—for from broad words, and 'cause he fail'd
His presence at the tyrant's feast, I hear,
Macduff lives in disgrace.   Sir, can you tell
Where he bestows himself?

Lord.   The son of Duncan,
From whom this tyrant holds the due of birth,   25
Lives in the English court; and is receiv'd
Of the most pious Edward with such grace,
That the malevolence of fortune nothing
Takes from his high respect.   Thither Macduff
Is gone to pray the holy King, upon his aid   30
To wake Northumberland, and warlike Siward;
That, by the help of these (with Him above
To ratify the work), we may again
Give to our tables meat, sleep to our nights,
Free from our feasts and banquets bloody knives,   35
Do faithful homage, and receive free honours,
All which we pine for now.   And this report
Hath so exasperate the King, that he
Prepares for some attempt of war.

Len.   Sent he to Macduff?

Lord. He did: and with an absolute " Sir, not I,"   40
The cloudy messenger turns me his back,

---

21. 'cause] *Pope;* cause *Ff.*   24. son] *Theobald;* Sonnes *Ff.*   26. Lives]
Live *F 2, 3, 4.*   31. Siward] *Theobald* (ed. 2), *Hanmer;* Seyward *Ff.*   38.
the] *Hanmer;* their *Ff.*

21. *broad*] open, plain. Cf. *Tim.*
III. iv. 64.

21. *fail'd*] Cf. III. iv. 127 *ante.*

22. *tyrant's*] " usurper's " (Clarendon); " Not *usurper's* but a bloodthirsty king's " (Wilson). I think
both senses are implied.

27. *Of*] by. Cf. III. vi. 4 *ante.*

30. *Is gone*] Perhaps, as Cuningham and others suggest, these words
ought to be printed at the end of the
previous line.

30. *upon his aid*] in his behalf.

35. *Free . . . knives*] i.e. free our
feasts and banquets from bloody

knives. Cf. *Temp.* Epil. 18: " frees
all faults," i.e. frees me from all
faults.

36. *free*] not bought by servility
and crime, but enjoyed in freedom.

38. *exasperate*] Cf. *T.C.* v. i. 34:
" Why art thou then exasperate? "
See Abbott, *Shaks. Gram.* §§ 341-2.

38. *the*] their—F. Presumably the
printer thought the king referred to
was Edward the Confessor.

40. *absolute.*] curt, peremptory. Cf.
Cor. III. i. 90.

41. *cloudly*] cloudy-visaged, sullen.
Cf. *1 Hen. IV.* III. ii. 83.

And hums, as who should say, " You 'll rue the time
That clogs me with this answer."
Len.   And that well might
Advise him to a caution, t' hold what distance
His wisdom can provide.   Some holy Angel   45
Fly to the court of England, and unfold
His message ere he come, that a swift blessing
May soon return to this our suffering country
Under a hand accurs'd!
Lord.   I'll send my prayers with him.
                                      [*Exeunt.*

44. caution, t'hold] *Ff;* caution, to hold *Camb.*

42. *hums*] cf. note on III. ii. 42.
43. *clogs*] The messenger knows he
will suffer for the bad tidings. Cf.
the reception of the messengers later
in the play, v. iii. 11 and v. v. 35.
44. *Advise . . . t'hold*] Cf. *Lear*, I. ii.
188: " I advise you to the best "
and *ib.* III. vii. 9.

48-9. *suffering . . . Under*] i.e.
country suffering under. Cf. *Rich.
II.* III. ii. 8: " As a long-parted
mother with her child."   Or " Under
a hand accurs'd " may be a kind of
relative clause, with " which is "
understood.

ACT IV

SCENE I.—*A dark cave. In the middle, a boiling cauldron. Thunder. Enter the three* Witches.

1 *Witch.* Thrice the brinded cat hath mew'd.
2 *Witch.* Thrice, and once the hedge-pig whin'd.
3 *Witch.* Harpier cries:—'Tis time, 'tis time.
1 *Witch.* Round about the cauldron go;
    In the poison'd entrails throw.—   5

ACT IV

Scene 1

S.D.] *Rowe, subst.*   2. hedge-pig] Hedges Pigge *F 2, 3, 4.*
5. throw.] *Rowe;* throw *Ff.*

Scene 1

1. *the brinded cat*] the first sister's familiar. Cf. " Graymalkin," i. i. 8 *ante.* " Brinded," i.e. branded, as if with fire, streaked, is the Elizabethan form of " brindled." Milton, *Paradise Lost*, vii. 466 speaks of the lion's " brinded mane."

2. *Thrice, and once*] " The Second Witch only repeats the number which the First had mentioned, in order to confirm what she had said; and then adds, that the *hedge-pig* had likewise cried, though but once. Or what seems more easy, the hedge-pig had whined *thrice*, and after an interval had whined once again " (Steevens). Theobald quotes Virgil, *Eclog.* viii. 75, " Numero deus impare gaudet " and Elwin says that " as even numbers were considered inappropriate to magical operations, the Second Witch makes the *fourth* cry of the hedge-pig an odd number by her method of counting. She tells three, and then begins a new reckoning." Jonson, however, used

even numbers in his *Masque of Queenes*, ed. Herford and Simpson, vii. 300:

> " Thou shalt haue three, thou
>   shalt haue foure,
> Thou shalt haue ten, thou shalt
>   haue a score."

3. *Harpier*] the third sister's familiar. Steevens suggested it was a corruption of " Harpy " which appears in Marlowe, *I Tamb.* ii. vii. 50, as " Harpyr " (1590), " Harpye " (1592) and " Harper " (1605). Cuningham thinks that Shakespeare took the word from Spenser, *Faerie Queene*, ii. xii. 36: " The hellish Harpyes prophets of sad destiny." The suggestion that the word may be derived from the Hebrew *Habar*, mentioned in Scot, *Discouerie of Witchcraft*, xii. 1 (Clarendon) is over-ingenious. R. Walker cites *Aen.* iii. which contains a description of harpies.

3. *'Tis time*] Harpier cries, i.e. gives them the signal, and therefore it is time for them to begin.

Toad, that under cold stone
Days and nights has thirty-one
Swelter'd venom, sleeping got,
Boil thou first i' th' charmed pot.

All. Double, double toil and trouble: 10
Fire, burn; and, cauldron, bubble.

2 *Witch.* Fillet of a fenny snake,
In the cauldron boil and bake;
Eye of newt, and toe of frog,
Wool of bat, and tongue of dog,   15
Adder's fork, and blind-worm's sting,
Lizard's leg, and howlet's wing,
For a charm of powerful trouble,
Like a hell-broth boil and bubble.

---

6. cold] *Ff;* the cold *Rowe (ed. 2);* coldest *Steevens (1793);* a cold *conj.*
Staunton.   7. has] *F 3, 4;* ha's *F 1, 2;* hast *Capell.* thirty-one] *Capell;*
thirty one: *Ff.*   10, 20. Double, double] *Steevens;* Double, double, *Ff.*

6. *cold*] various superfluous attempts have been made to emend this line; but it is not even desirable to regard the word as a dissyllable. The juxtaposed stresses on *cold stone* make the stone colder than Steevens' *coldest.*

8. *Swelter'd*] exuded, like sweat (*O.E.D.*).

8. *venom*] Topsell, *History of Serpents* (ed. 1658, p. 730) says: "All manner of toads, both of the earth and of the water, are venomous, although it be held that the toads of the earth are more poysonful than the toads of the water. . . . But the toads of the land, which do descend into the marishes, and so live in both elements, are most venomous. . . . The women-witches of ancient time which killed by poysoning, did much use Toads in their confections." The secretion of the skin-glands of the toad contains a poisonous substance (phrynin) acrid enough to be felt on tongue or eyes, and serving to protect the toad.

12. *Fillet . . . snake*] i.e. a slice of snake from the fens. Furness

thinks there may also be a reference to the other meaning of fillet, *head-band*, and he compares Lucan, *Pharsal.* vi. 656: "Et coma vipereis substringitur horrida sertis." The line comes in a passage about a witch, only a few lines from the quotation given in the note to III. v. 24. *ante.*

16. *fork*] i.e. double tongue. Cf. *M.M.* III. i. 16.

16. *blind-worm's sting*] Cf. *M.N.D.* II. ii. 11 and *Tim.* IV. iii. 182: "The eyeless venom'd worm." Drayton, *Noah's Floud,* 481-4, ed. Hebel, iii. 339, mentions that

"The small-ey'd slowe-worme held of many blinde . . .
Out of its teeth shutes the in-venom'd slime."

Topsell, *History of Serpents,* p. 763, says, "it receiveth name from the blindnesse and deafness thereof. . . . It is harmless except being provoked . . . for the poyson thereof is very strong." It is now known that both the slow-worm and the newt are harmless.

All. Double, double toil and trouble.
　Fire, burn; and, cauldron, bubble.   20
3 *Witch.* Scale of dragon, tooth of wolf;
　Witches' mummy; maw, and gulf,
　Of the ravin'd salt-sea shark;
　Root of hemlock, digg'd i' th' dark;   25
　Liver of blaspheming Jew;
　Gall of goat, and slips of yew,
　Sliver'd in the moon's eclipse;
　Nose of Turk, and Tartar's lips;
　Finger of birth-strangled babe,   30
　Ditch-deliver'd by a drab,

23. Witches'] *Theobald (ed. 2);* Witches *Ff;* Witch's *Singer.*　28. Sliver'd]
Silver'd *Rowe (ed. 3).*

23. *mummy*] " Egyptian mummy, or what passed for it, was formerly a regular part of the *Materia Medica* " (Nares). Johnson mentions there were two substances for medical use, which went under the same name, " the dried flesh of human bodies embalmed with myrrh and spice " and " the liquor running from such mummies when newly prepared, or when affected by great heat." Cf. *Oth.* III. iv. 74. Wilson has an appropriate quotation from James I, *Dæmonologie,* p. 43.　The Devil " causeth them to joynt dead corpses, and to make powders thereof, mixing such other thinges there amongst, as he giues vnto them " (*Workes,* 1616, p. 116).

23. *gulf*] stomach, voracious appetite. Cf. *Cor.* I. i. 101. *O.E.D.* quotes Spenser, *Shepherd's Calendar,* Sept. 184-5:
　　" a wicked Wolfe
　That with many a Lambe had
　　glutted his gulfe."
24. *ravin'd*] " glutted with prey " (Steevens); the maw of a shark glutted with human flesh has the right note of horror. Other explanations: " Used for *ravenous,* the passive participle for the adj." (Malone, Chambers) and " used

rather for the active participle ravening " (Cuningham).
25. *dark*] The time when an herb was gathered was supposed to affect its potency (Kittredge).
27. *yew*] The yew, which grows freely in churchyards, was regarded as poisonous by the ancients, by writers in the Middle Ages and by Shakespeare's contemporaries. Douce quotes Batman *Uppon Bartholome,* xvii. 161: " yew is altogether venomous, and against man's nature. The birdes that eate the redde berryes, eyther dye, or cast theyr fethers." Cf. *Rich. II.* III. ii. 117: " double-fatal yew."
28. *Sliver'd*] cut or sliced off. Cf. *Lear,* IV. ii. 34; and *Ham.* IV. vii. 174. According to Craig the word is still used in dialect and in America.
28. *moon's eclipse*] " A most unlucky time for lawful enterprises, and therefore suitable for evil designs " (Clarendon).
29. *Nose . . . lips*] Turks and Tartars were not only regarded as types of cruelty, as in *M.V.* IV. i. 32 (Craig) but also like the Jew (26) and the birth-strangled babe (30) they were *unchristened,* and hence valued by the witches. (Wilson).
31. *drab*] prostitute.

Make the gruel thick and slab:
Add thereto a tiger's chaudron,
For th' ingredience of our cauldron.
All. Double, double toil and trouble: 35
Fire, burn; and, cauldron, bubble.
2 *Witch.* Cool it with a baboon's blood:
Then the charm is firm and good.

[*Enter* HECATE, *and the other three Witches.*]

Hec. O, well done! I commend your pains,
And every one shall share i' th' gains.   40
And now about the cauldron sing,
Like elves and fairies in a ring,
Enchanting all that you put in.
[*Music and a song,* " Black spirits," etc.
[*Exeunt Hecate and the three other Witches.*]

34. ingredience] *Ff;* ingredients *Rowe.* 38. S.D.] *Ff; Enter Hecate Ritson;*
Enter Hecate to the other three witches Globe.   43. *Exeunt . . . Witches*]
Hecate retires Globe; Hecate goes Wilson; not in Ff.

32. *slab*] thick.

33. *chaudron*] entrails. Cf. Dekker, *Honest Whore,* Part I, sc. vii.: " Sixpence a meale, wench, as well as heart can wish, with Calves chaldrons and chitterlings."

34. *ingredience*] Cf. I. vii. 11.

37. *baboon*] With the accent on the first syllable. Cf. *Per.* IV. vi. 189. Nosworthy suggests " babione."

38. *Enter Hecate and the other three Witches*] Probably the appearance of Hecate with three additional witches was a non-Shakespearean interpolation. Some have thought the S.D. should read " Enter Hecate *to* the other three Witches." Hecate was not a witch, but might have been regarded as such by book-keeper or printer. The three spurious witches were needed for the song and perhaps for the " antic round " (132 *post*).

39-43. *O . . . put in*] The metre changes and " Like elves and fairies " is manifestly spurious.

43. *song*] It is given in *The Witch,* v. ii.:

" *Hec.* Black spirits and white, red
    spirits and gray,
  Mingle, mingle, mingle, you
    that mingle may!
  Titty, Tiffin,
    keep it stiff in;
  Firedrake, Puckey,
    Make it lucky;
  Liard, Robin,
    You must bob in.
Round, around, around, about
    about!
All ill come running in, all good
    keep out!
1 Witch. Here's the blood of a bat.
Hec. Put in that, O put in that!
2 Witch. Here's libbard's-bane.
Hec. Put in again!
1 Witch. The juice of toad, the oil
    of adder.
2 Witch. Those will make the
    younker madder.
Hec. Put in—there's all—and rid
    the stench.
Fire. Nay, here's three ounces of
    the red-hair'd wench.
All the Witches. Round, around,
    around, etc."

2 *Witch.* By the pricking of my thumbs,   44
      Something wicked this way comes.—   [*Knocking.*
      Open, locks,
      Whoever knocks.

Enter MACBETH.

Macb. How now, you secret, black, and midnight hags!
      What is't you do?
All.   A deed without a name.
Macb. I conjure you, by that which you profess,   50
      Howe'er you come to know it, answer me:
      Though you untie the winds, and let them fight
      Against the Churches; though the yesty waves
      Confound and swallow navigation up;
      Though bladed corn be lodg'd, and trees blown down;
      Though castles topple on their warders' heads;   56

46-7.] *two lines, Dyce; one line, Ff.*

It is to be hoped that this song was altered for *Macbeth*, as some lines are relevant only to the plot of Middleton's play. But the 1673 edition of *Macbeth* prints them without alteration. No exit is marked for Hecate and the spurious witches; but the sooner they depart the better. In the illustration of this scene in Rowe's edition, there are only three witches remaining at 112 *post*, though in Davenant's version Hecate speaks 125-32.

44. Shakespeare again.

44. *pricking*] " It is a very ancient superstition that all sudden pains of the body, which could not naturally be accounted for, were presages of somewhat that was shortly to happen " (Steevens).

48. *black . . . hags*] i.e. who practised the Black Art.

50. *conjure*] Here, as usually, with the accent on the first syllable.

50. *that . . . profess*] i.e. the Black Art.

51. *Howe'er . . . it*] e.g. by making a pact with the Devil.

52. *winds*] Scot, *The Discouerie of Witchcraft*, 1930, p. 1, says: " Such faithlesse people (I saie) are also

persuaded, that neither haile nor snowe, thunder nor lightening, raine nor tempestuous winds come from the heauens at the commandement of God; but are raised by the cunning and power of witches and conjurors."

53. *Against the Churches*] symbolically, as well as literally.

53. *yesty*] foaming, frothy, in a ferment. Cf. *Ham.* v. ii. 186; and *W.T.* III. iii. 94.

55. *bladed corn*] Scot, *Discouerie of Witchcraft*, p. 6, tells us that witches were thought to be able to " transferre corne in the blade from one place to another." Comenius, *Janua Linguarum*, 1673, ch. 32 (cited by Staunton) says: " As soon as standing corn shoots up to a blade, it is in danger of scathe by a tempest."

55. *lodg'd*] laid, beaten down. Cf. *2 Hen. VI.* III. ii. 176 and *Rich. II.* III. iii. 163.

56. *Though . . . heads*] Cf. Seneca, *Agam.*, tr. Studley, Chor. 1 :

" What castell strongly buylt, what
      bulwarke, tower or towne,
   Is not by mischyefes meanes,
      brought topsy turuye downe? "

See note on v. iii. 45 *post*.

Though palaces, and pyramids, do slope
Their heads to their foundations; though the treasure
Of Nature's germens tumble all together,
Even till destruction sicken, answer me   60
To what I ask you.

1 *Witch.*   Speak.

2 *Witch.*   Demand.

3 *Witch.*   We'll answer.

1 *Witch.* Say, if thou 'dst rather hear it from our mouths,
Or from our masters?

Macb.   Call 'em; let me see 'em.

1 *Witch.* Pour in sow's blood, that hath eaten
Her nine farrow; grease, that's sweaten   65

59. germens] *Globe; Germaine F 1, 2; germain F 3, 4; germen Delius;*
germains Pope; germins Theobald; german Elwin. all together] *Pope;*
altogether Ff.   62. thou'dst] *Capell; th' hadst Ff.*   63. masters?] *Pope;*
Masters. Ff; masters'? Capell.

57. *slope*] i.e. bend. Not used
elsewhere by Shakespeare. Capell
conj. " stoop," which, spelt " stope,"
might easily been misread.

59. *germens*] The collective form,
" germen," may be correct; but
cf. *Lear,* III. ii. 8: " Crack Nature's
moulds, all germens spill at once."
For the idea cf. *W.T.* IV. iv. 490:

" Let nature crush the sides o' th'
        earth together
And mar the seeds within."

Curry shows, *Shakespeare's Philo-*
sophical Patterns, pp. 31 ff., that
Nature's germens are the *rationes*
seminales, " the material essences
which correspond to the exemplars in
God's mind." He quotes Augustine,
De Trinitate; " But in truth, some
hidden seeds of all things that are
born corporeally and visibly, are
concealed in the corporeal elements
of this world. . . . For the Creator
of these invisible seeds is the Creator
of all things himself; since whatever
comes forth to our sight by being
born, receives the first beginnings of
its course from hidden seeds, and
takes the successive increments of its
proper size and its distinctive forms

from these as it were original rules."
Cf. note to I. iii. 58 *ante.* By being
willing to tumble the germens all
together in confusion, so that they
became barren or produced only
monstrosities Macbeth shows how far
he has declined since the beginning
of the play. Wilson (lxiii) thinks
that Macbeth dwells on the prospect
of such ultimate destruction with
delight. It is rather the *reductio ad*
absurdum of the principle that the
end justifies the means, of which the
equivocator in the Porter scene provides a mild example. Macbeth is
willing to sacrifice the future of the
universe to his own personal and
temporary satisfaction. Cf. III. ii. 16
ante, and Knight, *The Wheel of Fire,*
1949, p. 154.

60. *sicken*] i.e. through surfeit.

64. *sow's . . . eaten*] Steevens cites
Holinshed, *Hist. Scot.* 1585, p. 133
(on the laws of Kenneth II.): " If a
sow eate hir pigs, let hir be stoned to
death, and buried, so that no man
eate of hir fleshe."

65. *farrow*] litter. Holland, *Pliny,*
viii. 51 (cited Clarendon) says:
" One sow may bring at one farrow
twentie pigges."

From the murderer's gibbet, throw
Into the flame.
All.   Come, high, or low;
Thyself and office deftly show.

   Thunder. First Apparition, an armed head.

Macb. Tell me, thou unknown power,—
1 *Witch.*   He knows thy thought:
Hear his speech, but say thou nought.   70
1 *App.* Macbeth! Macbeth! Macbeth! beware Macduff;
Beware the Thane of Fife.—Dismiss me.—Enough.
            [Descends.
Macb. Whate'er thou art, for thy good caution, thanks:
Thou hast harp'd my fear aright.—But one word
  more:—
1 *Witch.* He will not be commanded.   Here's another,   75
More potent than the first.

68. S.D.] *Ff; Wilson adds like Macbeth's, rises from the cauldron.* 71.
one line, Rowe; two lines Ff.

65. *sweaten*] irregularly formed, to
rhyme with "eaten." Cf. Abbott,
op. cit. § 344.
 68, 76, 86. *an armed head, etc.*]
Upton, *Crit. Obs.* 1746, says: "The
armed head represents symbolically
Macbeth's head cut off and brought
to Malcolm by Macduff. The bloody
child is Macduff untimely ripped
from his mother's womb. The child
with a crown on his head, and a
bough in his hand, is the royal
Malcolm, who ordered his soldiers
to hew them down a bough and
bear it before them to Dunsinane."
 Crawford, *Modern Language Notes*,
xxxix, and Kittredge both think the
1st Apparition is Macduff. Knight,
The Imperial Theme, pp. 150-3, points
out "the vivid destruction-birth
sequence" in this scene. "The
Armed Head, recalling Macdonwald's head (I. ii. 23) . . . blends
with the 'chaos' and 'disorder'
thought throughout . . . and . . .
suggests both the iron force of evil
and also its final destruction." He

suggests that the order in which the
apparitions appear is important:
"Violent destruction, itself to be
destroyed; the blood-agony of birth
that travails to wrench into existence a force to right the sickening
evil; the future birth splendid in
crowned and accomplished royalty."
 69. *Tell . . . thought*] Grierson
calls attention to the irony of these
two sentences, as the apparition is
Macbeth's head.
 70. *say . . . nought*] Steevens
quotes Marlowe, *Faustus*, sc. x.
(ed. Brooke, p. 212):
  "demand no questions . . .
 But in dumbe silence let them
  come and goe."
 72. *Enough*] He is in torment.
Cf. *II Hen. VI.* I. iv. 38.
 74. *harp'd*] guessed.   Cotgrave
translates "Parler à taston" by "to
speak by ghesse or conjecture, onely
to harpe at the matter."
 76. *More potent*] This does not
necessarily mean that Macduff is
more potent than Macbeth, but

Thunder.   Second Apparition, a bloody child.

2 *App.* Macbeth! Macbeth! Macbeth!—
Macb. Had I three ears, I'd hear thee.
2 *App.* Be bloody, bold, and resolute: laugh to scorn
    The power of man, for none of woman born   80
    Shall harm Macbeth.   [*Descends.*
Macb. Then live, Macduff: what need I fear of thee?
    But yet I'll make assurance double sure,
    And take a bond of Fate: thou shalt not live;
    That I may tell pale-hearted fear it lies,   85
    And sleep in spite of thunder.—

*Thunder.   Third Apparition, a child crowned with a tree in
his hand.*

                        What is this,
    That rises like the issue of a king;
    And wears upon his baby brow the round
    And top of sovereignty?
All.   Listen, but speak not to 't.
3 *App.* Be lion-mettled, proud, and take no care   90

78-81. Had . . . Macbeth] *three lines, Var. 1803, ending* bold, man, Macbeth.
79. Be . . . scorn] *one line, Rowe; two lines, Ff.*   83. assurance double]
Pope; assurance: double *F 1;* assurance, double *F 2, 3, 4.* 86-7. What . . .
king] *so Rowe; one line, Ff.*   89. top] *type conj. Theobald.*

merely that the apparition is more
powerful than the other. The First
Witch has previously referred to
them as their " masters," which
can only mean the demons who
assume the shape of the apparitions. The phrase does not therefore dispose of Kittredge's theory
(cf. note to 68 *ante*) as Wilson
asserts.
    80. *for . . . Macbeth*] Cf. Holinshed
(Appendix, p. 182).
    83-4. *assurance . . . Fate*] Macbeth,
unwitting that Macduff is not in
the number of *woman born* is assured
that Macduff cannot harm him.
By killing him, Macbeth means to
bind fate to perform the promise

and make his own " assurance
double sure." Rushton, *Shakespeare
a Lawyer,* 1858, p. 20, says that the
allusion is to " a conditional bond,
under or by virtue of which when
forfeited, double the principal sum
was recoverable." Kittredge remarks
that Fate has to break two of her
fixed laws, produce a man never
born, and bring back a man from the
dead.
    89. *top*] " The crown not only
completes (especially in the eye of
Macbeth, the usurper) and rounds,
as with the perfection of a circle,
the claim to sovereignty, but it is
figuratively the top, the summit,
of ambitious hopes " (R. G. White).

Who chafes, who frets, or where conspirers are:
Macbeth shall never vanquish'd be, until
Great Birnam wood to high Dunsinane hill
Shall come against him.   [*Descends.*
Macb.   That will never be:
Who can impress the forest; bid the tree   95
Unfix his earth-bound root? Sweet bodements! good!
Rebellious dead, rise never, till the wood
Of Birnam rise; and our high-plac'd Macbeth

93. Birnam] *F 4;* Byrnam *F 1, 2, 3.*   97. Rebellious dead] *Ff;* Rebellious head   *Theobald (Warburton);*   Rebellion's head *Hanmer (conj.*
Theobald).   98. Birnam] Byrnan *F.*   our] your *conj. S. Walker.*

93. *Birnam*] a high hill near
Dunkeld, 12 miles W.N.W. of
Dunsinnan, which is 7 miles N.E.
of Perth
93 *Dunsinane*] now Dunsinnan.
The word here seems to be accented
on the second syllable; but elsewhere in the play on the first syllable.
Both pronunciations seem to have
been employed by all Scottish writers.
Wilson suspects from the pronunciation of " Dunsinane " here, the
use of " rise " (98), and the rhythm
of 105, the presence of an interpolator. R. Walker, *op. cit.* chap. 6,
suggests that " the unusual accentu-
ation . . . produced the startling
auditory sensation that the castle
of Macbeth is torn asunder by *sin,*
and therefore doomed to fall." This
is over-ingenious.
94. *That*] Macbeth continues the
oracle in rhyme, and thus identifies
himself with the lying spirits.
                   (Kittredge.)
97. *Rebellious dead*] Theobald's
emendation has been generally accepted, and Macbeth may be referring to " conspirers " (91 *ante*).
Perhaps " head " was suggested by
the Armed Head (Clarendon). For
" head " in the sense of armed force,
see *1 Hen. IV.* III. ii. 167 and *Ham.*
IV. v. 101. Halliwell, however,
thought that the Folio " dead "
referred to Banquo's ghost, which
would not stay buried (III. iv. 80

ante) and the original reading has
been defended by W. D. Sargeaunt,
Macbeth—a New Interpretation, 1937,
pp. 154-5, and by R. Walker, *op.
cit.* chap. 6. The latter argues that
the Folio reading links up better with
the reference to Banquo, 100-3 *post,*
and that Macbeth is afraid that the
dead will rise and drag him down
into the grave, or at least that
Banquo's son will avenge his father.
Walker also compares v. ii. 3-5 *post.*
On the whole there would seem to be
insufficient justification for emending
the Folio reading; cf. *T.L.S.* 23 Sept.
1949.
98. *Birnam*] With Folio spelling,
cf. Holinshed: " till the wood of
Bernane came to the castell of
Dunsinane."
98. *rise*] Probably copied by mistake from the previous line. Wilson
conj. " move." The text seems to
be corrupt here. Cf. next note.
98. *our . . . Macbeth*] Even if
" our " is a misprint for " your,"
the phrase would be queer in Macbeth's mouth. Cuningham interprets " ourself, Macbeth, the King."
Was Macbeth perhaps disguised, and
here pretending that he was not
Macbeth? Or, as Fleay suggests,
was this passage originally spoken
by one of the witches. Even as the
lines stand (96-100 " Sweet . . .
custom ") they might be given to
the First Witch, and we could then

Shall live the lease of Nature, pay his breath
To time, and mortal custom.—Yet my heart   100
Throbs to know one thing: tell me (if your art
Can tell so much), shall Banquo's issue ever
Reign in this kingdom?

All.   Seek to know no more.

Macb. I will be satisfied: deny me this,
And an eternal curse fall on you! Let me know.—   105
Why sinks that cauldron? and what noise is this?

                                        [*Hautboys.*

1 *Witch.* Show!
2 *Witch.* Show!
3 *Witch.* Show!
All. Show his eyes, and grieve his heart;   110
Come like shadows, so depart.

A show of eight Kings, the last with a glass in his hand;
                BANQUO *following.*

Macb. Thou art too like the spirit of Banquo: down!
Thy crown does sear mine eye-balls:—and thy hair,
Thou other gold-bound brow, is like the first:—
A third is like the former:—filthy hags!   115
Why do you show me this?—A fourth?—Start, eyes!

105-6. know.—Why] know. Why *Ff;* know Why *conj. S. Walker.* 111. S.D].
Hanmer subst. See note below.   113. hair,] haire *Ff;* air *Johnson;* heir
Jackson.   116. eyes!] eye *F 2, 3, 4.*

interpret the passage as another
example of "the equivocation of the
fiend That lies like truth."

   99. *the lease of Nature*] the term of
life.

   100. *mortal custom*] the custom of
mortality, natural death.

   106. *noise*] A concert or company
of musicians, usually three in number,
who attended taverns, etc., was
called a "noise." Cf. *2 Hen. IV.*
II. iv. 12.

   111. *A show . . . following*] The
S.D. in Folio "and Banquo last,
with a glasse in his hand" is inconsistent with 119 *post.*

   113. *hair*] Johnson's conj. "air"
is attractive. "As Macbeth ex-

pected to see a train of kings, and
was only inquiring from what race
they would proceed, he could not be
surprised that the hair of the second
was bound with gold like that of the
first; he was offended only that the
second resembled the first, as the
first resembled Banquo." Steevens
compares *W.T.* v. i. 128:
   "Your father's image is so hit in
        you,
   His very air, that I should call
        you brother."
But *O.E.D.* gives five quotations,
from 1387-1625 of "hair" used in
the sense "of one colour and ex-
ternal quality; . . . stamp, character."

What! will the line stretch out to th' crack of doom?
Another yet?—A seventh?—I'll see no more:—
And yet the eighth appears, who bears a glass,
Which shows me many more; and some I see,   120
That two-fold balls and treble sceptres carry.
Horrible sight!—Now, I see, 'tis true;
For the blood-bolter'd Banquo smiles upon me,
And points at them for his.—What! is this so?
1 *Witch.* Ay, Sir, all this is so:—but why   125
Stands Macbeth thus amazedly?—
Come, sisters, cheer we up his sprites,
And show the best of our delights.
I 'll charm the air to give a sound,
While you perform your antic round;   130
That this great King may kindly say,
Our duties did his welcome pay.
          [*Music. The Witches dance, and vanish.*

119. eighth] *F 3;* eight *F 1, 2.*   124. What! is] What? is *F 1;* What is
F 2, 3, 4; What, is *Pope.*

119. *the eighth*] Shakespeare refers
to kings only, omitting all mention
of Mary, Queen of Scots. Perhaps
we should retain the F reading. But
cf. l. 118.

119. *glass*] Not an ordinary mirror
in which King James could see himself (cf. Flatter, *T.L.S.* 23/3/51) but
a prospective, or magic, glass.

121. *two-fold . . . sceptres*] The
two-fold balls are usually taken to
refer to the double coronation of
James at Scone and at Westminster.
Chambers, *William Shakespeare,* I.
473, interprets " balls " to mean
the " mounds " borne on the English
and Scottish crowns; but surely it
is the orb, carried in the left hand.
The treble sceptres are the two
used for investment in the English
coronation, and the one used in
the Scottish coronation (Chambers).

123. *blood-bolter'd*] i.e. with the
hair in tangled knots, or clotted or
matted together in a coagulated
mass. According to Malone the

term was a provincialism, used in
Warwickshire. Other forms are
bolstred, used in *Arden of Fevershame,*
III. i. 73, and *balter* used in Holland's
Pliny, XII. xvii. 370 (cited Steevens),
referring to a goat's beard: " it
baltereth and cluttereth into knots
and balls."

125-32. *Ay . . . pay*] Possibly an
interpolation. See Introduction, p.
xxvii.

130. *antic round*] fantastic dance.
Wilson quotes Jonson's description
in *The Masque of Queenes:* " a
magicall Daunce full of praeposterous
change and gesticulation . . . daunc-
ing, back to back, hip to hip, theyr
handes joyn'd, and making theyr
circles backward to the left hand,
with strange, phantastique motions
of theyr heads and bodyes " (ed.
Herford and Simpson, vii. 301).

131. *this . . . king*] If the speech is
interpolated, this line may be addressed to a King in the audience
rather than to Macbeth.

Macb. Where are they? Gone?—Let this pernicious hour
　　Stand aye accursed in the calendar!—
　　Come in, without there!

Enter LENOX.

Len.　　　　　　　What's your Grace's will?　　135
Macb. Saw you the Weïrd Sisters?
Len.　　　　　　　No, my Lord.
Macb. Came they not by you?
Len.　　　　　　　No, indeed, my Lord.
Macb. Infected be the air whereon they ride;
　　And damn'd all those that trust them!—I did hear
　　The galloping of horse: who was't came by?　　140
Len. 'Tis two or three, my Lord, that bring you word,
　　Macduff is fled to England.
Macb.　　　　　　Fled to England?
Len. Ay, my good Lord.
Macb. [*Aside.*] Time, thou anticipat'st my dread exploits:
　　The flighty purpose never is o'ertook,　　145
　　Unless the deed go with it. From this moment,
　　The very firstlings of my heart shall be
　　The firstlings of my hand. And even now,

---

133. Where . . . hour] *so Rowe; two lines ending* Gone? houre, *Ff.*
136. Weïrd] *Theobald;* Weyard *F 1;* wizard *F 2, 3;* wizards *F 4.*　　144.
S.D.] *Johnson.*　　147. firstlings] *F 1;* firstling *F 2, 3, 4.*　　148. firstlings] *Ff;*
firstling *Rowe (ed. 2).*

138. *air . . . ride*] Cf. Scot, *The Discouerie of Witchcraft*, 1930, pp. 6, 19. "These can passe from place to place in the aire invisible . . . they ride and flie in the aire."
139. *damn'd . . . them*] As Macbeth does.
142. *Macduff . . . fled*] Kittredge notes that as in I. iii. "the predictions begin to fulfil themselves instantly, and thus their trustworthiness is established in Macbeth's mind."
143. *Ay . . . Lord*] Flatter, *op. cit.* p. 26, notes the significant pause before Macbeth speaks.
144. *anticipat'st*] forestallest.

145-6. *The flighty . . . it*] cf. II. iii. 29-37, "flighty" = swift, fleet. *O.E.D.* quotes Huloet (1552), "Flighty, *pernix.*" Cf. *A.W.* v. iii. 40:

　　"on our quick'st decrees,
The inaudible and noiseless foot
　　of Time
Steals ere we can effect them."

147-8. *firstlings . . . firstlings*] "the first conceptions of the heart and the first acts of the hand" (Clarendon). Cf. *T.C.* Prol. 27: "the vaunt and firstlings of those broils." *O.E.D.* quotes Coverdale (1535), *Prov.* iii. 9, "ye firstlinges of all thine encrease."

To crown my thoughts with acts, be it thought and
　　done:
The castle of Macduff I will surprise;　　　　　　　　150
Seize upon Fife; give to th' edge o' th' sword
His wife, his babes, and all unfortunate souls
That trace him in his line.　No boasting like a fool;
This deed I'll do, before this purpose cool:
But no more sights!—Where are these gentlemen? 155
Come, bring me where they are.　　　　　　[*Exeunt.*

SCENE II.—*Fife.　A room in Macduff's castle.*

Enter LADY MACDUFF, *her Son, and* ROSSE.

L. Macd. What had he done, to make him fly the land?
Rosse. You must have patience, Madam.
L. Macd.　　　　　　　　　　　　He had none:
His flight was madness: when our actions do not,
Our fears do make us traitors.

155. sights!] flights *Singer* (*ed. 2*).

Scene II

S.D. *Fife . . . castle*] *not in Ff.*　　　　1. L. Macd.] Wife *Ff passim,*

153. *trace*] in the sense of succeeding, following in, another's tracks, as
in *1 Hen. IV.* III. i. 47.

153-4. *No . . . cool*] Wilson,
following Fleay and others, thinks
this rhyming tag is spurious.

Scene II

Bradley says of this and the following scene, *Shakespearean Tragedy*, p.
391: "They have a technical value
in helping to give the last stage of
the action the form of a conflict
between Macbeth and Macduff.
But their chief function is of another
kind.　It is to touch the heart with
a sense of beauty and pathos, to
open the springs of love and tears."
But Knights, *op. cit.* pp. 26-7, points
out that this scene echoes in different
keys the theme of the false appearance, of doubt and confusion," and
" shows the spreading evil. . . .
There is much more in the death

of young Macduff than ' pathos ';
the violation of the natural order is
completed by the murder." Macduff
and his wife, says Fletcher, *Studies
of Shakespeare*, p. 166 (*ap.* Furness),
" are the chief representatives in
the piece of the interests of loyalty
and domestic affection, as opposed
to those of the foulest treachery and
. . . ambition."

1. *What . . . land?*] Masefield,
Thanks before Going, 1947, p. 172,
argues that in the uncut *Macbeth*,
Macduff, " debated with his wife
the policy of going and had her full
approval.　Her outcry against him
to Rosse, in the beginning of this
scene, is surely to divert suspicion
from herself . . . she knows that
spies are everywhere, and that Rosse
may be one." I think it more
likely that Macduff did not discuss
the matter with his wife, for fear of
implicating her.　There does not

Rosse.   You know not,
    Whether it was his wisdom, or his fear.   5
L. Macd. Wisdom! to leave his wife, to leave his babes,
    His mansion, and his titles, in a place
    From whence himself does fly? He loves us not:
    He wants the natural touch; for the poor wren,
    The most diminitive of birds, will fight,   10
    Her young ones in her nest, against the owl.
    All is the fear, and nothing is the love;
    As little is the wisdom, where the flight
    So runs against all reason.
Rosse.   My dearest coz,
    I pray you, school yourself: but, for your husband,   15
    He is noble, wise, judicious, and best knows
    The fits o' th' season. I dare not speak much further:
    But cruel are the times, when we are traitors,
    And do not know ourselves; when we hold rumour

---

10. diminitive] *F 1;* diminutiue *F 4.*   19. know] know't *Hanmer.*
19-20. we hold rumour . . . we . . . we] we bode ruin . . . we . . . we *or*
else the bold running . . . they . . . they *conj. Johnson.*

---

seem to be sufficient evidence for a
cut here. Nor, although Rosse
might well be suspect after his
time-serving, can I see any evidence
that Lady Macduff does suspect
him; and it is apparently the
murder of Lady Macduff which
finally makes him desert Macbeth.

4. *traitors*] " Our flight is considered as an evidence of our
treason " (Steevens).

7. *titles*] This is usually explained
to mean everything to which he was
entitled, i.e. his possessions.

9. *natural touch*] the feeling of
natural affection, " natural sensibility " (Johnson). Cf. *T.G.* II. vii.
18: " the inly touch of love ";
and *Temp.* v. i. 21: " Hast thou,
which art but air, a touch, a feeling."

9. *wren*] It need not worry us
that the wren is not the smallest of
birds, nor that it would not fight in

defence of its young. See Harting,
The Ornithology of Shakespeare, p. 91.

10. *diminitive*] variant of diminutive.

12. *All . . . love*] Noble, *Shake-*
speare's Biblical Knowledge, compares
1 John, iv. 18: " There is no feare
in loue, but perfect loue casteth out
feare: for feare hath painfulnesse:
and he that feareth is not perfect in
loue."

13. *wisdom*] cf. IV. iii. 15 *post.*

15. *school*] control.

17. *The fits o' th' season*] Steevens
explains as *the violent disorders* of the
season, its convulsions; and quotes
Cor. III. ii. 33: " the violent fit o'
the time." The metaphor is from
the fits of an intermittent fever.
Cf. III. ii. 23 *ante.* Rosse is hinting
at Macbeth's murderous fits.

19. *ourselves*] i.e. as such, " without
realizing it." Cuningham suggests
the word might mean " one another."

From what we fear, yet know not what we fear,   20
But float upon a wild and violent sea
Each way, and move—I take my leave of you:
Shall not be long but I'll be here again.
Things at the worst will cease, or else climb upward
To what they were before.—My pretty cousin,   25
Blessing upon you!
L. Macd. Father'd he is, and yet he's fatherless.
Rosse. I am so much a fool, should I stay longer,
It would be my disgrace, and your discomfort:
I take my leave at once.   [*Exit.*

21. sea] *F;* sea, *Arden (ed. 1), Wilson, etc.*   22. Each . . . move—]
conj. Johnson; each way, and moue. *Ff;* Each way and wave. *conj. Theobald;*
And move each way. *Capell;* And each way move. *Keightley (conj. Steevens);*
Each sway and move *conj. Staunton;* Each way it moves *Hudson (conj.
Daniel);* Each day a new one *conj. Ingleby;* Each way and none. *Wilson (conj.
Camb. substant.);* Each wayward move *conj. Leighton;* Each way we move *conj.
Rolfe.* 26-9. Blessing . . . discomfort] *lines end* yet Foole, disgrace, discom-
fort. *Walker.* 27. *so Rowe; two lines, divided after* is *Ff.*

19-20. *when . . . fear*] cf. *John,* IV.
ii. 144-6:
"I find the people strangely
    fantasied,
    Possess'd with rumours, full of
    idle dreams,
    Not knowing what they fear, but
    full of fear."
Rosse means: "When we entertain
rumours, inspired by our fears, and
those fears are themselves vague."
21-2. *But . . . move*—] This passage
is a field for much conjecture.
Knights argues for the punctuation
I have adopted: "The substitution
of a dash for the full stop after
'move' is the only alteration that
seems necessary in the Folio text.
The other emendations . . . ruin
both the rhythm and the idiom.
Rosse is in a hurry and breaks off.
. . . That the tide is about to turn
against Macbeth is suggested both
by the rhythm and the imagery of
Rosse's speech." Wilson, however,
argues that "moue" is a simple
minim error for "none" and com-

pares *A.C.* I. iv. 44-7. One might also
compare *A.C.* III. ii. 49. But Taylor,
Shakespeare's Debt to Montaigne, draws
attention to a parallel with a passage
in Florio, which seems to me decisive against the Camb. conj.,
accepted by Wilson:

"So are we drawne, as wood is
    shoved,
    By others sinnewes, *each way
    moved.*

We goe not, but we are carried:
as things that *flote,* now gliding
gently, now hulling *violently;* according as the water is, either stormy
or calme" (II. i. *Temple* iii. p. 4).
See Empson, *op. cit.* pp. 128-9.
23. *Shall not*] "It," "I" or
"And" understood; but Rosse is
in a hurry, and there are plenty of
examples in Elizabethan English of
the omission of the subject.
24-5. *Things . . . before*] Another
metaphor relating to the turn of
the tide.
29. *disgrace*] i.e. by weeping.

L. Macd.   Sirrah, your father's dead: 30
    And what will you do now?   How will you live?
Son. As birds do, mother.
L. Macd.   What, with worms and flies?
Son. With what I get, I mean; and so do they.
L. Macd. Poor bird! thou'dst never fear the net, nor lime,
    The pit-fall, nor the gin.   35
Son.   Why should I, mother?
    Poor birds they are not set for.
    My father is not dead, for all your saying.
L. Macd. Yes, he is dead: how wilt thou do for a father?
Son. Nay, how will you do for a husband?
L. Macd. Why, I can buy me twenty at any market.   40
Son. Then you'll buy 'em to sell again.
L. Macd. Thou speak'st with all thy wit;
    And yet, i' faith, with wit enough for thee.
Son. Was my father a traitor, mother?
L. Macd. Ay, that he was.   45
Son. What is a traitor?
L. Macd. Why, one that swears and lies.
Son. And be all traitors that do so?
L. Macd. Every one that does so is a traitor, and must be
    hang'd.   50

---

33. I mean] *not in F 2, 3, 4.*
Bird, *Ff.* lime] *F 1;* line *F 2, 3, 4.*
so Ff; Why . . . for. *one line,* Pope.
41. buy] *F 3;* by *F 1, 2.*
Pope.   42. with all] *F 2;* withall *F 1.*
after Traitor *Ff.*

34. *so* Theobald; *two lines, divided after*
35-6. The pit-fall . . . set for]
38. *one line,* Rowe; *two lines Ff.*
42-3. Thou . . . thee] *lines divided after* faith
49-50. *prose,* Pope; *lines divided*

30. *Sirrah*] " not always a term of reproach but sometimes used by masters to servants, parents to children, etc." (Malone).

32. *As birds do*] The boy is thinking of *Matt.* vi. 26.

32. *with*] i.e. on.

34. *lime*] bird lime.

35. *gin*] snare.

35. *Why . . . mother?*] All editors have followed Pope in detaching these words from this line, which they complete.

36. *Poor . . . for*] " In life traps are not set for the poor but for the rich " (Clarendon). " Poor " is emphatic, and " birds " is probably the object of " set for," " they " referring to the traps. But " they " may be in apposition to " birds." The boy is referring, of course, to his mother's epithet.

44-63. Wilson thinks this passage was added for a court performance after the hanging of Henry Garnet.

47. *one . . . lies*] cf. II. iii. 10-12 *ante.*

Son. And must they all be hang'd that swear and lie?

L. Macd. Every one.

Son. Who must hang them?

L. Macd. Why, the honest men.

Son. Then the liars and swearers are fools; for there   55
 are liars and swearers enow to beat the honest men,
 and hang up them.

L. Macd. Now God help thee, poor monkey! But how
 wilt thou do for a father?

Son. If he were dead, you'ld weep for him: if you would   60
 not, it were a good sign that I should quickly
 have a new father.

L. Macd. Poor prattler, how thou talk'st!

Enter a Messenger.

Mess. Bless you, fair dame! I am not to you known,
 Though in your state of honour I am perfect.   65
 I doubt, some danger does approach you nearly:
 If you will take a homely man's advice,
 Be not found here; hence, with your little ones.
 To fright you thus, methinks, I am too savage;
 To do worse to you were fell cruelty,   70

54. the] *not in F 3, 4.*   56. enow] *Ff;* enough *Hanmer.*   58-9. *so Pope; verse divided after* Monkie: *Ff.* 58. Now] *not in F 4.*   68-9. ones. To . . . thus,] *F 2, subst.;* ones To . . . thus. *F 1.*   70. worse to you] less, to you *Hanmer;* less to you, *Capell.*

57. *hang up them*] Cf. *R.J.* IV. ii. 41: "deck up her."

64-72. *Messenger*] He is a welcome reminder that all have not been corrupted by Macbeth's tyranny. There is no reason to believe, with Heath, that he is one of the murderers.

65. *state . . . perfect*] perfectly acquainted with your rank. Cf. *Rich. III.* III. vii. 120: "Your state of fortune, and your due of birth."

66. *doubt*] i.e. fear; a common usage. Cf. *Rich. II.* III. iv. 69; and Bacon, *Essays, Of Vicissitude of things:* "You may doubt the springing up of a *New Sect.*"

68. *little ones*] Cf. *Matt.* xviii. 6: "But whosoeuer shall offend one

of these little ones which beleeue in mee, it were better for him, that a millstone were hanged about his necke, and that he were drowned in the depth of the sea."

70. *To . . . cruelty*] Three explanations, of which I incline to the third: (i) "to fright you more, by relating all the circumstances of your dangers; which would detain you so long, that you could not avoid it" (Edwards); (ii) "to let her and her children be destroyed without warning" (Johnson); (iii) "It is too savage of me even to frighten you like this: to harm you would be the act of a monster—and such monsters, alas, are on your track" (Grierson).

Which is too nigh your person.   Heaven preserve you!
I dare abide no longer.   [*Exit.*
L. Macd.   Whither should I fly?
I have done no harm.   But I remember now
I am in this earthly world, where, to do harm
Is often laudable; to do good, sometime   75
Accounted dangerous folly: why then, alas!
Do I put up that womanly defence,
To say, I have done no harm?   What are these faces!

Enter Murderers.

Mur. Where is your husband?
L. Macd. I hope, in no place so unsanctified,   80
Where such as thou may'st find him.
Mur.   He's a traitor.
Son. Thou liest, thou shag-hair'd villain!
Mur.   What, you egg!
                                    [*Stabbing him.*

Young fry of treachery!
Son.   He has kill'd me, mother:
Run away, I pray you!   [*Dies.* 84

[*Exit Lady Macduff, crying* "*Murther!*" *and pursued by
the Murderers.*

72. Whither] *F 3, 4;* Whether *F 1, 2.*   78. *so Rowe; divided after*
harme? *Ff.* I have] *F 1;* I had *F 2, 3, 4.* I'd *Theobald;* I've *Dyce (ed. 2).*
82. shag-hair'd] *Singer (ed. 2), conj. Steevens;* shagge-ear'd *F 1, 2;* shag-ear'd
F 3, 4, Camb. S.D.] *Rowe; not in Ff.*

80. *unsanctified*] "We recall the
associations set up in III. vi., a scene
of choric commentary upon Macduff's flight . . . to the 'pious
Edward'" (Knights, *Explorations,*
p. 27).
     82. *shag-hair'd*] Steevens' conj. has
been generally adopted. The epithet
occurs in *2 Hen. VI.* III. i. 367 and

Sir Thomas More, Add. IV*c.* The
spelling *heare* is common in Shakespeare, and Wilson points out that
in his hand *g* and *h* are similar, so
that "shagheard" might be misread "shaggeard."
     82. *egg!*] Cf. *L.L.L.* v. i. 78:
"thou pigeon-egg of discretion."

SCENE III.—*England.*　*A room in the King's palace.*

Enter MALCOLM *and* MACDUFF.

Mal. Let us seek out some desolate shade, and there
　　Weep our sad bosoms empty.
Macd.　　　　　　　　　　　Let us rather
　　Hold fast the mortal sword, and like good men
　　Bestride our downfall birthdom.　Each new morn,
　　New widows howl, new orphans cry; new sorrows　　5
　　Strike heaven on the face, that it resounds
　　As if it felt with Scotland, and yell'd out
　　Like syllable of dolour.
Mal.　　　　　　　　　What I believe, I 'll wail;
　　What know, believe; and what I can redress,
　　As I shall find the time to friend, I will.　　　　10
　　What you have spoke, it may be so, perchance.
　　This tyrant, whose sole name blisters our tongues,
　　Was once thought honest: you have lov'd him well;

Scene III

S.D.] *England . . . palace*] *Rowe subst.*　　4. downfall] *F;* down-fall'n
Johnson.　　11. What] When *Chambers.*

Scene III

This scene is based on Holinshed (see Appendix, pp. 182 ff.) and it is the only considerable passage of dialogue in the *Chronicle* relating to Macbeth's reign.　The dialogue is also given prominence in Bellenden and Stewart.　Knights remarks of this scene that "Malcolm's suspicion and the long testing of Macduff emphasize the mistrust which has spread from the central evil of the play.　But the main purpose of the scene is obscured unless we realize its function as choric commentary.　In alternating speeches the evil which Macbeth has caused is explicitly stated, without extenuation.　And it is stated impersonally." (op. cit. p. 28).　Chambers, more representatively, regards the scene as

tedious.　It does not seem tedious today, perhaps, as Masefield suggests, because of the events of recent years.
　3. *mortal*] deadly.　Cf. I. v. 41 *ante.*
　4. *downfall*] i.e. downfallen.
　4. *birthdom*] i.e. native land.　The phrase means "defend our fatherland, as we would the body of a fallen comrade."
　6. *that*] so that.　Cf. I. ii. 60 *ante.*
　8. *Like . . . dolour*] Baldwin, *Shakespeare's Small Latine,* I. 570, shows that Shakespeare might have read in his *Accidence of Interjections;* "Some are of . . . Sorowe: as *Heu, hei.*"
　10. *to friend*] i.e. for friend, to befriend me.　Cf. *A.W.* v. iii. 182, and *J.C.* III. i. 143.
　12. *whose sole name*] the mere mention of whose name (Chambers).

He hath not touch'd you yet.   I am young; but some-
     thing
You may deserve of him through me, and wisdom   15
To offer up a weak, poor, innocent lamb,
T' appease an angry god.

Macd. I am not treacherous.

Mal.   But Macbeth is.
A good and virtuous nature may recoil,
In an imperial charge.   But I shall crave your
     pardon: 20
That which you are my thoughts cannot transpose:
Angels are bright still, though the brightest fell:
Though all things foul would wear the brows of grace,
Yet Grace must still look so.

Macd.   I have lost my hopes.

Mal. Perchance even there where I did find my doubts.   25
Why in that rawness left you wife and child

---

15. deserve] *Theobald (Warburton);* discerne *Ff.* of him] *not in conj.*
Steevens and wisdom] *F;* 'tis wisdom *Hanmer;* and wisdom is it *conj. Steevens;*
and 'tis wisdom *conj. Collier;* and wisdom bids *conj. Staunton;* and wisdom
'twere *Keightley;* and wisdom/Bids me remember it may be your wisdom *conj.*
Grierson; And wisdom 'tis *conj. Cuningham (lines 14-17 end, but me, weak god).*
16. To offer] 'Tis t'offer *Nicholson (ap. Camb.).*   17. T'appease] *Ff;* To
appease *many edd.*   23. wear] bear *F 4.*   25.] *so Rowe; divided after* there *Ff.*
26. child] Childe? *F;* children *F 2, 3, 4.*

14-17. *He hath ... god*] Cuningham
wished to alter the lineation of these
lines and to insert *'tis* after *wisdom.*
But *'tis* or *'twere* may be understood,
and need not be inserted.

15. *deserve*] Theobald's emendation is almost universally accepted,
but Upton's explanation of the
Folio "discerne" ("You may see
something to your advantage by
betraying me") is not impossible.

19-20. *recoil . . . charge*] give way
under pressure of a royal command.
For this use of "recoil" cf. v. ii. 23
and *Cym.* I. vi. 128.

20. *imperial*] royal. Cf. *M.N.D.*
II. i. 163.

20. *charge*] command; but the
word was suggested by "recoil," by
a quibble.

21. *transpose*] change. Cf. *M.N.D.*
I. i. 233: "Love can transpose to
form and dignity." The line means:
"my thoughts cannot alter what you
really are."

23-4. *Though . . . so*] "I do not
say that your virtuous appearance
proves you a traitor; for virtue must
wear its proper form, though that
form be counterfeited by villainy"
(Johnson).

23. *would*] should. Cf. I. vii. 34, etc.

24-5. *hopes . . . doubts*] Macduff is
thinking of an expedition against
Macbeth; Malcolm is suspicious of
Macduff's conduct in leaving his
wife and children.

26. *rawness*] unprotected condition.   He suspects Macduff of having
an understanding with Macbeth, or

(Those precious motives, those strong knots of love),
Without leave-taking?—I pray you,
Let not my jealousies be your dishonours,
But mine own safeties: you may be rightly just,   30
Whatever I shall think.

Macd.   Bleed, bleed, poor country!
Great tyranny, lay thou thy basis sure,
For goodness dare not check thee! wear thou thy
      wrongs;
The title is affeer'd!—Fare thee well, Lord:
I would not be the villain that thou think'st   35
For the whole space that's in the tyrant's grasp,
And the rich East to boot.

Mal.   Be not offended:
I speak not as in absolute fear of you.
I think our country sinks beneath the yoke;
It weeps, it bleeds; and each new day a gash   40
Is added to her wounds: I think, withal,
There would be hands uplifted in my right;
And here, from gracious England, have I offer

---

33. dare] *F 1, 2;* dares *F 3, 4, Wilson.*   34. The] Thy *Malone.*   affeer'd]
Hanmer; affear'd *F.*   35. think'st] think'st me *Keightley.*

he would not have left his family to
the tyrant's mercies. Cf. *Hen. V.*
iv. i. 147: " children rawly left."

27. *motives*] persons inspiring love
or devotion, as well as incentives.
Cf. *A.W.* iv. iv. 20 and *Tim.* v. iv. 27.

28. *Without . . . you*] Some editors
assume that something is missing.
But, as Abbott suggests, the pause
after "leave-taking" may be "explained by the indignation of Macduff, which Malcolm observes and
digresses to appease." Not that it is
necessary to explain every irregularity in the metre.

29. *jealousies*] suspicions.

33. *goodness . . . thee*] a criticism
of Malcolm's nervousness. Check =
hold in check, or call to account.

33. *wrongs*] ill-gotten gains.

34. *The . . . affeer'd!*] i.e. assured

or confirmed. " *Affeerers* . . . signifies in the common law such as
are appointed in Court-Leets, upon
oath, to set the fines on such as
have committed faults arbitrarily
punishable, and have no express
penalty appointed by statute "
(Cowell, *Interpreter*, cited Clarendon).
Ritson says: " To *affeer* is to assess,
or reduce to certainty. All amercia-
ments are by Magna Charta to be
affeered by lawful men, sworn to be
impartial." Originally a commercial
term, meaning " fix the market-
price." Elwin suggests that there is
a pun, the phrase meaning also
" Malcolm is afraid of asserting his
title to the throne."

37. *to boot*] in addition.

42. *my right*] mon droit.

43. *gracious England*] i.e. Edward
the Confessor.

Of goodly thousands: but, for all this,
When I shall tread upon the tyrant's head,   45
Or wear it on my sword, yet my poor country
Shall have more vices than it had before,
More suffer, and more sundry ways than ever,
By him that shall succeed.
Macd.   What should he be?
Mal. It is myself I mean; in whom I know   50
All the particulars of vice so grafted,
That, when they shall be open'd, black Macbeth
Will seem as pure as snow; and the poor State
Esteem him as a lamb, being compar'd
With my confineless harms.
Macd.   Not in the legions   55
Of horrid Hell can come a devil more damn'd
In evils, to top Macbeth.
Mal.   I grant him bloody,
Luxurious, avaricious, false, deceitful,
Sudden, malicious, smacking of every sin
That has a name; but there's no bottom, none,   60
In my voluptuousness: your wives, your daughters,
Your matrons, and your maids, could not fill up
The cistern of my lust; and my desire

---

44. thousands] thousands ten *conj. Cuningham.*   but] but yet *Hanmer.*   59.
smacking] *F 1;* smoaking *F 2, 3, 4.*

50-102. *It . . . spoken*] Knights, *Explorations,* p. 28, argues that Malcolm here " has ceased to be a person. His lines repeat and magnify the evils which have already been attributed to Macbeth, acting as a mirror wherein the ills of Scotland are reflected. And the statement of evil is strengthened by contrast with the opposite virtues."

52. *open'd*] i.e. like buds—suggested by " grafted."

55. *confineless*] boundless. Not used elsewhere by Shakespeare.

56-7. *devil . . . evils*] Pronounced as monosyllables.

58. *Luxurious*] In the now obsolete sense of " lascivious," " lustful," as always in Shakespeare. Lust, avarice and deceit are the three vices which Malcolm, as in Holinshed, proceeds to charge himself with. He only grants that Macbeth has these vices for the sake of argument. Shakespeare is showing the nature of royalty by describing its opposite.

59. *Sudden*] hasty, passionate, violent. Cf. *A.Y.L.I.* II. vii. 151: " sudden and quick in quarrel."

63. *cistern*] Cf. *Oth.* IV. ii. 61, where also the word is used in connection with lust. Holinshed here speaks of " the abhominable founteine of all vices."

All continent impediments would o'erbear,
That did oppose my will: better Macbeth,   65
Than such an one to reign.
Macd.   Boundless intemperance
In nature is a tyranny; it hath been
Th' untimely emptying of the happy throne,
And fall of many kings.   But fear not yet
To take upon you what is yours: you may   70
Convey your pleasures in a spacious plenty,
And yet seem cold—the time you may so hoodwink:
We have willing dames enough; there cannot be
That vulture in you, to devour so many
As will to greatness dedicate themselves,   75
Finding it so inclin'd.
Mal.   With this, there grows
In my most ill-compos'd affection such
A staunchless avarice, that, were I King,
I should cut off the nobles for their lands;
Desire his jewels, and this other's house: 80
And my more-having would be as a sauce
To make me hunger more; that I should forge

---

66. an] a *Capell.*   Boundless] *not in conj. Steevens.*   72. cold—] cold,
Theobald (Johnson); cold.   *Ff.*

64. *continent*]   restraining   and
chaste, a quibble on the two meanings. Cf. Lear, I. ii. 182, " continent
forbearance," *L.L.L.* I. i. 262,
" continent canon," and *W.T.* III. ii.
35, " as continent, as chaste."

65. *will*] desire, lust.

66-7. *Boundless . . . tyranny*] i.e.
want of control over the natural
appetites constitutes a tyranny or
usurpation in the " little kingdom "
of man's nature.

71. *Convey*] The word is used in
the corresponding passage in Holinshed (see Appendix, p. 183). It
means " arrange, manage secretly;"
cf. " hoodwink " (72). Staunton
quotes *The Plain Man's Pathway to
Heaven* (1599): " But verily, verily,
though the adulterer do never so
closely and cunningly *convey* his sin

under a canopy, yet . . ." etc.
" Convey " and " Conveyers " were
euphemisms for *theft* and *thieves*, as
in *M.W.* I. iii. 32: " ' Convey ' the
wise it call " and *Rich. II.* IV. i. 317:
" Conveyers are you all."

75. *dedicate*] See Murry, *Countries
of the Mind*, II. for an interesting essay
on Shakespeare's use of this word,
though I disagree with Murry's
chronology of the plays.

77. *affection*] disposition.

78. *staunchless*] insatiable.

80. *his*] i.e. one man's.

82-3. *forge   Quarrels*] Rushton,
*Shakespeare Illustrated by the Lex
Scripta*, quoted a statute of Henry IV's
reign about the making of faulty
arrow-heads and defective quarrels
(i.e. square-headed arrows for a
cross-bow) and argued that Malcolm

Quarrels unjust against the good and loyal,
Destroying them for wealth.

Macd.　　　　　　　　　　　This avarice
Sticks deeper, grows with more pernicious root　　　85
Than summer-seeming lust; and it hath been
The sword of our slain kings: yet do not fear;
Scotland hath foisons to fill up your will,
Of your mere own. All these are portable,
With other graces weigh'd.　　　　　　　　　　90

Mal. But I have none: the king-becoming graces,
As Justice, Verity, Temp'rance, Stableness,
Bounty, Perseverance, Mercy, Lowliness,
Devotion, Patience, Courage, Fortitude,
I have no relish of them; but abound　　　　　95
In the division of each several crime,
Acting it many ways. Nay, had I power, I should
Pour the sweet milk of concord into Hell,

---

85. Sticks] Strikes *Hanmer (conj. Theobald).*　　86. summer-seeming] *Ff;* summer-teeming *Theobald (Warburton);* summer-seeding *Steevens (1785), conj. Heath;* summer-seaming *conj. Staunton.*　　88. foisons] Poisons *F 3, 4.*　　98. Pour] Sow'r *Hanmer.* hell] hate *Hanmer.*

here and 137 *post* ("warranted quarrel") was using the word in a double sense, because the verbs "forge" and "warrant" might both be applied to arrows. I think this is very unlikely, though the double meaning might have been at the back of Shakespeare's mind.

85. *Sticks*] Theobald's change is unnecessary. Cf. III. i. 49 *ante,* and *M.M.* v. i. 480.

85. *root*] See Holinshed, Appendix, p. 184.

86. *summer-seeming*] i.e. either summer-beseeming, or summer-like. Lust fades with the winter of age, but avarice does not. Malone compared Donne's "Love's Alchymy":

　　"So, lovers dreame a rich and long
　　　　delight,
　　But yet a winter-seeming sum-
　　　　mer's night."

Here *winter-seeming* = winter-like, i.e.

long. Lust and summer are often juxtaposed in Shakespeare, e.g. *Oth.* IV. ii. 66.

87. *slain kings*] see Holinshed, Appendix, p. 184.

88. *foisons*] plenty, abundance. The plural form is unusual. Cf. *Temp.* IV. i. 110.

89. *Of your mere own*] i.e. royal property.

89. *portable*] Holinshed uses the word "importable" in this dialogue. See Appendix, p. 183.

90. *weigh'd*] i.e. counterbalanced.

93. *Perseverance*] The accent is on the second syllable.

95. *relish*] savour, trace. Cf. *Ham.* III. iii. 92:

　　　　　　"Some act
　　That hath no relish of salvation
　　　　in't."

96. *division*] variation, descant.

98. *milk of concord*] Cf. I. v. 17 *ante.*

Uproar the universal peace, confound
All unity on earth.
Macd.   O Scotland! Scotland!   100
Mal. If such a one be fit to govern, speak:
I am as I have spoken.
Macd.   Fit to govern?
No, not to live.—O nation miserable!
With an untitled tyrant bloody-scepter'd,
When shalt thou see thy wholesome days again,   105
Since that the truest issue of thy throne
By his own interdiction stands accus'd,
And does blaspheme his breed? Thy royal father
Was a most sainted King: the Queen, that bore thee,
Oft'ner upon her knees than on her feet,   110
Died every day she liv'd.   Fare thee well!

99. Uproar] Uproot *or* Uptear *conjs. Keightley.*   102-3. Fit . . . miserable!]
so Pope; one line Ff.   107. accus'd] *Grierson, Harrison, Wilson;* accust *F 1;*
accurst *F 2, 3, 4, most edd.*   111. liv'd] *Ff;* lived. *Capell, Wilson.*

99. *Uproar*] throw into confusion
(*O.E.D.*).
99-100. *confound . . . earth*] " This
is what Macbeth has done " (Knights,
op. cit. p. 29). As this is not in Holinshed, Wilson suspects an interpolation by Shakespeare to please
James I, who had ambitions as a
peacemaker and hoped for the unity
of Christendom. " It seems that
the crowning horror in Malcolm's
self-indictment is violent opposition
to James's cherished foreign policy."
Later (125-31) Malcolm recants
three vices—lechery, avarice, and
falsehood, as in Holinshed—though
he has not accused himself specifically of falsehood; and in his re-
cantation he does not mention his
hatred of peace. This is an ingenious
theory. But it should be noted that
Malcolm does accuse himself of lack
of verity (92) and that the " milk of
concord " is a main theme of the
play (cf. the chapter of that title in
Knight, *The Imperial Theme*). But
although there is insufficient evidence
of an insertion to please King James,
there may have been a cut at 89 or

90 of a passage in which Malcolm
spoke in detail of the third vice,
falsehood.
101. *such a one*] Cf. " such an one,"
66 *ante.*
107. *interdiction*] An interdiction
was normally an authoritative or
peremptory prohibition, particularly
in ecclesiastical matters; but it
seems here to be a term in Scots
law = " a restraint imposed upon a
person incapable of managing his
own affairs on account of unsound-
ness of mind, improvidence, etc."
(*O.E.D.*). Such an interdiction
might be " voluntary," when a man
resigned the conduct of his affairs to
another.
107. *accus'd*] Nearly all editors
follow F 2 reading, " accurst." But
" accus'd " (F 1 " accust ") makes
better sense if " interdiction " is
interpreted as above, and makes a
tolerable sense even if " interdiction " is interpreted in the ordinary
way.
108. *blaspheme*] slander, defame.
Cf. Bacon, *Advancement of Learning*,
I. ii. 9: " And as to the judgment

These evils thou repeat'st upon thyself
Hath banish'd me from Scotland.—O my breast,
Thy hope ends here!
Mal.   Macduff, this noble passion,
Child of integrity, hath from my soul   115
Wip'd the black scruples, reconcil'd my thoughts
To thy good truth and honour.   Devilish Macbeth
By many of these trains hath sought to win me
Into his power, and modest wisdom plucks me
From over-credulous haste: but God above   120
Deal between thee and me! for even now
I put myself to thy direction, and
Unspeak mine own detraction; here abjure
The taints and blames I laid upon myself,
For strangers to my nature.   I am yet   125
Unknown to woman; never was forsworn;
Scarcely have coveted what was mine own;
At no time broke my faith: would not betray
The Devil to his fellow; and delight
No less in truth, than life: my first false speaking   130
Was this upon myself.   What I am truly,
Is thine, and my poor country's, to command:

126. woman] women *F 2, 3, 4.* forsworn] foreswore *F 2, 3, 4.*

of Cato the Censor, he was well punished for his *blasphemy* against learning."

111. *Died . . . liv'd*] Malone compared 1 *Cor.* xv. 31: " I die dayly."

111. *liv'd*] Most editors correct this to " lived "; but although Shakespeare uses the dissyllabic word in *J.C.* III. i. 257, " That ever lived in the tide of times," it is better here to retain the Folio reading and assume a pause, which is natural and necessary. Cf. Flatter, *op. cit.* p. 43.

113. *Hath*] The change to modern syntax is unjustifiable. Macduff means either that Malcolm's sins, which he has just confessed, or the same sins in Macbeth, have banished him.

118. *trains*] stratagems, artifices,

plots. Cotgrave defines " Traine " as " a plot, practise, conspiracie, deuise." Cf. *1 Hen. IV.* v. ii. 21. In hunting and hawking the term was used for a bait trailed or drawn along the ground to entice an animal; or for a lure of some kind to reclaim a hawk. Baynes, *Shakespeare Studies,* 1896, p. 312, quotes Turberville, *Book of Hunting,* 1908, p. 210: " When a huntsman would hunt the wolfe, he must trayne them by these means . . . there lette them lay downe their traynes. And when the wolves go out in the night to pray and to feede, they will crosse upon the trayne and follow it."

123. *mine own detraction*] my detraction of myself.

125. *For strangers*] as being strangers.

Whither, indeed, before thy here-approach,
Old Siward, with ten thousand warlike men,
Already at a point, was setting forth.   135
Now we'll together, and the chance of goodness
Be like our warranted quarrel.   Why are you silent?
Macd. Such welcome and unwelcome things at once,
'Tis hard to reconcile.

Enter a Doctor.

Mal.   Well, more anon.
Comes the King forth, I pray you?   140
Doct. Aye, Sir; there are a crew of wretched souls,
That stay his cure: their malady convinces

133. thy] *F 2;* they *F 1.* here-approach] *Pope;* heere approach *F 1.*
135. Already] *Ff;* All ready *Rowe.* forth.] foorth? *F 2, 3.*   136-7. the
chance . . . quarrel] our chance, in goodness . . . quarrel *Hanmer;* the chance,
O goodness . . . quarrel *conj. Johnson;* the chance of good success Betide our
. . . quarrel *conj. Bailey;* the grace of Goodness Betide . . . quarrel *conj.*
Cuningham.   139. 'Tis . . . anon] *Muir;* Well, . . . you? *one line, Ff.*

133. *here-approach*] cf. "here-
remain," 148 *post.*
134. *Siward*] The son of Beorn,
Earl of Northumberland. He assisted King Edward the Confessor
in suppressing the rebellion of Earl
Godwin and his sons in 1053.
135. *at a point*] in readiness, prepared, in agreement. Clarendon
quote Foxe's *Acts and Monuments,*
1570, p. 2092: "The Register there
sittyng by. beying weery, belyke, of
tarying or els perceauyng the
constant Martyrs to be at a point,
called vpon the chauncelour in hast
to rid them out of the way, and to
make an end." Cf. *Ham.* I. ii. 200:
"armed at point."
136-7. *the chance . . . quarrel*] i.e.
may the chance of success be proportionate to the justice of our
cause. *goodness* = good fortune. (Or,
might it mean "may out just cause
be Goodness's (i.e. God's) opportunity to overthrow evil in the shape of
Macbeth"?)
139. *Well, more anon*] The pause
comes better after this phrase than

before it, for during the pause the
doctor comes down stage.
140-59. *Comes . . . grace*] Although
one motive for the introduction of
this passage may have been to flatter
James I, and although the fact that
"'Tis hard to reconcile" (139) and
"See who comes here" (159) might
be joined to make a line suggests
that the intervening lines might be
an interpolation, it can still be
justified on dramatic grounds. The
good supernatural described here is
a contrast to the evil supernatural
of the Weird Sisters (cf. Knight, *The*
Wheel of Fire, 1949, p. 148). Knights,
op. cit. p. 31, links the passage with
the disease imagery of Act V; and
there is an obvious contrast between
the holy king of England and the
unholy king of Scotland.   There has
been some preparation for the
account of Edward in III. vi. and in
the list of the king-becoming graces.
It is also arguable that the entrance
of Rosse, with his tragic news, comes
more dramatically after an undramatic interlude than it would

The great assay of art; but at his touch,
Such sanctity hath Heaven given his hand,
They presently amend.
Mal.   I thank you, Doctor.   145
                              [*Exit Doctor.*
Macd. What's the disease he means?
Mal.   'Tis call'd the Evil:
A most miraculous work in this good King,
Which often, since my here-remain in England,
I have seen him do.   How he solicits Heaven,
Himself best knows; but strangely-visited people,   150
All swoln and ulcerous, pitiful to the eye,
The mere despair of surgery, he cures;
Hanging a golden stamp about their necks,
Put on with holy prayers: and 'tis spoken,
To the succeeding royalty he leaves   155
The healing benediction.   With this strange virtue,
He hath a heavenly gift of prophecy;
And sundry blessings hang about his throne,
That speak him full of grace.

Enter ROSSE.

Macd.   See, who comes here.
Mal. My countryman; but yet I know him not.   160

148. here-remain] *Pope;* heere remaine *Ff.*   150. strangely-visited] *Pope;*
strangely visited *Ff.*   160. not] nor *F.*

at 139. The passage is based on the
account of Edward the Confessor in
Holinshed, *Hist. Eng.*, 195*a*: " As
hath beene thought he was inspired
with the gift of prophesie and also
to haue had the gift of healing infirmities and diseases. He vsed to
help those that were vexed with the
disease, commonlie called the kings
euill, and left that vertue as it were
a portion of inheritance vnto his
successors the kings of this realme."
   142. *convinces*] conquers.
   143. *great . . . art*] greatest effort
of medical skill.
   146. *the Evil*] the king's evil—
scrofula.

   148. *here-remain*] i.e. stay.
   149. *solicits*] prevails by entreaty.
King James in 1603 ascribed the
effect of his " touch " to prayer.
Cf. Gardiner, *History of England*, i.
152.
   152. *mere*] utter.
   153. *stamp*] i.e. stamped coin: an
angel. Cf. *W.T.* IV. iv. 747: " we
pay them for it with stamped coin."
The gift is not mentioned in Holinshed, but was customary in Shakespeare's day.
   156. *virtue*] healing power.
   160. *My countryman*] Malcolm recognizes him by his dress—Wilson
suggests a blue bonnet. There are

Macd. My ever-gentle cousin, welcome hither.
Mal. I know him now.   Good God, betimes remove
    The means that makes us strangers!
Rosse.   Sir, amen.
Macd. Stands Scotland where it did?
Rosse.   Alas, poor country!
    Almost afraid to know itself.   It cannot   165
    Be call'd our mother, but our grave; where nothing,
    But who knows nothing, is once seen to smile;
    Where sighs, and groans, and shrieks that rent the air
    Are made, not mark'd; where violent sorrow seems
    A modern ecstasy: the dead man's knell   170
    Is there scarce ask'd for who; and good men's lives
    Expire before the flowers in their caps,
    Dying or ere they sicken.
Macd.   O relation,
    Too nice, and yet too true!
Mal.   What's the newest grief?
Rosse. That of an hour's age doth hiss the speaker;   175
    Each minute teems a new one.

161. ever-gentle] *Pope;* euer gentle *Ff.*   163. The means] The meanes, the
meanes *F 2, 3, 4.*   makes] make *Hanmer.*   168. rent] *Ff;* rend *Rowe.*
173-4. O . . . true!] *so Theobald;* one line, *Ff.*   174. and . . . true] yet
true *conj. Steevens.*   174. What's] What is *Hanmer, etc.*   176-7. Each . . .
too] *lines end* one, children? too. *Arden (ed. 1).*

no signs of Scottish costume in the
earliest illustration to the play (1709)
and Macklin is reputed to have
introduced it in 1773.   R. Walker,
op. cit. chap. 7, suggests that Malcolm
refuses to know Rosse, diplomatically,
because he is a collaborator.   I
doubt this; but Walker also draws
a suggestive parallel between this
entry and Rosse's first entry in I. ii.:
" Again it is Ross who comes to the
King of Scotland, again with news
of a treacherous thane of Cawdor—
and again from Fife."
    167. *once*] ever, at any time.   Cf.
A.C. v. ii. 50.
    168. *rent*] used indifferently with
rend, as the present tense of the verb
(Clarendon).
    170. *A modern ecstacy*] i.e. a

commonplace emotion.   Cf. *R.J.*
III. ii. 120: " modern lamentation ";
A.W. II. iii. 2: " to make modern
and familiar things supernatural and
causeless."   For " ecstacy " see III.
ii. 22 *ante.*
    171. *who*] for " whom."
    172. *flowers*] H. Rowe thought
there might be a reference to the
way Highlanders stick heather in
their bonnets.
    174. *nice*] elaborate.   Cf. *R.J.*
v. ii. 18.   " The letter was not nice,
but full of charge."
    175. *hiss*] cause to be hissed.
    176. *teems*] Also in the active
sense in *Hen. V.* v. ii. 52:

      " nothing teems
But hateful docks, rough thistles."

Macd.　　　　　　　　　　　How does my wife?
Rosse. Why, well.
Macd.　　　　　　And all my children?
Rosse.　　　　　　　　　　　　Well too.
Macd. The tyrant has not batter'd at their peace?
Rosse. No; they were well at peace, when I did leave 'em.
Macd. Be not a niggard of your speech: how goes't?　　180
Rosse. When I came hither to transport the tidings,
　　Which I have heavily borne, there ran a rumour
　　Of many worthy fellows that were out;
　　Which was to my belief witness'd the rather,
　　For that I saw the tyrant's power afoot.　　　　185
　　Now is the time of help.　Your eye in Scotland
　　Would create soldiers, make our women fight,
　　To doff their dire distresses.
Mal.　　　　　　　　　　Be 't their comfort,
　　We are coming thither.　Gracious England hath
　　Lent us good Siward, and ten thousand men;　　190
　　An older, and a better soldier, none
　　That Christendom gives out.
Rosse.　　　　　　　　　Would I could answer
　　This comfort with the like!　But I have words,
　　That would be howl'd out in the desert air,
　　Where hearing should not latch them.
Macd.　　　　　　　　　　What concern they?　195

179. 'em] *Ff;* them *Capell.*　　180. goes't] *Capell;* gos't *Ff.*　　195. latch]
catch *Rowe.*　　　　　195-6. What . . . cause?] *Theobald;* What . . . they,
. . . cause, *Ff;* What? concern they The gen'ral cause? *Rowe.*

177. *well*] Cf. *A.C.* II. v. 32:
"We use To say, the dead are well."
Craig quotes Heywood, *Faire Maid
of the West* (ed. Pearson, ii. 299):
"Why well . . . He's well in heaven,
for, mistresse, he is dead."

177. *children*] The metrical pause
after this word suggests Rosse's
embarrassment.

179. *at peace*] Cf. "sent to peace,"
III. ii. 20 *ante,* and *Rich. II.* III. ii.
127-8.

181. *tidings*] i.e. of the murder of
Macduff's family.　Rosse twice shies
away from his message.

183. *out*] i.e. in the field, in rebellion.　The followers of the two
Pretenders were frequently spoken of
as "out" in the '15 and '45.

186. *Your*] i.e. Malcolm's.

188. *doff*] clothing image.　Cf.
33 *ante.*

189. *Gracious England*] cf. 43 *ante.*

192. *gives out*] proclaims.

194. *would*] should.

195. *latch*] i.e. catch.　See Palsgrave, *Lesclarcissement,* 1530, p. 604:
"I latche, I catche a thynge that is
throwen to me in my handes, *je
happe.*"　Cf. *Sonnet,* cxiii. 6.

The general cause? or is it a fee-grief,
Due to some single breast?
Rosse.   No mind that's honest
But in it shares some woe, though the main part
Pertains to you alone.
Macd.   If it be mine,
Keep it not from me; quickly, let me have it.   200
Rosse. Let not your ears despise my tongue for ever,
Which shall possess them with the heaviest sound,
That ever yet they heard.
Macd.   Humh! I guess at it.
Rosse. Your castle is surpris'd; your wife, and babes,
Savagely slaughter'd: to relate the manner,   205
Were, on the quarry of these murther'd deer,
To add the death of you.
Mal.   Merciful Heaven!—
What, man! ne'er pull your hat upon your brows:
Give sorrow words; the grief, that does not speak,
Whispers the o'er-fraught heart, and bids it break. 210
Macd. My children too?
Rosse.   Wife, children, servants, all
That could be found.

203. Humh!] Hum ! *Rowe;* Humh: *Ff;* Humph! *Malone.*   211-23. Wife
. . . too?] *so Capell; two lines, divided after* found *Ff.*

196. *fee-grief*] An estate in fee
simple is the largest estate in land
known to the English law, and
Shakespeare here may convey a
two-fold idea of boundless grief, i.e.
the utmost which could be contained
in "some single breast," and of
particular ownership as opposed to
ownership in common. But Shakespeare may have meant no more
than "a peculiar sorrow, a grief
which hath a single owner" (Johnson).
197. *Due to*] i.e. owned by.
198. *in . . . woe*] Continuation of
legal metaphor.
202. *possess*] inform precisely
(Dyce).
203. *Humh*] Cf. note on III. ii. 42
ante.

206. *quarry*] game killed in hunting or hawking. Cf. *Ham.* v. ii. 375.
206. *deer*] a pun.
209-10. *the grief . . . break*] a variation on one of the favourite lines
in Seneca, *Hippolytus,* 607: "Curae
leves loquuntur, ingentes stupent."
Florio, *Essayes,* I. ii., translates:
"Light cares can freely speake,
     Great cares heart rather breake."
Shakespeare uses the same rhyme.
Cf. Ford, *Broken Heart,* v. iii. 76:
"They are the silent griefs which
cut   the   heart-strings";   and
Webster, *White Divel,* II. i. 279:
"Those are the killing greifes which
dare not speake."
211-13. Perhaps the F lineation,
suggesting dramatic pauses in the
metrical gaps is preferable.

Macd.　　　　　　　And I must be from thence!
　　My wife kill'd too?
Rosse.　　　　　　　I have said.
Mal.　　　　　　　　　Be comforted:
　　Let's make us med'cines of our great revenge,
　　To cure this deadly grief.　　　　　　　　215
Macd. He has no children.—All my pretty ones?
　　Did you say all?—O Hell-kite!—All?
　　What, all my pretty chickens, and their dam,
　　At one fell swoop?
Mal. Dispute it like a man.　　　　　　　　220
Macd.　　　　　　　I shall do so;
　　But I must also feel it as a man:
　　I cannot but remember such things were,
　　That were most precious to me.—Did Heaven look on,
　　And would not take their part?　Sinful Macduff!
　　They were all struck for thee.　Naught that I am, 225
　　Not for their own demerits, but for mine,
　　Fell slaughter on their souls:　Heaven rest them now!
Mal. Be this the whetstone of your sword: let grief
　　Convert to anger; blunt not the heart, enrage it.

---

212. *must*] preterite.

214-15. *Let's . . . grief*] One passion was thought to drive out another. Cf. H. Craig, *The Enchanted Glass*, 1936, pp. 116 *seq.*

216. *He . . . children*] There are three explanations of this passage. (i) He refers to Malcolm, who if he had children of his own would not suggest revenge as a cure for grief. Cf. *John* III. iv. 91: "He talks to me that never had a son." This was supported by Malone and Bradley. (ii) He refers to Macbeth, on whom he cannot take an appropriate revenge (Clarendon, New Clarendon, Cuningham). (iii) He refers to Macbeth, who would never have slaughtered Macduff's children if he had had any of his own. Cf. *3 Hen. VI.* v. v. 63:

　　"You have no children, butchers
　　　if you had,

The thought of them would have
　　stirred up remorse."

(Delius).　I adhere to (ii).

217. *hell-kite*] Cf. note on III. iv. 71 *ante*, and *deer* (206), *chickens* (218), *slaughter, souls* (227).

218. *dam*] Used of birds as well as of quadrupeds.

219. *swoop*] i.e. of the hell-kite. But Wilson suggests there is also present the sense of losing all in a sweepstake. Cf. *Ham.* IV. v. 142.

220. *dispute*] struggle against.

225. *Naught*] wicked.

226. *Not . . . mine*] He is not blaming himself for his flight from Scotland, but for his sinful nature. The word " demerits " is used by Holinshed of Donwald (p. 151).

229. *Convert*] turn; here used intransitively, as in *Rich. II.* v. i. 66: " The love of wicked men converts to fear "; and *ibid.* v. iii. 64: " Thy

Macd. O! I could play the woman with mine eyes,   230
And braggart with my tongue.—But, gentle Heavens,
Cut short all intermission; front to front,
Bring thou this fiend of Scotland, and myself;
Within my sword's length set him; if he 'scape,
Heaven forgive him too!
Mal.   This tune goes manly.   235
Come, go we to the King: our power is ready;
Our lack is nothing but our leave.   Macbeth
Is ripe for shaking, and the Powers above

---

235. Heaven] *Ff;* The Heaven *Pope;* O God *or* Then God *or* May God *or* God, God *Camb.* tune] *Rowe (ed.* 3); time *Ff.*

---

overflow of good converts to bad."
Anderson, *Elizabethan Psychology and Shakespeare's Plays*, p. 99, comments that " to weep . . . is to make less the fuel of revenge."

232. *intermission*] interruption, delay, interval of time. Cf. *M.V.* III. ii. 201:

" You loved, I loved, for inter-
    mission
No more pertains to me, my
    lord, than you."

and *Lear*, II. iv. 33: " spite of inter-mission."

235. *Heaven*] " Probably the original MS. had ' May God,' or ' Then God,' or ' God, God,' as in v. i. 74, which was changed in the actors' copy to *Heaven* for fear of incurring the penalties provided by the Act of Parliament against profanity on the stage " (Clarendon). The Act 3 James I, cap. 21, *An Act to Restrain the abuses of Players*, " For the preventing and avoiding of the great abuse of the holy Name of God, in Stage-plays, Enterludes, May-games, Shews, and such-like," enacted that " if . . . any person do or shall in any Stage-play . . . jestingly or prophanely speak, or use the holy Name of God, or of Jesus Christ, or of the Holy Ghost,

or of the Trinity . . . shall forfeit for every such offence . . . ten pounds "; half of the fine going to the king and half to " him or them that will sue for the same." I suspect that " God " rather than the conjectures of the Cambridge and Clarendon editors, was what Shakespeare wrote.

235. *too*] because if he escapes, it will be a sign that my hatred is appeased. Wilson compares *Ham.* I. ii. 182-3, and III. iii. 73-95.

235. *tune*] Rowe's emendation for " time " is generally accepted. But Cuningham defends the Folio reading by quoting *Ham.* III. i. 166 (Q 2) " Like sweet bells jangled out of *time* and harsh " and two other passages from Elizabethan plays. Though the *Hamlet* " time " was probably a misprint, which was corrected in the Folio, and though the other passages quoted by Cuningham are not decisive, it is possible that Malcolm here means " time "; for the time of manly music would differ from that of a plaint or dirge.

236. *power*] army. Cf. 238 *post.*

237. *Our lack . . . leave*] i.e. we have only to take our leave of the king.

238. *ripe for shaking*] Noble compares *Nahum*, iii. 12: " All thy

Put on their instruments.　　Receive what cheer you
　　may;
The night is long that never finds the day.　　　　240
　　　　　　　　　　　　　　　　　　　　　　　　[*Exeunt.*

---

strong cities shall be like figge trees
with the first ripe figs: for if they
bee shaken, they fall into the mouth
of the eater."

238. *Powers*] Cf. note on II. i. 7 *ante.*

239. *Put . . . instruments*] i.e. arm
themselves; not " set us, their
instruments, to the work " (Steevens,
Clarendon, Cuningham).

239-40. *Receive . . . day*] Wilson
and others suspect the hand of the
interpolator; but the tag makes an
easier finish to the act, and the
alexandrine (239) is insufficient
evidence of an interpolation. Cuningham argues that " Put on " (239)
should be printed in the previous
line.

ACT V

SCENE I.—*Dunsinane. A room in the castle.*

Enter a Doctor of Physic and a Waiting-Gentlewoman

Doct. I have two nights watch'd with you, but can perceive no truth in your report. When was it she last walk'd?

Gent. Since his Majesty went into the field, I have seen her rise from her bed, throw her night-gown upon   5
her, unlock her closet, take forth paper, fold it, write upon't, read it, afterwards seal it, and again return to bed; yet all this while in a most fast sleep.

Doct. A great perturbation in nature, to receive at once the benefit of sleep, and do the effects of watching!   10
In this slumbery agitation, besides her walking and

ACT V

Scene I

S.D. *Dunsinane.*] *Capell. A . . . castle*] *Rowe (subst.)*   1. two]
too *F.*   9. nature,] *Ff;* nature,— *Dyce.*   10. watching!] *Dyce, Wilson;*
watching. *Ff.*

Scene I

4. *into the field*] Steevens complains that Shakespeare "forgot he had shut up Macbeth in Dunsinane and surrounded him with besiegers. That he could *not go into the field* is observed by himself with a splenetic impatience, v. v. 5-7." But Macbeth was not yet surrounded by besiegers; and in iv. iii. 186 Rosse speaks of having seen "the tyrant's power afoot," probably to suppress the rebels "that were out"; and Macbeth would not necessarily be beleaguered in his fortress until the arrival of the English forces under Siward. Holinshed mentions "light skirmishes." See Appendix, p. 185.

5. *night-gown*] See II. ii. 69 *ante.*

6. *closet*] private repository of valuables. Cf. *Lear*, III. iii. 11: "I have lock'd the letter in my closet."

6. *paper*] Critics suggest that she writes a letter to Macbeth; perhaps indicating that she still wishes to control him, though he no longer consults her. But it might be a confession.

6. *fold it*] probably to mark a margin. Cf. Florio's *Montaigne*, i. 39: "a sheete without folding or margine."

9. *perturbation in nature*] constitutional disorder (Wilson).

10. *watching*] i.e. waking. Cf. *R.J.* IV. iv. 8; and Holland, *Pliny,*

other actual performances, what, at any time, have
you heard her say?

Gent. That, Sir, which I will not report after her.

Doct. You may, to me; and 'tis most meet you should.   15

Gent. Neither to you, nor any one; having no witness to
confirm my speech.

Enter LADY MACBETH, *with a taper.*

Lo you! here she comes. This is her very guise; and,
upon my life, fast asleep. Observe her: stand close.

Doct. How came she by that light?   20

Gent. Why, it stood by her: she has light by her continually; 'tis her command.

Doct. You see, her eyes are open.

Gent. Ay, but their sense are shut.

Doct. What is it she does now? Look, how she rubs   25
her hands.

Gent. It is an accustom'd action with her, to seem thus
washing her hands. I have known her continue in
this a quarter of an hour.

---

14. report] *Ff;* repeat *conj. Warburton.*   17. S.D. Lady Macbeth] *Rowe;*
Lady *F.*   24. sense are] *Ff;* senses are *Keightley;* sense' are *Dyce conj.*
S. Walker, Arden (*ed. 1*); sense is *Rowe and many edd.*

---

xiv. 18 (cited Clarendon): " two
kindes of wine of contrary operations; the one procureth sleepe,
the other causeth watching."

11. *slumbery*] cf. Phaer, *Virgil* (sig.
i. 4, ed. 1620): " the place of
sleepe and slumbry night."

11. *agitation*] physical activity,
not mental. " slumbery agitation =
sleep-walking " (Wilson).

12. *actual*] exhibited in deeds
(*O.E.D.*).

15. *You may . . . should*] blank
verse.

16-17. *Neither . . . speech*] Liddell
comments: " The gentlewoman's
canny reluctance to shelter herself
under the physician's professional
privilege is probably due to Shakespeare's knowledge of law . . . her
unsupported statement as to what
Lady Macbeth has said would
amount to treason if the doctor
chose to betray her confidence."
This is most unlikely.

18. *Lo . . . guise*] blank verse.

18. *This . . . guise*] " This is the
way she has done it before " (New
Clarendon).

19. *close*] concealed. Cf. *J.C.* i. iii.
131.

21. *light*] Because she is now
terrified of the dark.

24. *are*] Often emended; but
Shakespeare probably wrote " are "
on account of the plural contained
in " their," and because the sense
of two eyes is referred to (Delius).
Walker compares *Sonnet,* cxii. 10-11.

" that my adder's sense
To critic and to flatterer stopped
are."

Lady M. Yet here's a spot.   30
Doct. Hark! she speaks.   I will set down what comes
  from her, to satisfy my remembrance the more
  strongly.
Lady M. Out, damned spot! out, I say!—One; two:
  why, then 'tis time to do't.—Hell is murky.—Fie,   35
  my Lord, fie! a soldier, and afeard?—What need
  we fear who knows it, when none can call our power
  to accompt?—Yet who would have thought the
  old man to have had so much blood in him?

32. satisfy] satisfie *F;* fortifie *Warburton.*   35. murky.] *Ff;* murky!
Steevens.   37-8. fear who . . . accompt?] feare? who . . . accompt: *F 1,
2;* fear who . . . account? *Theobald;* fear? who . . . account: *F 3, 4.*
39. him?] *Rowe;* him, *Ff;* him! *Knight.*

30. *spot*] Cf. II. ii. 67-8.
32. *satisfy*] furnish with sufficient
proof, i.e. support.   Cuningham
thinks it means "assure" and
quotes *Hen. V.* III. ii. 105; *T.N.*
III. iii. 22; and Coles, *Lat. Dict.*
(1677): "satisfied, certior factus."
34. *One; two*] Lady Macbeth
thinks she hears the clock strike—
not, I think, as Wilson suggests, the
bell she struck at II. i. 62; Cf.
Marston, *II Antonio and Mellida,*
I. i. 9.
34-65. *Out . . . to bed*] Lady Macbeth's speeches might be printed
as rough blank verse (cf. Bay-
field, *Shakespeare's Versification*) though
Shakespeare probably intended them
as prose.   The verse fossils (cf. notes
to 15, 19 *ante*) may indicate a revision of this scene.   It must be in
prose, writes J. Wilson, *Dies Boreales*
(Blackwood's, 1849) " because these
are the *ipsissima verba*—yea, the
escaping sighs and moans of the
bared soul.   There must be nothing,
not even the thin and translucent
veil of the verse, betwixt her soul
showing itself, and yours beholding."
35. *Hell is murky*] The Folio
punctuation, i.e. with the full stop,
is correct here and not Steevens'
emendation.   Bradley, *Shakespearean
Tragedy,* p. 334, remarks: " The

failure of nature in Lady Macbeth
is marked by her fear of darkness;
'She has light by her continually.'
And in the one phrase of fear that
escapes her lips even in sleep, it is
of the darkness of the place of torment that she speaks." Steevens
thought she imagined herself here
talking to Macbeth, who (she supposed) had first said *Hell is murky,*
and repeats his words in contempt
of his cowardice: and he punctuated with a note of exclamation
accordingly.   But, as Bradley further
remarks, " He would hardly in
those days have used an argument
or expressed a fear that could
provoke nothing but contempt."
In I. vii. Macbeth never appeals
to moral principles, and he would
jump the life to come.
37-8. *none . . . accompt*] Rushton,
Shakespeare a Lawyer (1858), p. 37,
says: " Reference seems to be here
made to the ancient and fundamental principle of the English
Constitution that the King can do
no wrong." Cuningham supported
this view by a quotation from
Blount's *Law Dictionary* (1670).   But
I agree with Case that " a more
ancient and fundamental principle
is that tyrant power cannot be
brought to book."

Doct. Do you mark that?   40
Lady M. The Thane of Fife had a wife: where is she
    now?—What, will these hands ne'er be clean?—
    No more o' that, my Lord, no more o' that: you
    mar all with this starting.
Doct. Go to, go to: you have known what you should not.   45
Gent. She has spoke what she should not, I am sure of
    that: Heaven knows what she has known.
Lady M. Here's the smell of the blood still: all the
    perfumes of Arabia will not sweeten this little hand.
    Oh! oh! oh!   50
Doct. What a sigh is there! The heart is sorely charg'd.
Gent. I would not have such a heart in my bosom, for
    the dignity of the whole body.
Doct. Well, well, well.
Gent. Pray God it be, sir.   55
Doct. This disease is beyond my practice: yet I have
    known those which have walk'd in their sleep, who
    have died holily in their beds.
Lady M. Wash your hands, put on your night-gown;
    look not so pale.—I tell you yet again, Banquo's   60
    buried: he cannot come out on's grave.
Doct. Even so?

---

44. this] *not in F 2, 3, 4.* starting] *F 1;* stating *F 2.*   45. Go . . . not.]
so Pope; two lines divided to:/You *Ff.*   52-3. the dignity] *F 1, 2;*
dignity *F 3, 4.*

41. *Fife . . . wife*] The doggerel
rhyme is used with superb effect.

42. *clean*] Imitated by Webster,
White Devil, v. iv. 76:
  " Heere's a white hand:
    Can bloud so soone bee washt
    out? "

44. *starting*] cf. III. iv. 62.

45. *Go . . . not*] This line is not
addressed to the Gentlewoman, as
some have imagined.

48. *smell*] Grierson contrasts Macbeth's visual imagination with Lady
Macbeth's sense of smell.

51. *sorely*] heavily.

53. *dignity*] worth, value. Cf. *T.C.*
I. iii. 204.

56. *practice*] art.

60-1. *I tell you . . . grave*] Adams
thinks that these words indicate
that a scene has been lost, because
there is nothing like it in the Banquet
scene. But Shakespeare does not
attempt to chronicle every hour of
the lives of his characters; and this
sentence is merely a retrospective
indication of the terrible dreams and
hallucinations which once afflicted
Macbeth nightly, but no longer.
Direness cannot once start him.
Cf. v. v. 9 *post.*

61. *on's*] i.e. of his. Cf. *Lear,* I. iv.
114: " two on's daughters "; and
" on " for " of ", I. iii. 84 *ante.*

Lady M. To bed, to bed: there's knocking at the gate.
    Come, come, come, come, give me your hand.
    What's done cannot be undone.   To bed, to bed,
    to bed.   [*Exit.*   65

Doct. Will she go now to bed?

Gent. Directly.

Doct. Foul whisp'rings are abroad.   Unnatural deeds
    Do breed unnatural troubles: infected minds
    To their deaf pillows will discharge their secrets.   70
    More needs she the divine than the physician.—
    God, God forgive us all!   Look after her;
    Remove from her the means of all annoyance,
    And still keep eyes upon her.—So, good night:
    My mind she has mated, and amaz'd my sight.   75
    I think, but dare not speak.

Gent.   Good night, good Doctor.
                                            [*Exeunt.*

72. God, God] *Ff;* God, God, *Theobald;* Good God *Pope.*

65. *What's . . . undone*] cf. iii. ii. 12.

68. *Foul whisp'rings*] insinuations, slanders, rumours.   Cf. *2 Cor.* xii. 20.

68-70. *Foul . . . secrets*] Knight, *New Adelphi*, 1927, pp. 69-73, compares *2 Hen. VI.* iii. ii. 374-6:

" he calls the King
And *whispers* to his *pillow*, as to him,
The *secrets* of his over-*charged* soul."

73. *annoyance*] injury, harm to herself; " annoy " and " annoyance " were used in a stronger sense than at present   This hint prepares us for Lady Macbeth's suicide.

75. *mated*] bewildered, confounded. Cotgrave's *Dict.* gives the two senses: " Mater: *To mate, or giue a mate unto; to . . . amate, quell, subdue, ouercome.*" Both senses are played upon in *C.E.* iii. ii. 54: " not mad but *mated.*" Cf. Marlowe, *I Tamb.* i. i. 107: " How now, my lord, what mated and amazed? "   The original form, *amate*, occurs in Greene, *Orlando Furioso*, ii. i. 488: " Hath love *amated* him? " Sidney, *Arcadia*, iii. vii. uses the expression " mated minde ".   (ed. Feuillerat i. 385).

SCENE II.—*The country near Dunsinane.*

Enter, with drums and colours, MENTETH, CATHNESS, ANGUS,
LENOX, *and Soldiers.*

Ment. The English power is near, led on by Malcolm,
His uncle Siward, and the good Macduff.
Revenges burn in them; for their dear causes
Would, to the bleeding and the grim alarm,
Excite the mortified man.
Ang.   Near Birnam wood   5
Shall we well meet them: that way are they coming.

Scene II

S.D. *The . . . Dunsinane.*] *Capell.*   4. bleeding] bleeding, *F.*   5.
Birnam] *F 3, 4;* Byrnan *F 1, 2.*   6. well] *not in F 3, 4, Chambers.*

Scene II

Angus] R. Walker, *op. cit.* chap. 9, remarks that the " re-appearance of Angus . . . in the rebel ranks in Scotland suggests an almost organic relationship between the invaders and the rebels, for Angus is almost as much Rosse as Rosse himself! The same qualities of Scottish manhood march with Malcolm and march to meet Malcolm, the union of the two armies is not merely an Anglo-Scottish alliance but an organic union of the sundered parts of the snake which Macbeth scotched but could not kill."

2. *His uncle Siward*] Holinshed speaks of him as the grandfather of Malcolm: " Duncane, hauing two sonnes by his wife which was the daughter of Siward, Earle of Northumberland." Cuningham points out that " nephew " with Elizabethans clearly meant " grandson " as well as our " nephew," as in Spenser, *Ruines of Rome*, 8:
" Of vertuous nephewes, that
          posteritie
Striuing in power their grand-
          fathers to passe."
But Duncan in the play seems to be at least as old as Siward; Shakespeare made him older than in the

Chronicle and made Siward Malcolm's uncle instead of grandfather to harmonize with the other alteration.

3. *Revenges*] Used in the plural, meaning either the desire for vengeance or the act of revenge. Cf. *Cym.* II. v. 24.

3. *dear causes*] heartfelt grounds of accusation, grievous wrongs (Wilson); or grounds of action; or grievous diseases (Liddell). The last meaning suggested " bleeding " (4) and " mortified " (5) and " cause " (15). Cf. *A.W.* II. i. 113: " toucht With that malignant cause."

4. *the bleeding . . . alarm*] i.e. the battlefield. But " bleeding " may have been suggested by the word " burn " in the previous line and by " causes," bleeding being the remedy for a fever (Liddell). But " bleeding " may also have been suggested by the superstition that the corpse of a murdered man bled afresh in the presence of the murderer (Clarendon), which Shakespeare might have been reminded of by Holinshed's account of Donwald, where it is mentioned.

5. *Excite . . . man*] Either (i) raise up the dead, or (ii) stir up the numbed. Cf. *J.C.* II. i. 324:

Cath. Who knows if Donalbain be with his brother?

Len. For certain, Sir, he is not. I have a file
      Of all the gentry: there is Siward's son,
      And many unrough youths, that even now   10
      Protest their first of manhood.

Ment.   What does the tyrant?

Cath. Great Dunsinane he strongly fortifies.
      Some say he's mad; others, that lesser hate him,
      Do call it valiant fury: but, for certain,
      He cannot buckle his distemper'd cause   15
      Within the belt of rule.

Ang.   Now does he feel
      His secret murthers sticking on his hands;
      Now minutely revolts upbraid his faith-breach:
      Those he commands move only in command,
      Nothing in love: now does he feel his title   20
      Hang loose about him, like a giant's robe
      Upon a dwarfish thief.

10. unrough] *Theobald;* vnruffe *F;* unruff'd *Pope.*   11. tyrant?] *F 4;*
Tyrant. *F 1, 2, 3.*

"Thou, like an exorcist, hast
   conjured up
My mortified spirit."
" Excite " (from *excitare*) would thus
mean " call forth " or " quicken."
The whole passage is discussed in
Modern Language Notes, xxix. 94-5,
and thus paraphrased: " The justice
of their cause should rouse even the
dead to an interest in the bloodshed
and din of the battle." This is, I
believe, what Shakespeare meant,
though there may have been unconscious or concealed puns.
   8. *file*] list, roll. Cf. III. i. 94 *ante.*
   10. *unrough*] unbearded.
   11. *Protest*] proclaim. Cf. III. iv.
105 *ante,* and *M.A.* v. i. 149.
   15-16. *He . . . rule*] For the metaphor compare *T.C.* II. ii. 30:
   " And buckle in a waist most
      fathomless
   With spans and inches so dimin-
      utive
   As fears and reasons."
Cf. note to 3 *ante: cause* = sickness.

It may mean that Macbeth, like a
man with dropsy who cannot get
his belt on (cf. Falstaff), cannot
restrain his passions (cf. " mad ").
Or, it may mean that the kingdom
which he rules is sick and rebellious.
Cf. *2 Hen. IV.* III. i. 38 ff.:
   " the body of our kingdom
   . . . is but as a body, yet dis-
   temper'd."
   17. *sticking*] Cf. note on II. ii.
59-63 *ante.*
   18. *minutely*] adj. " very frequent."
   18. *upbraid*] used with accusative
of things as well as of persons. Cf.
T.C. III. ii. 198: " Upbraid my
falsehood."
   18. *his faith-breach*] i.e. his own
treason.
   19. *in command*] i.e. under orders.
   21-2. *Hang . . . thief*] The same
image is repeated in different forms
several times in the course of the
play. Cf. I. iii. 107-8 and I. iii.
145. Traversi, *Approach to Shakespeare,*
p. 100, comments: " Before the ad-

Ment.   Who then shall blame
His pester'd senses to recoil and start,
When all that is within him does condemn
Itself, for being there?
Cath.   Well; march we on,   25
To give obedience where 'tis truly ow'd:
Meet we the med'cine of the sickly weal;
And with him pour we, in our country's purge,
Each drop of us.
Len.   Or so much as it needs
To dew the sovereign flower, and drown the weeds.   30
Make we our march towards Birnam.
                                        [*Exeunt, marching.*

SCENE III.—*Dunsinane.   A room in the castle.*

Enter MACBETH, *Doctor, and Attendants.*

Macb. Bring me no more reports; let them fly all:
Till Birnam wood remove to Dunsinane,
I cannot taint with fear.   What's the boy Malcolm?
Was he not born of woman?   The spirits that know

Scene III

S.D. *Dunsinane . . . castle*] *Capell.*   2. Birnam] *F 3, 4;* Byrnane
F 1; Byrnam *F 2.*   3. taint] faint *conj. S. Walker.*

---

vancing powers of healing good, evil has shrunk to insignificance."

23. *pester'd*] embarrassed, troubled, Cotgrave gives: "Empestrer. *To pester, intricate, intangle, trouble, incomber.*" The original sense was "to hobble a horse, or other animal, to prevent it straying." Cf. *1 Hen. IV.* I. iii. 50: "To be so pester'd with a popinjay" and *T.C.* v. i. 38: "pester'd with such water flies."

27. *med'cine*] Probably used in the sense of doctor (Fr. *médecin*), though Shakespeare usually uses it in the sense of drug. Cuningham points out that Minsheu's *Spanish Dictionary* (1599) and Cotgrave's *French Dictionary* (1611) have only the word in the latter sense. In either case Malcolm is meant.

28. *purge*] The blood they shed,

absorbed by the earth, will act as a purgative drug. Wilson explains the whole passage: "they are ready to help . . . Malcolm purge the land of its fever, even if it means bleeding themselves to the last drop of their blood."

30. *dew*] bedew. Cf. *2 Hen. VI.* III. ii. 340.

30. *sovereign*] "Two ideas are suggested by this epithet, royal or supreme, and powerfully remedial, the latter continuing the metaphor of 27-9" (Clarendon). Fleay and Wilson suspect that the couplet is interpolated.

Scene III

1. *them*] the thanes.
3. *taint*] go rotten, become weak, wither. Cf. *T.N.* III. iv. 145.

All mortal consequence have pronounc'd me thus: 5
"Fear not, Macbeth; no man that's born of woman
Shall e'er have power upon thee."—Then fly, false
   Thanes,
And mingle with the English epicures:
The mind I sway by, and the heart I bear,
Shall never sag with doubt, nor shake with fear.   10

Enter a Servant.

The devil damn thee black, thou cream-fac'd loon!
Where gott'st thou that goose look?
Serv. There is ten thousand—
Macb.   Geese, villain?
Serv.   Soldiers, Sir.
Macb. Go, prick thy face, and over-red thy fear,
Thou lily-liver'd boy. What soldiers, patch?   15

5. consequence] *Singer (ed. 1), Wilson;* Consequences *Ff;* consequents *Steevens (1793).*   12. goose look?] *Capell;* Goose-looke. *Ff.*

Liddell quotes Comenius, *Janua linguarum,* 106: "failing of that moisture it flags, tainteth, and by and by drieth away."

4. *spirits*] not the witches but their. "masters" who appear as the apparitions in IV. i.

5. *consequence*] As Shakespeare does not elsewhere use the plural form, and as the rhythm is improved by using the singular form here, "used collectively and comprising in its meaning all subsequent circumstances," I have adopted Singer's emendation.

5. *me*] "in my case" or "me to be circumstanced."

8. *epicures*] Perhaps suggested by Holinshed, 1587, pp. 179-80, who says that "The Scottish people before had no knowledge nor understanding of fine fare or riotous surfet . . . those superfluities came into the realme of Scotland with the *English-men.* . . . For manie of the people abhorring the riotous maners and superfluous gormandizing brought in among them by the *Englishmen,*

were willing inough to receiue this Donald for their King, trusting . . . they should by his severe order in gouernement recouer againe the former temperance of their old progenitors."

9. *sway*] control myself, direct my actions. Cf. *T.N.* II. iv. 32.

10. *sag*] droop. Not used elsewhere by Shakespeare, but in Golding, Ovid's *Metam.* xi. 198: "And made them downe to sag."

11. *loon*] a rogue or worthless rascal. F 4 spelling and *Oth.* II. iii. 95, "lown" corresponds to the Southern pronunciation.

12. *goose*] Cf. II. iii. 16 *ante.* Armstrong, *Shakespeare's Imagination,* p. 60, suggests that the black and white imagery was "almost certainly aroused by the thought of writing with a goose-quill on white paper." He also shows that prick (14), lily-livered (15), sick (19), water (51), and sere (23) all appear elsewhere in Shakespeare in goose contexts.

15. *patch*] properly, a domestic

Death of thy soul! those linen cheeks of thine
Are counsellors to fear.   What soldiers, whey-face?
Serv. The English force, so please you.
Macb. Take thy face hence.   [*Exit Servant.*]—Seyton!—I am
    sick at heart,
When I behold—Seyton, I say!—This push   20
Will cheer me ever, or disseat me now.
I have liv'd long enough: my way of life

19. Seyton] *Ff;* Seton *Wilson.*   21. cheer] cheere *F 1, 2;* chair *Dyce (conj. Percy).* disseat] *Steevens (conj. Jennens and Capell);* dis-eate *F 1;* disease *F 2, 3, 4;* disseize *conj. Bailey;* defeat *conj. Daniel;* dis-ease *Furness.* 22. way] May *Steevens (1778), (conj. Johnson).*

fool or clown. It is also used as a term of contempt. It is perhaps derived from Ital. *pazzo,* or from the fool's wearing a "patched," or parti-coloured, coat. Cf. *M.N.D.* III. ii. 9: "a crew of patches." An unconscious pun on "patch" (= also *plaster*) would suit the associations of *goose* and *disease,* Cf. note on 12 *ante.*

17. *Are . . . fear*] prompt others to fear (Kittredge).

20. *push*] crisis, assault of fortune, attack. Cf. III. iv. 81 *ante* and *J.C.* v. ii. 5.

21. *cheer*] Probably a quibble on *cheer* and *chair* (which Percy proposed). The former links up with "sick at heart" and the latter with "disseat" (Wilson). Cuningham points out that *cheer* is misprinted *chair* in *Cor.* IV. vii. 52 and that it is quite common in the Folio to find *heare* for *hair;* a proof that the pronunciation of our *hair* in Shakespeare's day must have been close to *heer.* So, Cuningham argues, the *cheere* of the Folio might easily represent a phonetic spelling of *chair.* "Chair" in the sense of throne is common enough in Shakespeare. Cf. *Rich. III.* v. iii. 251. But Cuningham's arguments for emendation are more powerful as arguments for a quibble.

22. *way of life*] course of life. Cf. Horace, *Epistles,* I. xvii. 26. Baldwin,

Shakespeare's Small Latine, II. 518, thinks Shakespeare was recalling the context. Johnson supporting his conjecture, argued that there was no relation between "way of life" and "fallen into the sere," and that Shakespeare had "May" in the same sense elsewhere (e.g. *M.A.* v. i. 76 and *Rich. II.* III. iv. 48-9). Steevens, in support of Johnson, quoted Sidney, *Astrophel and Stella,* xxi: "If now the May of my years much decline." The Clarendon editors object to the mixture of metaphors in the Folio reading; and Cuningham points out that "may" is misprinted for "way" at II. i. 57 *ante.* But the lines from *Sonnet* 73, which Cuningham cites in support of Johnson, are used by Wilson in support of Folio.

"That time of year thou may'st
    in me behold
When yellow leaves, or few, or
    none, do hang. . . . "

Wilson also quotes Seneca, *Her. Fur.* 1258-9:

"Cur animam in ista luce de-
    tineam amplius
Morerque nihil est; cuncta iam
    amisi bona."

The parallel is not very close. But certainly no emendation is desirable. The image "way of life" is not sufficiently vivid to conflict with the image of "the yellow leaf" and may refer also to the "process

Is fall'n into the sere, the yellow leaf;
And that which should accompany old age,
As honour, love, obedience, troops of friends,   25
I must not look to have; but in their stead,
Curses, not loud, but deep, mouth-honour, breath,
Which the poor heart would fain deny, and dare not.
Seyton!—

Enter SEYTON.

Sey. What's your gracious pleasure?
Macb.   What news more?   30
Sey. All is confirm'd, my Lord, which was reported.
Macb. I'll fight, till from my bones my flesh be hack'd.
     Give me my armour.
Sey.   'Tis not needed yet.
Macb. I'll put it on.
     Send out moe horses, skirr the country round;   35
     Hang those that talk of fear.   Give me mine armour.—
     How does your patient, Doctor?

32. be] *F 1;* is *F 2, 3, 4.*   35. moe] *F 1, 2;* more *F 3, 4.*   skirr]
skirre *F 1, 2;* skir *F 3, 4.*   36. talk of] *F 1;* stand in *F 2, 3, 4.*   armour.—]
S.D. *Seton goes to fetch it Wilson.*

of the seasons " (*Sonnet* 104, in which Shakespeare mentions " Three beauteous springs to yellow autumn turn'd "). See Empson, *op. cit.* pp. 104-6.

23. *sere*] the withered state (Onions, who points out in *T.L.S.*, 24 Oct., 1935, that the word is printed with a capital in the Folio, that Shakespeare often converted adjs. into nouns, and that " the withered state, i.e. yellow-leaf state " makes better sense than " the withered, i.e. the yellow, leaf.")

25. *As*] i.e. namely.

27. *mouth-honour*] Cf. *Isa.* xxix. 13: " Because this people come neere vnto me with their mouth, and honour me with their lippes, but haue remooued their heart farre from me."

29. *Seyton*] French, *Shakespeare Genealog.* p. 296, says: " The Setons of Touch were (and are still) hereditary armour-bearers to the Kings of Scotland; there is thus a peculiar fitness in the choice of this name." One critic suggests wildly that Shakespeare intended a quibble on *Satan*.

35. *moe*] Shakespeare used both forms, *moe* and *more;* the former usually relating to number, the latter to size. But the distinction, if any there really were, was not always observed.

35. *skirr*] move rapidly, scour. Cf. *Hen. V.* IV. vii. 64.

37. *How . . . doctor?*] Cuningham suggests that the doctor should enter at this point. As there is no occasion for his presence until now, and as the names of characters who appear in a scene are sometimes given at the beginning, though they do not appear until later, I agree.

Doct.　　　　　　　　　　Not so sick, my Lord,
As she is troubled with thick-coming fancies,
That keep her from her rest.

Macb.　　　　　　　　　　Cure her of that:
Canst thou not minister to a mind diseas'd,　　　　　40
Pluck from the memory a rooted sorrow,
Raze out the written troubles of the brain,
And with some sweet oblivious antidote
Cleanse the stuff'd bosom of that perilous stuff
Which weighs upon the heart?

39. Cure her] *F 2, 3;* Cure *F 1.*　of] *F 1, 2;* from *F 3.*　　44. stuff'd]
Theobald; stufft *F 1;* stuft *F 2, 3, 4.*　stuff] *F 3;* stuffe *F 1, 2.*　*Cf. note
below.*

40. *Canst . . . diseas'd*] Cf. Seneca,
Her. Fur. 1261-2:

"nemo polluto queat
Animo mederi."

Heywood translates:

"no man may heale and loose
from gylty bandes
My mynd defyled."

42. *written . . . brain*] "written"
and hence fixed or permanent. Cf.
Ham. I. v. 103.

43. *oblivious*] Cotgrave, *Dict.,* "Ob-
livieux: *causing forgetfulnesse.*" Cf.
Horace, *Odes,* II. vii. 21: "*Ob-
livioso* levia Massico Ciboria exple."
Other critics quote Spenser, *F.Q.* IV.
iii. 43; Virgil, *Aen.* VI. 714-15.
See note to II. ii. 34 *ante,* and compare the following lines from Seneca,
Herc. Fur. 1077-81:

"placidus fessum lenisque fove,
preme devinctum torpore gravi;
sopor indomitos alliget artus
nec torva prius pectora linquat,
quam mens repetat pristina
cursum."

Heywood translates:

"Keepe him fast bound with
heavy sleepe opprest,
Let slomber deepe his Limmes
untamed bynde,

Nor soner leave his unright
raginge breaste
Then former mynd his course
agayne may fynd."

44. *stuff'd . . . stuff*] Editors suspect
that one of these words is a corruption. For "stuff'd" (F "stufft")
numerous words have been proposed:
full, foul, steep'd, fraught, clogged,
slufft, press'd, charg'd. For "stuff"
the following: load, matter, freight,
fraught, slough, sluff. Wilson voted
for *charged,* and failing that, *pressed* =
oppressed. Cf. *2 Hen. VI.* III. ii.
376: "the secrets of his over-
charged soul" (cf. note v. i. 51 *ante*)
and *3 Hen. VI.* II. v. 78: "o'er-
charged with grief." *Oth.* III. iv. 177:
"I have this while with leaden
thoughts been pressed," and *Per.* III.
ii. 84: "the o'erpressed spirits."
I think we should rule out words
which rhyme with "stuff" as the
jingle would be more offensive than
the repetition. But I believe that
Shakespeare wrote the text as printed.
If an alteration were necessary,
"fraught" for "stuff'd" would be
comparatively harmless. The Folio
spelling "stufft" might conceivably
have been a misreading of "fraught,"
the initial *fr* being read as *st* and

Doct.   Therein the patient   45
     Must minister to himself.
Macb. Throw physic to the dogs; I'll none of it.—
     Come, put mine armour on; give me my staff.—
     Seyton, send out—Doctor, the Thanes fly from me.—
     Come, sir, despatch.—If thou couldst, Doctor, cast   50

46. to] *F 1;* unto *F 2, 3, 4.*
armourer, who presently begins to equip Macbeth.
the concluding *ght* as *fft.* Cf. *Oth.*
III. iii. 449: " Swell bosom with
thy fraught, for 'tis of aspics'
tongues "; and *Macb.* IV. iii. 210,
" o'erfraught."
    45. *Which . . . heart*] There would
seem to be echoes in this scene and
in Scene v. of Seneca, *Agam.* tr.
Studley (Chorus 1):

    " Sleepe that doth ouercome and
         breake the bonds of griefe,
    It cannot ease theyr heartes, nor
         mynister reliefe."

(cf. " minister " (46) *post* and II. ii.
36-8 *ante*). " Can not bestow on
them her safe and quiet rest " (cf.
39 *ante*) " No banners be displayed."
Cf. v. v. 1: " Hang out our banners." " castell strongly built."
Cf. v. v. 2: " castle's strength."
" From high and proude degre
driues downe in dust to lye." Cf.
v. v. 24: " The way to dusty death."
It may be added that the " paynted
pomp " and wretchedness of the
monarch described in the chorus
may be compared with Macbeth's
speech, v. iii. 22 ff.; that the
repetition of " fear " (3, 10, 14, 17,
36 *ante*) may have been suggested
by the lines:

    " Fayne would they dreaded bee,
         and yet not settled so,
    When as they feared are, they
         feare, and lyue in woe ";

that v. v. 19 ff. resembles

    " To-morrow shall we rule, as wee
         haue done to-day.
    One clod of croked care another
         bryngeth in,

S.D. *Seton returns with armour and an
Wilson.*   48. mine] my *F 4.*
    One hurly burly done, another
         doth begin "—

the " clod of croked care " being
" the perilous stuff " (44 *ante*) and
the " hurly burly " is echoed in
I. i. 3; and finally that " those
Erennys wood turmoyles " links up,
by a quibble, with Birnam wood
(2, 60, *ante* and *post*). It may be
worth noting that the same chorus
contains the phrase " light and
vaine conceipt " (cf. *Rich. II.* III. ii.
166), the line

    " The bloudy Bellon those doth
         haunt with gory hand "

(cf. *Macb.* I. ii. 55 and II. ii. 61) and
a parallel with IV. i. 56. Cf. note
on that line.
    45-6. *Therein . . . himself*] Baldwin
quotes from *Ciceronis Sententiae,* which
Shakespeare may have read at
school: " Corpora curari possunt,
animorum nulla medicina est."
Timothy Bright, *Treatise on Melancholy,* p. 189, says: " Here no
medicine, no purgation, no cordiall,
no tryacle or balme are able to assure the afflicted soule and trembling
heart, now painting (i.e. panting)
vnder the terrors of God."
    50. *cast*] The term employed in
the diagnosis of ailments by in-
spection of the urine. Shakespeare
would find it in Lyly, *Euphues* (ed.
Arber) 296: " An Italian . . .
casting my water . . . commaunded
the chamber to be voyded "; and
in Greene, *Menaphon* (ed. Arber),
p. 35: " Able to cast his disease
without his water." Cf. *T.N.* III.
iv. 114.

The water of my land, find her disease,
And purge it to a sound and pristine health,
I would applaud thee to the very echo,
That should applaud again.—Pull 't off, I say.—
What rhubarb, cyme or what purgative drug,   55
Would scour these English hence?—Hear'st thou of
    them?
Doct. Ay, my good Lord: your royal preparation
    Makes us hear something.

---

52. pristine] *F 2;* pristiue *F 1.*   55. cyme] *F 1;* Cæny *F 2, 3;* senna *F 4;*
Sirrah *conj. Bulloch; cf. note below.*

52. *purge*] Cf. III. iv. 75.

55. *cyme*] Some think that this word is a misprint of *cynne*, an earlier spelling of senna. Hunter defends F 2, whose spelling "correctly represents the pronunciation." Cotgrave spells it *Sene* and *Senne*, and Dodoens, *New Herball*, 1586, mentions that "The cods and leaues of Sena taken in the quantitie of a dram do loose and purge the belly, scoure away fleume and choler, especially blacke choler and melancholie." The curious may be referred to a long controversy in *Modern Language Notes*, where the following suggestions were made: *Tyme* (liv), *sium* = wild parsley (lvi), a doublet of *cumin* (lvii), and *Ocyme* = basil (lx). The last, which is mentioned in Burton's *Anatomy of Melancholy* is superficially attractive because, as Gerard, *Herbal*, p. 548, says, "the seede cureth the infirmities of the hart, taketh away sorrowfulnesse which cometh of melancholie, and maketh a man merrie and glad." This links up with Macbeth's previous speech (40-5 *ante*) but it does not suggest a purgative drug, which the sense requires. The various Herbals I have consulted make no mention of the use of basil as a purge. Dodoens, *op. cit.* p. 272, is typical: "The later writers say, that it doth fortifie and strengthen the hart and the brayne, and that it reioyceth and recreateth the spirits, and is good against melancholie and sadnesse, and that if it be taken in wine, it cureth an old cough." *Cynne* or *senna* therefore gives the best sense. But as Rea points out (*Modern Language Notes*, xxxv) the word *cyme* is used in Holland's *Pliny*, 1634, Bk. xix, Vol. 2, p. 26: "Moreouer, like as Coleworts may be cut at all times of the yeare for our vse, so may they be sown and set all the yere long. . . . The tender crops called Cymæ after the first cutting, they yeeld the Spring next following: now are these Cymæ nothing els but the yong delicat tops or daintier tendrils of the maine stem . . . and yet none put forth their Cymes or tender buds more than they." Coleworts (*op. cit.* pp. 48-9) "be good for the stomack, and gently loosen the belly . . . they purge cholerick humours, being taken with sweet grosse wine." Rea comments: that the reading of the First Folio is perfectly intelligible, "meaning the tops and tendrils of the Colewort." But *cyme* is the top of any plant, not specifically of the Colewort (cf. *O.E.D.*). The later contributors to *Modern Language Notes* seem not to have noticed this passage.

Macb.   Bring it after me.—
I will not be afraid of death and bane,
Till Birnam forest come to Dunsinane.   [*Exit.*

Doct. [*Aside.*] Were I from Dunsinane away and clear,   61
Profit again should hardly draw me here.   [*Exeunt.*

SCENE IV.—*Country near Dunsinane.   A wood in view.*

Enter, with drum and colours, MALCOLM, *old* SIWARD, *and his
Son,* MACDUFF, MENTETH, CATHNESS, ANGUS, LENOX,
ROSSE, *and Soldiers, marching.*

Mal. Cousins, I hope the days are near at hand,
That chambers will be safe.

Ment.   We doubt it nothing.

Siw. What wood is this before us?

Ment.   The wood of Birnam.

Mal. Let every soldier hew him down a bough,
And bear't before him: thereby shall we shadow   5
The numbers of our host, and make discovery
Err in report of us.

Soldier.   It shall be done.

Siw. We learn no other but the confident tyrant

---

60. Birnam] Birnane *F.*

Scene IV

S.D. Country . . . view] *Capell subst.*   1. Cousins] Cousin *F 3, 4.*
3. Birnam] *F 3, 4;* Byrnam *F 2;* Birnane *F 1.*

58. *it*] i.e. some part of his armour.
61-2. *Were . . . here*] Fleay thought this couplet spurious and beneath the dignity of tragedy. " But when Shakespeare saw a chance to salt the meats of his plays with such touches he did not stand upon tragic dignity " (Granville-Barker).

Scene IV

2. *chambers . . . safe*] Shakespeare may refer to the espionage men-

tioned in III. iv. 130-1. But there is more likely to be a reference to Duncan's murder, the phrase meaning: " When we can sleep in our beds without fear of being murdered."
4-7. *Let . . . us*] This incident is in Holinshed, and there is therefore no point in tracing its origins to the *Romance of Alexander* or to the battle of Lamberkine, in 1332.
6. *discovery*] i.e. reconnaissance. Cf. *Lear* v. i. 53.

Keeps still in Dunsinane, and will endure
Our setting down before 't.

Mal.　　　　　　　　　'Tis his main hope;　　　10
For where there is advantage to be gone,
Both more and less have given him the revolt,
And none serve with him but constrained things,
Whose hearts are absent too.

Macb.　　　　　　　　Let our just censures
Attend the true event, and put we on　　　15
Industrious soldiership.

Siw.　　　　　　　　The time approaches,
That will with due decision make us know
What we shall say we have, and what we owe.
Thoughts speculative their unsure hopes relate,
But certain issue strokes must arbitrate;　　　20
Towards which advance the war.　　*[Exeunt, marching.*

11. advantage to be gone,] *Capell, Wilson;* aduantage to be giuen, *Ff;* advantage to be gone, *conj. Johnson;* advantage to be got *conj. Steevens;* advantage to be gotten *Collier (ed. 2);* advantage to be ta'en *Dyce (ed. 2. conj) S. Walker.* advantage to 'em given, *conj. Clar.*　　　14-15. Let our just Censures Attend] *F 1;* Let our best Censures Before *F 2, 3, 4.*

9. *endure*] allow.
10. *setting down before*] i.e. laying siege to. Cf. *Cor.* I. ii. 28:

"Let us along to guard Corioli:
If they set down before's."

Cuningham thinks that the above should read *sit* and the *Macbeth* passage *sitting.*
11. *advantage*] opportunity.
11. *gone*] Johnson's conj. makes sense, which the Folio reading does not. The compositor's eye obviously hit on the "giuen" in the followng line. This means that "giuen" is more likely to be wrong than "to be," so that the Clarendon conj. should be rejected. Kittredge retains F, and explains: "Wherever the circumstances are such that an opportunity can offer itself."

12. *more and less*] great and small. Cf. *2 Hen. IV.* I. i. 209.
14-15. *Let . . . event*] i.e. we shall know after the battle if the rumours about the morale of Macbeth's army are true or not.
19. *Thoughts . . . relate*] Siward, as well as Macduff, warns Malcolm of the dangers of optimism.
20. *certain . . . arbitrate*] i.e. actual fighting must decide the issue and make it a certainty. Steevens cites Chapman, *Odyssey,* bk. xviii: "Can arbitrate a war of deadliest weight." Fleay thought that this and the preceding couplet could not be Shakespeare's, and Wilson suspected 19-20 because "due decision" (17) makes a good antecedent to "which" (21). But "certain issue" (20) is an equally good antecedent.

SCENE V.—*Dunsinane. Within the castle.*

Enter, with drum and colours, MACBETH, SEYTON, *and Soldiers.*

Macb. Hang out our banners on the outward walls;
The cry is still, "They come!" Our castle's strength
Will laugh a siege to scorn: here let them lie,
Till famine and the ague eat them up.
Were they not forc'd with those that should be ours, 5
We might have met them dareful, beard to beard,
And beat them backward home. What is that noise?
    [A cry within, of women.
Sey. It is the cry of women, my good Lord.   *[Exit.*
Macb. I have almost forgot the taste of fears.
The time has been, my senses would have cool'd 10
To hear a night-shriek; and my fell of hair
Would at a dismal treatise rouse, and stir,
As life were in't. I have supp'd full with horrors:

Scene v

    S.D. *Dunsinane . . . castle.*] *Malone subst.*   1-2.] Hang . . . banners!
On . . . walls The cry is still, "They come!" *Keightley;* Hang . . . banners!
On . . . walls The cry is still, "They come." *Robert Nichols.*   5. forc'd]
'forc'd *Hanmer.*   8. S.D.] *Dyce; not in Ff.*   9. fears] tears *conj.* Bayliss.

Scene v

1-2. *Hang . . . cry*] Keightley justified his emended punctuation by declaring that it was from the keep, not the walls, that the banner was hung. But the rhythm of the line is against Keightley and Nichols. Cf. also *1 Hen. VI.* i. vi. 1: "Advance our waving colours on the walls."

5. *forc'd*] reinforced, strengthened. In *T.C.* v. i. 64, "wit larded with malice and malice forced with wit," where forced = farced, stuffed, the metaphor is from the kitchen. In the present passage there is a quibble on the two meanings.

6. *dareful*] bold or boldly; or defiantly. Not used elsewhere by Shakespeare.

8. *cry*] Lady Macbeth has not died a natural death.

10. *cool'd*] Used in a stronger sense than at present. Cf. *John* II. i. 479, and Florio's *Montaigne,* iii. 5: "In like case, incorporeal pleasures, is it not injustice to quaile and coole the minde, and say it must thereunto be entrained as unto a forced bond, or servile necessity?" (Temple ed. v. 179). Collier's reading "quail'd" may have come first to Shakespeare's mind, and may then have recalled the word near it in the Florio context.

11. *fell of hair*] skin with the hair on. Florio, *Worlde of Wordes,* for "Vello" has "a fleese of wooll, a fell or skin that hath wooll on." Cf. *Job,* IV. 15.

12. *treatise*] story, recital. Cf. *M.A.* I. i. 317 and *V.A.* 774.

13. *with*] cf. IV. ii. 32 *ante.*

Direness, familiar to my slaughterous thoughts,
Cannot once start me.

Re-enter SEYTON.

Wherefore was that cry?   15
Sey. The Queen, my Lord, is dead.
Macb. She should have died hereafter:
There would have been a time for such a word.—
To-morrow, and to-morrow, and to-morrow,
Creeps in this petty pace from day to day,   20
To the last syllable of recorded time;

15. S.D.] *Dyce; not in Ff.*   17-18. died hereafter: There] died: hereafter
There *Jackson.*

14-15. *Direness . . . me*] Horror can
never make me start.

17. *She . . . hereafter*] This apparently simple statement is ambiguous. Either " She would have
died sometime " (Wilson, Arrow-
smith) or " Her death should have
been deferred to a more peaceful
hour; had she lived longer, there
would have been a more convenient time for such a word." On
this, Johnson's interpretation, Murry,
Shakespeare, p. 335, comments:
" Macbeth's meaning is stranger
than that. 'Hereafter,' I think,
is purposely vague. It does not
mean 'later'; but in a different
mode of time from that in which
Macbeth is imprisoned now. ' Hereafter '—in the not-Now: *there* would
have been a time for such a word
as ' The Queen is *dead.*' But the
time in which he is caught is to-
morrow, and to-morrow, and to-
morrow—one infinite sameness, in
which yesterdays have only lighted
fools the way to dusty death. Life
in this time is meaningless—a tale
told by an idiot—and death also.
For his wife's death to have meaning
there needs some total change—a
plunge across a new abyss into a
Hereafter." That Shakespeare would
have been puzzled by this explanation is not necessarily a condemna-

tion of it. Perhaps " should " is
used indifferently to denote either
what will be or what ought to be;
cf. 31 *post.*

18. *time . . . word*] i.e. such a
phrase, expression, intelligence, as
" the queen is dead." Cf. *Rich. II.*
I. iii. 152: " The hopeless word
of 'never to return ' "; and *Ecc.*
iii. 2, " a time to die."

19-28. *To-morrow . . . nothing*]
" Expresses in Shakespeare's terms
the hopelessness of a hardened sinner,
to whom the universe has now no
meaning . . ."; " merely implies the
atheism . . . which has resulted
from his gradual hardening in
crime " (Bethell, *Shakespeare and the
Popular Dramatic Tradition,* pp. 74, 98).
See Introduction, p. xlviii. Halliwell thought the lines were suggested
by " a remarkable engraving " in
Barclay's *Ship of Fooles,* 1570, p. 61:
" They folowe the crowes crye to
     their great sorowe,
  Cras, cras, cras, to-morrowe we
     shall amende."
Cuningham thinks Shakespeare may
have been influenced by his recent
perusal of Florio's *Montaigne,* I. xix:
" That to Philosophie, is to learne
how to die."

21. *recorded time*] the record of
time (Hudson). This seems to be
the best and simplest explanation.

And all our yesterdays have lighted fools
The way to dusty death.   Out, out, brief candle!
Life's but a walking shadow; a poor player,
That struts and frets his hour upon the stage,   25
And then is heard no more: it is a tale
Told by an idiot, full of sound and fury,
Signifying nothing.

23. dusty] study *F 2, 3, 4;* dusky *Hanmer (conj. Theobald).*   28-30.
Signifying . . . Lord] *two lines, ending* tongue, Lord, *conj. Lettsom.*

Johnson suggests: " the time fixed
in the decrees of Heaven for the
period of life." Steevens thinks
recorded was used for *recording* or
recordable. Elwin thinks the line
means " till the last judgment."
Cf. *Rev.* x. 5, 6.
    22. *fools*] Not " foules " = crowds,
as Hunter conjectured, but just
ordinary foolish people.
    23. *dusty*]   Theobald's   conj.
" dusky " has little to recommend
it; cf. *Ps.* xxii. 15: " dust of
death." Steevens suggests that *dusty*
refers to " dust to dust " of the
burial service.   Collier cites Copley,
Fig for Fortune (1596, Spenser *Soc.*,
p. 55): " Inviting it to dusty death's
defeature." But Cuningham supports *dusky* on the ground that
Shakespeare often uses the word in
connection with death. He cites
1 Hen. VI. II. ii. 27; *2 Hen. VI.*
III. ii. 104; *Rich. III.* IV. iv. 70:
" dusky graves." Cuningham proceeds to summarize Elwin's arguments: Light lights folly on its
way to darkness; this is connected
with the idea of darkness as a
shadow; the living man is the
shadow walking between the light
and that dusky death to which it is
lighting him. Life has only a delusive resemblance to an endurable
substance, and the poor player is
but the shadow of the substance or
reality whose semblance he has
assumed. I agree with some of
Elwin's analysis of the passage, but
not with his conclusion: " With
the term *dusty* the shadow has no affin-

ity: and by retaining this word
the otherwise exquisitely preserved
unity of thought would consequently
be destroyed." Shakespeare would
cheerfully violate a unity of impression for his own purposes—in
this case to extend the associations
of the word " death."
    23. *candle*] Cf. *Job* xviii. 6: " The
light shall be darke in his dwelling,
and his candle shall be put out with
him." Cf. *Ps.* xviii. 28. Wilson
contrasts *Prov.* xx. 27.
    24. *shadow*] Cf. *Ps.* xxxix. 7: " For
man walketh in a vain shadow ";
Job viii. 9: " For wee are but of
yesterday, and are ignorant: for
our dayes vpon earth are but a
shadow."
    24. *player*] suggested by *shadow.*
Cf. *M.N.D.* v. i. 213: " The best
in this kind are but shadows "; and
M.N.D. v. i. 430. *Poor* player does
not mean a *bad actor*—or not primarily—but one who is to be pitied
because his appearance on the stage
of life is so brief (Kittredge).
    26-7. *it . . . Told*] Cf. *Ps.* xc. 9:
" We bring our years to an end as
a tale that is told."
    28. *Signifying nothing*] " The theme
of the false appearance is revived—
with a difference. It is not only that
Macbeth sees life as deceitful, but
the poetry is so fine that we are
almost bullied into accepting an
essential ambiguity in the final
statement of the play, as though
Shakespeare were expressing his own
' philosophy ' in the lines. But the
speech is ' placed ' by the tendency

Enter a Messenger.

Thou com'st to use thy tongue; thy story quickly.

Mess. Gracious my Lord,   30
I should report that which I say I saw,
But know not how to do't.

Macb.   Well, say, sir.

Mess. As I did stand my watch upon the hill,
I look'd toward Birnam, and anon, methought,
The wood began to move.

Macb.   Liar, and slave!   35

Mess. Let me endure your wrath, if 't be not so.
Within this three mile may you see it coming;
I say, a moving grove.

Macb.   If thou speak'st false,
Upon the next tree shalt thou hang alive,
Till famine cling thee: if thy speech be sooth,   40
I care not if thou dost for me as much.—
I pull in resolution; and begin
To doubt th' equivocation of the fiend,
That lies like truth: "Fear not, till Birnam wood

30. Gracious my] My gracious *F 2, 3, 4.*   30-1. Gracious . . . which]
one line, Keightley.   34, 44. Birnam] *F 4;* Byrnam *F 2, 3;* Byrnane *F 1.*
37. may you] *F 1, 2;* you may *F 3, 4.*   39. shalt] shall *F.*   42. pull]
Ff. pall *conj. Johnson, A. Hunter, Wilson.*

of the last Act (order emerging from
disorder, truth emerging from deceit) " (knights, *op. cit.* p. 36.)

28-30. *Signifying . . . my lord*] The
text could be printed in two lines,
the first ending with " use " or
" tongue."

31. *should*] cf. 17 *ante.*

32. *say*] Pope's insertion of " it "
is essential neither to the rhythm nor
the meaning of the line.

37. *mile*] Cf. *M.W.* III. ii. 33:
" This boy will carry a letter
twenty mile "; and *M.A.* II. iii.
17: " he would have walked ten
mile afoot."

39. *the next tree*] cf. *Temp.* III. ii. 42.

40. *cling*] shrink up, wither. Used
of the drawing together and shrinking up of animal or vegetable tissue;
and still used in dialect. *O.E.D.*

quotes *Cov. Myst.* 54: " My heart
doth clynge and cleve as clay."

42. *pull in*] rein in. Kittredge explains: " I can no longer give free
rein to confidence and determin-
ation ". He cites as illustration of
alternative meanings Dekker, *Old
Fortunatus,* Prol. (" feare . . . makes
her pull in her fainting pinions ")
and Fletcher, *The Sea Voyage.* III.;
(" All my spirits . . . Pull in their
powers "). Johnson's conj. " pall " is,
however, possible. Cf. *Ham.* v. ii. 9
and *A.C.* II. vii. 88.

43. *equivocation*] Cf. II. iii. 9;
Introduction, pp. xvi-xxviii; Scot,
The Discouerie of Witchcraft, XIII. xv.
(" How men have beene abused with
words of equivocation, with sundrie
examples thereof ") and *2 Hen. VI.*
I. iv. 60-75.

Do come to Dunsinane ";—and now a wood   45
Comes toward Dunsinane.—Arm, arm, and out!—
If this which he avouches does appear,
There is nor flying hence, nor tarrying here.
I 'gin to be aweary of the sun,
And wish th' estate o' th' world were now undone.—   50
Ring the alarum bell!—Blow, wind! come, wrack!
At least we'll die with harness on our back.

                                                            [*Exeunt.*

SCENE VI.—*The same.   A plain before the castle.*

Enter, with drum and colours, MALCOLM, *old* SIWARD,
       MACDUFF, *etc., and their army, with boughs.*

Mal. Now, near enough: your leavy screens throw down,
And show like those you are.—You, worthy uncle,
Shall, with my cousin, your right noble son,
Lead our first battle: worthy Macduff, and we,

48. nor flying] *F 1, 2;* no flying *F 3, 4.*

S.D. *A plain . . . castle.*] *Rowe, subst.*
Rowe; two lines Ff.   leavy] *Ff;* leafy *Collier.*

47-50.] The Clarendon Editors
thought these lines were interpolated.
47. *avouches*] cf. III. i. 119 *ante.*
50. *estate o' th' world*] the universe.
Cf. III. ii. 16 *ante:* "frame of
things." Wilson suggests that the
phrase implies both structure and
organisation.
51. *Ring . . . bell!*] Theobald believed these words to be a "Stage-
direction crept from the Margin into
the text" because the line was
"deficient without them, occasioned
probably by a Cut that had been
made in the Speech by the Actors.
They were a Memorandum to the
Prompter to ring the *Alarum-bell.*"
I see no sufficient warrant for
Theobald's belief in this instance,
though I think he was right on
II. iii. 81 *ante.*
51. *wrack!*] The usual spelling in
Shakespeare. Cf. I. iii. 114.

1. now . . . down,] *so*

52. *At . . . back*] If Macbeth had
not sallied forth the attackers might
have stayed "till famine and the
ague eat them up." By leaving the
castle, he enables the prophecies to
be fulfilled.
52. *harness*] gear, equipage, furniture, and specifically, armour for a
man or horse. Shakespeare uses it
in both senses. See Bible (A.V.),
1 Kings xxii. 34.

1. *leavy*] Cf. *M.A.* II. iii. 75 where
the word rhymes with "heavy."
Cotgrave has "Feuillu: *leauie.*"
2. *uncle*] See note to v. ii. 2 *ante.*
4. *battle*] Nares defines as "the
main or middle body of an army,
between the van and the rear."
But it is often used of a whole army
in order of battle, e.g. *John* IV. ii. 78.

Shall take upon 's what else remains to do,   5
According to our order.
Siw.   Fare you well.—
Do we but find the tyrant's power to-night,
Let us be beaten, if we cannot fight.
Macd. Make all our trumpets speak; give them all breath,
Those clamorous harbingers of blood and death.   10
              [*Exeunt. Alarums continued.*

SCENE VII.—*The same. Another part of the plain.*

Enter MACBETH.

Macb. They have tied me to a stake: I cannot fly,
But, bear-like, I must fight the course.—What's he,
That was not born of woman? Such a one
Am I to fear, or none.

Enter young SIWARD.

Yo. Siw. What is thy name?
Macb.   Thou 'lt be afraid to hear it.   5
Yo. Siw. No; though thou call'st thyself a hotter name
Than any is in hell.
Macb.   My name's Macbeth.
Yo. Siw. The devil himself could not pronounce a title
More hateful to mine ear.
Macb.   No, nor more fearful.
Yo. Siw. Thou liest, abhorred tyrant: with my sword   10
I'll prove the lie thou speak'st.
             [*They fight, and young Siward is slain.*

Scene VII
S.D.] *Capell, subst.*   10. abhorred] *F 1*; thou abhorred *F 2, 3, 4.*

Probably Shakespeare took the word from Holinshed. See Appendix, p. 175.

9-10. *Make . . . death*] Fleay regarded this couplet as an interpolation.

10. *harbingers*] Cf. note on I. iv. 45.

Scene VII

2. *bear-like . . . course*] Bear-baiting was a favourite old English sport; and a "course" was the technical term for a bout or round between the bear and the dogs. Cf. *Lear*, III. vii. 54: "I am tied to the stake, and I must stand the course."

Macb.   Thou wast born of woman:—
But swords I smile at, weapons laugh to scorn,
Brandish'd by man that's of a woman born.   [*Exit.*

Alarums.   Enter MACDUFF.

Macd. That way the noise is.—Tyrant, show thy face:
If thou be'st slain, and with no stroke of mine,   15
My wife and children's ghosts will haunt me still.
I cannot strike at wretched Kernes, whose arms
Are hir'd to bear their staves: either thou, Macbeth,
Or else my sword, with an unbatter'd edge,
I sheathe again undeeded. There thou shouldst be; 20
By this great clatter, one of greatest note
Seems bruited. Let me find him, Fortune!
And more I beg not.   [*Exit.   Alarum.*

Enter MALCOLM *and old* SIWARD.

Siw. This way, my Lord;—the castle's gently render'd:
The tyrant's people on both sides do fight;   25

12. swords] words *conj. Daniel.*

11. *born of woman*] Cf. *Job* xiv. 1,
and the Burial Service: "Man
that is born of a woman."

13. *born*] "Shakespeare designed
Macbeth should appear invincible
till he encountered the object destined
for his destruction" (Steevens).

17. *Kernes*] Cf. I. ii. 13 *ante.* Macbeth has to rely on Irish mercenaries,
upon whom Macdonwald had relied
before (Wilson).

18. *staves*] spear-shafts. Cf. *Rich.
III.* v. iii. 341.

18. *thou*] Commentators have worried themselves over the grammar.
"We must supply some words like
must be my antagonist" (Clarendon).

20. *undeeded*] i.e. not having performed any deeds: the word was
probably coined by Shakespeare.

21. *clatter*] another word not found
elsewhere in Shakespeare's works.

22. *bruited*] announced, reported,
with the idea of clamour. Cf. *1 Hen.
VI.* II. iii. 68: "I find thou art no
less than fame hath bruited."

22. *Let*] Although the line wants a
foot, we need not assume that a
word has dropped out. There is
room for a pause, a move, or a
gesture after *bruited.*

23. *Enter Malcolm and old Siward*]
Siward does not notice his son's
body; and we hear later (v. ix. 10)
that it has been "brought off the
field." This was, perhaps, just
before the entrance of old Siward,
as Macduff should obviously enter
immediately after the exit of Macbeth. In which case 24-29 would
be virtually a separate scene, its
effectiveness depending mainly on
the ironical juxtaposition of the
removal of young Siward's body
and the entrance of his father.
Granville-Barker, however, suggests
(Preface, xxxi) that young Siward
has been killed in the gallery, and
that his body is concealed by the
drawing of a curtain.

24. *gently render'd*] i.e. tamely surrendered.

The noble Thanes do bravely in the war.
The day almost itself professes yours,
And little is to do.
Mal.   We have met with foes
That strike beside us.
Siw.   Enter, Sir, the castle.
                                    [*Exeunt. Alarum.*

SCENE VIII.—*Another part of the field.*

Enter MACBETH.

Macb. Why should I play the Roman fool, and die
On mine own sword? whiles I see lives, the gashes
Do better upon them.

Re-enter MACDUFF.

Macd.   Turn, Hell-hound, turn!
Macb. Of all men else I have avoided thee:
But get thee back, my soul is too much charg'd
With blood of thine already.
Macd.   I have no words;
My voice is in my sword: thou bloodier villain
Than terms can give thee out!   [*They fight.*
Macb.   Thou losest labour:
As easy may'st thou the intrenchant air
With thy keen sword impress, as make me bleed: 10

Scene VIII

S.D.] *Dyce. Scene vii continued Ff, Rowe, Arden (ed. 1); sc. viii Pope, Camb.
etc.*

29. *strike beside us*] i.e. by our side.
Some, however, interpret ' deliber-
ately miss us ' and cite *3 Hen. VI.*
II. i. 130-2.

Scene VIII

S.D. There is no scene division in
the Folio at this point, but most
editors follow Pope and Johnson in
beginning a new scene. Siward
and Malcolm enter the castle, and

Macbeth is obviously on another
part of the field.
1. *Roman fool*] e.g. Cato, Brutus,
Antony.
5-6. *my . . . already*] " the only
touch of real remorse in Macbeth "
(Chambers). Or is he rationalizing
his fear?
9. *intrenchant*] incapable of being
cut: the active in a passive sense.
Shakespeare uses *trenchant* in an
active sense in *Tim.* IV. iii. 115:
" trenchant sword."

Let fall thy blade on vulnerable crests;
I bear a charmed life; which must not yield
To one of woman born.
Macd.   Despair thy charm;
And let the Angel, whom thou still hast serv'd,
Tell thee, Macduff was from his mother's womb   15
Untimely ripp'd.
Macb. Accursed be that tongue that tells me so,
For it hath cow'd my better part of man:
And be these juggling fiends no more believ'd,
That palter with us in a double sense;   20
That keep the word of promise to our ear,
And break it to our hope.—I 'll not fight with thee.
Macd. Then yield thee, coward,
And live to be the show and gaze o' th' time:
We 'll have thee, as our rarer monsters are,   25

22-3] *lines end* hope! coward, *and read* I will *for* I'll S. *Walker.*

12. *charmed life*] Cf. Spenser, *Faerie Queene*, I. iv. 50:
"he beares a charmed shield,
And eke enchaunted armes, that
none can perce";
and *Cym.* v. iii. 68.

13. *Despair*] i.e despair of; the preposition being omitted after verbs regarded as transitive.

14. *Angel*] i.e. bad angel, demon.

16. *Untimely ripp'd*] Furness quoted Virgil, *Aen.* x. 315:
"Inde Lichan ferit, exsectum jam
matre perempta
Et tibi, Phoebe, sacrum."
Shakespeare may have read the passage in Virgil; but he probably relied on Holinshed; see Appendix A p. 186. Flatter, *op. cit.* p. 27, notes that the line is filled out by a pause, before Macbeth's speech.

18. *better part*] This seems to mean simply the mind, soul, or spirit: not "the better part of my manhood" (Clarendon). Cf. *Sonnet*, lxxiv. 8: "My spirit is thine, the better part of me"; and Peele's *Arraignment of Paris*, II. i. 76:

"And look how much the mind,
the better part,
Doth overpass the body in
desert."

19-20. *these . . . sense*] Simpson (*ap.* Wilson) cites Spenser, *Faerie Queene*, III. iv. 28:
"So tickle be the termes of mortall
state,
And full of subtile sophismes,
which doe play
With double sences, and with
false debate,
T'approue the vnknown purpose
of eternal fate."

20. *palter*] shuffle, equivocate. Cf. *J.C.* II. i. 125:
"Secret Romans, that have spoke
the word,
And will not palter."
Cotgrave has "*Harceler: to haggle, hucke, dodge, or paulter long in the buying of a commoditie.*"

22-3. *I'll . . . coward*] S. Walker's arrangement may be right.

24. *show*] Cf. *A.C.* IV. xii. 36: "most monster-like be shown."

Painted upon a pole, and underwrit,
" Here may you see the tyrant."
Macb.   I will not yield,
To kiss the ground before young Malcolm's feet,
And to be baited with the rabble's curse.
Though Birnam wood be come to Dunsinane,   30
And thou oppos'd, being of no woman born,
Yet I will try the last: before my body
I throw my warlike shield: lay on, Macduff;
And damn'd be him that first cries, " Hold, enough! "
   [*Exeunt, fighting. Alarums. Re-enter fighting, and
    Macbeth slain.*

SCENE IX.—*Within the castle.*

Retreat. Flourish. Enter, with drum and colours, MALCOLM,
   old SIWARD, ROSSE, *Thanes, and Soldiers.*

Mal. I would the friends we miss were safe arriv'd.
Siw. Some must go off; and yet, by these I see,
So great a day as this is cheaply bought.
Mal. Macduff is missing, and your noble son.
Rosse. Your son, my Lord, has paid a soldier's debt: 5

30. Birnam] *F 4;* Byrnam *F 2, 3;* Byrnane *F 1.*   31. being] be *Theobald.*   34. S.D.] *Ff subst.* Re-enter . . . slain] *not in Pope, etc.; restored by Wilson.*

Scene IX

S.D.] *Pope, Wilson (conj. Kittredge); sc. vii. continues, F.*

26. *Painted . . . pole*] i.e. painted on a cloth or board suspended on a pole. Cf. Benedick's jest, *M.A.* I. i. 267: " and let me be vilely painted." Craig conj. that *Painted* should be *Paunched* = disembowelled. But Macduff threatens Macbeth with life in captivity.

32-3. *before . . . shield*] Clarendon editors thought this sentence must be interpolated. It would certainly be improved by Hilton's conj. (*ap.* Wilson) of " warlock " for " warlike."

34. *Hold*] The cry of the heralds, " Ho! Ho! " commanding the cessation of a combat, is probably corrupted from " Hold, hold " (Clarendon).

34. S.D. I have retained the substance of the Folio directions. On the Elizabethan stage the fight would be concluded either on the inner stage (Wilson), or in the gallery (Granville-Barker, *op. cit.* p. xxxii), in either case the curtain being drawn on Macbeth's body.

Scene IX

S.D. I follow Kittredge and Wilson in assuming that a new scene begins at this point, inside the castle. There is no reason to believe that Shakespeare intended

He only liv'd but till he was a man;
The which no sooner had his prowess confirm'd,
In the unshrinking station where he fought,
But like a man he died.

Siw.   Then he is dead?

Rosse. Ay, and brought off the field.   Your cause of sorrow
Must not be measur'd by his worth, for then   11
It hath no end.

Siw.   Had he his hurts before?

Rosse. Ay, on the front.

Siw.   Why then, God's soldier be he!
Had I as many sons as I have hairs,
I would not wish them to a fairer death:
And so, his knell is knoll'd.

Mal.   He's worth more sorrow,
And that I 'll spend for him.

Siw.   He's worth no more;
They say he parted well and paid his score:
And so, God be with him!—Here comes newer comfort.

Re-enter MACDUFF, *with* MACBETH'S *head.*

Macd. Hail, King! for so thou art.   Behold, where stands
Th' usurper's cursed head: the time is free.   21
I see thee compass'd with thy kingdom's pearl,

20. Hail . . . stands] *so Rowe; two lines Ff.*   22. pearl] peers *Rowe;*
pearls *Var. '73.*

Malcolm to leave the castle once he
had entered it.   The Clarendon
editors questioned the authenticity
of the whole of this scene; but it
has been convincingly defended by
Nosworthy, *Review of English Studies,*
April 1948, p. 139.

2. *go off*] a stage metaphor,
signifying the exit from life's stage.
Cf. *A.C.* IV. xiii. 6, and the similar
expressions, I. vii. 20 and III. i. 104
ante.

7. *prowess*] Probably a monosyllable, though elsewhere in Shakespeare it is a dissyllable.   Butler,
Hudibras, III. iii. 357 rhymes *prowess*
and *cows.*

8. *unshrinking station*] i.e. the
station whence he did not shrink.

9-10. *he died . . . dead?*] Nosworthy

compares Laertes' reception of Ophelia's death.

12-15. *Had he . . . death*] Shakespeare closely follows Holinshed.
See Appendix A, p. 187.

15. *Had . . . hairs*] quibble on
hairs/heirs.   Nosworthy compares
Marlowe, *Doctor Faustus,* 339: "Had
I as many soules as there be starres."

18. *parted*] Cf. *Hen. V.* II. iii. 12
(of the death of Falstaff): "a'
parted even just between twelve and
one."

20-1. *stands . . . head*] "vpon a
pole" (Holinshed).

21. *the time*] See I. v. 63 and IV.
iii. 72 *ante,* etc.

22. *pearl*] used collectively for
the nobles of Scotland, and probably
suggested by "the row of pearls

That speak my salutation in their minds;
Whose voices I desire aloud with mine,—
Hail, King of Scotland!
All.　　　　　　　　Hail, King of Scotland!　　[*Flourish.*
Mal. We shall not spend a large expense of time,
Before we reckon with your several loves,
And make us even with you. My Thanes and kinsmen,
Henceforth be Earls; the first that ever Scotland
In such an honour nam'd. What's more to do,　　30
Which would be planted newly with the time,—
As calling home our exil'd friends abroad,
That fled the snares of watchful tyranny;
Producing forth the cruel ministers
Of this dead butcher, and his fiend-like Queen,　　35
Who, as 'tis thought, by self and violent hands
Took off her life;—this, and what needful else
That calls upon us, by the grace of Grace,
We will perform in measure, time, and place.
So thanks to all at once, and to each one,　　40
Whom we invite to see us crown'd at Scone.
　　　　　　　　　　　　[*Flourish.　Exeunt.*

26. expense] extent *conj. Steevens;* expanse *conj. Singer.*　　28. My] *not in Pope.*
37. what]. what's *Hanmer.*

which usually encircled a crown"
(Clarendon). Florio, *Worlde of
Wordes*, called Southampton " Braue
Earle, bright Pearle of Peeres."
Cf. *Ham.* IV. vii. 93: "he is the
brooch indeed and gem of all the
nation."

26. *spend . . . expense*] Cf. *C.E.*
III. i. 123: "This jest shall cost
me some expense," and *Numb.*
xxiii. 10: "die the death of the
righteous." There is no reason to
think that the passage is corrupt.

26. *time*] Cf. 21 *ante,* 31, 39 *post.*

27-8. *Before . . . you*] Before we
reward you for your services, so
that we are no longer in your debt.

29. *Earls*] From Holinshed. See
Appendix A, p. 187.

34. *Producing forth*] bringing out
of hiding.

36. *self and violent hands*] Cf. *Rich.
II.* III. ii. 166: "Infusing him with
self and vain conceit." "Self is
used by Shakespeare as an adjective,
as in *T.N.* I. i. 39, 'one self king,'
so that he felt no awkwardness in
separating it from the substantive,
whose sense it modifies, by a second
epithet " (Clarendon).

38. *the grace of Grace*] Theobald
compares *T.G.* III. i. 146; *A.W.*
II. i. 163. Cuningham compares
his own emendation for IV. iii. 136:
" the grace of Goodness."

39. *measure*] due proportion (Wilson).

40. *So . . . one*] Manly suggested
that this was addressed to the
audience rather than the *dramatis
personæ.*

41. *Scone*] See note on II. iv. 31
ante.

APPENDIX A

HOLINSHED

HOLINSHED in his *Chronicles of Scotland* describes how various noblemen were put to death for conspiring with witches against King Duff. Amongst them were certain kinsmen of Donwald, " capteine of the castell," who " has been persuaded to be partakers with the other rebels, more through fraudulent counsell of diuerse wicked persons, than of their owne accord: whervpon the foresaid Donwald lamenting their case, made earnest labor and sute to the king to haue begged their pardon; but hauing a plaine deniall, he conceiued such an inward malice towards the king (though he shewed it not outwardlie at the first), that the same continued still boiling in his stomach, and ceased not, till through setting on of his wife, and in reuenge of such vnthankefulnesse, hee found meanes to murther the king within the foresaid castell of Fores where he vsed to soiourne. For the king being in that countrie, was accustomed to lie most commonlie within the same castell, hauing a speciall trust in Donwald, as a man whom he neuer suspected.

" But Donwald, not forgetting the reproch which his linage had susteined by the execution of those his kinsmen, whome the king for a spectacle to the people had caused to be hanged, could not but shew manifest tokens of great griefe at home amongst his familie: which his wife perceiuing, ceassed not to trauell with him, till she vnderstood what was the cause of his displeasure. Which at length when she had learned by his owne relation, she as one that bare no lesse malice in hir heart towards the king, for the like cause on hir behalfe, than hir husband did for his friends, counselled him (sith the king often-times vsed to lodge in his house without anie gard about him, other than the garrison of the castell, which was wholie at his commandement) to make him awaie, and shewed him the meanes wherby he might soonest accomplish it.

" Donwald thus being the more kindled in wrath by the
words of his wife, determined to follow hir aduise in the execution of so heinous an act.   Whervpon deuising with himselfe for
a while, which way hee might best accomplish his curssed
intent, at length gat opportunitie, and sped his purpose as
followeth.   It chanced that the king vpon the daie before he
purposed to depart foorth of the castell, was long in his oratorie
at his praiers, and there continued till it was late in the night.
At the last, comming foorth, he called such afore him as had
faithfullie serued him in pursute and apprehension of the rebels,
and giuing them heartie thanks, he bestowed sundrie honorable
gifts amongst them, of the which number Donwald was one,
as he that had been euer accounted a most faithfull seruant
to the king.

" At length, hauing talked with them a long time, he got him
into his priuie chamber, onelie with two of his chamberlains,
who hauing brought him to bed, came foorth againe, and
then fell to banketting with Donwald and his wife, who had
prepared diuerse delicate dishes, and sundrie sorts of drinks
for their reare supper or collation, wherat they sate vp so
long, till they had charged their stomachs with such full gorges,
that their heads were no sooner got to the pillow, but asleepe
they were so fast, that a man might haue remooued the chamber
ouer them, sooner than to haue awaked them out of their
droonken sleepe.

" Then Donwald, though he abhorred the act greatlie in
heart, yet through instigation of his wife hee called foure of his
seruants vnto him (whome he had made priuie to his wicked
intent before, and framed to his purpose with large gifts) and
now declaring vnto them, after what sort they should worke the
feat, they gladlie obeied his instructions, & speedilie going
about the murther, they enter the chamber (in which the king
laie) a little before cocks crow, where they secretlie cut his
throte as he lay sleeping, without anie buskling at all: and
immediatlie by a posterne gate they caried foorth the dead
bodie into the fieldes. . . .

" Donwald, about the time that the murther was in dooing,
got him amongst them that kept the watch, and so continued
in companie with them all the residue of the night.   But in the
morning when the noise was raised in the kings chamber how
the king was slaine, his bodie conueied awaie, and the bed all
beraied with bloud; he with the watch ran thither, as though
he had knowne nothing of the matter, and breaking into the

chamber, and finding cakes of bloud in the bed, and on the floore about the sides of it, he foorthwith slue the chamberleins, as guiltie of that heinous murther, and then like a mad man running to and fro, he ransacked euerie corner within the castell, as though it had beene to haue seene if he might haue found either the bodie, or anie of the murtherers hid in anie priuie place: but at length comming to the posterne gate, and finding it open, he burdened the chamberleins, whome he had slaine, with all the fault, they hauing the keies of the gates committed to their keeping all the night, and therefore it could not be otherwise (said he) but that they were of counsell in committing of that most detestable murther.

" Finallie, such was his ouer earnest diligence in the seuere inquisition and triall of the offendors heerein, that some of the lords began to mislike the matter, and to smell foorth shrewd tokens, that he should not be altogether cleare himselfe. But for so much as they were in that countrie, where he had the whole rule, what by reason of his friends and authoritie togither, they doubted to vtter what they thought, till time and place should better serue thereynto, and heerevpon got them awaie euerie man to his home. For the space of six moneths togither, after this heinous murther thus committed, there appeered no sunne by day, nor moone by night in anie part of the realme, but still was the skie couered with continuall clouds, and sometimes such outragious windes arose, with lightenings and tempests, that the people were in great feare of present destruction. . . .

" Monstrous sights also that were seene within the Scotish kingdome that yeere were these: horsses in Louthian, being of singular beautie and swiftnesse, did eate their owne flesh, and would in no wise taste anie other meate. In Angus there was a gentlewoman brought foorth a child without eies, nose, hand, or foot. There was a sparhawke also strangled by an owle. Neither was it anie lesse woonder that the sunne, as before is said, was continuallie couered with clouds for six moneths space. But all men vnderstood that the abhominable murther of king Duffe was the cause heereof." (pp. 149-52).

A later passage describes a mysterious voice after King Kenneth had slain his nephew:

" Thus might he seeme happie to all man, hauing the loue both of his lords and commons; but yet to himselfe he seemed most vnhappie, as he that could not but still liue in continuall feare, least his wicked practise concerning the death of Malcolme

Duffe should come to light and knowledge of the world. For so commeth it to passe, that such as are pricked in conscience for anie secret offense committed, haue euer an vnquiet mind. And (as the fame goeth) it chanced that a voice was heard as he was in bed in the night time to take his rest, vttering vnto him these or the like woords in effect: ' Thinke not Kenneth that the wicked slaughter of Malcolme Duffe by thee contriued, is kept secret from the knowledge of the eternall God: thou art he that didst conspire the innocents death, enterprising by traitorous meanes to doo that to thy neighbour, which thou wouldest haue reuenged by cruell punishment in anie of thy subiects, if it had beene offered to thy selfe. It shall therefore come to passe, that both thou thy selfe, and thy issue, through the iust vengeance of almightie God, shall suffer woorthie punishment, to the infamie of thy house and familie for euermore. For euen at this present are there in hand secret practises to dispatch both thee and thy issue out of the waie, that other maie inioy this kingdome which thou doost indeuour to assure vnto thine issue.'

" The king, with this voice being striken into great dread and terror, passed that night without anie sleepe comming in his eies " (p. 158).

" After Malcolme succeeded his nephue Duncane the sonne of his daughter Beatrice: for Malcolme had two daughters, the one which was Beatrice, being giuen in mariage vnto one Abbanath Crinen, a man of great nobilitie, and thane of the Iles and west parts of Scotland, bare of that mariage the foresaid Duncane; the other called Doada, was maried vnto Sinell the thane of Glammis, by whom she had issue one Makbeth a valiant gentleman, and one that if he had not beene somewhat cruell of nature, might haue beene thought most woorthie the gouernement of a realme. On the other part, Duncane was so soft and gentle of nature, that the people wished the inclinations and maners of these two cousins to haue beene so tempered and interchangeablie bestowed betwixt them, that where the one had too much of clemencie, and the other of crueltie, the meane vertue betwixt these two extremities might haue reigned by indifferent partition in them both, so should Duncane haue prooued a woorthie king, and Makbeth an excellent capteine. The beginning of Duncans reigne was verie quiet and peaceable, without anie notable trouble; but after it was perceiued how negligent he was in punishing offendors, manie misruled persons tooke occasion thereof to trouble the peace and quiet state of the common-wealth, by seditious commotions which first had their beginnings in this wise.

"Banquho the thane of Lochquhaber, of whom the house of the Stewards is descended, the which by order of linage hath now for a long time inioied the crowne of Scotland, euen till these our daies, as he gathered the finaunces due to the king, and further punished somewhat sharpely such as were notorious offenders, being assailed by a number of rebelles inhabiting in that countrie, and spoiled of the monie and all other things, had much a doo to get awaie with life, after he had receiued sundrie grieuous wounds amongst them. Yet escaping their handes after hee was somewhat recouered of his hurts and was able to ride, he repaired to the court, where making his complaint to the king in most earnest wise, he purchased at length that the offenders were sente for by a sergeant at armes, to appeare to make answer vnto such mater as shoulde be laid to their charge: but they augmenting their mischiefous act with a more wicked deede, after they had misused the messenger with sundrie kindes of reproches, they finallie slew him also.

"Then doubting not but for such contemptuous demeanor against the kings regall authoritie, they should be inuaded with all the power the king could make, Makdowald one of great estimation among them, making first a confederacie with his neerest friends and kinsmen, tooke vpon him to be chiefe capteine of all such rebels as would stand against the king, in maintenance of their grieuous offenses lately committed against him. Manie slanderous words also, and railing tants this Makdowald vttered against his prince, calling him a faint-hearted milkesop, more meet to gouerne a sort of idle moonks in some cloister, than to haue the rule of such valiant and hardie men of warre as the Scots were. He vsed also such subtill persuasions and forged allurements, that in a small time he had gotten togither a mightie power of men: for out of the westerne Iles there came vnto him a great multitude of people, offering themselues to assist him in that rebellious quarell, and out of Ireland in hope of the spoile came no small number of Kernes and Galloglasses, offering gladlie to serue vnder him, whither it should please him to lead them."

Makdowald defeats an army sent against him and beheads its captain, Malcolm. Duncan thereupon called a council.

"At length Makbeth speaking much against the kings softnes, and ouermuch slacknesse in punishing offendors, whereby

they had such time to assemble together, he promised notwithstanding, if the charge were committed vnto him and vnto
Banquho, so to order the matter, that the rebels should be
shortly vanquished & quite put downe, and that not so much
as one of them should be found to make resistance within the
countrie.

" And euen so it came to pass: for being sent foorth with
a new power, at his entring into Lochquhaber, the fame of his
comming put the enimies in such feare, that a great number of
them stale secretlie awaie from their capteine Makdowald,
who neuerthelesse inforced thereto, gaue battell vnto Makbeth,
with the residue which remained with him: but being ouercome, and fleeing for refuge into a castell (within the which
his wife & children were inclosed) at length when he saw how
he could neither defend the hold anie longer against his enimies,
not yet vpon surrender be suffered to depart with life saued,
hee first slue his wife and children, and lastlie himselfe, least
if he had yeelded simplie, he should haue beene executed in
most cruell wise for an example to other."

Macbeth entered the castle and found Makdowald lying
dead with the rest of the corpses:

" which when he beheld, remitting no peece of his cruell
nature with that pitifull sight, he caused the head to be cut off,
and set vpon a poles end, and so sent it as a present to the king.
. . . Thus was iustice and law restored againe to the old accustomed course, by the diligent means of Makbeth. Immediatlie wherevpon woord came that Sueno king of Norway
was arriued in Fife with a puissant armie, to subdue the whole
realme of Scotland " (pp. 168-9).

" The crueltie of this Sueno was such, that he neither spared
man, woman, nor child, of what age, condition or degree soeuer
they were. Whereof when K. Duncane was certified, he set
all slouthfull and lingering delaies apart, and began to assemble
an armie in most speedie wise, like a verie valiant capteine:
for oftentimes it happeneth, that a dull coward and slouthfull
person, constreined by necessitie, becommeth verie hardie and
actiue. Therefore when his whole power was come togither,
he diuided the same into three battels. The first was led by
Makbeth, the second by Banquho, & the king himselfe gouerned
in the maine battell or middle ward, wherein were appointed
to attend and wait vpon his person the most part of all the
residue of the Scotish nobilitie.

" The armie of Scotishmen being thus ordered, came vnto

Culros, where incountering with the enimies, after a sore and cruell foughten battell, Sueno remained victorious, and Malcolme with his Scots discomfited.   Howbeit the Danes were so broken by this battell, that they were not able to make long chase on their enimies, but kept themselues all night in order of battell, for doubt least the Scots assembling togither againe, might haue set vpon them at some aduantage.   On the morrow, when the fields were discouered, and that it was perceiued how no enimies were to be found abrode, they gathered the spoile, which they diuided amongst them, according to the law of armes.   Then was it ordeined by commandement of Sueno, that no soldier should hurt either man, woman, or child, except such as were found with weapon in hand readie to make resistance, for he hoped now to conquer the realme without further bloudshed.

" But when knowledge was giuen how Duncane was fled to the castell of Bertha, and that Makbeth was gathering a new power to withstand the incursions of the Danes, Sueno raised his tents & comming to the said castell, laid a strong siege round about it.   Duncane seeing himself thus enuironed by his enimies, sent a secret message by counsell of Banquho to Makbeth, commanding him to abide at Inchcuthill, till he heard from him some other newes.   In the meane time Duncane fell in fained communication with Sueno, as though he would haue yeelded vp the castell into his hands, vnder certaine conditions, and this did he to driue time, and to put his enimies out of all suspicion of anie enterprise ment against them, till all things were brought to passe that might serue for the purpose.   At length, when they were fallen at a point for rendring vp the hold, Duncane offered to send foorth of the castell into the campe great prouision of vittels to refresh the armie, which offer was gladlie accepted of the Danes, for that they had beene in great penurie of sustenance manie daies before.

" The Scots heerevpon tooke the iuice of mekilwoort berries, and mixed the same in their ale and bread, sending it thus spiced & confectioned, in great abundance vnto their enimies. They reioising that they had got meate and drinke sufficient to satisfie their bellies, fell to eating and drinking after such greedie wise, that it seemed they stroue who might deuoure and swallow vp most, till the operation of the berries spread in such sort through all parts of their bodies, that they were in the end brought into a fast dead sleepe, that in manner in was vnpossible to awake them.   Then foorthwith Duncane sent vnto Makbeth, commanding him with all diligence to come and set vpon the enimies, being in easie point to be ouercome. Makbeth making no delaie, came with his people to the place, where his enimies were lodged, and first killing the watch, afterwards entered the campe, and made such slaughter on all sides without anie resistance, that it was a wonderful matter to behold, for the Danes were so heauie of sleepe, that the most part of them were slaine and neuer stirred: other that were awakened either by the noise or other waies foorth, were so amazed and dizzie headed vpon their wakening, that they were not able to make anie defense; so that of the whole number there escaped no more but onelie Sueno himselfe and ten other persons, by whose helpe he got to his ships lieng at rode in the mouth of Taie " (pp. 169-70).

Holinshed goes on to describe how Sueno escaped with only one ship back to Denmark. While the Scots were rejoicing in their victory word was brought that a new Danish fleet had arrived at Kingcorne, sent by Canute, king of England, to avenge his brother Sueno's overthrow.

" To resist these enimies, which were alreadie landed, and busie in spoiling the countrie; Makbeth and Banquho were sent with the kings authoritie, who hauing with them a con-uenient power, incountred the enimies, slue part of them, and chased the other to their ships. They that escaped and got once to their ships, obteined of Makbeth for a great summe of gold, that such of their friends as were slaine at this last bickering, might be buried in saint Colmes Inch. In memorie whereof, manie old sepultures are yet in the said Inch, there to be seene grauen with the armes of the Danes, as the maner of burieng noble men still is, and heeretofore hath beene vsed.

" A peace was also concluded at the same time betwixt the Danes and Scotishmen, ratified (as some haue written) in this wise: That from thenceforth the Danes should neuer come into Scotland to make anie warres against the Scots by anie maner of meanes. And these were the warres that Duncan had with forren enimies, in the seventh yeere of his reigne. Shortlie after happened a strange and vncouth woonder, which afterward was the cause of much trouble in the realme of Scotland as ye shall after heare. It fortuned as Makbeth and Banquho iournied towards Fores, where the king then laie, they went sporting by the waie togither without other company, saue onelie themselues, passing thorough the woods and fields, when suddenlie in the middest of a laund, there met them three women in strange and wild apparell, resembling creatures of elder world, whome when they attentiuelie beheld, woondering much at the sight, the first of them spake and said: All haile Makbeth, thane of Glammis (for he had latelie entered into that dignitie and office by the death of his father Sinell). The second of them said: Haile Makbeth thane of Cawder. But the third said: All haile Makbeth that heereafter shalt be king of Scotland.

" Then Banquho: What manner of women (saith he) are you, that seeme so little fauourable vnto me, whereas to my fellow heere, besides high offices, ye assigne also the kingdome, appointing foorth nothing for me at all? Yes, (saith the first of them) we promise greater benefits vnto thee, than vnto him, for he shall reigne in deed, but with an vnluckie end: neither shall he leaue anie issue behind him to succeed in his place, where contrarilie thou in deed shalt not reigne at all, but of thee those shall be borne which shall gouern the Scotish king-dome by long order of continuall descent. Herewith the fore-said women vanished immediatlie out of their sight. This was reputed at the first but some vaine fantasticall illusion by Mackbeth and Banquho, insomuch that Banquho would call Mackbeth in iest, king of Scotland; and Mackbeth againe would call him in sport likewise, the father of manie kings. But afterwards the common opinion was, that these women were either the weird sisters, that is (as ye would say) the goddesses of destinie, or else some nymphs or feiries, indued with knowledge of prophesie by their necromanticall science, bicause euerie thing came to passe as they had spoken. For shortlie after, the thane of Cawder being condemned at Fores of treason against the king committed; his lands, liuings, and offices were giuen of the kings liberalitie to Mackbeth.

" The same night after, at supper, Banquho iested with him and said: Now Mackbeth thou hast obteined those things which the two former sisters prophesied, there remaineth onelie for thee to purchase that which the third said should come to passe. Wherevpon Mackbeth reuoluing the thing in his mind, began euen then to deuise how he might atteine to the kingdome; but yet he thought with himselfe that he must tarie a time, which should aduance him thereto (by the diuine prouidence) as it had come to passe in his former preferment. But shortlie after it chanced that king Duncane hauing two sonnes by his wife which was the daughter of Siward earle of Northumberland, he made the elder of them called Malcolme prince of Cumberland, as it were thereby to appoint him his successor in the kingdome, immediatlie after his deceases. Mackbeth sore troubled herewith, for that he saw by this his hope sore hindered (where, by the old lawes of the realme, the ordnance was, that if he that should succeed were not of able age to take the charge vpon himselfe, he that was next of bloud vnto him should be admitted) he began to take counsell how he might vsurpe the kingdome by force, hauing a just quarrell so to doo (as he tooke the matter) for that Duncane did what in him lay to defraud him of all manner of title and claime, which he might in time to come, pretend vnto the crowne.

" The woords of the three sisters also (of whom before ye haue heard) greatlie incouraged him herevnto, but speciallie his wife lay sore vpon him to attempt the thing, as she that was verie ambitious, burning in vnquenchable desire to beare the name of a queene. At length therefore, communicating his purposed intent with his trustie friends, amongst whome Banquho was the chiefest, vpon confidence of their promised aid, he slue the king at Enuerns, or (as some say) at Botgosuane, in the sixt yeare of his reigne. Then hauing a companie about him of such as he had made priuie to his enterprise, he caused himselfe to be proclaimed king, and foorthwith went vnto Scone, where (by common consent) he receiued the inuesture of the kingdome according to the accustomed maner. The bodie of Duncane was first conueied vnto Elgine, & there buried in kinglie wise; but afterwards it was remoued and conueied vnto Colme-kill, and there laid in a sepulture amongst his predecessors, in the yeare after the birth of our Sauiour, 1046.

" Malcolme Canmore and Donald Bane the sons of king Duncane, for feare of their liues (which they might well know that Mackbeth would seeke to bring to end for his more sure confirmation in the estate) fled into Cumberland, where Malcolme remained, till time that saint Edward the sonne of Etheldred recouered the dominion of England from the Danish power, the which Edward receiued Malcolme by way of most friendlie enterteinment: but Donald passed ouer into Ireland, where he was tenderlie cherished by the king of that land. Mackbeth, after the departure thus of Duncanes sonnes, vsed great liberalitie towards the nobles of the realme, thereby to win their fauour, and when he saw that no man went about to trouble him, he set his whole intention to mainteine iustice, and to punish all enormities and abuses, which had chanced

through the feeble and slouthfull administration of Duncane "
(pp. 170-1).

Holinshed gives a number of examples of Macbeth's reforms
and mentions that among the thanes who were slain for sedition
was Ros. After giving a list of some of Macbeth's laws, Holinshed adds:

" These and the like commendable lawes Makbeth caused
to be put as then in vse, gouerning the realme for the space of
ten yeares in equall iustice. But this was but a counterfet
zeale of equitie shewed by him, partlie against his naturall
inclination to purchase thereby the fauour of the people.
Shortlie after, he began to shew what he was, in stead of equitie
practising crueltie. For the pricke of conscience (as it chanceth
euer in tyrants, and such as atteine to anie estate by vnrighteous
means) caused him euer to feare, least he should be serued
of the same up, as he had ministred to his predecessor. The
woords also of the three weird sisters, would not out of his mind,
which as they promised him the kingdome, so likewise did they
promise it at the same time vnto the posteritie of Banquho.
He willed therefore the same Banquho with his sonne named
Fleance, to come to supper that he had prepared for them,
which was indeed, as he had deuised, present death at the
hands of certeine murderers, whom he hired to execute that
deed, appointing them to meet with the same Banquho and
his sonne without the palace, as they returned to their lodgings,
and there to slea them, so that he would not haue his house
slandered, but that in time to come he might cleare himselfe,
if anie thing were laid to his charge vpon anie suspicion that
might arise. It chanced yet by the benefit of the darke night,
that though the father were slaine, the sonne yet by the helpe
of almightie God reseruing him to better fortune, escaped
that danger: and afterwards hauing some inkeling (by the
admonition of some friends which he had in the court) how his
life was sought no lesse than his fathers, who was slaine not by
chancemedlie (as by the handling of the matter Makbeth woold
haue had it to appeare) but euen vpon a prepensed deuise:
wherevpon to auoid further perill he fled into Wales " (p. 172).

Holinshed goes on to describe how the founder of the
Stuart dynasty, Walter Steward, who married the daughter
of Robert Bruce, and also " the earles of Leuenox and Dernlie,"
were descended from Fleance.

" But to returne vnto Makbeth, in continuing the historie,
and to begin where I left, ye shall vnderstand that after the

contriued slaughter of Banquho, nothing prospered with the foresaid Makbeth: for in maner euerie man began to doubt his owne life, and durst vnneth appeare in the kings presence; and euen as there were manie that stood in feare of him, so likewise stood he in feare of manie, in such sort that he began to make those awaie by one surmized cauillation or other, whome he thought most able to worke him anie displeasure.

"At length he found such sweetnesse by putting his nobles thus to death, that his earnest thirst after bloud in this behalfe might in no wise be satisfied: for ye must consider he wan double profite (as hee thought) hereby: for first they were rid out of the way whome he feared, and then againe his coffers were inriched by their goods which were forfeited to his vse, whereby he might the better mainteine a gard of armed men about him to defend his person from iniurie of them whom he had in anie suspicion. Further, to the end he might the more cruellie oppresse his subiects with all tyrantlike wrongs, he builded a strong castell on the top of an hie hill called Dunsinane situate in Gowrie, ten miles from Perth, on such a proud height, that standing there aloft, a man might behold well neere all the countries of Angus, Fife, Stermond and Ernedale, as it were lieng vnderneath him. This castell then being founded on the top of that high hill, put the realme to great charges before it was finished, for all the stuffe necessarie to the building, could not be brought vp without much toile and businesse. But Makbeth being once determined to haue the worke go forward, caused the thanes of each shire within the realme, to come and helpe towards that building, each man his course about.

"At the last, when the turne fell vnto Makduffe thane of Fife to builde his part, he sent workemen with all needfull prouision, and commanded them to shew such diligence in euerie behalfe, that no occasion might bee giuen for the king to find fault with him, in that he came not himselfe as other had doone, which he refused to doo, for doubt least the king bearing him (as he partlie vnderstood) no great good will, would laie violent handes vpon him, as he had doone vpon diuerse other. Shortly after, Makbeth comming to behold how the worke went forward, and bicause he found not Makduffe there, he was sore offended, and said: I percieue this man will neuer obeie my commandments, till he be ridden with a snaffle: but I shall prouide well inough for him. Neither could he afterwards abide to looke vpon the said Makduffe, either for that he thought his puissance ouer great; either

else for that he had learned of certeine wizzards, in whose words
he put great confidence (for that the prophesie had happened
so right, which the three faries or weird sisters had declared
vnto him) that he ought to take heed of Makduffe, who in time
to come should seeke to destroie him.

" And suerlie herevpon had he put Makduffe to death,
but that a certeine witch, whom hee had in great trust, had
told that he should neuer be slaine with man borne of anie
woman, nor vanquished till the wood of Bernane came to
the castell of Dunsinane. By this prophesie Makbeth put all
feare out of his heart, supposing he might doo what he
would, without anie feare to be punished for the same, for by
the one prophesie he beleeued it was vnpossible for anie man
to vanquish him, and by the other vnpossible to slea him.
This vaine hope caused him to doo manie outragious things,
to the greeuous oppression of his subiects. At length Makduffe,
to auoid perill of life, purposed with himselfe to pass intoe
England, to procure Malcolme Canmore to claime the crowne
of Scotland. But this was not so secretlie deuised by Makduffe,
but that Makbeth had knowledge giuen him thereof: for
kings (as is said) haue sharpe sight like vnto Lynx, and long
ears like vnto Midas. For Makbeth had in euerie noble mans
house one slie fellow or other in fee with him, to reueale all
that was said or doone within the same, by which slight he
oppressed the most part of the nobles of his realme.

" Immediatlie then, being aduertised whereabout Makduffe
went, he came hastily with a great power into Fife, and foorthwith besieged the castell where Makduffe dwelled, trusting to
haue found him therein. They that kept the house, without
anie resistance opened the gates, and suffered him to enter,
mistrusting none euill. But neuertheless Makbeth most cruellie
caused the wife and children of Makduffe, with all other whom
he found in that castell, to be slaine. Also he confiscated the
goods of Makduffe, proclaimed him traitor, and confined him
out of all the parts of his realme; but Makduffe was alreadie
escaped out of danger, and gotten into England vnto Malcolme
Canmore, to trie what purchase hee might make by means of
his support to reuenge the slaughter so cruellie executed on his
wife, his children, and other friends. At his comming vnto
Malcolme, he declared into what great miserie the estate
of Scotland was brought, by the detestable cruelties exercised
by the tyrant Makbeth, hauing committed manie horrible
slaughters and murders, both as well of the nobles as commons,

for the which he was hated right mortallie of all his liege people, desiring nothing more than to be deliuered of that intollerable and most heauie yoke of thraldome, which they susteined at such a caitifes hands.

" Malcolme hearing Makduffe's woordes, which he vttered in verie lamentable sort, for meere compassion and verie ruth that pearsed his sorrowful hart, bewailing the miserable state of his countrie, he fetched a deepe sigh; which Makduffe perceiuing, began to fall most earnestlie in hand with him, to enterprise the deliuering of the Scotish people out of the hands of so cruell and bloudie a tyrant, as Makbeth by too manie plaine experiments did shew himselfe to be: which was an easie matter for him to bring to passe, considering not onelie the good title he had, but also the earnest desire of the people to haue some occasion ministred, whereby they might be reuenged of those notable iniuries, which they dailie susteined by the outragious crueltie of Makbeths misgouernance. Though Malcolme was verie sorowfull for the oppression of his countrie-men the Scots, in maner as Makduffe had declared; yet doubting whether he were come as one that ment vnfeinedlie as he spake, or els as sent from Makbeth to betraie him, he thought to haue some further triall, and therevpon dissembling his mind at the first, he answered as followeth.

" I am trulie verie sorie for the miserie chanced to my countrie of Scotland, but though I haue neuer so great affection to relieue the same, yet by reason of certeine incurable vices, which reigne in me, I am nothing meet thereto. First, such immoderate lust and voluptuous sensualitie (the abhominable founteine of all vices) followeth me, that if I were made king of Scots, I should seeke to defloure your maids and matrones, in such wise that mine intemperancie should be more importable vnto you than the bloudie tyrannie of Makbeth now is. Heerunto Makduffe answered: this suerly is a verie euill fault, for manie noble princes and kings haue lost both liues and kingdomes for the same; neuerthelesse there are women enow in Scotland, and therefore follow my counsell. Make thy selfe king, and I shall conueie the matter so wiselie, that thou shalt be so satisfied at thy pleasure in such secret wise, that no man shall be aware thereof.

" Then said Malcolme, I am also the most auaritious creature on the earth, so that if I were king, I should seeke so manie waies to get lands and goods, that I would slea the most part of all the nobles of Scotland by surmized accusations, to the end

I might inioy their lands, goods, and possessions; and therefore to shew you what mischiefe may insue on you through
mine vnsatiable couetousnes, I will rehearse vnto you a fable.
There was a fox hauing a sore place on him ouerset with a swarme
of flies, that continuallie sucked out hir bloud: and when one
that came by and saw this manner, demanded whether she
would haue the flies driuen beside hir, she answered no: for
if these flies that are alreadie full, and by reason thereof sucke
not verie egerlie, should be chased awaie, other that are emptie
and fellie an hungred, should light in their places, and sucke
out the residue of my bloud farre more to my greeuance than
these, which now being satisfied doo not much annoie me.
Therefore saithe Malcolme, suffer me to remaine where I am,
least if I atteine to the regiment of your realme, mine inquench-
able auarice may prooue such; that ye would thinke the dis-
pleasures which now grieue you, should seeme easie in respect
of the vnmeasurable outrage, which might insue through my
comming amongst you.

" Makduffe to this made answer, how it was a far woorse
fault than the other: for auarice is the root of all mischiefe,
and for that crime the most part of our kings haue beene slain
and brought to their finall end. Yet notwithstanding follow
my counsell, and take vpon thee the crowne. There is gold
and riches inough in Scotland to satisfie thy greedie desire.
Then said Malcolme againe, I am furthermore inclined to
dissimulation, telling of leasings, and all other kinds of deceit,
so that I naturallie reioise in nothing so much, as to betraie
& deceiue such as put anie trust or confidence in my woords.
Then sith there is nothing that more becommeth a prince than
constancie, veritie, truth, and iustice, with the other laudable
fellowship of those faire and noble vertue which are comprehended in soothfastnesse, and that lieng vtterlie ouerthroweth
the same; you see how vnable I am to gouerne anie prouince
or region: and therefore sith you haue remedies to cloke and
hide all the rest of my other vices, I praie you find shift to cloke
this vice amongst the residue.

" Then said Makduffe: This yet is the woorst of all, and
there I leaue thee, and therefore saie; Oh ye vnhappie and
miserable Scotishmen, which are thus scourged with so manie
and sundrie calamities, ech one aboue another! Ye haue one
curssed and wicked tyrant that now reigneth ouer you, without
anie right or title, oppressing you with his most bloudie crueltie.
This other that hath the right to the crowne, is so replet with

the inconstant behauiour and manifest vices of Englishmen, that he is nothing woorthie to inioy it: for by his owne confession he is not onelie auaritious, and giuen to vnsatiable lust, but so false a traitor withall, that no trust is to be had vnto anie woord he speaketh. Adieu Scotland, for now I account my selfe a banished man for euer, without comfort or consolation: and with those woords the brackish tears trickled downe his cheekes verie abundantlie.

"At the last, when he was readie to depart, Malcolme tooke him by the sleeue, and said: Be of good comfort Makduffe, for I haue none of these vices before remembered, but haue iested with thee in this manner, onelie to prooue thy mind: for diuerse times heeretofore hath Makbeth sought by this manner of meanes to bring me into his hands, but the more slow I haue shewed my self to condescend to thy motion and request, the more diligence shall I vse in accomplishing the same. Incontinentlie heereupon they imbraced ech other, and promising to be faithfull the one to the other, they fell in consultation how they might best prouide for all their businesse, to bring the same to good effect. Soone after, Makduffe repairing to the borders of Scotland, addressed his letters with secret dispatch vnto the nobles of the realme, declaring how Malcolme was confederat with him, to come hastilie into Scotland to claime the crowne, and therefore he required them, sith he was right inheritor thereto, to assist him with their powers to recouer the same out of the hands of the wrongfull vsurper.

" In the meane time, Malcolme purchased such fauor at king Edwards hands, that old Siward earle of Northumberland, was appointed with ten thousand men to go with him into Scotland, to support him in this enterprise, for recouerie of his right. After these newes were spread abroad in Scotland, the nobles drew into two seuerall factions, the one taking part with Makbeth, and the other with Malcolme. Heereevpon insued oftentimes sundrie bickerings, & diuerse light skirmishes: for those that were of Malcolmes side, would not ieopard to ioine with their enimies in a pight field, till his comming out of England to their support. But after that Makbeth perceiued his enimies power to increase, by such aid as came to them foorth of England with his aduersarie Malcolme, he recoiled backe into Fife, there purposing to abide in campe fortified, at the castell of Dunsinane, and to fight with his enimies, if they ment to pursue him; howbeit some of his friends aduised him, that it should be best for him, either to make some agreement with Malcolme, or else to flee with all speed into the Iles, and to take his treasure with him, to the end he might wage sundrie great princes of the realme to take his part, & reteine strangers, in whome he might better trust than in his owne subiects, which stale dailie from him: but he had such confidence in his prophesies, that he beleeued he should neuer be vanquished, till Birnane wood were brought to Dunsinane; not yet to be slaine with anie man, that should be or was borne of anie woman.

"Malcolme following hastilie after Makbeth, came the night before the battell vnto Birnane wood, and when his armie had rested a while there to refresh them, he commanded euerie man to get a bough of some tree or other of that wood in his hand, as big as he might beare, and to march foorth therewith in such wise, that on the next morrow they might come closelie and without sight in this manner within viewe of his enimies. On the morrow when Makbeth beheld them comming in this sort, he first maruelled what the matter ment, but in the end remembred himselfe that the prophesie which he had heard long before that time, of the comming of Birnane wood to Dunsinane castell, was likelie to be now fulfilled. Neuertheless, he brought his men in order of battell, and exhorted them to doo valiantlie, howbeit his enimies had scarsely cast from them their boughs, when Makbeth perceiuing their numbers, betooke him streict to flight, whom Makduffe pursued with great hatred euen till he came vnto Lunfannaine, where Makbeth perceiuing that Makduffe was hard at his backe, leapt beside his horsse, saieng: Thou traitor, what meaneth it that thou shouldest thus in vaine follow me that am not appointed to be slaine by anie creature that is borne of a woman, come on therefore, and receiue thy reward which thou hast deserued for thy paines, and therewithall he lifted vp his swoord thinking to haue slaine him.

"But Makduffe quicklie auoiding from his horsse, yet he came at him, answered (with his naked swoord in his hand) saieng: It is true Makbeth, and now shall thine insatiable crueltie haue an end, for I am euen he that thy wizzards haue told thee of, who was neuer borne of my mother, but ripped out of her wombe: therewithall he stept vnto him, and slue him in the place. Then cutting his head from his shoulders, he set it vpon a pole, and brought it vnto Malcolme. This was the end of Makbeth, after he had reigned 17 yeeres ouer the Scotishmen. In the beginning of his reigne he accomplished manie woorthie acts verie profitable to the commonwealth (as ye haue heard), but afterward by illusion of the diuell, he defamed the same with most terrible crueltie. He was slaine in the yeere of the incarnation 1057, and in the 16 yeere of king Edwards reigne ouer the Englishmen.

" Malcolme Canmore thus recouering the relme (as ye haue heard) by support of king Edward, in the 16 yeere of the same Edwards reigne, he was crowned at Scone the 25 day of Aprill, in the yeere of our Lord 1057. Immediatlie after his coronation he called a parlement at Forfair, in the which he rewarded them with lands and liuings that had assisted him against Makbeth, aduancing them to fees and offices as he saw cause, & commanded that speciallie those that bare the surname of anie offices or lands, should haue and inioy the same. He created manie earles, lords, barons, and knights. Manie of them that before were thanes, were at this time made earles, as Fife, Menteth, Atholl, Leuenox, Murrey, Cathnes, Rosse, and Angus. These were the first earles that haue beene heard of a amongst the Scotishmen (as their histories doo make mention) " (pp. 174-6).

" It is recorded also, that in the foresaid battell, in which earle Siward vanquished the Scots, one of Siwards sonnes chanced to be slaine, whereof although the father had good cause to be sorrowfull, yet when he heard that he died of a wound which he had receiued in fighting stoutlie in the forepart of his bodie, and that with his face towards the enimie, he greatlie reioised thereat, to heare that he died so manfullie. But here is to be noted, that not now, but a little before (as *Henrie Hunt* saith) that earle Siward went into Scotland himselfe in person, he sent his sonne with an armie to conquere the land, whose hap was there to be slaine. When his father heard the newes he demanded whether he receiued the wounds whereof he died, in the forepart of the bodie, or in the hinder part: and when it was told him that he receiued it in the forepart; I reioise (saith he) euen with all my heart, for I would not wish either to my sonne nor to my selfe any other kind of death " (*History of England*, p. 192).

Miss Muriel Bradbrook pointed out in a lecture, printed in *Shakespeare Survey* 4, that Shakespeare may have derived some hints for the character of Lady Macbeth and particularly for her speech I. vii. 54 ff. from Holinshed's *Description of Scotland* prefixed to the *Chronicles*: " And sith it was a cause of suspicion of the mothers fidelitie toward hir husband, to seeke a strange nurse for hir children (although hir milke failed) each woman would take intollerable paines to bring vp and nourish hir owne children. They thought them furthermore not to be kindlie fostered, except they were so well nourished after their births with the milke of their brests, as they were before they were borne with the bloud of their owne bellies, nay they feared least they should degenerat and grow out of kind, except they gaue them sucke themselues, and eschewed strange milke, therefore in labour and painfulnesse they were equall, and neither sex regarded the heat in summer or cold in winter. . . . In these daies also the women of our countries were of no lesse courage than the men; for all stout maidens and wiues (if they were not with child) marched as well in the field as did the men, and so soone as the armie did set forward, they slue the first liuing creature that they found, in whose bloud they not onelie bathed their swords, but also tasted thereof with their mouthes, with no lesse religion and assurance conceiued, than if they had alreadie been sure of some notable and fortunate victorie. When they saw their owne bloud run from them in the fight, they waxed neuer a whit astonished with the matter, but rather doubling their courages, with more egernesse they assailed their enimies" (ed. 1587 p. 21).

APPENDIX B

Extracts from Buchanan's *Rerum Scoticarum Historia*. Translated by J. Aikman (1827).

XXII. . . . When Donald, the governor of the castle, requested the release of some of his relations, and was denied their pardon, he conceived the most unbounded rage against the king; and, as if he had received a signal affront, turned all his thoughts upon revenge, for he valued the services he had rendered Duff so highly, that he imagined he ought to be refused nothing which he chose to ask. Donald's wife, too, when she found that some of her own relations were condemned to death, inflamed her already incensed husband, not only by her bitter speeches, but by her persuasion incited him to murder the king; telling him that as keeper of the royal castle he had the life and death of his sovereign in his hands, and that he might thereby not only perpetrate the act, but conceal it when it was done. Wherefore, after the king, fatigued with business, had fallen into a deep sleep, and his attendants, who had been made drunk by Donald, were also overcome with drowsiness, assassins were secretly admitted, who murdered the king, and carried out the body so circumspectly by a back way, that not a single drop of blood betrayed the deed. . . . Next day, when the report was spread abroad that the king was nowhere to be found, and that the bed was spotted with blood, Donald, as if suddenly struck with the atrocious act, rushed into the bedchamber, and apparently transported with anger, murdered the servants, and then diligently searched everywhere round about to see if any traces of the dead man could be found. . . .

XXXVIII. (The following passage refers to King Kenneth.)

His soul, disturbed by a consciousness of his crime, permitted him to enjoy no solid or sincere pleasure; in retirement the thoughts of his unholy deed rushing upon his recollection, tormented him; and, in sleep, visions full of horror drove repose from his pillow. At last, whether in truth an audible voice from heaven addressed him, as is reported, or whether it were the suggestion of his own guilty mind, as often happens with the wicked, in the silent watches of the night he seemed thus to be admonished: " Dost thou think that the murder of the innocent

Malcolm, perpetrated secretly by thee with the most consummate villany, is either unknown to me, or can remain longer unpunished? Even now snares are spread for thy life, which thou canst not escape. Nor shalt thou leave, as thou imaginest, a stable and secure throne to thy posterity. They shall inherit an agitated and tempestuous kingdom."

IV. Macbeth was a man of penetrating genius, a high spirit, unbounded ambition, and, if he had possessed moderation, was worthy of any command, however great; but in punishing crimes he exercised a severity which, exceeding the bounds of the laws, appeared oft to degenerate into cruelty.

VIII. After this tide of success, both at home and abroad, when peace was re-established throughout the whole of Scotland, Macbeth, who had always despised the inactivity of his cousin, cherished secretly the hope of seizing the throne, in which he is said to have been confirmed by a dream. On a certain night, when he was far distant from the king, three women appeared to him of more than human stature, of whom one hailed him thane of Angus, another, thane of Moray, and the third saluted him king. His ambition and hope being strongly excited by this vision, he revolved in his mind every way by which he might obtain the kingdom, when a justifiable occasion, as he thought, presented itself. Duncan had two sons, by the daughter of Sibard, governor of Northumberland, Malcolm Canmore (great head) and Donald Bane (white). Of these he made Malcolm, while yet a boy, governor of Cumberland. This appointment highly incensed Macbeth, who thought it an obstacle thrown in the way of his ambition, which—now that he had obtained the two first dignities promised by his nocturnal visitors—might retard, if not altogether prevent, his arriving at the third, as the command of Cumberland was always considered the next step to the crown. His mind, already sufficiently ardent of itself, was daily excited by the importunities of his wife, who was the confidant of all his designs. Wherefore, having consulted with his most intimate friends, among whom was Bancho, and having found a convenient opportunity, he waylaid the king at Inverness, and killed him, in the seventh year of his reign; then, collecting a band together, he proceeded to Scoon, where, trusting to the favour of the people, he proclaimed himself king. The children of Duncan, amazed at this sudden misfortune, their father slain, and the author of the murder upon his throne, surrounded on every side by the snares of the tyrant, who sought, by their

death, to confirm the kingdom to himself, for some time endeavoured to save themselves by flight, and shifting frequently the
places of their concealment. But when they saw they could be
no where safe, if within the reach of his power, and having no
hope of mercy from a man of so barbarous a disposition, they fled
in different directions, Malcolm into Cumberland, and Donald to
his relations in the Æbudæ.

LXXXV. MACBETH

IX. Macbeth, in order to establish himself on the throne he
had so iniquitously acquired, won the favour of the nobles by
large gifts. As he was secure of the king's children, on account of
their age, and of the neighbouring kings, on account of their
mutual animosities, having gained the more powerful, he
determined to procure the affection of the people by his equity,
and retain it by his strict administration of justice. Wherefore,
he determined to punish the robbers, who had grown insolent
through the lenity of Duncan. But when he saw that this could
not be effected without raising a great commotion, he contrived,
by men selected for the purpose, to scatter the seeds of dissension
among them, and induce them to challenge each other to decide
their disputes by battle, in small parties of equal numbers, in
places widely distant, and upon the same day. On which day,
when they assembled according to appointment, they were all
seized by trusty officers, whom the king had stationed for
apprehending them, and their execution struck terror into the
rest. He, likewise, put to death the thanes of Caithness, Ross,
Sutherland, and Nairn, together with some other powerful chieftains, by whose feuds the people were terribly harassed. He,
afterwards, went to the Æbudæ, where he executed severe justice,
and returning thence, he summoned repeatedly Macgill, or
Macgild, the most powerful chief of Galloway, to stand trial. But
he—Macgill—more afraid of being charged with having belonged
to the party of Malcolm, than dreading any crime of which he
could have been accused—refused to obey; on which, Macbeth
sent some detachments against him, who, having vanquished him
in battle, put him to death. By these means, perfect tranquillity
being restored, he applied himself to frame laws, an object which
had been much neglected by the preceding kings, and enacted
very many and very useful statutes, which now, to the great
detriment of the public, are allowed to remain unnoticed, and
almost unknown. Thus, for ten years, he so governed the

kingdom, that, if his obtaining it by violence were forgotten, he would be esteemed inferior to none of the kings who preceded him.

X. But when he had strengthened himself by so many safe-guards, and thus gained the favour of the people; the murder of the king—as is very credible—haunting his imagination, and distracting his mind, occasioned his converting the government which he had obtained by perfidy, into a cruel tyranny. He first wreaked his unbounded rage on Bancho, his accomplice in the treason, instigated, as is reported, by the prophecy of some witches, who predicted that Bancho's posterity would enjoy the kingdom. Wherefore, fearing that so powerful and active a chief, who had already dipt his hands in royal blood, might imitate the example which he himself had set, he familiarly invited him, along with his son, to an entertainment, and caused him to be assassinated on his return, in such a manner, as if he had been accidentally killed in a sudden affray. Fleanchus, his son, being unknown, escaped in the dark, but, informed by his friends that his father had been killed by the treachery of the king, and that his own life was sought after, fled secretly to Wales. This murder, so cruelly and perfidiously committed, inspired the nobles with such dread, each for his own safety, that they all departed to their houses, few of them, and they but rarely, ever venturing to court; so that the cruelty of the king, being openly exercised upon some, and secretly suspected by all, mutual terror produced mutual hatred between him and his nobles, and then, when concealment became impossible, he began to exhibit an undisguised tyranny. He publicly executed the most power-ful chieftains, upon the most frivolous pretences, and frequently upon fictitious accusations; and with the produce of their confiscations, he supported a band of ruffians, under the name of Royal Guards.

XI. The king, however, not yet thinking his life sufficiently protected, commenced building a castle upon Dunsinnan hill, whence there is an extensive prospect upon every side; and when the building proceeded but slowly, on account of the difficulty of the carriage of the materials, he commanded all the thanes, throughout the whole kingdom, to provide by turns for the work labourers and carriages, and ordered that they should themselves superintend the operations, as inspectors. Macduff, thane of Fife, was then exceedingly powerful, but not daring to trust his life in the king's hands, frequently sent workmen thither, and, likewise, several of his most intimate friends to urge their labour. The king, either desirous to see how the work proceeded, as he pretended, or, as Macduff feared, to apprehend him, came to view the building, when, by chance, a yoke of oxen, unequal to the task, could not drag a load over a steep ascent. The king eagerly seized the occasion to vent his indignation, threatening that he would subdue the contumacious spirit of the thane, which was already well known to him, and place the yoke on his own neck, which speech being reported to Macduff, he commended his family to his wife, and, without delay, passed over to Lothian, in a little vessel hastily rigged out for the occasion, and thence proceeded to England. Macbeth, having heard of his intended flight, proceeded immediately with a strong force to Fife, if possible to prevent him. At his arrival, he was immediately admitted into Macduff's castle, but not finding the thane, he wreaked his vengeance upon his wife, and his children who remained. He confiscated also his estate, proclaimed himself a rebel, and threatened to inflict a severe punishment on any one who dared to hold any communication with him. He likewise behaved with great cruelty towards the rest of the rich, and the powerful, without distinction; and, in contempt of his nobility, administered the internal affairs of the kingdom, by the advice of his household, without ever deigning to consult them.

XII. In the meantime, Macduff, having arrived in England, found Malcolm living in a royal style, at the court of king Edward; for Edward having been recalled from exile to the throne, when the power of the Danes was broken in England, was for many reasons interested in behalf of Malcolm, who had been presented to him by his maternal grandfather, Sibard, either because his father and grandfather, when they commanded in Cumberland, were always attached to his ancestors, or, because a similarity of circumstances, and a recollection of their mutual dangers, had produced a mutual friendship, for both kings had been driven into exile unjustly, by tyrants, or, because the misfortunes of kings easily interest the minds of the greatest strangers. The thane, therefore, as soon as he could find a proper opportunity, addressed Malcolm in a long speech, in which he lamented the unhappy necessity of his flight, represented the cruelty of Macbeth towards all ranks, and the universal hatred of all ranks towards him, and strongly urged Malcolm to attempt the recovery of his paternal throne, especially, as he could not without the greatest guilt leave the impious murder of his father unpunished, neglect the miseries of a people committed to him by God himself, or turn a deaf ear to the just petitions of his friends. Besides, he might rely on the assistance of his ally, the excellent king Edward, and on the affections of the people, who hated the tyrant, nor would the favour of the Deity, to aid a just cause against the wicked, be withheld. In fine, nothing would be wanting, if he were not wanting to himself. Malcolm, who had often before been solicited to return, by spies, sent from Macbeth to draw him into a snare, determined, before he should commit himself to fortune in so great an affair, to prove the fidelity of Macduff. He therefore replied, I am not indeed ignorant of what you tell me, but I am afraid that you are wholly unacquainted with me, whom you invite to assume the crown; for the same vices which have destroyed many kings, lust and avarice, exist in me also, and although now hid in a private station, would break forth in the licence of a regal state. Beware then, lest you do not rather invite me to destruction, than to a kingdom. Macduff answered, that licentious desires after variety, might be counteracted by a lawful marriage, and avarice removed, by being placed above the fear of penury. Malcolm rejoined, that he now rather chose to confess to him ingenuously as a friend, than hereafter to be caught in faults, which might prove dangerous to both; that he did not believe in the existence, either of truth or sincerity; that he confided in no man; that he was apt to change his designs with every breath of suspicion, and, that from the inconstancy of his own disposition, he formed his judgment of every other person. On which, Macduff exclaimed, away! dishonour of thy royal blood and name, more fit to dwell in a desert, than to reign; and was about to retire in anger, when Malcolm taking him by the hand, explained to him the reason of his simulation, that he had so often been deceived by the emissaries of Macbeth, that he dared not rashly trust himself to every body, but with regard to Macduff, his lineage, his manners, his character, and his circumstances, claimed his confidence. Then mutually plighting their faith, they proceeded to consult on the means for accomplishing the destruction of the tyrant. Having, by secret messengers, sent previous information of their design to their friends, they received from King Edward, ten thousand soldiers, under the command of Sibard, Malcolm's maternal grandfather.

XII. The report of this army's march, excited a great commotion in Scotland, and many daily flocked to the new king. Macbeth, being almost wholly deserted, when in this so sudden defection he saw no better alternative, shut himself up in the castle of Dunsinnan, and sent his friends with money into the Æbudæ, and Ireland, to procure soldiers. Malcolm hearing of his intentions, marched directly against him, accompanied, wherever he went, by the acclamations of the people, and their prayers for his success. The soldiers joyfully seized this as an omen of victory, and placing green boughs in their helmets, represented an army rather returning in triumph, than marching to battle. Astonished at this confidence of the enemy, Macbeth immediately fled and the soldiers, deserted by their leader, surrendered to Malcolm, Macduff having followed the tyrant, overtook him, and slew him. Here some of our writers relate a number of fables, more adapted for theatrical representation, or Milesian romance, than history, I therefore omit them. Macbeth reigned seventeen years over Scotland, during the first ten of which, he performed the duty of the best of kings, but in the seven last, he equalled the cruelty of the most barbarous tyrants.

APPENDIX C

Extracts from John Leslie's *De Origine, Moribus, et Rebus Gestis Scotorum*. Translated by C. Collard.

Chapter lxxxiv: DUNCAN

Malcolm's grandson Duncan then became king with the assent of all; * a man whose nature was unmarked by any roughness, resentment or bitterness, he was of the sort which does not retaliate even when provoked by the most grievous outrage. The common people shamefully abused this remarkable and merciful disposition of their king, and indulged their wicked cravings like wild beasts freed of all bonds; because Duncan was himself quite unable to act otherwise than mercifully, he entrusted his powers of government to Macbeth, a man a little more disposed to stern measures. Macbeth seized the earliest opportunity to repress the general lawlessness of the nation by inflicting the harshest punishment on the inhabitants of Lochaber (they had despoiled Banquo, the Royal Thane of Lochaber, of the royal estates and of much money, besides wounding him severely). Macbeth also drove into Lochaber Castle MacDonald of the Isles, who supported these robbers and had fought stubbornly for them; he was there put under so close a siege that no way of escape was left to him. MacDonald became so terrified by the imagination of the penalties he would suffer if he fell into his enemies' hands, and so blinded by obstinacy of kind, that he took the lives both of himself and of his family.

Meanwhile the King of Norway crossed to Scotland with an army, bringing about a wholly unjustifiable war on the pretext of avenging an ancient massacre of his countrymen. Besieging Duncan in Perth Castle he pressed him so hard that he would without doubt have been forced to surrender to his enemy, had he not taken quick advantage of a chance to attack the Danes while they were buried in their drinking. Not long after, Macbeth came to his help with reinforcements; thereupon King Sven hastily broke camp and fled to his ships, for he had not only sustained a great defeat but was himself in extreme danger of his life. Duncan did not allow the opportunity to destroy the

* Malcolm was murdered at Glamis, 1040 (end. of chap. lxxxiii).

196

Danes to slip away, but with Macbeth's counsel and assistance overcame and scattered their fleet at Kingorn. The tombs of the Danes survive there to this day, and memorials graven in stone mark the everlasting glory of the action.

Within a few days, however, Macbeth had become so swollen with vainglory, and his resolution so tortured by a mad lust for power, that he hideously murdered Duncan his most holy King, who had rewarded him with such great honours, in the sixth year of his reign; though fearful of the deed, his wife urged him to it with high promises of its happy outcome. Duncan's two sons Malcolm Canmoir and Donald were seized by fear upon their father's murder, and most wisely decided to flee the country.

Chapter lxxxv: MACBETH

Thus Macbeth forcibly seized the throne; he was the son of Doada, the daughter of Malcolm the Second.

Though Macbeth was famed for his prowess in war, and by nature disposed to cruelty, he thought to secure his ill-won kingdom by favouring the nobles through total suppression of brigandage, and indulging the common people with beneficial laws; thus he might bind both to himself in the closest ties of goodwill. In the end, however, the conscience of his hideous deeds so worked upon him and caused him such fear for his life from those about him, that his mildness changed to ruthlessness. He began either openly to execute his nobles or to induce them by his cunning to intrigue one another's deaths.

Banquo and, above all, Macduff he thought particularly dangerous. He destroyed Banquo at the first opportunity, while he contrived to ensnare Macduff by cunning. In short, like any tyrant, he went in fear of all men, and all men of him. The people thereupon wisely grew concerned for the state of their kingdom, and for their own safety; they sent Macduff to England, where Malcolm Canmoir was in exile, to invite him to recover his rightful inheritance and to assure him under holy oath of their allegiance to him against Macbeth. At this news Malcolm was generously furnished with 10,000 English soldiers by King Edward. Returning to Scotland, he pursued Macbeth in a number of fierce engagements first to Dunsinane, and then to Lumphanan. There Macduff, the Earl of Fife, had Macbeth put to death (he had a little before ordered the execution of Macduff's wife and children), and took his head to Malcolm, who gave him fine praise and abundant reward. Macbeth's death occurred in the sixth year of his tyranny.

APPENDIX D

AFFINITIES WITH *MACBETH*

(i) *The Rape of Lucrece*

SEVERAL critics have noted parallels between *Macbeth* and *Lucrece*. Whiter, in *Specimen of a Commentary*, pp. 160-84, compared the use of stage imagery in *Lucrece* (764-805) with II. iv. 4-9. Warburton compared the setting of Duncan's murder with that of Lucrece's rape (cf. note to II. i. 55). Dover Wilson has pointed out a number of parallels, e.g. I. v. 53 and L. 788, 801, II. ii. 54 and L. 245, II. ii. 32 and L. 341-3. See also Muriel Bradbrook, *Shakespeare Survey* 4. We may also notice the reference to " foul usurper " (412); winking at things too terrible for the eye, which Caroline Spurgeon mentioned as a characteristic image in *Macbeth* (375, 458, 1138-9); the reference to bird, fear and lime (IV. ii. 34; L. 88); the parallel between IV. iii. 81-2 and L. 148-54; the resemblance between Macbeth's temptation by his wife and Tarquin's by himself (L. 127-54, 246-52); the reference to the staining of water with blood (II. ii. 62; L. 655); the stanza about insomnia (974-80); the comparison of death to the cancellation of a bond (III. ii. 49; L. 1729); the turning of Macduff's and Collatine's grief to revenge (IV. iii. 228-40; L. 1808-55); and compare Macbeth's remarks on the blessings of old age (v. iii. 24-5) with Tarquin's fear of losing them (L. 141-7).

(ii) *II Henry VI*

Wilson Knight pointed out some resemblances between *Macbeth* and *II Henry VI* in *The New Adelphi* (1927). Cf. *Modern Language Notes*, xxxviii, for a brief article on the same subject. The Duchess of Gloucester (in I. ii) and Queen Margaret have both been compared with Lady Macbeth; and it has even been suggested that the Duchess' penitential taper (II. iv) may be compared with Lady Macbeth's (v. i). Suffolk counterfeits surprise after the murder of Gloucester as Macbeth does after the murder of Duncan. The Cardinal on his death-bed has been compared with Macbeth when confronted by the ghost of Banquo. There is a witch scene and an equivocating prophecy (I. iv). There is a reference to kerns and gallowglasses (IV. ix. 26). Queen Margaret uses an image of the flower and the snake

(III. i. 228; cf. *Mac.* I. v. 64-5) and Gloucester of a prologue (III. i. 151; cf. *Mac.* I. iii. 128). See also note to v. i. 68. The parallels are probably due to the fact that the theme of witch-craft called up the earlier associations.

(iii) *Richard III*

F. M. Smith, *P.M.L.A.* (1945), pp. 1003 ff., has written on the relation between the two plays. Both heroes are tyrants, usurpers, and murderers; both aspiring and ambitious, both courageous, cruel, and treacherous, and both are called ' hell-hound.' Margaret is called a witch. Some of Smith's parallels seem rather forced, and I do not agree with all he says about the resemblances between the two plays. He compares the following passages: M. II. i. 63-4; R. v. iii. 312-3; M. III. ii. 18-9, R. I. iii. 225-7; M. III. iv. 135-7, R. IV. ii. 65-6; M. III. i. 141, R. I. i. 119-20; M. IV. iii. 209-10, R. IV. iv. 129-31; M. v. iii. 24-6, R. v. iii. 200-1. See also notes on I. ii. 31, 55 and compare Macbeth's vacillation (v. iii. 48-60) with Richard's (IV. iv. 440-56) as their enemies close in. Tillyard, *Shakespeare's History Plays*, p. 316, has some remarks on the resemblances between the two plays.

APPENDIX E

ADDITIONAL NOTES (1951-61)

The Royal Play of Macbeth by Henry N. Paul (1950) appeared after the 1951 edition had gone to press. Notes from this book are distinguished by P. Notes from other sources are ascribed to their authors.

1. *Date* (cf. p. xvi)

Shakespeare was probably in Oxford in the summer of 1605, and he would then have heard that the King disliked long plays and approved of Gwinn's *Tres Sibyllae*, with its reference to his ancestry. He may also have heard that one of the subjects debated before the King was " whether the imagination can produce real effects." He was thus provided with a plot and with a method of dealing with it. On his return to London in the late autumn of 1605, the poet began his play. The last two acts seem to show the influence of the Profanity Statute and must therefore have been written after 27 May, 1606. The play was first performed at Hampton Court on 7 August, 1606, and not performed at the Globe until the autumn of the same year. (P)

A parallel between Daniel's pastoral play, *The Queenes Arcadia*, (1240-51) and v. iii. 39-45 suggested that Shakespeare may have seen the performance at Oxford before the Queen of *Arcadia, Reformed*, as it was then called, on 30 August, 1605. (M)

Mr. Seronsy, *N.Q.*, ccv, p. 328, compares these lines from *The Queenes Arcadia*—

> Custome, who takes from vs our priuiledge
> To be our selues, rendes that great charter too
> Of nature and would likewise cancell man—

with III. ii. 49-50. It may be added that six lines earlier (2558) Daniel uses the phase " bonds of mischiefe " which may have linked up with " that great charter " to form Shakespeare's " that great bond." There is, however, an even closer parallel (as G. K. Hunter points out) in the episode in Montemayor's *Diana* which was the probable source of *The Two Gentlemen of Verona*, as translated by B. Yonge (1598). See Bullough, *Narrative and Dramatic Sources of Shakespeare*, I. 252:

How small account would I make of my life (my deerest *Felismena*) for cancelling that great bond, wherein (with more then life) I am for ever bound unto thee.

Shortly before this Montemayor speaks of the knight's " pale visage."

2. *Music*

J. M. Nosworthy informs me that the *Macbeth* music attributed to Matthew Locke was an elaboration of music written for *The Witch* by Robert Johnson.

3. *The Hecate Scenes* (cf. p. xxxv)

W. Farnham, *Shakespeare's Tragic Frontier* (1950), pp. 74 ff., shows that both *hag* and *witch* could mean a demon, as well as a human being who had made a compact with the devil; and that in the three spurious passages Shakespeare's superhuman witches are changed into human witches. " They are compared to fairies when they cease to be fairies."

4. *Sources* (cf. p. xxxix)

Parallels between Studley's version of Seneca's *Agamemnon* and two speeches of Macbeth (I. iii. 127-42 and II. i. 31-64) support the view expressed on p. 154 that Shakespeare knew the translation. (M)

Jane H. Jack, *ELH* (1955), pp. 173 ff., argues that Shakespeare was influenced by James I's *Fruitful Meditation*, though the scriptural passages in that book could have been echoed directly from the Bible.

Sir James Fergusson of Kilkerran, Bart., *Shakespeare's Scotland* (1957), p. 6, points out that the Table of all the Kings of Scotland was reprinted in London in *Certeine Matters concerning the Realme of Scotland* (1603). He also suggests that *Macbeth* may have been influenced by some details in the career of James Stewart of Bothwellmuir, who fell from power in 1585 and met his death in 1595. He became Earl of Arran and was spurred on by the ambition of a wicked wife. The " highland oracles " had shown her that " Gowrie should be ruined," but she " helped the prophecy forward as well as she could." Stewart was slain by a kinsman of the Regent Morton

> of whose ruin and death he had been the primary agent; he too tried to avoid the circumstances which it had been prophecied would attend his death; and his " cursed head," like Macbeth's, was cut off by his slayer and set on a pole.

Stewart's wife was suspected of trafficking with witches and she was described as " a meete matche for such a spouse, depending upon the response of witches, and enemie of all human societie " (Wardlaw MS., 182). Shakespeare may have been ignorant of these matters but they provide further evidence that the atmosphere of the play was not alien to Shakespeare's contemporaries.

5. *Notes on Individual Passages*

I. ii. 17-20] Possibly " Like Valour's minion " should be substituted for " Disdaining Fortune," the lines being printed as three. (P)

I. ii. 25. *reflection*] turning-back (*O.E.D.*) at the vernal equinox. (P)

I. ii. 31. *Norweyan*] Shakespeare, in deference to King Christian, suppresses mention of the Danes. (P)

I. ii. 36-9] Paul thinks that l. 37 was an afterthought, referring to the cannonade fired by the Danish ships as the two Kings were rowed up the Thames, and that the lines should read:

> If I say sooth, I must report that they
> Doubly redoubled strokes upon the foe,
> As cannons over-charg'd with double cracks.

I. ii. 64. *dollars*] Paul scents a reference to the 10,000 dollars presented by King Christian to " the officers above the stairs." Shakespeare, as groom of the outer chamber, was one of these officers. But would his gratitude quite submerge his artistic conscience?

I. iv. 2-11] Possibly a reference to the execution of Sir Everard Digby for complicity in the Gunpowder Plot, on 30 January, 1606. (P)

I. v. 17. *milk*] One of the subjects debated at Oxford in August 1605 was the nurse's influence on the baby's character. James I was interested in the subject as his own nurse had been a drunkard as well as a protestant. Cf. other references to milk. (P)

I. v. 65. *serpent*] The medal commemorating the Gunpowder Plot depicts a serpent lurking among flowers. (P)

I. vii. 64-8] Schanzer, *M.L.R.* (1957), argues that as warder was not used in the sense of jailor in Shakespeare's day, we should emend to "warden." He then gives an interpretation based on A. Davenport's:

> " The full meaning of the alchemic methaphor that follows seems never to have been brought out by commentators. 'Receipt' appears to comprise both the meaning of ' container,' suggested by the theory that reason occupies a separate ventricle of the brain, and that of the receiver at the bottom of the still in which the end-product is gathered and condensed. ' Limbeck' here clearly refers not to the head or cap of the still, the alembic proper, as it is often explained, but to the retort or cucurbit, the vessel in which the liquids to be distilled are heated. This

seems to have been the more common use of ' limbeck ' or ' alembic ' in
Shakespeare's day. The full meaning of the image is therefore that the
receptacle which should collect only the pure drops of reason, the final
distillate of the thought-process, will be turned into the retort in which
the crude undistilled liquids bubble and fume.''

II. i. 59. *horror*] Edvard Beyer points out that Niels Hauge in his
translation of *Macbeth* into Norwegian (1855) takes the word
" horror " to mean the murder. Beyer supports this interpretation as an effective crescendo in the sequence of
" horrid image " (I. iii. 35), " horrid deed " (I. vii. 24) and
by the fact that Macbeth constantly avoids the word
" murder." I doubt whether the meaning should be
limited in this way.

II. ii. 3. *bellman*] Paul takes this to be a reference to Robert Dow's
gift in May 1605 to pay for visits of the bellman to condemned
prisoners in Newgate.

II.ii. 34] James I suffered from insomnia (P); but it is difficult
to believe that Shakespeare introduced the subject for that
reason.

II. iii. 4. *farmer*] Possibly suggested by Sordido in Jonson's *Every
Man out of his Humour*, III. ii. (P)

II. iii. 55] Possibly an allusion to the hurricane of 29-30 March,
1606. (P)

III. i. 5. *root*] This may have been suggested by the Banquo tree in
Leslie, *op. cit.* Cf. III. i. 49 " stick deep." (P)

III. i. 60-3] This part of the prophecy is not found in Shakespeare's
presentation of the scene but only in Holinshed's account.
Shakespeare omitted it from the earlier scene because " the
prospect of kingship must appear at this moment entirely
unclouded." (Schanzer)

III. i. 69. *seed*] We ought, perhaps, to retain the F plural. (P)

III. i. 92. *hounds*] James I was notoriously fond of dogs. (P)

III. ii. 13. *snake*] Possibly suggested by the serpentine trunk of the
Banquo tree in Leslie's book. Cf. III. iv. 28. (P)

III. iv. 40] Banquo's Ghost may have been suggested by De
Loier's *Treatise of Spectres* (1605), p. 113, where King Thierry
" on an evening as he sat at supper " is haunted by the ghost
of a man he has slain. (P)

III. iv. 75. *purg'd*] This and other images of purging may have
been suggested by James I's *Counter-Blaste to Tobacco:* " For
remedie whereof, it is the kings part (as the proper Phisician

of his politicke-bodie) to purge it of all those diseases, by Medicines meete for the same." (P)

III. iv. 123-5] Schanzer argues that these lines refer to tell-tale birds as in *Per.* IV. iii. 21-3: " understood relations " means " reports which could be understood " because they were delivered in human language.

III. v. 23-9] These lines can mean that " with the aid of her magic potion Hecate will fashion phantom figures " or else that she will " use her magic potion to call up powerful demons, just as is done with the magic ingredients of the witches' cauldron." " Artificial " would then mean (*N.E.D.* ii. 9) " Displaying artifice; artful, cunning, deceitful." The second explanation is the more likely one. (Schanzer)

IV. i. 3. *Harpier*] Possibly an owl, the Third Witch's familiar. There are references to the owl before the three murders of Duncan, Banquo and Lady Macduff. Cf. II. ii. 3; II. iii. 60; II, iv. 13; III. ii. 53; IV. ii. 11. (P)

IV. i. 12. *snake*] This and the howlet's wing have been suggested by Ovid, *Metam.*, vii. 269, 272. (P)

IV. i. 46. *locks*] This word suggests that the traditional cave is a wrong setting for this scene. (P)

IV. ii. 19. *rumour*] On 22 March, 1606, there was a rumour that the King had been stabbed with a poisoned knife. (P)

IV. ii. 41. *sell*] This may have a secondary sense of *cheat*. (P)

IV. iii. 153. *stamp*] Paul supposes that Shakespeare, on Buck's suggestion, inserted this reference to the coin in order to overcome the King's reluctance to use it in the ceremony. This is improbable.

IV. iii. 170. *modern ecstasy*] This may mean a sham trance or fit of hysteria, and allude to the counterfeit demoniacs described in Harsnett's *Declaration*, a book used by Shakespeare in *King Lear*. (P)

V. i. 6. *paper*] Paul suggested that Lady Macbeth is writing to warn Lady Macduff and that the Messenger (IV. ii. 64) had been sent by her to warn her friend. But there is no evidence that Lady Macbeth was friendly with Lady Macduff.

ADDITIONAL NOTE (1964)

Mr James O. Wood argues (*Notes and Queries*, July 1964, pp. 262–4) that the author of III.v. made use, as Shakespeare did, of Leslie's *De Origine Moribus et Rebus Gestis Scotorum*, and suggests that "profound" (III.v.) is derived from "instillato perfundere" (Leslie, p. 193) and means "profounded" (i.e. poured out, immersed).